Acknowledgements

We wish to give our thanks to the members of the Ladies Auxiliaries and their Commands from across Canada who sent their recipes to enable us to compile this cookbook. Thank you, also, to Derksen Printers of Steinbach, Manitoba for without their assistance this book would not have been possible.

Ladies Auxiliary to Royal Canadian Legion
Branch #190, P.O. Box 3519
Steinbach, Manitoba R0A 2A0

October 1984

ISBN: 0-919673-79-1

Published by the Ladies Auxiliary to Royal Canadian Legion

Printed by Derksen Printers (1982) Ltd., Steinbach, Manitoba R0A 2A0

Contents

Appetizers, Snacks, Dips & Beverages

Appetizers & Snacks

Pizza Mix

1-15 oz. can tomato sauce
1 tin ripe olives, chopped
1 lb. medium cheese, grated
½ cup Mazola oil
1 onion, chopped fine
1 tin mushrooms, chopped
garlic salt
salt and pepper to taste

Mix together and store in fridge. Use on bread rolls, hamburger or hot dog buns. Broil under grill.

Squamish, B.C.
Branch No. 277

Filling For Egg Rolls

4 cups cabbage
1 cup diced chicken
½ cup onion, chopped
½ cup celery, chopped
1 tbsp. corn oil
2 tsp. salt
½ tsp. pepper
1 tbsp. soya sauce

Let stand 20 minutes. Drain. Cover edges of pastry with beaten egg. Deep fry for 3 minutes.

Happy Valley, Labrador, Nfld.
Branch No. 51

Cheese Ball

2-8 oz. pkgs. Philadelphia
    Cream Cheese
2 cups (8 oz.) cheddar cheese
2 tsp. Worchestershire Sauce
1 tsp. lemon juice
1 tbsp. green pepper, chopped
1 tbsp. onion, chopped
1 tbsp. pimento, chopped
dash of cayenne
dash of salt

Blend well; roll in chopped walnuts or parsley.

Penticton, B.C.
Branch No. 40

Meat Balls and Franks

1½ lbs. ground chuck
1 egg, slightly beaten
1 large onion, grated
2 tsp. salt

Mix and shape into meatballs (50-60). Brown on cookie sheet in oven at 400°F. for 10 minutes.

1 lb. frankfurters,
    diagonally cut
1-20 oz. jar grape jelly
1-12 oz. jar chili sauce

Combine jelly and chili sauce and simmer until jelly melts. Add meatballs and franks; simmer about 10 to 15 minutes. Can be frozen.

Clarks Harbour, N.C.
Branch No. 148

Breakfast Cheese Ball

1 pkg. cream cheese, softened,
    (250 g)
½ cup cottage cheese (125 ml)
1 tsp. lemon juice (5 ml)
¼ tsp. salt (1 ml)
½ cup chopped dried apricots
    or 1 chopped apple and raisins (125 ml)
½ cup all-bran cereal (125 ml)
sugar to taste

In large mixing bowl, beat cream cheese and cottage cheese until smooth. Stir in lemon juice, salt, dried apricots or apples and raisins. Add sugar if desired. Chill until stiff. Shape into a ball and roll in cereal. Chill. Serve with crackers, vegetable sticks or fruit.

Ste. Anne, Man.
Ladies Auxiliary Branch No. 220

Corn Fritters

1 cup flour
1 tsp. baking powder
¾ tsp. salt
2 eggs, beaten
2 tbsp. chopped parsley (optional)
1½ cups cooked corn

Mix batter and drop by heaping tablespoons into hot oil. Cook until golden brown. Serve hot. Excellent with homemade soups and stews!

Sanford, Man.
Branch No. 171

Summer Sausage

1 tsp. mustard seed
3 tbsp. Tender Quick
1 cup cold water
¼ tsp. garlic salt
½ tsp. onion salt
1/8 tsp. pepper
1½ tsp. liquid smoke, "hickory"
2 lbs. hamburger

Mix all seasonings in cold water, pour over hamburger. Mix and shape into roll. Wrap in foil, pressing together tightly. Let stand in fridge 24 hours. Bake 1 hour in a 350°F. oven on a cookie sheet. Cool in foil and slice as sausage. Store in fridge in plastic bag. Keeps for weeks.

Sioux Lookout, Ontario
Branch No. 78

Cheese Whiz

½ lb. cream cheese
¼ lb. butter or margarine
2 eggs, well beaten
½ tsp. dry mustard

Slowly melt cheese and butter. When warm add beaten eggs and mustard. Mix well till smooth and pour in jar.

Lundar, Man.
Legion Auxiliary Branch No. 185

Fried Cheese Puffs

1-10 oz. pkg. cheese (sharp or extra sharp), cut in ¾" cubes
2 eggs, beaten
¾ cup dry bread crumbs
1 tsp. sesame seed oil

Dip cheese in egg. Coat with crumbs and sesame seeds. Repeat. Fry in deep hot oil (350°F.), for 1 to 2 minutes, or until browned.

Trenton, N.S.
Branch No. 29

Broiled Mushrooms

1 lb. large mushrooms
¼ lb. melted butter
1 large pkg. cream cheese
½ tsp. garlic salt
4 tbsp. sour cream
½ tsp. salt

After washing mushrooms and removing stems, brush outside of mushrooms with butter and broil until light brown. Blend sour cream, cream cheese and seasonings. Turn mushrooms over and fill with mixture. Broil an additional 5 minutes and serve hot.

Edmonton, Alta.
Norwood Branch No. 178

Lobster Stuffed Eggs

6 hard cooked eggs
1 cup cooked lobster
1 tsp. prepared mustard
2 tbsp. mayonnaise
salt and pepper
paprika

Cut egg in half and remove yolks to a bowl. Mash yolks well and stir in lobster, mustard, mayonnaise and seasonings. Spoon into the egg whites and sprinkle top with paprika. Chill before serving.

St. John's, Nfld.
Branch No. 1

Cracker Spread

Philadelphia Cream Cheese
onion, chopped fine
celery, chopped fine
touch of Miracle Whip

Blend these four ingredients to whatever amount you wish to make. Then add salmon, tuna or shrimp, whichever you prefer. Mix well and chill. Spread on crackers for a snack.

Ignace, Ont.
Ladies Auxiliary Branch No. 168

Hot Crab Spread

1-8 oz. pkg. cream cheese
1 tbsp. milk
½ tsp. horseradish
2 tbsp. onion
1 can crab meat
salt to taste
⅓ cup slivered almonds

Soften cheese with milk, add other ingredients and top with almonds. Bake at 375°F. for 15 minutes. Serve warm with Triscuits.

Winnipeg, Man.
St. Vital Branch No. 16

Bacon-Stuffed Cherry Tomatoes

2 lbs. bacon
½ cup green onion, finely chopped
½ cup mayonnaise
24 cherry tomatoes

Dice bacon and fry until crisp. Drain and cool on paper towels. In medium bowl, mix bacon, onion and mayonnaise. Remove stems from tomatoes. Place tomatoes stem side down on cutting board. Cut a thin slice off the top of each tomato. With a small spoon, scoop out pulp. Invert tomatoes on paper towels 30 minutes to drain. Fill tomatoes with bacon mixture. Refrigerate several hours or overnight. Makes 24 appetizers. They won't roll on the platter if you scoop out the bottoms and stand them stem side down.

Durham River, Man.
Branch No. 77

Party Marinated Vegetables

1 lb. carrots, sliced
1 head cauliflower (broken into flowerets, and sliced)
½ cup white vinegar
½ cup Mazola oil
½ lb. mushrooms, sliced
3 green onions, thinly sliced
1 tbsp. sugar
1 tbsp. lemon juice
¼ tsp. salt
¼ tsp. dried thyme leaves

Cook carrots and cauliflower separately, until just tender. Drain, reserving ½ cup carrot liquid. Place carrots, cauliflower and mushrooms in separate bowls, set aside. Stir together reserved liquid and remaining ingredients. Pour ⅓ of mixture over each vegetable. Cover; chill at least 3 hours. Drain and serve on lettuce. Makes 8 servings.

Ste. Anne, Man.
Ladies Auxiliary Branch No. 220

Cheese And Shrimp Puffs

½ cup butter
1 cup water
1¾ cups flour
6 eggs
2 cups shredded gouda cheese (1 roll)
1 cup shrimp, finely diced (1 tin)
2 tbsp. chopped onion
salt and pepper to taste
few drops tabasco sauce (optional)
oil for frying

Heat butter and water till boiling, let cool. Add flour all at once. Stir till batter leaves sides of pan. Add eggs, one at a time. Beat thoroughly after each addition. Stir in shrimp, cheese and onion. Heat oil to 375-400°F. Drop mixture in by teaspoon. Cook till golden brown. Heat in oven at 200°F. to serve or in microwave at defrost.

The Pas, Man.
Ladies Auxiliary Branch No. 19

Cream Mushrooms on Toast

1 lb. fresh mushrooms
3 tbsp. butter
1 tbsp. onion, grated
1 small clove garlic, minced
2 tsp. lemon juice
2 tbsp. flour
1 tsp. salt
¼ tsp. pepper
1 tsp. celery seeds
1 cup chicken stock
½ cup light cream
hot buttered toast

Wash and slice mushrooms. Heat butter; add onion and garlic and cook gently for 2 minutes. Add mushrooms and lemon juice, cover and cook gently until mushrooms are tender (approx. 3 minutes), stirring occasionally. Sprinkle in flour, salt, pepper and celery seeds, stir to blend and let bubble up. Remove from heat, add chicken stock and cream all at once. Stir to blend and return to heat. Cook gently, stirring constantly until thick and smooth. Serve immediately over hot buttered toast.

Montreal, Que.
Mazeppa Branch No. 183

Pickled Eggs

1 dozen eggs
1 tbsp. salt
2 cups white vinegar
1 cup cold water
1 tbsp. mixed whole spices
   (tied in a bag)

Put eggs and salt in cold water. Bring to a boil. Shut off heat; let stand for 5 minutes. Drain. Place in cold water and let cold water run while peeling. Let eggs stand till cold. Mix together the remaining ingredients. Let boil and then cool. Make sure eggs and vinegar are cold before putting in jar. Leave 24 hours before eating pickled eggs.

Ignace, Ont.
Ladies Auxiliary Branch No. 168

Filling For Buns

¼ lb. cheddar cheese, grated
3 hard boiled eggs
1-7 oz. can tuna
2 tbsp. green pepper, chopped
2 tbsp. onion, chopped
2 tbsp. stuffed green olives, chopped
2 tbsp. sweet pickle, chopped
½ cup mayonnaise

Heat in a slow oven (300°F.) for 30 minutes on a cookie sheet covered with foil.

Strathclair, Man.
Branch No. 154

Shrimp Cocktail

4 tins shrimp
1 large bottle chili sauce
1 large jar salad olives
1-48 oz. can tomato juice
1 green pepper, cut fine
1 cup celery, cut fine
1 spanish onion, cut fine
1 tbsp. Worcestershire Sauce
½ tsp. Tabasco Sauce

Mix all ingredients together. Will keep well.

Keewatin, Ont.
Branch No. 13

Toaster Oven Treats

3 slices whole wheat or white bread
1 cup Swiss or medium cheddar cheese, grated
½ tsp. Dijon mustard
1 tbsp. each of red and green pepper, finely chopped

Remove crusts from bread if you like. Cut bread in half. Toast until crisp. Mix remaining ingredients together. Thickly spread over bread, right to the edges. Grill until cheese is melted and bubbly. About 81 calories per half slice. Makes 3 to 6 servings.

Milltown, N.B.
Branch No. 48

Jellied Shrimp and Grapefruit

3 large grapefruit
2-4½ oz. cans shrimp
2 pkgs. lemon-flavored gelatin
2 cups boiling water
1 cup grapefruit juice (from fruit above)
½ cup mayonnaise
1 tbsp. lemon juice
1 tsp. salt
chopped parsley

Cut grapefruit in half and remove seeds. Cut around inside edge as close to shell as possible. Separate grapefruit segments from membrane. Lightly squeeze shells to collect remaining juice. Use spoon to remove membrance from shell. Save shells. Cut grapefruit segments into small pieces and drain. Save juice.

Drain shrimp. Save 12 for garnish. Flake rest of shrimp with a fork.

Dissolve gelatin in boiling water. Add 1 cup saved grapefruit juice, mayonnaise, lemon juice and salt. Blend with beater. Chill until partially set. Fold in drained grapefruit and flaked shrimp. Fill grapefruit shells level. Top each with a square of waxed paper and chill until firm (4 hours or overnight).

To serve: remove waxed paper. Cut grapefruit halves in half. Arrange each on a small plate. Spread a little mayonnaise on edge of each saved shrimp and roll in chopped parsley. With colored cocktail pick impale to filled grapefruit wedge. Yields 12 servings.

Wetaskiwin, Alta.
Branch No. 86

Avocado with Bacon and Mushrooms

3 ripe avocados
6 oz. mushrooms
8 slices bacon
1 tbsp. chopped parsley
oil
vinegar
seasonings

Slice mushrooms and cook in a vinaigrette dressing made with 1½ tbsp. wine vinegar and 5 tbsp. good oil, salt, pepper and a slice of onion. When cooked remove onion and allow to cool (this can be done ahead of time). Cook bacon and crumble into tiny pieces. Cut avocados in half, scoop out flesh, leaving skins intact. Cut flesh into teaspoon-size pieces, add to mushrooms. Add chopped parsley, taste for seasoning. Fill shells with mixture and sprinkle bacon on top.

Winnipeg, Man.
St. Vital Branch No. 16

Cherry Tomatoes Stuffed with Crab

36 medium size cherry tomatoes
½ lb. crab meat
4 tbsp. mayonnaise
½ tsp. salt
½ tsp. pepper
½ tsp. thyme
1½ tsp. lemon juice
1 tsp. dill weed
paprika

Slice top end off of each cherry tomato. Scoop out pulp and seeds. Wash tomatoes, sprinkle lightly with salt and invert them on paper towelling to drain, about 30 minutes. Flake crab meat, watching for any bits of shell. Mix thoroughly with all remaining ingredients except paprika. Use small spoon and carefully stuff tomatoes with crab mixture. Sprinkle with

paprika. Arrange on platter and keep in fridge until serving time.

Sioux Lookout, Ont.
Branch No. 78

Coconut Bananas

4 bananas, peeled
4 tbsp. lemon juice
1 pint dairy sour cream
1½ cups shredded coconut

Cut bananas into 1″ pieces; place lemon juice, sour cream and coconut in separate bowls. Dip banana pieces in lemon juice. Roll in sour cream and then coconut, making sure all sides are coated. Cover with plastic wrap and refrigerate several hours or overnight. Makes about 24 pieces.

Jacquet River, N.B.
Durham Branch No. 77

Sausage Party Rolls

¾ cup milk
1¼ tsp. salt
¼ cup shortening
½ cup warm water
1 tbsp. sugar
2 pkgs. yeast
3¾ cups flour

Let yeast rise in mixture of warm water and sugar. Mix in remaining ingredients like bread. Let rise, then punch down and proceed.

Filling:
1 lb. sausage meat
1 cup onion, chopped
¼ cup ketchup

Fry sausage meat and onion, add ketchup and let cool.
Roll out dough in small circles and put 1 tbsp. meat into one side, shape in half-moons and seal edges. Let rise. Bake in hot oven for 20 minutes or until they are brown like bread buns. Remove and brush with butter. These are really delicious.

Red Rock, Ont.
Branch No. 226

Shrimp Mold

1 can tomato soup
2 small pkgs. cream cheese
1½ tbsp. gelatin
½ cup cold water
¾ cup onion, chopped
¾ cup celery, chopped
1 cup mayonnaise
1-7 oz. can shrimp
Crisco to grease mold

Bring soup to a boil and add cheese and heat until melted. Add gelatin in water, mix and cool. Add onion, celery and mayonnaise. Let stand until it begins to thicken. Drain shrimp and add to mixture. Grease mold (4½ cup) and pour in mixture. Chill. Serve with crackers. For variety change the tomato soup to cream of mushroom and the shrimp to crab.

Bowser, N.B.
Branch No. 211

Tuna Burgers

1 cup white tuna
1 onion, diced
1 tbsp. green pepper, chopped
3 hard boiled eggs, chopped
½ cup Miracle Whip
½ lb. Cheese Whiz
1 tbsp. green relish
salt and pepper to taste

Mix and spread on opened burger buns. Top with ¼ slice of cheese. Brown lightly in oven.

Grand Manan, N.B.
Branch No. 44

Pizza Snack

⅓ cup cheese, grated
1 can mushrooms
2 tsp. chopped onion
1 can tomato soup
¼ cup oil
few grains garlic

Mix all ingredients together and place in fridge to thicken. Spread on hamburger bun halves and broil until bubbly.

Minnedosa, Man.
Auxiliary Branch No. 138

Crabmeat Mushroom Hats

1 lb. crabmeat
24 large mushrooms
1 tbsp. flour
½ tsp. salt
¼ tsp. pepper
dash of cayenne pepper
¼ tsp. celery salt
½ cup melted butter
½ cup canned milk or cream
4 tbsp. chopped mushroom
   stems
1 tsp. chopped parsley
1 tbsp. sherry
2 tbsp. parmesan cheese,
   grated
paprika

Wash mushrooms, dry and cut off stems. Chop stems and reserve for later. Blend flour and seasonings to taste in melted butter. Add cream, stirring constantly, and cook until mixture is thick and smooth. Add mushroom stems, parsley and sherry. Mix well and add crabmeat. Stuff the mushroom caps with crab mixture. Top with cheese and paprika to taste. Place in a well-greased baking tin and bake at 350°F. for 20 minutes or until lightly browned.

Montreal, Que.
Mazeppa Branch No. 183

Pizza Buns

1 lb. sausage meat or hamburger
½ cup onion, chopped
½ cup green pepper, finely chopped
1 small can tomato paste
1 can mushrooms
¼ tsp. garlic salt or to taste
¼ tsp. chili powder or to taste

Brown the first 3 ingredients in frying pan, then add remaining ingredients. Cook over low heat. Spread mixture on buns, top with mozzarella cheese and place under broiler. Mixture freezes well.

Morris, Man.
Branch No. 111

Empanadas

Pastry:
   2 cups flour, sifted
   2 tsp. baking powder
   ½ tsp. salt
   ⅔ cup shortening
   ½ tsp. chili powder
   ⅔ cup milk

Sift dry ingredients together and cut in shortening. Stir just until dough follows fork around bowl. Knead two or three times on floured board and roll out about ¼" thick. Cut in circles (size desired).

Filling:
   1 lb. ground beef
   1 tsp. chili powder
   ½-1 tsp. chilies, crushed
   1 clove garlic, crushed, or 1 onion, cut up
   ½ tsp. pepper

Sauté meat, add spices and simmer. Place 1 tbsp. of meat on half the circle of dough, fold over, crimp edges with fork. Bake at 400°F. for 12 to 15 minutes or until slightly brown, as for any kind of pastry. May be frozen, wrapped in saran wrap. Unfreeze before baking.

Canning, N.S.
Branch No. 73

Nuts and Bolts

Mix in large roaster:
   1 box Shreddies
   1 box Cheerios
   2 bags pretzels, straight ones
   1 large bag peanuts (various kinds of nuts may be used, also sunflower seeds)

Mix:
   1 pint Mazola oil
   ½ cup melted butter
   ½ tsp. garlic powder
   1 tsp. celery salt
   1 tsp. onion salt
   ¼ tsp. curry powder

Season to taste. Pour over dry ingredients. Bake 2 hours at 200-250°F., stirring from bottom every 20 minutes. I added raisins after mixture was cooked.

Elkhorn, Man.
Branch No. 58

Anti-Pasta

2 lbs. fresh cauliflower, chopped
2 lbs. green beans, cooked or 2-28 oz. cans
2 lbs. red peppers, chopped
2 lbs. green peppers, chopped
2 lbs. mushrooms, canned bits and pieces or fresh chopped
4-20 oz. bottles ketchup
1 cup vinegar
1 cup salad oil
2 lbs. pickled white onions, chopped (2 pint jars)
2 lbs. pickled cucumbers (sweet pickles 1 qt. and 1 pint jar)

Cook the above for 5 minutes. Mix in another pot:

6 or 7 tins solid white tuna
1 large or 4 small tins anchovies, cut fine
2-16 oz. tins pitted black olives
2 jars stuffed green olives (1-12 oz. and 1-16 oz.)
2 tbsp. salt

Add to first mixture, bring to boil again. Pack in sealers and process in large pot or canner for 20 minutes. Yields 21 to 23 pints.

Fort McMurray, Alta.
Branch No. 165

Cheese Snacks

1 cup margarine
½ lb. Imperial Cheese (sharp) (in red tub)
½ tsp. salt
1½ cups flour
4 cups Rice Krispies

Leave margarine and cheese out overnight to become soft. Beat together with salt until creamed. Spoon in flour. Add Rice Krispies by folding into above. Roll small balls and press down with fork on ungreased cookie sheet. Bake at 375°F. for 8 to 10 minutes. Watch carefully so they'll not burn.

Winnipeg, Man.
Ladies Auxiliary
Imperial Veterans in Canada
Branch No. 84

Scotch Eggs

1 lb. sausage meat (500 mls)
2 tbsp. chili sauce (30 mls)
2 tsp. worcestershire sauce
   (10 mls)
¼ tsp. salt (1 ml)
6 hard boiled eggs
2 eggs, well beaten
1-1½ cups fine dry bread
   crumbs (300 mls)
oil for frying

Combine sausage meat, chili sauce, worcestershire sauce and salt on waxed paper. Press meat mixture into six thin patties; wrap around hard boiled eggs. Dip in breads crumbs, then in beaten eggs. Dip again in bread crumbs. Chill 1 hour. Deep fry until well browned. Serve with tossed salad.

Port Hawkesbury, N.S.
Branch No. 43

Mushroom Delights

Pastry:
1-8 oz. pkg. cream cheese
½ cup butter or margarine
1½ cups flour

Knead and let stand in fridge for 1 hour.

Filling:
2 cans sliced mushrooms, well
   drained and chopped fine
1 onion, chopped fine

Sauté mushrooms and onion with 2 tbsp. butter, add 2 tbsp. flour, ¼ cup sour cream, garlic (to suit taste) and cook for 1 minute. Cool. Roll out pastry and make as perogies. Top with filling and cover. Wet edges of pastry with water before pinching to avoid breaking open while cooking. Make small slit in top. Bake at 350°F. for 10 to 15 minutes. May be frozen uncooked.
Option: Brush with white of eggs and cover with sesame seeds.

Gilbert Plains, Man.
Branch No. 98

Mushroom Turnovers

1 cup butter, softened
1-8 oz. pkg. cream cheese
½ tsp. salt
2 cups flour
1 egg yolk, beaten with 2 tsp.
   milk or cream
mushroom filling

To make pastry, combine first three ingredients in mixing bowl and beat until well blended and smooth. Add flour and stir until well blended and smooth. Put dough on a piece of double wax paper and flatten to form an 8x6" triangle. Wrap and chill overnight. Remove from fridge 8 to 10 minutes before rolling. Divide in half and roll each half in a 9x6" rectangle. Fold over in thirds, roll, fold over again and roll dough to 1/8" thickness. Cut in 2½" rounds. Reroll trimmings. Put level teaspoonful of filling in center of each round. Moisten edges with water and fold double. Press edges with floured fork to seal. Place on ungreased cookie sheet. Brush with egg yolk mixture and chill one hour. Bake in preheated 350°F. oven 25 to 30 minutes, or until golden. Serve warm, cold or reheated. Can be frozen. Makes 5-6 dozen.

Mushroom Filling:
2-4 oz. cans mushrooms,
   minced
2 tbsp. butter
½ tsp. salt
1/8 tsp. pepper
2 tbsp. minced onion
1 tsp. lemon juice
2 tbsp. flour
½ cup cream
1 tbsp. sherry or dry vermouth
   (optional)

In small saucepan, sauté mushrooms and butter 5 minutes. Sprinkle with next 4 ingredients; stir and simmer 2 minutes longer. Gradually stir in cream and simmer, stirring until thickened and smooth. Stir in sherry if desired; chill.

Waverly, N.S.
Dieppe Branch No. 90

Nutty Cheese Log

500 g cream cheese, softened
1-14 oz. can crushed pineapple, drained
1-7¾ oz. can flakes of ham,
   flaked, (tuna, salmon or
   shrimp)
1 tbsp. lemon juice
1 tbsp. horseradish, less if desired
½ tsp. pepper
1 cup chopped parsley
¼ cup chopped walnuts or
   almonds

Soften cream cheese, to this add the well drained pineapple, then your flakes of meat or fish. Add lemon juice, horseradish, pepper and nuts. Mix well. This will be sticky, so turn out on saran wrap and form into a log shape. Chill overnight. Before serving remove saran wrap and roll in chopped parsley. Serve with crackers or melba toast.

Winnipeg, Man.
Ladies' Auxiliary
Imperial Veterans in Canada
Branch No. 84

Tartlets
Salmon, tuna or lobster

1 can salmon
1 egg
canned peas
tart shells
buttered bread crumbs
1 tsp. minced parsley
salt and pepper
1 cup white sauce

Pick over and flake salmon. Season. Place a spoonful of mixture in each pastry shell, cover with a layer of canned peas, then a layer of white sauce, top with buttered bread crumbs. Bake until mixture is heated through and crumbs are brown.

Wedgeport, N.S.
Branch No. 155

Salmon Balls

1-7½ oz. can salmon
1-8 oz. pkg. cream cheese
1 tbsp. lemon juice
2 tsp. onion, grated
1 tsp. horseradish
¼ tsp. salt

Mix well until creamy. Shape into two round balls. Put in saran wrap and chill for several hours.

St. Peters, N.S.
Branch No. 47

Drumstick Canapes

3 pbs. small chicken wings
   (about 15)
½ tsp. ginger
¼ tsp. pepper
⅔ cup water
½ cup sugar
3 tbsp. cornstarch
½ tsp. salt
⅓ cup lemon juice
¼ cup soya sauce

Cut wings in half at joint. Discard tips. Place on broiler rack and bake at 400°F. for 15 minutes. Turn and bake an additional 15 minutes.
Mix sugar, cornstarch, salt, ginger and pepper. Add liquids. Cook, stirring constantly over medium heat until mixture thickens. Boil 2 minutes. Brush over wings and continue baking at 400°F. for about 35 minutes. During baking brush soya sauce mixture on wings frequently. Serve in chafing dish.

Oak River, Man.
Branch No. 150

Cheese Rarebit

2 cups cheddar cheese, diced
2 tbsp. flour
1 tsp. dry mustard
½ tsp. salt
1 tbsp. margarine
⅔ cup hot milk

Combine in double boiler over simmering water until smooth. Serve on toast, muffins, etc.

New Glasgow, N.S.
Ladies Auxiliary
Normandy Branch No. 34

Chicken-Bacon Nuggets

2 whole large chicken breasts
¼ cup orange marmelade
2 tbsp. soya sauce
½ tsp. salt
½ tsp. ground ginger
1/8 tsp. garlic powder
1-8 oz. pkg. sliced bacon
about 24 toothpicks

Cut each chicken br .ast lengthwise, remove skin and bones; then cut each half into 6 chunks. In bowl mix chicken, marmelade, soya sauce, salt, ginger and garlic; set aside. Arrange bacon slices on rack in broiling pan. Broil bacon 4 minutes or until partially cooked, turning once. Cut each slice crosswise in half.
Wrap each piece of chicken with a piece of bacon, secure with toothpick. Place on rack in broiling pan; broil 5 minutes or until chicken is fork-tender, turning nuggets once and brushing with mixture remaining in bowl. Remove toothpicks before serving.

The Pas, Man.
Branch No. 19

Crab Quickies

1-5 oz. can crabmeat
¼ cup mayonnaise
¼ cup grated parmesan
   cheese
¼ tsp. Worcestershire Sauce
dash Tabasco Sauce
dash garlic salt
round melba toast
tiny strips pimento
tiny sprigs of parsley

Drain crabmeat and flake with fork. Add mayonnaise, cheese, Worcestershire Sauce, Tabasco Sauce and garlic salt; chill until shortly before serving time. Turn on broiler, spread rounds of melba toast thickly with crab mixture, spreading right to edges. Set on broiler rack. Broil about 2 minutes or until hot. Cool slightly and top each with

a tiny strip of pimento and a sprig of parsley. Makes about 2 dozen.

Montreal, Que.
Mazeppa Branch No. 183

Pizza Buns

1-14 oz. can tomato sauce
1 medium onion, chopped
1 can mushroom stems and
   pieces
pepperoni, as much as you
   like, chopped
½ lb. cheddar cheese, grated
oregano to taste

Spread on buns and top with grated mozzarella cheese. Heat till melted and hot.

Crystal City, Man.
Branch No. 35

Homemade Onion Rings

onion rings
1 cup flour
1 tsp. baking powder
1 tsp. salt
1 egg
1 cup milk
¼ cup cooking oil

Mix all ingredients, except onion rings together. Dip onion rings in mixture and deep fry until golden.

Stonewall, Man.
Branch No. 52

Salmon Log

1-7 oz. can red salmon,
   drained
2-8 oz. pkgs. cream cheese,
   room temperature
1 tsp. lemon juice
½ tsp. horseradish
1 tsp. grated onion
chopped walnuts or pecans

Flake salmon, removing bones and skin; combine all ingredients in bowl, chill several hours, shape into 8x2″ log and roll in chopped nuts, coating well. Chill thoroughly. Serve with assorted crackers.

Winnipeg, Man.
Transcona Branch No. 7

Cheese Ball

1-8 oz. pkg. cream cheese
handful corned beef, chopped
   fine
1¼ cups chopped dill pickles
   or olives
1 tsp. horseradish
2 shakes Worcestershire Sauce
1¼ cups cheddar cheese,
   grated

Mix together, shape into ball
and chill. Roll in crushed walnuts. Delicious!

Miami, Man.
Branch No. 88

Dips

Shrimp Dip

1 can broken shrimp
1-8 oz. pkg. cream cheese
1 cup Miracle Whip
minced onion, to taste
red pimento, to taste
ketchup (to color)
dash garlic salt

Mix all ingredients together
well, except the shrimp. Add
shrimp and mix carefully so
shrimp will remain in pieces.

Penticton, B.C.
Branch No. 40

Shrimp Mould

Salad for Dip

1 can tomato soup
1-8 oz. Philadelphia cream
   cheese
½ cup salad dressing
1-2 cans shrimp
1 envelope gelatin
¼ cup cold water
¼ cup finely chopped onion
¼ cup finely chopped celery

Bring tomato soup to a boil.
Add cream cheese, onion,
celery, salad dressing and
shrimp. Mix thoroughly with
beater. Dissolve gelatin in the ¼
cup cold water and mix into the
above. Pour into mould and let
set. Unmold onto large tray and
serve with fresh vegetables such
as green peppers, carrots,
cucumbers, celery, cauliflower
and green onions. Also good as
a cracker or chip dip.

Nipigon, Ont.
Branch No. 32

Chip, Cracker or Vegetable Dip

1-8 oz. pkg. cream cheese
2 tbsp. mayonnaise
3 tsp. lemon juice
salt
¼ cup milk
Pimento cream cheese spread
   to taste

Mix all ingredients together
well.

Perth Andover, N.B.
Branch No. 36

Dip

⅔ cup mayonnaise
⅔ cup sour cream
1 tbsp. Beaumonde spice
1 tbsp. dill weed
1 tsp. chives
1 tsp. parsley

Mix all ingredients together
well. Great with raw vegetables.
Beaumonde spice may be pur-
chased at health food stores.

Ontario Provincial Command
Ladies Auxiliary

Sour Cream Dip

1 small container sour cream
5-6 tbsp. Miracle Whip
   (heaping)
4-5 shakes garlic salt
2-3 shakes seasoning salt

Mix together in small bowl. Put
in fridge about one hour before
serving, to let the dip get a bit
stiff. It's great with raw vegetables, potato chips, etc.

Houston, B.C.
Ladies Auxiliary
Branch No. 249

Salmon Dip

1 can salmon
1-8 oz. pkg. cream cheese
3 tbsp. green onion
1 tsp. Accent meat tenderizer
pinch garlic powder
Worcestershire Sauce
chopped almonds

Mix thoroughly in a bowl. Can
be used with crackers, chips,
melba toast, bread sticks, etc.

Happy Valley, Labrador, Nfld.
Branch No. 51

Garlic Cheese Dip

2-3 oz. pkgs. cream cheese
2 cups dairy sour cream
1 pkg. garlic-cheese salad
   dressing mix
dash Tabasco Sauce

Soften cream cheese; blend in
sour cream. Add remaining ingredients and beat smooth.

Minitonas, Man.
Branch No. 47

Guacamole Dip

3 avocados, peeled, seeded
   and mashed
1 tsp. salt
1 tbsp. lemon juice
1/8 tsp. Tabasco Sauce
1 clove garlic, crushed or
   garlic salt to taste
2 medium tomatoes, peeled
   and chopped

Mix, chill and serve with tortilla
or corn chips.

Edmonton, Alta.
Norwood Branch No. 178

Magic Mayonnaise

1 can Eagle Brand milk
½ cup vinegar
1¼ tsp. dry mustard
1 tsp. salt
1 egg
½ cup salad oil or melted
   butter

Place all ingredients in a quart
sealer and shake well.

Justice, Man.
Auxiliary Branch No. 233

My Favorite Dip

dash garlic powder
few drops lemon juice
1 tbsp. minced onion
1 cup sour cream
½ cup Miracle Whip
1 tbsp. parsley
a little less than a tbsp. of dill
   weed

Mix and let stand for two hours
before serving.

Winnipeg, Man.
Branch No. 117

Raw Vegetable Dip

1 cup mayonnaise, yogurt or
  blended cottage cheese
1 tsp. horseradish
1 tsp. dry mustard
1 tsp. curry powder
dash lemon juice
2 tbsp. sour cream
fresh or dried herbs to taste

Mix well and chill. Serve with an assortment of raw vegetables.

Ste. Anne, Man.
LaVerendrye Branch No. 220

Herb and Curry Dip

1 cup mayonnaise or salad
  dressing
1/2 cup sour cream
1 tsp. fine herbs, crushed
1/4 tsp. salt
1/8 tsp. curry powder
1 tbsp. chopped parsley
1 tbsp. grated onion
2 tsp. lemon juice
1/2 tsp. Worcestershire Sauce

Combine all ingredients and mix well. Chill before serving. Makes about 1 1/2 cups dip.

Stonewall, Man.
Branch No. 52

Vegetable Garden Dip

1 cup sour cream
1/2 cup mayonnaise
1/4 cup chopped radishes
1/4 cup chopped green pepper
1/4 cup chopped green onion
1/4 cup chopped cucumbers,
  unpeeled
1 tbsp. sugar
dash pepper
dash garlic salt

Combine all ingredients together and chill at least 2 hours.

Oxford, N.S.
Oxford Branch No. 36

Ham and Cheese Dip

1-5 oz. jar pimento-cheese
  spread
1-2 1/4 oz. can devilled ham
1/2 cup salad dressing
2 tbsp. minced parsley
1 tbsp. minced onion
dash monosodium glutamate
4 drops Tabasco Sauce

Blend well with electric mixer. Chill.

Minitonas, Man.
Branch No. 47

Cottage Cheese Dip

1-12 oz. carton creamed
  cottage cheese
1 tbsp. mayonnaise
1 tsp. salad-spice-and-herb
  mix
parsley snips

Blend together all ingredients except parsley snips. Chill. Top with parsley. Make 1 1/2 cups.

Minitonas, Man.
Branch No. 47

Beverages

Slush

8 cups water
3 cups sugar
8 oz. lemon juice
1-48 oz. can unsweetened
  orange juice (or frozen
  orange juice)
1-48 oz. can unsweetened
  pineapple juice
1-25 oz. Gilbey's Lemon Gin
  Collins or Dry Gin

Combine water and sugar. Boil 20 minutes in covered pot. Cool with lid on. Then add other ingredients. Mix well and freeze. Makes 2 gallons. To serve scoop out frozen drink into glasses and pour 7-Up or Sprite over frozen mixture. Add a straw for drinking.

Lac du Bonnet, Man.
Branch No. 164

Singapore Sling Slush

12 oz. gin
1/2 cup cherry brandy
1/2 cup grenadine
1/2 cup lemon juice
1 small can frozen lemonade
4 cups water
1/2 cup sugar
6 oz. cherry juice (reserve
  cherries for garnish in
  fridge)
1-19 oz. can pineapple juice

Combine all ingredients in a 4 litre ice cream pail and set in deep freeze overnight. Stir several times while freezing. Fill glass 3/4 full and then add Sprite, 7-Up or Ginger Ale.

Foxwarren, Man.
Legion Auxiliary Branch No. 152

Concentrated Lemonade

3 large lemons
1 large orange
1 1/2 lbs. sugar
1 pint water
1 oz. citric acid

Wash fruit well. Peel with potato peeler. Put peelings, juice and citric acid in a large bowl. Boil water and sugar together, and pour over fruit, juice and peelings. Let stand overnight. Strain and put into bottle. To use, put about 1/2" in a glass, fill with cold water. Adjust to taste.

Morin Heights, Que.
Branch 171

Hot Chocolate Mix

4 cups powdered milk
3/4 cup cocoa
1 1/2 cups sugar
1/8 tsp. salt

Combine all ingredients and mix well. Then put into fast turning blender and mix till fluffy. Store in dry jar. Mix 2 cups at a time. Keeps well. Put 3 tsp. in one cup hot water. Tastes like bought hot chocolate mix.

Wells, B.C.
Wells Branch No. 128

Pina Colada Slush

1 large can unsweetened pine-apple juice
1 tin coconut syrup
26 oz. vodka

Combine all ingredients and freeze. Serve with gingerale or 7up.

Justice, Man.
Justice Auxiliary
Branch No. 233

Punch

3 small bottles ginger ale
2 lemons
1 jar cherries
4 cups lemonade
2 cups cranberry cocktail
1 cup orange juice
ice cubes

Combine all ingredients. Spike if desired.

Boiestown, N.B.
Normandy Branch No. 78

Special Tea
Ideal for hot weather.

1-48 oz. pkg. orange Tang
1-24 oz. pkg. lemon
½-1 cup sugar
½ cup instant tea
1 tsp. cinnamon
1 tsp. cloves

Blend and serve cold. Use 2 tsp. in a mug. 1-1½ tsp. in a cup.

Valemount, B.C.
Branch No. 266

Apple Juice

3 qts. crab apples
5 qts. water
8 tsp. cream of tartar
2 cups sugar

Cut up crab apples. Pour boiling water over. Mix in cream of tartar and let stand 24 hours. Seal in sterilized jars.

Winnipeg Beach, Man.
Ladies Auxiliary
Branch No. 61

Little Joe Summer Drink

8 cups boiling water
6 cups sugar
4½ tbsp. citric acid (2 oz.)
2½ tbsp. tartaric acid (1 oz.)
Juice and rind of 3 oranges
Juice and rind of 2 lemons

Dissolve sugar and acids in boiling water. Stir until completely dissolved. Add juice and rind of oranges and lemons. Let stand 8 hours. Makes 3 quarts. Put 2 tbsp. per glass of water.

Squamish, B.C.
Branch No. 277

Reception Punch

1-6 oz. can frozen orange juice
1-6 oz. can frozen lemonade
1-6 oz. can frozen pineapple concentrate or 24 oz. pine-apple juice
1 large bottle ginger ale

Dilute frozen juices with water according to directions. Just before serving add one bottle ginger ale and some ice cubes. This makes 24 4 oz. servings.

Abbey, Sask.
Branch No. 222

Newfoundland Punch

2 cups strong tea
1 cup sugar
1 cup orange juice
½ cup lemon juice
1 cup cranberry juice
1 cup pineapple juice
Ginger Ale

Heat tea and sugar until sugar is dissolved. Add rest of ingredients except ginger ale. Cool. When ready to serve, add ginger ale to taste. Pour into punch bowl, adding round of ice made by putting water into a mold and scattering red and green cherries before freezing.

Springdale, Nfld.
Branch No. 40

Sparkling Pink Punch

2 qts. chilled lemonade
2 bottles Asti-Spumante wine, chilled
½ cup grenadine
thinly sliced lemon

Combine well-chilled ingredients just before you are ready to serve. Float thinly sliced lemon on top. Serve in champagne glasses. Makes 1 gallon.

Snow Lake, Man.
Branch No. 241

Egg Nog

9 egg yolks
6 tbsp. sugar
¾ of a 1/5 Brandy
2 tbsp. rum
1 qt. milk
1 qt. heavy cream, lightly beaten
9 egg whites

In large bowl beat yolks until flufffy, add sugar gradually, beating at low speed for 5 minutes, adding rum, brandy and milk. Blend in cream. Beat egg whites until stiff and fold into the first mixture. Cover and chill for several hours. Serve with a dash of nutmeg on top.

Grand Manan, N.B.
Branch No. 44

Punch

10 oz. Captain Morgan white rum
10 oz. Captain Morgan dark rum
6 oz. apricot brandy
12 oz. sweetened orange juice
12 oz. sweetened pineapple juice

Place lots of ice cubes in punch bowl, then pour the above mixture over them. Serves 12-15 people.

Shubenacadie, N.S.
Branch No. 111

Potato Champagne

1 apple
2 oranges
3 lemons
4 potatoes, peeled
5 lbs. sugar
1 pkg. yeast
1 gallon hot water

Thoroughly dissolve sugar in 1 qt. hot water. Dice all fruits and potatoes. Pour 3 qts. hot water in crock. Add dissolved sugar and add yeast, fruit and potato mixture. Mixture should be luke warm when yeast, fruit and potato are added and stirred together. Stir once a day for 10 days. Siphon Champagne off and bottle.

Houston, B.C.
Ladies Auxiliary
Branch No. 249

Dogberry Wine

2 qts. dogberries
12 apples, cut in pieces
4 qts. water
8 cups sugar

Cook apples and berries in water. Strain, then add 1 pkg. yeast. Store in bottle about two months, then put in smaller bottles.

Carbonear, Nfld.
Branch No. 23

Creamy Coffee Punch

½ cup Sanka instant coffee
⅓ cup sugar
5 cups cold water
2 tsp. vanilla
1 cup light cream, or half and half cream
4 eggs, well beaten
1 qt. vanilla ice cream, softened

Dissolve coffee and sugar in water, stir in vanilla. Stir cream into well beaten eggs. Add coffee mixture. Beat in softened ice cream. Chill at least one hour. Just before serving, beat to blend. Sprinkle with nutmeg, if desired. Makes about 2½ qts. or 20 servings.

Montreal, Que.
Maisonneuve Branch No. 66

Tia Maria

3 cups brown sugar
2 cups water

Boil sugar and water for 8 minutes, then cool. Add:
26 oz. vodka
5 tbsp. camp coffee
1 tsp. vanilla
½ cup dark rum

Mix all ingredients together. Make 2 26 oz. bottles. Can be used immediately.

Prince George, B.C.
Branch No. 43

Beet Wine

½ gallon beets
1 gallon water
1½ lemons
1½ oranges
3 lbs. sugar

Cut beets in cubes, boil for 3 hours, strain and add the oranges and lemons cut fine, add sugar, then boil for ½ hour. Let get warm and add ¼ yeast. Let stand 2 weeks, then strain and put in bottles tightly capped. This is a good wine and will keep for a long time.

St. John's, Nfld.
Branch No. 1

Durhams Favorite Punch

1 qt. bottle Beefeater Dry Gin
2 bottles dry table wine
2 large bottles 7-Up or Sprite
1 large can fruit punch
2 lemons, sliced
2 oranges, sliced
1 small bottle cherries, including juice
Ice cubes
¼ cup grenadine

Mix in large punch bowl, let stand until ice cubes are partly dissolved.

Jacquet River, N.B.
Durham Branch No. 77

TAKE TIME FOR TEN THINGS

1. TAKE TIME TO WORK—
   it is the price of success.
2. TAKE TIME TO THINK—
   it is the source of power.
3. TAKE TIME TO PLAY—
   it is the secret of youth.
4. TAKE TIME TO READ—
   it is the fountain of knowledge.
5. TAKE TIME TO WORSHIP—
   it is the highway of reverence and washes the dust of the earth from our eyes.
6. TAKE TIME TO HELP AND ENJOY FRIENDS—
   it is the source of happiness.
7. TAKE TIME TO LOVE—
   it is the one sacrament of life.
8. TAKE TIME TO DREAM—
   it hitches the soul to the stars.
9. TAKE TIME TO LAUGH—
   it is the singing that helps with life's loads.
10. TAKE TIME TO PLAN—
   it is the secret of being able to have time to take time for the first nine things.

Yeast Breads & Buns

Bread and Rolls
How Lucky we are Today!

Eight points in Bread Making

1. Good Wheat Flour— Some varieties of wheat are deficient in gluten which will not make good flour.

2. **A Good Miller to Grind the Wheat— The bread-maker should be sure to find The Good Miller.**

3. The Wheat— Should not be ground when very dry. Choose a "wet spell" for the grinding.

4. **The Flour— Should be sifted before using, to separate the particles.**

5. Good Yeast— This made from new hops. Stale hops, will not, with certainty, make lively yeast.

6. **Thorough Kneading— After it has had enough, knead it awhile longer.**

7. Do not let the dough rise too much. Nine out of every ten bread-makers in this country let their bread "rise" until its sweetness has been destroyed.

8. **The Oven can be too hot as well as too cool. The "happy medium" must be determined and selected.**

Good Luck in
your Bread Making!

Western Shore, N.S.
Branch No. 144

White Bread

1 pkg. yeast
½ cup warm water
½ tsp. sugar
4 cups warm water
3 tbsp. shortening
2 tsp. sugar
3 tsp. salt
flour

Soak yeast in ½ cup warm water and ½ tsp. sugar. Put 4 cups warm water in pan and add shortening, sugar and salt. Add enough flour to make a batter and add yeast, then enough flour until dough is not sticky and is easy to handle. Let rise until double, knead down. Let rise again until double in size. Put in pans and let rise. Bake at 350°F. for 30 minutes. Makes 5 loaves.

Oak River, Man.
Branch No. 150

Cheese and Beer Wheat Bread

1½ cups or 12 oz. beer
⅔ cup warm water (105-115°)
½ cup cooking oil
1½ cups whole wheat flour
4½-5 cups all-purpose flour
½ cup sugar
½ cup wheat germ
2 tsp. salt
1 pkg. yeast
1 egg
2 cups or 8 oz. cheddar cheese cut into ¼ to ½" cubes

Dissolve yeast in ⅔ cup warm water and let sit for 10 minutes. In saucepan warm beer to same temperature as yeast water. Pour into large bowl, add oil, yeast which is now risen, whole wheat flour, sugar, wheat germ, salt and egg; beat 2 minutes with mixer. Stir in remaining flour by hand. Knead about 5 minutes on floured surface, place in greased bowl and let rise until double, 60 to 75 minutes.
Line two 1 qt. casseroles or 9x5" loaf pans with foil; grease well. On well floured surface, work cheese cubes into dough, half at a time, until evenly distributed. Shape into 2 loaves, covering cheese cubes as much as possible. Put in greased casseroles, cover and let rise until light and doubled, 45 to 60 minutes.
Heat oven to 350°F. Bake 40 to 50 minutes or until loaf sounds hollow when lightly tapped. Remove from pans and cool. Here is a really delicious "special occasion bread"!

St. John's, Nfld.
Branch No. 1

Air Buns

½ cup warm water
1 tsp. sugar
1 pkg. yeast
3⅓ cups lukewarm water
½ cup sugar
½ cup melted lard
1 tsp. salt
1 tbsp. vinegar
9-10 cups flour

In the ½ cup warm water, put 1 tsp. sugar and the yeast. Let rise for 10 minutes in a warm place. In pot or bowl with lid put the 3⅓ cups lukewarm water, ½ cup sugar, lard and salt. Add yeast to this and the vinegar. Add flour, one cup at a time, just enough so the dough is not sticky. Grease the bowl and let rise for 2 hours. Knead down and let rise one hour. Form into buns and place on greased cookie sheets. Let rise 3 hours and bake at 400°F. for 10 to 12 minutes. Delicious!

Evansburg, Alta.
Branch No. 196

Pizza Dough

1 tsp. sugar
1 cup warm water
1 tbsp. yeast
1 tbsp. oil
2½-3½ cups flour
1 tsp. salt

Sprinkle yeast and sugar over warm water and let rise for 10 minutes. Mix in 2½ cups flour and the rest as needed to roll out.

Grand Manan, N.B.
Branch No. 44

Christmas Bread

1 pkg. granular yeast
½ cup lukewarm water
1 tsp. sugar
1 cup cereal cream or milk
½ cup sugar (second amount)
½ cup margarine, room temperature
1 tsp. salt
about 3½ cups unsifted flour
1 egg
1 tbsp. brandy extract
¼ cup mixed fruit
¼ cup raisins
¼ cup chopped almonds
½ tsp. cinnamon
½ tsp. grated orange or lemon rind
Glaze (see below)

Soak yeast and 1 tsp. sugar in warm water for 10 minutes. Scald cream. Add the ½ cup sugar, margarine and salt to cool. Add cream mixture, 1 cup flour, egg and extract to risen yeast liquid. Beat to blend. Beat in 2 more cups flour, for 2 minutes. Cover and let rise till double. Punch down on floured board with last ½ cup of flour. Press down dough. Cover with fruit, nuts, cinnamon and rind. Knead well into dough. Shape into roll; cut in 3 even pieces, roll each to 14″ length and braid together on greased cookie sheet. Let rise till puffy (take 2 to 3 hours). Bake at 350°F. for 35 to 45 minutes. Cool on rack. Can be frozen till needed, then thaw and reheat at 250°F. for 15 minutes. Glaze does not melt. Bread pans or angel food cake tin may be used.

Glaze:
1 cup icing sugar
½ tsp. vanilla
5 tsp. milk

Combine all ingredients and drizzle over bread.

Drumheller, Alta.
Branch No. 22

Olie Bollen

3 pkgs. dry yeast
1 tsp. sugar
1 cup lukewarm water
8 cups flour
5 tsp. salt
4 eggs
4 cups lukewarm water
3 cups raisins
2 cups currants
4 apples, peeled and diced
frying oil

Sprinkle yeast and sugar over lukewarm water. Let stand until yeast is completely softened. Mix with eggs and lukewarm milk. Sift flour and salt, add to yeast, eggs and milk mixture. Add raisins, currants and apples. Cover bowl and let rise 1½ hours. Drop by tablespoonful into hot frying oil. Turn if necessary. Some balls will turn by themselves when cooking. Remove from oil with fork and drain excess oil. Sprinkle with icing sugar while still hot. Delicious hot or cold.

Saulnierville, N.S.
Clare Branch No. 52

Fermipan Yeast Buns

Mix dry:
    2 tbsp. yeast
    4 cups flour
In a separate bowl mix:
    ½ cup sugar
    1 tsp. salt
    2 beaten eggs
    ⅓ cup oil
    3 cups warm water

Mix and add to flour mixture. Add 4-5 cups more flour. Let rise 15 minutes in warm place. Knead. Let rise 15 minutes. Knead and let rise 15 minutes more; then put in pans and let rise one hour. Bake at 350°F. for 15 to 20 minutes.

Frobisher, Sask.
Branch No. 343

Overnight Buns

1 pkg. yeast
½ cup warm water
1 tsp. sugar
1 cup sugar
1 tbsp. salt
1 cup vegetable oil
2 eggs
10-12 cups flour

At 5 p.m. set yeast, warm water and 1 tsp. sugar. Let stand 10 minutes. In large mixing bowl mix together all remaining ingredients except flour. Beat together and add 2 cups boiling water. Mix well and add 2 cups cold water. Mixture should now be lukewarm. Add yeast mixture. Add flour. Mix and knead until dough is no longer sticky. Let rise until 8 p.m. Punch down. Let rise until 10 p.m. Put in pan and let rise overnight at room temperature. Bake in the morning at 375°F. Makes 6½-7 dozen buns.

Emo, Ont.
Ladies Auxiliary
Branch No. 99

Butter Flaked Rolls

1 tbsp. yeast
1 tbsp. warm water
1 cup hot water
1 tbsp. butter or shortening
½ cup sugar
1 egg
3½ cups flour
1 tsp. salt

Add salt, sugar and shortening to hot water, cool. Add yeast dissolved in warm water and then add beaten egg. Beat in flour, let rise. Pinch off in small pieces and shape. Put in pan brushed with butter. Let rise again until double (about one hour). Bake at 425°F. for 12 to 15 minutes. (Batter will be quite soft, but do not add more flour.) Flour the board to make them easier to handle.

Sydney, N.S.
Branch No. 128

Sugarplum Bread

1 tsp. suagar
1 cup warm water (105-115°)
2 pkgs. active dry yeast
½ cup sugar
½ cup melted butter
2 tsp. salt
1 tsp. grated lemon rind
5½-6 cups flour
4 eggs
1 cup raisins
¾ cup mixed candied fruit
⅓ cup slivered almonds
vanilla glaze or icing sugar

Dissolve 1 tsp. sugar in warm water in large mixer bowl. Sprinkle in yeast. Let stand 10 minutes; then stir well. Add ½ cup sugar, melted butter, salt, lemon rind and 2 cups flour. Beat for 2 minutes on medium speed of electric mixer. Add 2 cups more flour and eggs; beat 3 minutes. Stir in almost all remaining flour, using enough flour to make a soft dough. Knead dough on floured board until smooth and elastic, about 8 minutes. Place in lightly greased bowl. Cover with greased waxed paper and tea towel. Let rise in warm place (75-85°F.) until doubled in size, about 2 hours. Punch down. Turn out on lightly floured board and knead in raisins, candied fruit and nuts. Shape into 2 round loaves. Place each in a well greased 9″ round cake pan. Cover with tea towel and let rise in warm place until doubled, 1-1½ hours. Bake at 350°F. for 45 to 55 minutes. Remove from pans immediately. Cool on wire racks. To serve spread with vanilla glaze or dust with icing sugar, if desired. Decorate with cherries or toasted slivered almonds. Makes 2 round loaves.

Waverley, N.S.
Dieppe Branch No. 90

90 Minute Rolls

1 cup hot water
1 tsp. salt
6 tsp. shortening
¼ cup sugar
1 yeast cake, dissolved in warm water
1 egg, beaten
3¼-4 cups flour

Combine hot water, salt, sugar and shortening in bowl; let stand till cool; add egg and yeast. Add flour until mixture handles easily. Let stand 5 minutes and shape in rolls. Let rise until double in bulk. Bake at 350°F. for 30 minutes.

Canning, N.S.
Habitant Branch No. 73

Ukrainian Easter Babba

½ cup lukewarm water
2 pkgs. yeast
1 tsp. sugar
2 cups scalded milk
½ lb. butter, melted
1 tbsp. salt
1¼ cups sugar
5 whole eggs
10 egg yolks
juice and rind of one orange
1 cup golden raisins
flour to make soft dough, about 7 cups

Dissolve the sugar in lukewarm water, sprinkle the yeast over and let stand 10 minutes. Beat the eggs and the egg yolks, adding the sugar a little at a time. Add the salt, orange juice, milk, rind and the yeast to beaten eggs. Blend well, gradually mix in flour, adding the melted butter a little at a time to make soft dough. Knead dough. Cover and let rise. Knead and let rise again. Grease tins. Fill and let rise. Bake at 350°F. for 25 to 30 minutes, then reduce heat to 300°F. Brush with 1 egg beaten and a little water added before baking.

Sydney, N.S.
Branch No. 128

Hot Cross Buns

1 yeast cake or 1 envelope
2 cups milk
6 cups flour
⅓ cup shortening
½ cup white sugar
1 cup currants or raisins
½ tsp. cinnamon or more spices if desired
1 tsp. salt

Scald milk, pour over sugar, salt and shortening. Let cool till lukewarm. Add yeast which has been dissolved in water and sugar. Add well beaten eggs, flour, spices and currants. Mix well. Let rise until double in bulk. Spread on a lightly floured board and cut with cutter. Place on greased cookie sheets, not too close together. Let rise 1½ hours. Bake at 400°F. for about 25 minutes.
If desired, brush with syrup consisting of ¼ cup white sugar and 2 tbsp. water when done.

Donkin, N.S.
Branch No. 5

Brown Bread

2 yeast cakes
1 cup lukewarm water
2 tsp. sugar
2 cups oatmeal
4 cups boiling water
1½ cups molasses
12 cups flour
2 tbsp. shortening
1 tsp. salt

Combine yeast, lukewarm water and sugar in bowl. Let rise. Soat oatmeal for 30 minutes in half the 4 cups of water, then add remaining water, molasses, shortening and salt; stir well. Add yeast mixture. Stir in flour until thick, then work in remaining flour. Knead well. Let rise until double in bulk, put in pans and let rise one hour. Bake at 350°F. for 40 minutes.

Milltown, N.B.
Branch No. 48

Brown Bread

½ cup warm water
1 tsp. sugar
1 tbsp. yeast
6 cups white flour
6 cups whole wheat flour
4 tsp. salt
¼ cup lard, melted
4 cups warm water
¼ cup molasses.

Set yeast with ½ cup warm water and 1 tsp. sugar. Let rise 10 minutes. In large bowl mix the white flour, whole wheat flour and the salt. Add lard melted in the 4 cups warm water and molasses. Add yeast. Mix and knead into a soft dough, adding more flour if necessary. Cover and put in warm place to rise until double in bulk. Punch down and let rise about one hour. Divide into 4 and put into greased bread pans. Let rise again. Bake at 375-400°F. for about 45 minutes.

Hint: Rub a little lard on top of dough so it doesn't harden while rising.

Teulon, Man.
Branch No. 166

Never Fail Buns

3 cups lukewarm water
½ cup sugar
2 pkg. or 2 tbsp. dry yeast
2 tsp. salt
4 eggs
½ cup oil
10 cups flour

Combine first four ingredients together. When yeast has risen, add the next 3 ingredients. Mix and knead well. Let rise until double in size, about 1½ hours. Punch down and let rise 10 minutes. Form into buns on greased cookie sheet and let rise one hour. Bake at 350°F. for 20 minutes. When baked, brush top with butter. Makes about 4 dozen.

Fort Assiniboine, Alta.
Branch No. 210

Paska
(Easter Bread)

1 tsp. sugar
1 cup lukewarm water
1 pkg. yeast
3 cups scalded milk
5 cups flour
6 eggs, beaten
⅓ cup sugar
½ cup melted butter
1 tbsp. salt
9-10 cups flour

Dissolve sugar in water and add yeast. Let stand 10 minutes. Combine yeast with warm milk and 5 cups flour. Beat well until smooth. Cover and let rise. Add the beaten eggs, sugar, melted butter, salt and mix. Stir in enough flour to make a dough that is neither too soft nor too stiff. Knead the dough until the dough no longer sticks. Knead until smooth. Let rise. Punch down and let dough rise again. Divide the dough into three equal parts. Make designs with one. Let dough rise, brush with beaten egg and 2 tbsp. water. Bake at 400°F. for 15 minutes, reduce heat to 350°F. and continue baking for 40 minutes. Cover with tin foil the last 10 minutes to keep the crust a light brown.

Sydney, N.S.
Ladies Auxiliary
Branch 128

Raised Doughnuts

2 cups margarine
1 cup sugar
1 tsp. salt
8 egg yolks
16 cups flour
juice and rind of 1 lemon
6 cups scalded milk, cooled
1 cup lukewarm water
2 pkgs. yeast
2 tsp. sugar

Prepare yeast according to pkg. instructions. Add milk to sugar, margarine and salt mixture. Add lemon rind and juice. Add beaten egg yolks and yeast when milk is cooled. Add flour until

stiffness for buns (about 16 cups). Let rise 1½ hours in large bowl. Knead and let rise 1 more hour. Roll dough and cut. Let rise 1½-2 hours. Fry in deep fat until golden brown.

Glaze:
1½ cups milk
2 cups sugar
1 cup margarine

Boil about 2 minutes. Remove from heat and add 2 cups icing sugar and 2 tsp. vanilla. Dip warm doughnuts in hot glaze. Place on platter to drain and then on waxed paper. Scrape glaze from platter back into pot and re-heat. Glaze will thicken if it gets cool, so set pot in hot water to keep it hot.

Bowsman, Man.
Branch No. 51

Truck Shop Cinnamon Buns

1 oz. or 2 tbsp. yeast
½ cup warm water
2 tbsp. sugar
2 cups boiling water
2 tbsp. margarine, melted
2 tbsp. salt
3 tbsp. sugar
2-3 cups flour
3 eggs, beaten
3¼ cups flour
⅓ cup margarine, melted
1 cup sugar
1½ tsp. cinnamon

Soften yeast in ½ cup warm water and 2 tbsp. sugar. Let stand 10 minutes. Mix together the 2 cups boiling water, 2 tbsp. margarine, salt and sugar. Let cool. Add 2-3 cups flour and beat to a smooth batter. Add yeast mixture and the eggs beaten with 3¼ cups flour. Mix until smooth. This makes a soft dough. Let rise one hour.

Melt ⅓ cup margarine in a dish. Cut dough into golf ball size pieces. Stretch to length of 4 or 5 inches. Dip in margarine. Roll in sugar and cinnamon. Tie in knot. Place on greased baking sheet. Let rise 45 minutes. Bake at 375°F. for 30 minutes.

Fort McMurray, Alta.
Branch No. 165

Vegetable Bread

8-9 cups whole wheat flour
½ cup warm water
2 tbsp. dry yeast
2 tsp. sugar
½ cup cooking oil
2 eggs
1 cup evaporated milk
1 stalk celery
2 large carrots
1 cup fresh parsley
    or 3 tbsp. dry parsley
1 inch wedge cabbage
3 tbsp. honey
1 tbsp. salt

Put warm water, yeast and sugar in bowl. Let stand 10 minutes. Put cooking oil, eggs, canned milk, celery, carrots, parsley, cabbage and honey in blender and liquidize thoroughly. Put this liquid in mixer bowl, add flour and salt, mix and knead till pliable consistency. Let rise till double in bulk. Punch down and form into 3 loaves. Put in greased bread pans. Let rise till double in bulk. Bake at 400°F. for 15 minutes, reduce heat to 350°F. and continue baking for 25 to 35 minutes, or till loaves sound hollow when tapped.

I use the dry yeast that is to be mixed with the flour (fermipan). If the vegetables are mixed all together and put in the blender half at a time, it liquidizes better.

Glenboro, Man.
Branch No. 71

Additional Recipes

Quick Breads, Coffee Cakes, Muffins, Donuts, Scones & Pancakes

Quick Breads

Pumpkin Bread

3 cups flour
2 tsp. baking soda
4 tsp. cinnamon
2 cups sugar
1-14 oz. can pumpkin pie filling
2 tsp. baking powder
½ tsp. salt
1½ cups butter or margarine
4 eggs

Beat eggs and set aside. Sift dry ingredients together. Combine sugar, butter and eggs. Mix well. Add dry ingredients slowly, then add pumpkin pie filling. Bake at 350°F. for one hour. Yields 2 loaves.

Twillingate, Nfld.
Branch No. 21

Christmas Cherry Loaf

1-6 oz. jar red maraschino cherries
1 egg, beaten
2¼ tsp. baking powder
2 cups flour
½ cup walnut pieces
¾ cup sugar
½ cup melted butter
¼ tsp. salt
milk

If desired, half green and half red cherries may be used for more color. Drain the cherries, reserving the syrup. Cut cherries in halves. Add enough milk to cherry juice to make one cup. Combine sugar, butter, egg and milk-juice mixture. Beat well. Add sifted dry ingredients and stir only until mixed. Add nuts. Fold in the cherries last. Bake at 350°F. for about one hour.

Calgary, Alta.
Alta. and N.W.T. Provincial Command
Ladies Auxiliary

Cherry Pound Loaf

½ cup butter
5/8 cup sugar
2 eggs, well beaten
½ tsp. vanilla
½ tsp. almond extract
½ tsp. lemon extract
2 tbsp. milk
1¼ cups all-purpose flour
1 tsp. baking powder
¼ tsp. salt
2 tsp. lemon juice
¼ cup almonds
¾ cup glace or well-drained maraschino cherries, halved

Cream butter, with an electric mixer, until fluffy. Add sugar and continue beating until the mixture becomes creamy. Add eggs. Mix in flavourings and milk. Sift the flour, baking powder and salt together. Add to the above mixture. Add the almonds and cherries. Fold in until well combined. Add lemon juice and stir in. Pour into a greased 9x5" loaf pan. Bake at 325°F. for one hour.

Calgary, Alta.
Ladies Auxiliary
Alta. and N.W.T. provinces Command

Orange Bread

½ cup Crisco
1 cup sugar
2 eggs
½ cup milk
rind and juice of one large orange
1½ cups flour
½ tsp. salt
1 tsp. baking powder

Combine ingredients in the order listed. Bake at 350°F. for 40 to 50 minutes.

Amhurst, N.S.
Branch No. 10

Pineapple and Cherry Bread

¾ cup sugar
½ cup butter
2 eggs, beaten
2 cups, flour
¼ tsp. baking soda
3 tsp. baking powder
½ tsp. salt
⅓ cup pineapple juice
¾ cup crushed pineapple
1 tsp. grated orange rind
½ cup cherries
1 tsp. vanilla

Drain pineapple and cherries well. Cream butter, sugar and beaten eggs. Add sifted dry ingredients with juice. Fold in pineapple and cherries. Bake at 350°F. for one hour.

Halifax, N.S.
Branch No. 25

Beet and Carrot Loaf

1 cup Crisco oil
1½ cups sugar
3 egg yolks
1 cup grated carrots
1 cup grated beets
2 tsp. baking powder
½ tsp. salt
2 cups flour
1 tsp. cinnamon
½ cup chopped nuts
3 stiffly beaten egg whites

Beat together oil, sugar, and egg yolks; add carrots and beets. Mix dry ingredients together with nuts and blend in. Fold in egg whites. Grease and flour loaf pans. Bake at 350°F. for one hour. Recipe may be doubled. Freezes well.

Domain, Man.
Branch No. 208

Boston Brown Bread

2½ cups flour
2 cups cold water
2 tsp. baking soda
1½ cups cornmeal
1 cup molasses
¼ tsp. salt

Mix all ingredients together, beat well and bake at 300-350°F. for 1½ to 2 hours. Bread will leave the sides of pan when done.

Tantallon, N.S.
St. Margaret's Bay Branch No. 116

Cherry All-Bran Bread

1 tbsp. butter
½ cup brown sugar
⅔ cup maraschino cherries, diced
¾ cup pecans or walnuts, chopped
2 cups sifted flour
4½ tsp. baking powder
¾ cup sugar
1 tsp. salt
1 tsp. vanilla
1 egg
1¼ cups milk
2 tbsp. melted butter
1 cup all-bran
⅓ cup maraschino cherries, diced

Melt 1 tbsp. butter in 9x6½" loaf pan or round pan. Sprinkle with the brown sugar, then the ⅔ cup diced maraschino cherries. Sprinkle with ½ cup of the chopped nuts.

Sift dry ingredients together into a bowl; make a well in centre. Melt 2 tbsp. butter in small pot; add egg and beat well; add milk; and stir into dry mixture to which balance of nuts and ⅓ cup cherries have been mixed. Stir well and put on top of first mixture. Bake at 350°F. for 50 to 60 minutes.

Penticton, B.C.
Branch No. 40

Irish Soda Bread

4 cups sifted flour
1½ tsp. baking soda
1 tsp. salt
2 tbsp. caraway seed
1½ cups buttermilk
¾ cup sugar
1 cup raisins
2 tbsp. melted butter
2 eggs, lightly beaten

Into bowl sift flour, baking soda and salt. Add caraway seed, sugar and raisins. Mix together melted butter, beaten eggs and buttermilk (or 1 cup buttermilk and ½ cup beer). Stir into flour mixture. Form into a round loaf and place into a round, well-greased 2 qt. pan (can use a 9" round iron frying pan). Cut a cross on top of loaf. Bake at 350°F. for 1¼ hours. Test with cake tester. Cool and wrap in foil. Freezes well. If you use a loaf pan, bake for 45 minutes.

Chateauguay, Que.
Branch No. 108

Banana-Apricot Bread

¼ cup chopped dried apricots
¼ cup good sherry or brandy
1 cup unbleached flour
¾ cup whole wheat flour
2 tsp. double acting baking powder
½ tsp. salt
3 tbsp. walnut or peanut oil
⅓ cup sugar
1 egg, beaten
1 cup mashed banana (3 small)
½ cup chopped nuts

Soak apricots overnight in sherry or brandy. Sift together the flour, baking powder and salt. Blend together oil and sugar and beat into the egg and mashed banana. Add sifted dry ingredients, a litle at a time. Fold in walnuts and apricots. Pour into greased loaf pan and bake at 350°F. for about 60 minutes.

Rouge River, Que.
Branch No. 192

Strawberry Festival Loaf

1¾ cups flour
1 cup sugar
⅓ cup oil
½ cup chopped nuts
1 tsp. baking soda
2 large eggs
1-10 oz. pkg. frozen strawberries, sweetened and undrained

In small bowl, stir together flour, baking soda and sugar. In large bowl beat eggs and oil together. Add strawberries with juice and beat slightly at low speed until berries are broken up. Add flour mixture and beat at low speed or by hand until batter is smooth, with bits of strawberries still whole. Fold in nuts. Pour into greased 9x5x3" loaf pan. Bake at 350°F. for one hour or until tested done.

Ear Falls, Ont.
Branch No. 238

Poppy Seed Bread

3 eggs
⅔ cup oil
1¼ cups evaporated milk
1 tsp. vanilla
2¼ cups flour
1½ cups sugar
4½ tsp. baking powder
¾ cup poppy seed

Preheat oven to 350°F. Grease and flour two 9x5" loaf pans. Lightly beat eggs in large bowl. Add oil, milk and vanilla; beat well. Add dry ingredients and poppy seed, beating until smooth. Turn into pans. Bake about 40 to 50 minutes or until it tests done.

Thunder Bay, Ont.
Ortona Branch No. 113

Prune Loaf

1 lb. prunes
3 cups water
2 cups white or brown sugar
¾ cup shortening
2 cups prune juice (add water to make 2 cups if needed)
2 tsp. cinnamon
½ tsp. nutmeg
½ tsp. cloves
½ tsp. salt
2 eggs, beaten
4 cups flour
2 tsp. baking soda

Soak prunes overnight in water. Drain, reserving juice from prunes. Pit prunes and cut into bits. Put in pan with sugar, shortening, prune juice, spices and salt. Bring to a boil and simmer for 5 minutes. Cool. Beat eggs and add to prune mixture alternately with flour; putting baking soda in last ½ cup of flour and mix well. Fill loaf pans ⅔ full. Bake at 350°F. for about one hour or until bread pulls away from pans. You can use 14 oz. pans, fill ⅔ full; makes 7 to 8, 14 oz. round loaves.

Winnipeg, Man.
Transcona Branch No. 7

Blueberry Casserole Bread

2 cups sifted all-purpose flour
1 cup sugar
1½ tsp. baking powder
½ tsp. baking soda
1 tsp. salt
1 tbsp. grated orange rind
1 cup fresh or frozen blueberries
¾ cup orange juice
2 tbsp. shortening
1 egg

Combine flour, sugar, baking powder, baking soda, salt, orange rind and blueberries. Add orange juice, shortening and egg. Beat until smooth. Pour into well greased casserole. Bake at 350°F. for 55 to 65 minutes.

Yarmouth, N.S.
Branch No. 61

Beer Bread

3 cups flour
3 tsp. cream of tartar
1½ tsp. baking soda
or substitute the following:
3 cups flour
4 tsp. baking powder
1½ tsp. salt
2 tbsp. sugar
1 bottle beer, room temperature

Put all ingredients into a large bowl. Mix as well as possible in about 17 strokes — do not knead. Push dough into a well greased loaf pan. Bake at 350°F. for 1 to 1¼ hours. The top will be crispy — I usually wrap the loaf in foil as soon as it is baked to make a softer crust. The bread is best eaten warm. For variations add:
raisins
dill seed
dry onion soup mix

Winnipeg, Man.
Duke of Kent Memorial Branch No. 119

Pineapple Cheese Loaf

2 cups flour
¾ cup sugar
3 tsp. baking powder
½ tsp. baking soda
1 tsp. salt
1 cup crushed pineapple, undrained
1 egg, beaten
2 tbsp. oil
½ cup cheddar cheese, shredded
½ cup chopped walnuts

Combine flour, sugar, baking powder, baking soda and salt. Mix together the crushed pineapple, beaten egg and oil; add to flour mixture. Fold in shredded cheese and walnuts. Pour into greased 9x5″ loaf pan. Let set for 20 minutes. Bake at 350°F. for 55 to 60 minutes.

Coquitlam, B.C.
Branch No. 263

Green Tomato Bread

8-10 medium green tomatoes
⅔ cup seedless raisins
⅔ cup boiling water
⅔ cup shortening or margarine
2⅔ cups white sugar
4 eggs
3⅓ cups flour
½ tsp. baking powder
2 tsp. baking soda
1½ tsp. salt
1 tsp. cinnamon
¼ tsp. cloves
⅔ cup chopped walnuts

Peel and core tomatoes. Run cut up pieces through blender until smooth and creamy (yields 2 cups pulp). Set raisins to soak in ⅔ cup boiling water, set aside to cool. In a large bowl, cream shortening and sugar until fluffy. Add eggs, two cups tomato pulp, raisins and water in which they were soaked. Beat well. In another bowl, combine flour, soda, salt, baking powder, cinnamon, cloves and nuts. Mix together with liquid ingredients. Divide batter into two loaf pans. Bake at 350°F. for 70 minutes or until cooked through. This freezes well.

Carberry, Man.
Ladies Auxiliary
Branch No. 153

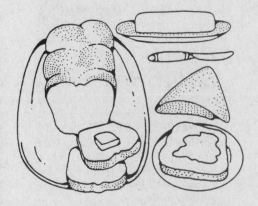

Moir's Pound Cake

3 cups flour
1 tsp. salt
1½ tsp. baking powder
2 cups sugar
½ lb. butter
3 eggs
1 cup scalded milk
flavouring
½ lb. cherries
1 lb. sultanas

Cream butter, sugar and eggs, add sifted flour, salt and baking powder alternately with scalded milk, lastly add flavouring and fruit. Bake at 325-350°F. for 1½ hours or more.

Clarenville, Nfld.
Branch No. 27

Rhubarb Bread

1 cup rhubarb, finely cut
1½ cups sugar
1 cup brown sugar
¼ cup melted butter
1 beaten egg
½ cup orange juice
grated rind of one orange
2½ cups flour
4½ tsp. baking powder
½ tsp. salt
½ cup nuts

Cream sugar and butter; mix in egg and beat well. Mix in orange juice and rind. Mix in dry ingredients well. Stir in nuts and rhubarb. Pour in well greased 9x5x2″ pan. Bake at 350°F. for one hour.

Petitcodiac, N.B.
Branch No. 41

Peanut Butter Bread

2 cups flour
2 tsp. baking powder
1 tsp. salt
⅓ cup sugar
¾ cup peanut butter
1 egg, well beaten
1 cup milk

Preheat oven to 350°F. Grease a 4x8″ loaf pan. Sift the flour, baking powder, salt and sugar together. Work in the peanut butter, using a pastry blender or fork, until crumbly. Combine the beaten egg and milk; add to the mixture, mixing thoroughly. Pour into greased pan. Bake about one hour.

Murdochville, Que.
Branch No. 218

No Egg Carrot Loaf

1⅓ cups water
1 cup sugar
1 cup grated carrots
1 cup raisins
1 tsp. nutmeg
1 tsp. cinnamon
½ tsp. cloves
4 tsp. butter

Boil all above ingredients for 5 to 10 minutes. Cool. Add:

2 cups flour
1 tsp. baking powder
1 tsp. baking soda
1 tsp. salt
½ cup walnuts

Bake at 325°F. for one hour.

Mafeking, Man.
Branch No. 93

Mexican Wedding Bread

½ lb. butter
4 tbsp. sugar
2 cups flour
¼ tsp. salt
1 cup pecans, chopped fine
1 tsp. vanilla

Cream butter, salt and sugar till light and fluffy. Add vanilla, flour and nuts to make a stiff dough. Divide dough in half. Roll about ½″ thick. Chill in freezer for 10 minutes. Cut in slices or with cookie cutter. Bake at 350°F. for 20 minutes. Cool slightly. While still warm dip into icing sugar. Place on wax paper to cool.

Carman, Man.
Branch No. 18

Date and Nut Loaf

1 cup dates, chopped
½ cup boiling water
1 cup brown sugar
1 tsp. baking soda
2 cups flour
½ cup butter
2 eggs
½ cup walnuts, chopped

Boil dates and water until dates are soft. Add remaining ingredients and blend well. Bake in greased loaf pan at 350°F. for 1½ hours.

Boissevain, Man.
Branch No. 10

Glazed Lemon Loaf

2 cups all-purpose flour
3 tsp. baking powder
½ tsp. salt
1 cup sugar
½ cup melted butter or
   margarine
2 eggs, slightly beaten
1 cup milk
grated peel of ½ a lemon
½ tsp. vanilla

Preheat oven to 350°F. Lightly grease 9x5″ loaf pan. Combine flour, baking powder, salt and sugar. Combine remaining ingredients. Add the liquid ingredients all at once to the dry ingredients. Stir just until moistened. Turn into prepared pan and bake at 350°F. for 60 to 65 minutes or until a toothpick inserted in centre comes out clean. When cool top with Lemon Glaze.

Lemon Glaze:
2 tbsp. sugar
2 tbsp. lemon juice

Combine sugar and lemon juice and mix until sugar is dissolved. When loaf is almost cool spoon mixture over top.

Salmon River, N.S.
Clare Branch No. 52

Pecan Rolls

½ cup sweetened condensed milk
2 tbsp. soft butter
¼ tsp. salt
½ tsp. vanilla
2½ cups icing sugar
½ cup glace cherries, chopped red and/or green

Blend softened butter with milk, add salt and vanilla and work in sugar to make a firm mixture that will hold its shape. Work in the chopped cherries. Form into rolls about 4″ long and 1½″ in diameter.

Caramel Coating:
1 cup brown sugar
3 tbsp. corn syrup
⅔ cup sweetened condensed milk
½ cup butter

Put all ingredients into a large heavy pot. Cook over low heat, stirring constantly until a few drops tested in cold water forms a firm ball. Cool slightly. Pour over rolls or dip rolls into mixture; then roll in nuts. Chill thoroughly before cutting.

Aunt Peg's Hints: The first time you make these you may think you don't want to try again — it is a bit messy.
1. Make the first part ahead of time and freeze. Easier to handle.
2. If making more than a single recipe, more than one person advisable. Good family Christmas project.
3. Have nuts (any type nuts are good) spread on buttered wax paper.
4. Dip roll in caramel and then in nuts. Will flatten but can be re-shaped.
5. Packaged cherries are preferred, but if using the bottled ones, dry them as much as possible. Extra icing sugar may have to be used.

Edmonton, Alta.
Jasper Place Branch No. 255

Chocolate Zucchini Loaf

2½ cups all-purpose flour, unsifted
½ cup cocoa
2½ tsp. baking powder
1½ tsp. baking soda
1 tsp. salt
1 tsp. cinnamon
¾ cup soft butter or margarine
2 cups sugar
3 eggs
2 tsp. vanilla
2 tsp. grated orange peel
2 cups coarsely shredded zucchini, unpeeled
1 cup milk
1 cup pecans or walnuts, chopped

Combine all dry ingredients and set aside. Beat together butter and sugar until well blended. Add eggs, one at a time, beating well after each addition. With spoon, stir in vanilla, orange peel and zucchini, alternately stir in dry ingredients and milk into zucchini mixture, adding nuts with last addition. Pour batter into a greased and floured 10″ tube pan or Bundt pan or 2 loaf pans. Bake at 350°F. for about one hour or until a toothpick inserted in centre of cake comes out clean. Cool in pan for 15 minutes, turn out on cake rack to cool thoroughly. Glaze if you wish.

Glaze:
2 cups icing sugar
2 tbsp. milk
1 tsp. vanilla

Mix together and beat until smooth. Drizzle glaze over cake. Slice thin. Freezes well.

Vernon, B.C.
Ladies Auxiliary
Branch No. 25

Coffee Cakes

Sour Cream Coffee Cake

1 cup sour cream
2 eggs, well beaten
1 tsp. baking soda
½ cup. soft butter
1 cup white sugar
1 tsp. vanilla
1¾ cups sifted cake flour
2 tsp. baking powder

Topping:
¼ cup brown sugar
1 tbsp. cinnamon
2 tbsp. chopped nuts

Grease and flour an 8″ square pan. Preheat oven to 350°F. Combine sour cream and baking soda in a bowl. It will double in volume. Blend butter and sugar; add eggs and vanilla, beat well. Add sifted dry ingredients and sour cream. Spread half of the batter in prepared pan. Sprinkle with half the topping mixture. Cover with remaining batter. Sprinkle with remainder of topping. Bake for 45 to 50 minutes. Serve warm or wrapped in foil.

Channel, Nfld.
Channel Branch No. 11

Rhubarb Coffee Cake

½ cup butter
1½ cups brown sugar
1 egg
1 cup sour milk
2 cups flour
1 tsp. baking soda
½ tsp. salt
3 cups rhubarb, diced

Blend together butter, sugar and egg. Sift flour, baking soda and salt. Mix diced rhubarb into flour mixture; then add to batter and sour milk. Sprinkle batter with ½ cup granulated sugar and 1 tbsp. cinnamon. Bake at 350°F. for 35 to 45 minutes.

Lundar, Man.
Branch No. 185

Cinnamon Coffee Cake

¾ cup sugar (180 ml)
¼ cup shortening (60 ml)
1 egg
½ cup milk (125 ml)
1½ cups flour (375 ml)
2 tsp. baking powder (10 ml)
½ tsp. salt (2 ml)

Topping:
½ cup brown sugar
1½ tsp. cinnamon

Preheat oven to 375°F. Grease and flour a 9x9″ cake pan. Cream shortening, add sugar and egg. Mix well. Stir in milk. Measure flour, baking powder and salt. Sift into mixture. Blend well. Spread batter in pan. Sprinkle with topping. Bake 3O to 35 minutes.

Port Hawkesbury, N.S.
Branch No. 43

Poppy Seed Coffee Cake

½ cup margarine
½ cup cooking oil
1½ cups sugar
4 eggs, separated
2½ cups flour
1 tsp. baking soda
2 tsp. baking powder
1 tsp. vanilla
¼ cup poppy seed
1 cup buttermilk

Soak poppy seed in buttermilk for 15 minutes. Cream margarine, add oil, sugar and egg yolks. Beat well. Add dry ingredients and then add poppy seed mixture and vanilla. Beat egg whites stiff and fold into the above.

Sprinkle on top:
⅓ cup white sugar
2 tsp. cocoa
1 tsp. cinnamon

Mix in with knife. Bake at 350°F. for 50 minutes.

Stony Mountain, Man.
Branch No. 142

Quick Coffee Ring

2 cups flour
2 tsp. baking powder
2 tbsp. sugar
1 egg
½ cup milk
6 tbsp. shortening

Filling:
¼ cup butter
½ cup brown sugar
1 tbsp. cinnamon
½ cup nuts
½ cup raisins
½ tsp. allspice

Cream sugar and shortening; add egg and beat. Add dry ingredients with milk. Brush butter on rolled out dough. Put on filling and roll, forming into a ring. Bake at 425°F. for 15 minutes. Ice if desired.

Crystal City, Man.
Branch No. 35

Peach Coffee Cake

¾ cup sugar
½ cup shortening
2 eggs
1 cup sour cream
2 cups flour
1 tsp. baking powder
1 tsp. baking soda
2 cups peaches, drained
1 tsp. vanilla
½ tsp. salt

Combine dry ingredients. Cream sugar and shortening until light and fluffy, add eggs, sour cream and vanilla, then add dry ingredients and lastly, fold in peaches by hand. Pour in angel food cake pan and bake at 325°F. for 40 minutes. Serves 6 to 8.
This is delicious served warm with cream or ice cream, but can be served plain.

Mahone Bay, N.S.
Branch No. 49

Cranberry Streusel Coffee Cake

Streusel:
¾ cup lightly packed brown sugar
½ cup all-purpose flour
1 tsp. cinnamon
¼ cup butter

Cake:
½ cup soft butter
1 cup white sugar
2 eggs
1 tsp. vanilla
2 cups all-purpose flour
1 tsp. baking powder
1 tsp. baking soda
½ tsp. salt
1 cup dairy sour cream
2 cups cranberries, fresh or frozen

To make streusel: Mix together sugar, flour and cinnamon; blend in butter until crumbly.
To make cake: Cream butter with sugar until light and fluffy. Beat in eggs, one at a time, then vanilla. Sift together flour, baking powder, baking soda and salt. Add to creamed mixture alternately with sour cream. Spread half the batter in a greased and floured 10″ springform pan. Sprinkle with half the streusel mixture, then half the cranberries. Spread with remaining batter. Sprinkle evenly with remaining cranberries, then remaining streusel. Bake at 350°F. for about one hour or until skewer inserted in centre comes out clean. Cool in pan 10 minutes, then remove pan.
A variation: Bake coffee cake in a 13x9″ cake pan; instead of layering the mixtures, simply spread batter in pan, then sprinkle with cranberries and streusel evenly over top. Bake about 45 minutes. Serve warm. Makes about 12 servings.
To reheat coffee cake, wrap in foil and heat about 20 minutes in a 350°F. oven.

Howick, Que.
Howick Branch No. 123

Apple Cheddar Coffee Cake

1½ cups flour
2 tsp. baking powder
¼ tsp. salt
¼ cup butter
½ cup sugar
1 egg
1 tsp. vanilla
½ cup milk
1 cup grated cheddar cheese
4 cups apples, thinly sliced

Topping:
2 tbsp. flour
¼ cup brown sugar
½ tsp. cinnamon
2 tbsp. butter

Preheat oven to 375°F. Sift flour, baking powder and salt. Cream butter and sugar; beat in egg and vanilla. Add dry ingredients with milk and vanilla and blend well. Turn half the batter into an 8″ square pan. Add in layers, half the cheese, half the apples, then remaining cheese, batter and end with apples. Make crumbs of topping and sprinkle over apples. Bake 30 minutes. Serve warm. To reheat put in 350°F. oven for 15 minutes.

Campobello, N.B.
Ladies Auxiliary
Branch No. 83

Apple Strudel Cake

1½ cups flour
¼ cup shortening
3 tsp. baking powder
1 tsp. cinnamon
¼ tsp. salt
½ cup milk
½ cup sugar
1 egg
2 large apples, chopped

Mix flour with baking powder, salt, sugar and cinnamon. Beat egg, add milk and melted shortening and pour into dry ingredients. Add chopped apples and

mix well. Pour into greased pan. Mix topping and pour over batter.

Topping:
¼ cup brown sugar
2 tbsp. flour
¼ tsp. butter
½ tsp. cinnamon

Bake at 350°F. for 45 minutes.

Tarrace Bay, Ont.
Branch No. 223

Pancakes

Pancakes

2 eggs
1/8 cup sugar
1 tsp. vanilla
¼ cup Mazola oil
1 cup flour
½ cup milk
1 tsp. baking powder
1/8 tsp. salt

Beat eggs and sugar together. Add sifted dry ingredients. Beat well; add oil and milk. Beat until batter is smooth. Drop on a hot griddle or frying pan.

Glenboro, Man.
Branch No. 71

Cottage Cheese Pancakes

3 eggs, beaten
1 cup dry cottage cheese
½ tsp. salt
1 cup milk
1 cup flour
2-3 tsp. sugar

Beat eggs well, blend in milk and cottage cheese, then add rest of ingredients, beating just to blend. Preheat skillet well, grease lightly and spoon batter onto pan, browning pancakes on both sides. Serve hot with sour cream and fresh sweetened berries or serve with your favorite apple sauce or fruit.

Winnipeg, Man.
General Monash
Branch No. 115

Maple syrup

1 cup boiling water
2 cups white sugar
½ tsp. maple extract

Boil water and sugar until clear and sugar is dissolved. Add maple extract.

Waskada, Man.
Brancho No. 92

Apple Pancakes

1 tin apple pie filling
2 cups flour
1 cup sugar
1½ tsp. baking soda
1 tsp. salt
2 eggs
1 tsp. vanilla
⅔ cup oil

Spread apple filling in 9x12″ pan. Mix flour, sugar, soda and salt together. Sprinkle over apples. Beat oil, eggs and vanilla together; pour over mixture in pan. Stir all together. Mix ½ cup brown sugar and 1 tsp. cinnamon and sprinkle over top. Bake at 350°F. for 45 minutes.

Winnipeg, Man.
Ladies Auxiliary
West Kildonan Branch No. 30

Corn Fritters

1 egg, slightly beaten
1⅓ cups all-purpose flour
1 tsp. salt
1½ tsp. baking powder
2½ cups cream style corn

Heat fat for deep-frying. Mix and sift dry ingredients. Add corn and egg, stirring very little. Drop fritter mixture in a generous tablespoon into hot fat and fry until golden brown. Turn and brown. Serve hot. Maple syrup may be poured over fritters when served. Yields 18 fritters.

Salisbury, N.B.
Branch No. 31

English Tea Pancakes

2 cups flour
½ cup sugar
3 tsp. baking powder
½ tsp. salt
1 egg, beaten
¼ cup melted butter
1¾ cups milk

Beat all ingredients together until smooth. Pour 1 tbsp. for each pancake onto hot griddle. Flip quickly as they cook quickly. Butter and serve hot or cold; or fill with jam or jelly and roll up.

Valemount, B.C.
Branch No. 266

Potato Pancakes

1 large onion, finely grated
6 large potatoes, peeled and
    finely grated
3 eggs, slightly beaten
¼ cup flour
1 tsp. salt
1 tsp. baking powder
2 tbsp. vegetable oil

Combine ingredients. Use ¼ cup batter for each pancake. Fry in greased hot frying pan until nicely browned; turn and brown other side. Makes about 2 dozen pancakes .
Serve with sour cream or butter. Bacon goes very nice as well.

Mafeking, Man.
Branch No. 93

Fluffy Pancakes

4 eggs, separated
1 cup sour cream
1 cup small curd cottage
    cheese
¾ cup flour
¾ tsp. baking powder
½ tsp. salt
1 tbsp. sugar

Beat egg whites until stiff. Beat yolks creamy, add sour cream and cottage cheese. Sift flour with baking powder, salt and sugar; add to cheese mixture. Gently fold in egg whites. Makes 20, 4″ pancakes.

Domain, Man.
Branch No. 208

Nalysnyky
(Rolled Pancakes)

4 eggs
1 cup flour
1 cup milk
½ tsp. salt
3 tbsp. water

Beat eggs in blender till light. Add milk and remaining ingredients. Beat till smooth. Butter frying pan lightly, pour a few tablespoons of batter in pan and spread really thin, when lightly browned on bottom, remove the cakes to a warm plate. Cook one side only. Butter pan each time. Fill with one of the following fillings. Pour either fried cream and onions over rolled pancakes or just straight cream. Bake in oven for 20 to 30 minutes.

Cottage Cheese Filling:
   2 cups cottage cheese
   2 tbsp. rich cream
   2 egg yolks
   salt and sugar to taste
   chopped dill or green onions
     (optional)

Mash cheese, add rest of ingredients. Place 1 tablespoon of filling on one side of cake roll and place in buttered shallow casserole dish.

Mushroom Filling:
   1½ cups finely chopped
     mushrooms
   1 tsp. onion
   2 tbsp. butter
   2 tbsp. sour cream
   salt and pepper

Cook onion till transparent. Add sour cream and cook a little longer. Season.

Cabbage Filling:
   3 cups finely shredded
     cabbage
   1 tbsp. grated onion
   2 tbsp. butter
   salt and pepper

Cook onions till tender. Add cabbage, season with salt and pepper; cook till just tender. Vary by adding one of the following: chopped ham, cooked crisp bacon or chopped mushrooms.

Enderby, B.C.
Branch No. 98

Oatmeal Pancakes

1½ cups rolled oats
2 cups milk
½ cup whole wheat flour
½ cup all-purpose flour
1 tbsp. brown sugar
1 tbsp. baking powder
1 tsp. salt
½ tsp. cinnamon
2 eggs, beaten
¼ cup melted butter

In a large mixing bowl, blend rolled oats and milk; let stand 5 minutes. Stir together flours, baking powder, salt and cinnamon. Add dry ingredients, eggs and melted butter to oats, stirring until combined. Pour ¼ cup batter for each pancake onto a hot lightly greased griddle. Cook each pancake until edges become dry and surface is covered with bubbles. Turn and cook second side until golden brown. Makes 16 to 18 pancakes.

Glenboro, Man.
Branch No. 71

Scones

Jam Buns

2 cups flour
4 level tsp. baking powder
1 cup butter or part shortening
3 tbsp. white sugar
1 egg
pinch of salt
½ cup milk
1 tsp. vanilla

Mix flour, baking powder, salt, sugar and butter as for pastry. Beat egg, add milk and vanilla. Roll out as for cookies. Cut with good sized cutter in rounds. Put teaspoon raspberry or strawberry jam on each round, draw up to centre. Put in greased muffin pans and bake in 350°F. oven for 20 to 25 minutes.

Kelwood, Man.
Ladies Auxiliary
Kelwood Branch No. 50

Onion Cheese Supper Bread

½ cup chopped onion
1 egg, beaten
½ cup milk
1½ cups Bisquick
1 cup cheddar cheese, shredded
2 tbsp. melted butter

Cook onion in a small amount of hot oil till tender but not brown. Combine egg, milk and Bisquick, stirring until moist. Add onion and half of cheese. Grease muffin tins and fill about half full. Sprinkle with remaining cheese. Drizzle melted butter over top. Bake at 400°F. for 20 minutes or until toothpick inserted in centre comes out clean. This makes about 8 large biscuits or it can also be baked in a bread pan. Great with a salad!

Wainwright, Alta.
Worthington Branch No. 29

Sour Cream Biscuits

2 cups sifted all-purpose flour
2 tbsp. sugar
1 tbsp. baking powder
½ tsp. baking soda
½ tsp. salt
3 tbsp. cold butter
1 egg
1 cup sour cream

Glaze:
light cream
sprinkle of sugar

Dust baking sheet with flour and preheat oven to 450°F. Sift together dry ingredients and cut in butter. In another bowl, beat egg and mix with sour cream, then mix in dry ingredients. Pat ¾" thick and cut with cutter. Makes one dozen. Glaze if desired. Bake 15 minutes or until done.

West Pubnico, N.S.
Ladies Auxiliary
Branch No. 66

Biscuits, Dumplings, Pancakes, etc.

9 cups flour
1 lb. shortening
1½ tsp. salt
¼ cup baking powder

Mix together and keep in airtight container. Just add milk when needed. This will keep for a long time.

Strathclair, Man.
Branch No. 154

Molasses Buns

½ cup butter
¼ cup sugar
1 egg
1 tsp. salt
1 tsp. vanilla
½ cup molasses
2¼ cups flour
½ tsp. baking powder
1 tsp. baking soda
¼ cup hot water
1 cup raisins
½ tsp. cloves
½ tsp. cinnamon

Cream butter and sugar, add egg and beat well. Add vanilla, and molasses. Add soda to hot water and fold in mixture. Add flour, spices, salt and baking powder, then raisins. Bake at 350°F. for 20 minutes.

Milltown, Bay D'Espoir, Nfld.
Centennial Branch No. 61

Mile High Biscuits

3 cups flour
¾ tsp. cream of tartar
¾ tsp. salt
1 egg
4½ tsp. baking powder
2 tbsp. sugar
¾ cup shortening
1 cup milk

Mix all ingredients in order given, except egg, which is added to the milk. Knead 3 minutes. Cut with round cookie cutter and bake at 450°F. for 12 minutes.

Morden, Man.
Branch No. 11

Jiffy Cinnamon Rolls

2 cups flour
2 tbsp. sugar
4 tsp. baking powder
1 tsp. salt
¼ cup cold margarine
1 cup cold milk
⅓ cup margarine
1 cup brown sugar
3 tsp. cinnamon
⅓ cup raisins

Glaze:
½ cup icing sugar
milk or water

Cut ¼ cup margarine into flour, sugar, baking powder and salt. Add milk and stir until it becomes a soft dough. Knead on floured board 8 to 10 times. Roll into rectangle. Cream together ⅓ cup margarine, brown sugar and cinnamon. Drop one teaspoon into 12 greased muffin tins. Spread rest on rectangle and sprinkle with raisins. Roll up and cut into 12 slices. Bake at 400°F. for 20 to 25 minutes. Turn out on tray. Mix glaze and drizzle over rolls.

Fairview, Alta.
Branch No. 84

Cottage Cheese Biscuits

2 cups flour
4 tsp. baking powder
2 tbsp. margarine
1 tsp. salt
1 egg, beaten
¼ cup milk
1 cup cottage cheese

Mix together first four ingredients. Combine beaten egg, milk and cottage cheese. Stir with fork until moist, and mix together. Roll out ½" thick, cut into squares and place on lightly greased pan and bake at 425°F. for 12 minutes.

Selkirk, Man.
Branch No. 42

Sour Milk Biscuits

4 cups flour
1 cup sugar or ¼ or ½ cup or
   even none if one prefers it
   not sweet
1 tsp. salt
2 tsp. baking powder
1 small tsp. baking soda
4 large tbsp. shortening
1 cup currants
buttermilk or artificially
   soured milk

Sift dry ingredients together. Rub in the shortening, add currants and enough sour milk to make a soft dough. Cut with a floured biscuit cutter. Bake at 400°F. for 12 to 14 minutes.

Cypress River, Man.
Branch No. 188

Irish Griddle Farls

2 cups flour
2 tsp. baking soda
¼ tsp. salt
1 scant cup buttermilk or
   sour milk

Mix together all ingredients, making a soft dough. Knead gently. Form into circle and pat down until about ¾" thick. Cut into 4 triangles. Place on heated griddle on medium heat. Cook about 15 minutes on one side, turn and cook until done.

Donkin, N.S.
Branch No. 5

Biscuits

6 cups flour
1 cup shortening
½ cup sugar
salt
2 tsp. baking soda
4 tsp. cream of tartar
5 to 6 tsp. baking powder
2 cups milk, may need more

Blend all ingredients together. Roll out dough on floured board and cut. Bake at 400°F. until done.

Joggins, N.S.
Branch No. 4

Biscuit Mix

7 cups flour
¼ cup baking powder
1 tbsp. salt
1 cup shortening

Mix well and store in plastic bag in fridge until needed. For biscuits take out required amount and add milk. Stir until smooth and roll out on a floured board. Bake at 400°F. for 15 minutes.

Foxwarren, Man.
Branch No. 152

Bannock

4 cups flour
½ cup lard
4 tsp. baking powder
1½ cups cool water
pinch of salt

In large bowl combine ingredients and mix well, kneading into a huge cookie size and place on cookie sheet. Bake at 450°F. for ½ hour.

Hodgson, Man.
Branch No. 158

Tea Scones

2 cups flour
¼ cup sugar
3 tsp. baking powder
1 tsp. salt
⅓ cup butter
¼ cup currants
½ cup milk
2 eggs

Stir together flour, sugar, baking powder and salt. Cut in butter with pastry blender until it resembles course meal. Stir in currants. Add milk, 1 egg plus yolk from second egg (reserve one egg white). Mix together till moist. Turn out and knead on slightly floured board. Roll out dough ½" thick. Brush with beaten egg and sprinkle with sugar; cut out scones and bake on ungreased baking sheet at 425°F. for 12 to 15 minutes. Serve warm with butter. Makes 1 dozen.

Dominion City, Man.
Roseau Valley Branch No. 160

Cinnamon Rolls

3 cups bread flour
6 tsp. baking powder
1 tsp. salt
6 tbsp. shortening or margarine
1 cup milk

Blend all ingredients together. Handle like biscuit dough. Roll out to ¼" thick. Spread with plenty of butter or margarine. Sprinkle with white sugar; over this sprinkle heavily with cinnamon. Roll like Jelly roll. Slice and bake.

New Ross, N.S.
Branch No. 79

Tea Biscuits

4 cups flour
4 tsp. baking powder (heaping)
½ tsp. baking soda
1 tsp. salt
¼ cup sugar
4 heaping tbsp. lard
2 cups milk

Mix dry ingredients together. Work in lard and add milk. Bake in a 450° to 500°F. oven until lightly brown.

Sydney, N.S.
Branch No. 12

Scotch Scones

2 cups bread flour
1 tsp. white sugar
1 level tsp. baking soda
1 heaping tsp. baking powder
2 tsp. shortening
1 tsp. salt
1½ cups buttermilk or sour
   milk

Mix together dry ingredients. Rub shortening into flour mixture. Add buttermilk and blend well. Cook in electric frying pan at 360°F. for 12 to 15 minutes on each side.

Digby, N.S.
Branch No. 20

Scotch Scones

1¾ cups quick rolled oats (450 ml)
1½ cups all-purpose flour (375 ml)
¼ cup sugar (50 ml)
1 tbsp. baking powder (15 ml)
½ tsp salt (2 ml)
½ cup margarine or butter, melted (125 ml)
⅓ cup milk (75 ml)
1 egg
¼ cup currants (50 ml)

Combine rolled oats, flour, sugar, baking powder, salt and currants in large mixing bowl. Beat together margarine, milk and egg. Stir liquid ingredients into flour, just until combined. Do not overmix. Turn mixture onto a lightly floured surface and pat or roll into a rectangle 9x12″. Cut into 9 rectangles, then cut each again diagonally to form 18 triangles. Place on lightly greased baking sheet. Bake at 425°F (220°C.) for 12 to 14 minutes or until golden brown. Serve warm.

Erickson, Man.
Branch No. 143

Muffins

Bran Muffins

4 cups flour
4 cups bran
1¾ cups white sugar
2 tsp. baking powder, heaping
2 tsp. baking soda, heaping
1 tsp. salt
2 cups raisins
2 cups strong black coffee or orange juice
2 cups cold milk
2 cups oil
2 tsp. vanilla
5 eggs

Mix dry ingredients well. Add liquids. Stir and let stand 5 hours. Can be kept in fridge up to three weeks. Bake at 375°F. for 20 minutes.

Morden, Man.
Branch No. 11

Zucchini Muffins

2¼ cups flour
½ tsp baking soda
1-2 cups grated zucchini
½ cup shortening
1 tsp. vanilla
1 tsp. cinnamon
2½ tsp. baking powder
2 eggs, beaten
½ tsp. salt
1 cup white sugar
¼ cup sour milk
½ tsp nutmeg

Mix in usual manner. Makes 16 to 18 muffins.

Topping:
¼ cup brown sugar
½ cup crushed walnuts

Bake at 350°F. for 15 to 20 minutes.

Minnedosa, Man.
Branch No. 138

Never Fail Bran Muffins

2 cups 100% bran cereal
2 cups boiling water
3 cups sugar
1 cup shortening
4 eggs
4 cups flour
1½ cups Pro-Gro or Sunny Boy
5 tsp. baking soda
1 tsp. salt
4 cups 40% bran flakes
chopped raisins

Mix the 100% bran cereal with the boiling water. Stir and cool. In another bowl mix the sugar, and shortening; stir in eggs. In another bowl sift together flour, Pro-Gro, baking soda and salt. Mix bran and sugar mixtures together; add flour mixture and 1 qt. buttermilk. Add bran flakes. Stir to make mixture. Add raisins. Bake at 400°F. for 20 to 25 minutes. This muffin mixture will keep in a covered bowl four weeks in your fridge. These are super good.

Lumby, B.C.
Branch No. 167

If you enjoy hot muffins in the morning, you may want to try this convenient Bran Muffin recipe. The batter can be made ahead of time and stored in the refrigerator until needed. Just spoon out the desired number of muffins into cups and bake for 20 minutes (while you're washing or dressing for the day ahead).

Muffins are low in sugar and fat content; they're good breakfast food or snacks. Bran muffins provide essential carbohydrates for energy, as well as fibre and B Vitamins. With raisins or dates, they give an added bonus of iron.

Refrigerator Bran Muffins

3 cups whole bran cereal
1 cup boiling water
2 eggs, slightly beaten
½ cup molasses
2 cups buttermilk or sour milk
½ cup salad oil
1 cup raisins, dates, currants or prunes
2 tsp. baking powder
2 tsp. baking soda
½ tsp. salt
1 cup brown sugar
2½ cups flour, unsifted (may use 1½ cups whole wheat flour with scant cup enriched white flour)

Pour boiling water over bran in a large bowl; stir to moisten evenly. Allow to cool. Add eggs, molasses, buttermilk, salad oil and dried fruit. Blend well. Stir together baking soda, salt, sugar and flour, then stir into bran mixture. Store in tightly covered plastic container in the refrigerator for up to five weeks. When desired, spoon batter into greased muffin cups and bake at 425°F. for 20 minutes.

Vegreville, Alta.
Branch No. 39

Crumb Muffins

2 cups flour
1½ tsp. baking powder
1 tsp. baking soda
¼ tsp. salt
1 cup sugar
¾ cup margarine

Blend ingredients together and reserve half for topping. Add:

1 cup sweet milk
1 egg
a little vanilla may be used
½ cup chocolate chips, raisins or nuts

Fill muffin tins a little over half full. Bake at 350°F. for 30 minutes.

Ladies Auxiliary
Brant Argyle Branch No. 222

Carrot Muffins

2 eggs
1 cup white sugar
⅔ cup oil
½ tsp. salt
1 tsp. vanilla
1 tsp. cinnamon
1 tsp. baking powder
1 tsp. baking soda
1½ cups flour
1 cup grated carrots
½ cup crushed pineapple

Beat eggs, then mix ingredients in order given. Bake in greased muffin tins at 325°F. for 25 minutes.

Boissevain, Man.
Branch No 10

Muffins

2½ cups flour
4 tsp. baking powder
1½ tsp. salt
1¾ cups sugar
¾ cup shortening
1¼ cups milk
1 tsp. lemon extract
3 large eggs

Sift together dry ingredients. Cream shortening and sugar; add eggs and flavoring. Beat well. Add dry ingredients alter-

nately with milk. Bake at 350°F. until brown. You can add chocolate chips, coconut, blueberries or raisins.

Louisbourg, N.S.
Branch No. 62

Carrot and Pineapple Muffins

1½ cups flour
1 cup white sugar
1 tsp. cinnamon
½ tsp. salt
⅔ cup Crisco oil
1 tsp. baking powder
1 tsp. baking soda
2 eggs, well beaten
½ cup crushed pineapple, drained
1 tsp. vanilla
1 cup grated carrot

Sift dry ingredients, add carrots; then add remaining ingredients. Bake at 350°F. for 25 to 30 minutes. Makes 18 muffins.

Gilbert Plains, Man.
Branch No. 98

Applesauce Oatmeal Muffins

½ cup margarine
¾ cup brown sugar, lightly packed
1 egg
1 cup flour
½ tsp. cinnamon
1 tsp. baking powder
¼ tsp. baking soda
¼ tsp. salt
¾ cup applesauce
½ cup raisins
1 cup rolled oats
½ cup chopped nuts

Cream margarine and sugar. Beat in egg. Add sifted dry ingredients alternately with applesauce. Stir in raisins, oats and nuts. Fill greased muffin tins ¾ full. Bake at 350°F. for 25 to 30 minutes. Yields 12 muffins.

Morris, Man.
Branch No. 111

Melt-Your-Heart Blueberry Oat Muffins

1 cup rolled oats
1 cup buttermilk
1 cup flour
½ tsp. salt
1 egg, beaten
¾ cup brown sugar
½ tsp. baking powder
½ tsp. baking soda
¼ cup melted butter
1 cup fresh or frozen blueberries, thawed

Combine oats and buttermilk in a small bowl. Let stand. Combine flour, baking powder, baking soda, salt and brown sugar. Stir well to blend. Add eggs and melted butter to oat mixture. Mix well; add oat mixture all at once to dry ingredients. Stir just until all ingredients are moistened. Gently fold in blueberries. Fill well-greased muffin cups ¾ full. Bake at 400°F. for 15 to 22 minutes. Makes one dozen.

Winnipeg Beach, Man.
Branch No. 61

Pumpkin Muffins

1½ cups flour
½ cup sugar
2 tsp. baking powder
½ tsp. salt
½ tsp. cinnamon
½ tsp. nutmeg
½ cup milk
½ cup canned pumpkin
¼ cup melted butter
1 egg
½ cup raisins

Mix in order given. Fill muffin tins ⅔ full. Sprinkle ¼ tsp. sugar over batter in each cup. Bake at 400°F. for 18 to 20 minutes. Makes 1 dozen muffins.

Wolfville, N.S.
Branch No. 74

Eileen's Bran Muffins

1 cup dates, cut up
1½ tsp. baking soda
2 cups boiling water
2 eggs
1 cup white sugar
⅔ cup oil
½ tsp. salt
2 cups cooking bran
2 cups flour
2 tsp. baking powder

Mix together dates, 1½ tsp. baking soda and boiling water. Let stand till cool. (Being as dates have gotten so expensive, I make 1 lb. do 3 batches and they are just as nice.) In mixing bowl stir together the eggs, sugar, oil and salt. Mix and add dates. Add remaining ingredients. Bake at 350°F. for 10 minutes, reduce heat to 325°F. and bake for another 10 minutes. This makes 2 dozen large muffins.

Hamiota, Man.
Branch No. 174

Spiced Apple Muffins

2 cups flour
3½ tsp. baking powder
½ tsp. salt
½ cup sugar
1 cup chopped apple, peeled
1 egg, slightly beaten
1 cup milk
⅓ cup melted butter or shortening

Topping:
2 tbsp. brown sugar
¼ tsp cinnamon
¼ tsp. nutmeg

In mixing bowl sift flour, baking powder, salt and sugar. Stir in apple. Combine egg, milk and melted butter; add liquid to dry ingredients, stirring just until moistened, do not overmix. Spoon into prepared muffin tins, filling ¾ full. Combine sugar, cinnamon and

nutmeg. Sprinkle over top of muffins. Bake at 400°F. for 15 to 20 minutes.

Louisbourg, N.S.
Branch No. 62

Mincemeat Muffins

1 cup white sugar
¾ cup Mazola oil
2 eggs
2 cups milk
1 cup bran
2 cups flour
2 tsp. baking powder
2 tsp. baking soda
1 tsp. salt
1 cup mincemeat

Beat together sugar, oil and eggs. Add milk and bran and beat well. Add remaining ingredients. Bake at 350°F. for 15 to 18 minutes. Will keep in fridge for up to three weeks.

Penticton, B.C.
Branch No. 40

Oatmeal Muffins

½ cup butter or shortening
1 egg
1 tsp. baking soda
2 cups flour
¼ tsp. salt
1 cup brown sugar
1 cup sour milk
1 tsp. baking powder
1 cup rolled oats
1 tsp. vanilla

Cream butter and sugar, add well beaten eggs and vanilla. Add flour, salt, baking soda, baking powder, sifted together, alternately with sour milk. Add oatmeal. Bake in muffin tins in quick oven.

Waskada, Man.
Branch No. 92

Honey Blueberry Muffins

¼ cup margarine
¼ cup honey
¼ cup sugar
1 egg
1 cup blueberries

1½ cups flour
2 tsp. baking powder
½ tsp. salt
⅓ cup milk

Cream margarine, sugar and honey. Add egg, then milk. Blend in flour, baking powder and salt. Fold in blueberries. Bake at 375°F. for 20 to 25 minutes.

Petitcodiac, N.B.
Branch No. 41

Banana Bran Muffins

1¼ cups flour
½ cup natural bran
¼ cup wheat germ
1 tsp. baking powder
1 tsp. baking soda
pinch salt
½ cup butter
½ cup brown sugar
⅔ cup mashed bananas
½ cup buttermilk or sour milk
1 tbsp. molasses
¾ cup raisins
1 egg
¼ cup walnuts

Mix all dry ingredients and add to creamed mixture with liquid. Add raisins. Bake at 375°F. for 20 to 25 minutes.

Grand Manan, N.B.
Branch No. 44

Aloha Muffins

1 whole orange
1 egg
1½ cups flour
1 tsp. baking soda
¾ cup sugar
½ cup orange juice
½ cup chopped pitted dates
½ cup butter
1 tsp. baking powder
1 tsp. salt

Cut the orange into sections and blend until finely ground. Add juice, egg, dates and butter; blend. Mix dry ingredients in a separate bowl. Pour orange mixture over dry ingredients and stir lightly. Drop into 15 muffin cups and bake at 400°F. for 15 minutes.

Montreal, Que.
Maisonneuve Branch No. 66

Pineapple Muffins

⅓ cup shortening
¾ cup sugar
1 egg
1½ cups flour
1 tsp. salt
½ tsp. baking soda
1 tsp. baking powder
½ tsp. cinnamon
¼ tsp. ground cloves
1 cup crushed pineapple

Cream shortening and sugar; add egg and beat well. Sift together dry ingredients. Add pineapple to shortening, sugar and egg mixture and blend. Add dry ingredients. Bake at 350°F. in greased muffin tins until lightly browned.

Salisbury, N.B.
Branch No. 31

Rhubarb Muffins

1¼ cups brown sugar, packed
½ cup salad oil
1 egg
2 tsp. vanilla
1 cup buttermilk or sour milk
1½ cups diced rhubarb
2½ cups flour
1 tsp. baking soda
1 tsp. baking powder
½ tsp. salt

In large bowl combine sugar, oil, egg, vanilla and buttermilk. Beat well. Stir in rhubarb. In separate bowl stir together flour, baking soda, baking powder and salt till thoroughly blended. Stir dry ingredients into rhubarb mixture just until blended. Spoon batter into greased muffin tins, filling about ⅔ full. Scatter cinnamon topping over and press lightly into batter. Bake at 400°F. for 20 to 25 minutes.

Topping:
1 tbsp. melted butter
⅓ cup sugar
1 tsp. cinnamon

Havelock, N.B.
Branch No. 86

Donuts
Drop Doughnuts Snowballs

2 eggs
½ cup sugar
1 tbsp. Crisco
1 cup milk
1 tsp. vanilla
3½ cups flour
2 tsp. baking powder
pinch of salt

Beat eggs until light; add sugar, melted Crisco, milk and vanilla. Sift flour, baking powder and salt together. Stir into first mixture. Drop by spoonfuls into hot fat (360 to 370°F.). Fry like doughnuts. When cool, dust with powdered sugar.

Westlock, Alta.
Ladies Auxiliary
Branch No. 97

Raised Donuts

1 pkg. yeast
2½ cups warm water
1 cup white sugar
½ cup shortening, melted
1½ tsp. salt
3 eggs, beaten
vanilla
nutmeg

Set yeast to rise. Cream together the water, sugar, shortening and salt. Then add the remaining ingredients. Add yeast and melted shortening to creamed mixture. Mix in flour to make a soft dough. Let rise till triple in bulk. Roll out to ¼ to ½" thick and let rise ¾ to 1 hour. Fry in hot oil (375°F.).

Holland, Man.
Victoria Branch No. 121

Whole Wheat Doughnuts

3 eggs, beaten
2 cups sugar
1 tsp. ginger
½ tsp. nutmeg
5 tbsp. melted shortening or oil
1 tsp. salt
2 cups milk
5 tsp. cream of tartar
3 tsp. baking soda
3 cups white flour
3 cups whole wheat flour

Blend all ingredients together, adding the white flour to the mixture before the whole wheat. Set for couple of hours or more before rolling out. This recipe can be halved, except I use two eggs.

Grand Manan, N.B.
Branch No. 44

Donuts

1¾ cups flour
1 tsp. baking powder
½ tsp. baking soda
¼ tsp. cinnamon
¼ tsp. nutmeg
½ tsp. salt
1 egg
1½ tbsp. oil
½ cup sugar
⅓ cup milk
1 tsp. vinegar

Sift dry ingredients together twice. Add vinegar to milk. In a large bowl, beat egg until frothy. Add oil, sugar and milk. Add the sifted dry ingredients to the egg mixture. Mix well with a spoon or using your hands. Roll dough out to ½" thickness on lightly floured surface. Deep fry until golden brown on both sides. Use medium-low heat only, otherwise outside will cook and inside will stay raw. Drain on paper towels. Roll in cinnamon-sugar or icing sugar

Stony Mountain, Man.
Ladies Auxiliary
Branch No. 142

Raised Glazed Doughnuts

6 cups warm water
2 cups lard or margarine
6 eggs
1 cup sugar
1 tbsp. salt
2 pkgs. yeast

Dissolve yeast according to pkg. instructions. Melt exactly 2 cups lard; cool. Add sugar and salt, yeast and water; mix. Beat the eggs and add to water and sugar mixture. Add enough flour to make quite a soft dough. Knead for at least 10 minutes. Cover, put in warm place to rise. Let rise once and punch down, let rise again and repeat a third time. Cut into donuts and maple bars and let rise. Fry in hot fat and dip in glaze while hot.

Glaze:
½ cup butter
1 cup white sugar
¾ cup milk
1 cup icing sugar
½ tsp. salt
½ tsp. vanilla

Boil butter, sugar and milk for exactly one minute; then add remaining ingredients.

Maple icing:
2 cups icing sugar
2 tbsp. butter
milk
maple extract

Blend icing sugar and butter together, stir in enough milk to make a medium frosting. Add maple extract to flavor.

Yields 15 dozen.

Vavenby and District, B.C.
Branch No. 259

Strawberry or Raspberry Donut Rings

3 cups strawberries or rasp-
berries, washed and drained
¾ cup sugar
1 cup water
1 tbsp. lemon juice
1 cup flour
1 tbsp. baking powder
½ tsp. salt
½ cup butter
1 egg
3 tbsp. milk

Cream butter, add dry ingredients alternately with milk and beaten egg. Refrigerate. In saucepan mix water and sugar and bring to a boil, stirring lightly. Add berries (sliced strawberries or whole raspberries). Simmer 10 minutes, add lemon juice. Drop dough on berries. Cover and cook slowly on very low heat for about 20 minutes. Serve hot.

Cowansville, Que.
Branch No. 99

Chrusty

oil for frying
6 egg yolks
1 egg
3 tbsp. icing sugar
1 glass rum or brandy liqueur
1 tbsp. vinegar
1½ cups flour
pinch of salt

Blend together egg yolks, egg, sugar, rum, vinegar and pinch of salt; beat well with fork. Sift flour and add to mixture in small amounts, beating well between each addition with fork. When finished put dough on board and knead well. Heat oil slowly. Roll the dough very thin. Cut diagonally into 1½" pieces, slit in center and invert one end into the slit. Do not let them dry, put them in oil for 2 minutes until golden brown. When fried drain on paper towelling.

Montreal, Que.
Ladies Auxiliary
Mazeppa Branch No. 183 (Ukrainian)

Baked Spicy Doughnuts

¼ cup soft butter
6 tbsp. white sugar
1 egg
½ tsp. vanilla
1¼ cups flour
2 tsp. baking powder
1/8 tsp. salt
¼ tsp. nutmeg
⅓ cup milk

Coating:
½ cup melted butter
½ to ⅔ cup white sugar
1 to 1½ tsp. cinnamon

Butter 16 small muffin cups. Beat butter till creamy; add sugar, egg and vanilla. Beat till fluffy. Sift dry ingredients and stir in with the milk. Fill muffin cups ⅔ full and bake about 15 minutes at 375°F. When doughnuts are baked, roll in melted butter, then sugar and cinnamon while still warm.

Shubenacadie, N.S.
Ladies Auxiliary
Branch No. 111

Astar Bollur

Icelandic doughnuts

oil for deep frying
2 eggs
¾ cup sugar
2 tbsp. soft butter
⅔ cup milk
1 tsp. vanilla
2 cups sifted flour
2 tsp. baking powder
½ tsp. salt
½ tsp. nutmeg

Icing:
½ cup sugar
½ tsp. cinnamon

Heat oil to 375°F. Beat eggs well; beat in sugar and butter. Add milk and vanilla. Sift flour, baking powder, salt and nutmeg together into first mixture and blend well. Drop dough into hot fat from a teaspoon (do only four at a time, since they will puff quite large). Fry 3 minutes or until well browned. Drain on paper towelling and roll in mixture of sugar and cinnamon. Makes 2½ dozen.

Erickson, Man.
Branch No. 143

Maple Crullers

½ cup warm water
2 tsp. sugar
2 pkg. dry yeast
1½ cups milk, scalded and
    cooled to lukewarm
½ cup sugar
2 tsp. salt
2 eggs, beaten
½ cup shortening
7 cups flour
oil for deep frying

Measure water into mixing bowl; add 2 tsp. sugar and stir to dissolve. Sprinkle yeast over water and let stand 10 minutes. Stir well. Add milk, ½ cup sugar, salt, eggs, shortening and about half of the flour. Mix thoroughly with a spoon. Add enough of the remaining flour to make a soft but not sticky dough. Mix with hand to blend well. Turn out onto floured board and knead until smooth and elastic and small bubbles appear under the surface. Put in greased bowl, cover with a damp cloth and let rise in a warm place until double (about 1½ hours). Punch down and let rise again until nearly double (30 to 45 minutes).

Turn dough out onto floured board and roll ½" thick. Cut in strips ¾" wide and 10" long. Turn strips in opposite directions from each end to form twists and press ends together to fasten. Let rise until very light (30 to 45 minutes). Heat oil to 375°F. (have oil 3 to 4" deep). Drop twists of dough into hot fat and fry until golden, turning once. Drain in paper towelling. Dip in Maple Glaze while warm and cool on racks. Note: If desired, dough can be rolled as directed and cut with a doughnut cutter.

Maple Glaze:
⅔ cup maple syrup
2 tbsp. water
2 cups icing sugar

Heat maple syrup and water to boiling. Put icing sugar in a broad flat dish (a large pie pan is fine). Gradually blend in hot syrup mixture, stirring until glaze is smooth.

Hodgson, Man.
Branch No. 158

Additional Recipes

_____

_____

_____

_____

_____

_____

_____

_____

_____

_____

_____

_____

_____

_____

Soups, Salads, Sauces & Dressings

Soups

Garden Salad Soup

2 tbsp. butter
1 cup potatoes, sliced thin
1 cup chopped green onion
3 cups chicken broth
1 large cucumber, diced
2 cups shredded lettuce
1 tsp. dill
salt and pepper
1-8 oz. plain yogurt
thin radish slices

Fry potatoes and onion till tender. Stir in broth, cucumber, lettuce, dill, salt and pepper. Heat to boiling; simmer covered for 15 minutes. Remove and add yogurt. Blend till smooth. Serve hot or cold. Garnish with radish slice.

Minitonas, Man.
Branch No. 47

Soup

3 oz. butter
2 oz. lentils (preferably brown)
5 oz. carrots, sliced thin
10 oz. turnip, chopped fine
5 oz. onion, chopped fine
2 oz. cabbage, shredded fine
2 oz. flour
1 qt. chicken stock
parsley
salt and pepper

Cover lentils with water and bring to a boil, then simmer for 30 minutes. Melt butter in pot. Add vegetables and sauté 5 minutes, do not brown. Add flour and mix well. Add chicken stock, stirring slowly. Continue stirring until soup reaches a boil. Add drained lentils and simmer 30 minutes. Check lentils for softness. Add salt, pepper and parsley to taste. Serves 6.

Winnipeg, Man.
Charleswood Branch No. 100

Meal-in-a-Soup

1 tsp. butter or margarine
¼ lb. hamburger
2 medium onions, sliced
3 celery stalks, sliced
2 large carrots, sliced
1 medium pota.o, diced
1¼ cups cauliflower flowerettes
1-19 oz. can tomatoes, or
2 cups chopped fresh tomatoes (approx. 5)
1½ tsp. salt
1/8 tsp. pepper
6 cups water
¾ cup macaroni or small shells

Melt butter in a large pot. Add hamburger and brown slightly. Add all remaining ingredients, except the pasta. Cover and bring to a boil. Reduce heat and simmer 30 Minutes. Add pasta just before end of cooking time. Yields about 12 cups.

Wells, B.C.
Branch No. 128

Kapusniak
Sauerkraut Soup

1 lb. spareribs
1 medium onion, chopped
1 or 2 carrots, diced
2 cups sauerkraut
salt and pepper to taste
1 or 2 potatoes, diced, if desired

Cook spareribs for 30 minutes. Add remaining ingredients and Cook till vegetables and meat are tender. Serve. Instead of spareribs, a ham bone may be used, or bone from roast of pork or some of the liquid in which a ham was cooked.

Ste. Anne, Man.
La Verendrye Branch No. 220

French Pea Soup

1 cup whole yellow peas
6 cups water
1 small onion, diced
¼ cup diced carrots
¼ cup diced turnip
½ small stalk celery, diced
4-8 oz. cubed pork or cracked ham bone

Wash peas, then place in boiling water and cook to puree (about 75 minutes). Add remaining ingredients and salt to taste.

Langruth, Man.
Branch No. 162

Manhattan Clam Chowder

2 lbs. fresh clams (approx.)
¼ cup chopped bacon or salt pork
½ cup chopped onion
½ cup chopped green pepper
1 cup chopped celery
1 cup clam liquor and water
1 cup diced potatoes
½ cup diced carrots
¼ tsp. thyme
1 small bay leaf
1 tsp. salt
dash cayenne
2 cups tomato juice

Allow clams to thaw for 3 hours, if necessary, save the liquor. Chop clams. Fry bacon until lightly brown; add onion, green pepper and celery; cook until tender. Add clam liquor, potatoes, carrots, seasonings and clams. Cook about 25 minutes until potatoes are tender. Add tomato juice and heat. Do not boil. Canned clams could be used. I use 1 can stewed tomatoes and 1 can tomato soup instead of tomato juice. Delicious soup.

Vavenby and District, B.C.
Branch No. 259

Doukabour Borscht

2½ qts. water
7 medium potatoes
1 small beet, sliced
1 large carrot, chopped
1 stalk celery, chopped
1 small green pepper
1 tsp. dill
½ lb. butter
1 large can tomatoes
1 medium cabbage, shredded

Put 4 halved potatoes in boiling water with carrots and beet, salt to taste. Fry onion with 6 tbsp. butter until golden brown, add tomatoes and fry. When potatoes are done, remove from water and mash with 6 tbsp. butter and half the contents of frying pan. Peel remaining 3 potatoes and cube, add to pot. Add remaining contents of frying pan to pot with 1 tbsp. butter. Let boil 5 minutes. Add chopped pepper, celery and 1 cup shredded cabbage to pot. Fry remainder of cabbage with rest of butter until golden brown, stirring constantly after celery and pepper have boiled about 2 minutes. Add mashed potatoes and dill. Cook for 2 minutes. When cabbage is ready, remove soup from heat and add fried cabbage. Serve hot. Add cream when serving if desired.

Grand Forks, B.C.
Branch No. 59

Hamburg Soup

1½ lbs. hamburger
1 medium onion, chopped
1-28 oz. can tomatoes
3-10 oz. cans consommé soup
1-10 oz. can tomato soup
2 cups water
4 carrots, chopped
3 stalks celery, chopped
1 bay leaf
½ tsp. thyme
4 tbsp. barley
parsley

Fry hamburger and onion. Drain off fat, and add remaining ingredients. Simmer for 2 hours or more.

Keewatin, Ont.
Branch No. 13

French Onion Soup

2 cans Campbell's Onion Soup
1 can water
1 can beer
1 large onion slice in half-moon
4 slices crusty bread, cut in ¾ " slices
shredded mozarella cheese
paprika

Mix first four ingredients together. Place slice of bread in each dish. Pour over the soup mixture and cover with cheese. Sprinkle with paprika. Broil until cheese is melted.

Montreal, Que.
Maisonneuve Branch No. 66

Homemade Egg Noodles
(For Soup)

2 cups flour
1 tsp. salt
4 eggs
chicken broth

Knead flour, salt and eggs together until it becomes a firm ball. Add a little flour if needed. Place on a well-floured board. Roll up very thin and flour well. Roll up as for a jelly roll and cut thinly. Drop into boiling broth and stir for 15 minutes.

Westlock, Alta.
Branch No. 97

Cabbage Soup

4 cups shredded cabbage
1-28 oz. can tomatoes
1 large onion
2 tbsp. vinegar
1 large clove garlic
1 tbsp. salt
½ tsp. pepper
2½ qts. water

Place all ingredients in large pot. Simmer until cabbage is cooked. Serve.

Sydney, N.S.
Branch No. 128

Mushroom and Leek Soup

½ cup butter
2 bunches leeks
½ lb. fresh mushrooms, chopped
¼ cup flour
1 tsp. salt
dash cayenne pepper
1 cup chicken broth
3 cups milk
1 tbsp. dry sherry or lemon juice

Wash leeks well; slice and use white part only. In ¼ cup butter sauté leeks until tender, but not brown. Remove and set aside. In remaining butter, sauté mushrooms until soft, about 10 minutes. Blend in flour, salt and cayenne. Gradually stir in broth and milk. Cook, stirring until thickened and it comes to a boil. Add leeks and lemon juice. Simmer for 10 minutes. Makes 6 servings.

Schreiber, Ont.
Branch No. 109

Seafood Chowder

2 medium potatoes
1 medium onion
1½ cups milk
1 cup heavy cream or condensed milk
1-5 oz. can shrimp
1-5 oz. can lobster or crab
1 large can baby clams
½ lb. cooked or canned haddock
2 tbsp. butter
salt and pepper

Cook potatoes and onion; mash, or use leftover potatoes. Add remaining ingredients and cook slowly for 10 minutes.

Grand Manan, N.B.
Branch No. 44

Scotch Soup

**1 or 2 lbs. lean shank beef
(depending on amount of
meat preferred)
6 cups of water, or enough
to cover meat
¼ cup peas
1 tbsp. salt
1 tsp. pepper**

On low heat bring above ingredients to a slow boil. One hour later add the following, still cooking on low heat:

**2 tbsp. pearl barley
2 tbsp. red lentils**

Prepare the following vegetables and add one hour later:

**½ cup diced carrots
¾ cup diced turnips
1 cup chopped leeks**

30 minutes later add the following:

**¼ cup grated carrot
¼ cup parsley (dried or fresh)
¾ cup chopped tomatoes
(fresh or canned)**

Continue simmering for another 30 minutes, a total of 3 hours. Meat can be diced after two hours. This soup is very substantial. It can be frozen and is a meal in itself.

Montreal, Que.
Maisonneuve Branch No. 66

Cape Breton Fish Chowder

**1 onion, sliced
6 potatoes, cubed
1 pt. boiling water
fat pork or bacon (omit for
salt fish; use 1 tbsp. butter)
pepper
2 cups cooked cod, flaked
(salt, fresh or frozen)
1 qt. milk**

Add onion to salt pork fat or butter and brown lightly in pan. Add potatoes, fish and water; simmer 20 minutes. Add milk and pepper. Heat to boiling. Serves 6. Bacon can be crumbled and added to chowder.

Port Morien, N.S.
Branch No. 55

Clam Chowder

**2 cups clams
½ cup chopped onion
2 cups clam liquor or salted
water
½ tsp. salt
¼ cup diced salt pork or
bacon
1 cup diced potatoes
2 cups milk
1/8 tsp. pepper**

Fry salt pork and remove scraps. Reserve for garnish. Add onions and cook slowly. Add clam juice and potatoes and simmer until potatoes are tender. Add clams, milk and seasoning. Garnish with salt pork scraps and a small piece of butter.

Clarenville, Nfld.
Branch No. 27

Newfoundland Pea Soup

**salt beef, salt pork or ham
bone
dried split peas
chopped carrots
chopped turnip
chopped onion
potatoes**

Soak piece of meat overnight. Soak dried split peas overnight. In the morning, put on to cook in fresh water. Add vegetables except potatoes and boil together. About 20 minutes before serving, put in whole potatoes. Serve with dumplings.

**Dumplings:
2¼ cups flour
1 tsp. salt
3 tsp. baking powder
2 tsp. butter
1 cup milk**

Sift together flour, salt and baking powder. Cut in butter, add milk. Mix until smooth. Drop by spoonfuls on hot soup. Cover tightly. Cook 10 to 12 minutes without removing cover.

Clarenville, Nfld.
Branch No. 27

Cream of Broccoli Soup

**1 bunch broccoli
¼ cup butter
2 onions, chopped
1 cup celery, chopped
1 clove garlic (or more)
chopped
½ cup flour
4 cups milk
4 cups chicken broth
½ tsp. thyme
½ tsp. marjoram
salt and pepper**

Trim broccoli and cut into ½" thick pieces. Cook in boiling salted water until tender; drain. In large saucepan melt butter and sauté onion, garlic and celery until golden brown. Stir in flour, gradually add milk, broth and herbs. Stir over low heat until soup thickens slightly and bubbles. Add cooked broccoli, salt and pepper. Continue heating until piping hot. Serve with toasted sliced almonds and finely chopped ripe tomatoes.

Montreal, Que.
Mazeppa Branch No. 183

Creamy Quick Borscht

**2 tbsp. butter
¼ cup chopped onion
1 bay leaf
1/8 tsp. thyme
1-16 oz. can beets
3-10½ oz. cans beef broth
1 cup water
2 tbsp. lemon juice
1 cup sour cream**

Melt butter in saucepan. Add onion, bay leaf and thyme. Cook over low heat. Add beets, broth, water and lemon juice. Heat thoroughly. Remove and discard bay leaf. Blend in sour cream gradually. Serve warm.

Sydney, N.S.
Branch No. 128

Chili Bean Soup

1 lb. ground beef
1 cup chopped onion
½ cup chopped green pepper
2 tbsp. chili powder
2 cups kidney beans, un-
  drained
3 cups V8 juice
½ tsp. salt

In a large saucepan sauté beef, onion and green pepper until vegetables are tender. Add remaining ingredients, bring to a boil. Reduce heat and simmer 45 minutes. Makes 4 servings.

Hantsport, N.S.
Lucknow Branch No. 109

Salads

Salmon Mousse

1-7 oz. tin red salmon
¼ pt. whipping (35%) cream
1 tbsp. sherry
½ cucumber, cooked until
  tender
1 tbsp. salad dressing
pepper to taste

Mix together all ingredients in a blender. Add 1 pkg. melted gelatin and chill. Decorate with paprika and cucumber slices.

Rouge River, Que.
Branch No. 192

Cottage Cheese Salad

1 pkg. lemon Jello
1 pkg. lime Jello
¼ cup sugar
12 oz. or 1 carton creamed
  cottage cheese
¾ cup whipping cream, not
  whipped
½ cup crushed pineapple

Dissolve Jello and sugar in one cup boiling water. Let cool. Then add remaining ingredients. Stir well and pour in mould to set.

Boiestown, N.B.
Normandy Branch No. 78

Marinated Carrot

2 lbs. serving size carrots
1 or more large Spanish
  onions
1 large green pepper
1-10 oz. can tomato soup,
  undiluted
1 cup white sugar
1 tsp. salt
1 tsp. pepper
1 tsp. dry mustard
½ cup salad oil
¾ cup vinegar

Pare and cook carrots until tender and crisp. Slice onions in thin rings. Slice pepper into rings, removing seeds and membrane. Combine remaining ingredients in a saucepan, bring to a boil, stirring to dissolve sugar. Pour over vegetables. Cool in fridge and store in covered container until needed.

Piney, Man.
Branch No. 176

Jellied Salad

Juice of 1 lemon
Juice of 1 can pineapple tidbits, drained well
Juice of 1 can mandarin
  oranges, drained well
½ cup sugar
1 egg, beaten

Bring juices and sugar to a boil. Add the beaten egg and bring to a boil again. Take some of the hot liquid and add cornstarch to it to thicken. Add the cornstarch mixture to the rest of the hot liquid and bring it all to a boil. Take the mixture off the stove and let it cool to almost cold before adding your fruit.

Fruit:
  Pineapple tidbits, apples (not
  peeled, but cored), mandarin
  orange slices, bananas (on the
  green side) and seedless
  grapes

Put in as much fruit as you desire. Keep salad in fridge until serving time.

Snow Lake, Man.
Branch No. 241

Frozen Cranberry Salad

1 cup white sugar
2 cups miniature marsh-
  mallows
1 pint whipped cream
2 cups apples, ground
1 lb. fresh cranberries (ground
  in blender)

Combine cranberries, marshmallows, sugar and apples; let stand for 30 minutes. Add whipped cream, freeze in plastic container. 15 servings.

Wedgeport, N.S.
Branch No. 155

Fruit Salad

1 pkg. Jello instant lemon
  pudding
2 cups buttermilk
500 ml. container Cool Whip
1 can fruit cocktail
1 can mandarin orange slices
1 can pineapple chunks

Combine pudding and buttermilk; then add Cool Whip. Let stand for 5 minutes. Add fruit, which is well drained. Refrigerate for several hours before using. Will keep well until next day.

Emerson, Man.
Branch No. 77

Curried Salt Cod

1 lb. or 2 cups watered salt cod
  cooked, cooled and then
  flaked
1 cup chopped celery
1 cup diced apple
1 tbsp. lemon juice
½ cup raisins
½ cup chopped onion
½ cup salad dressing
1½ tsp. curry powder

Pour lemon juice over apples. Blend curry powder into salad dressing. Stir together. Mix with remaining ingredients.

Gander, Nfld.
Branch No. 8

Crab Macaroni Salad

1 cup shell macaroni
2-7 oz. cans crab, drained
1 cup sliced celery
¼ cup drained pickle relish
¾ cup salad dressing
¼ cup Russian dressing
1 tbsp. lemon juice
½ tsp. salt
1/8 tsp. pepper
few drops onion juice
1 hard cooked egg, sliced

Cook macaroni according to pkg. directions. Drain. Break crabmeat. Combine macaroni and crab, celery, and relish. In another bowl, blend together remaining ingredients, except for egg slices. Add to crab mixture and toss lightly. Garnish with egg slices.

Twillingate, Nfld.
Branch No. 21

Winter Fruit Salad

3 bananas, sliced
¾ cup pineapple juice
1 cup diced, unpeeled red
   apples
1 cup tangerine sections
3 tbsp. chopped peanuts
shredded lettuce
salad dressing

Sprinkle sliced bananas with pineapple juice. Combine with diced apples and tangerines. Add peanuts. Toss with shredded lettuce and French dressing.

Lawrencetown, N.S.
Branch No. 112

Crabmeat or Lobster Salad

2 cups crab or lobster meat
½ onion, chopped
1 stalk celery, chopped
⅓ cup mayonnaise
½ tsp. salt

Combine all ingredients in a bowl. Serve on lettuce cups with potato salad and sliced tomatoes.

Clarenville, Nfld.
Branch No. 27

Cranberry Pineapple Jelly Salad

1 can crushed pineapple,
   drained, reserve juice and
   add enough water to make
   1½ cups liquid
2 pkgs. lemon Jello
¼ cup lemon juice
grated rind of one orange
drained pineapple
1 can whole cranberry sauce
¼ cup chopped walnuts

Heat pineapple juice and water to boiling; pour over lemon Jello. Add remaining ingredients and turn into 8″ ring mould and let set.

Argyle, Man.
Brandt Argyle Branch No. 222

Cucumber Salad

1 pkg. lime Jello
¾ cup salad dressing
8 oz. creamed cottage cheese
1 cucumber, peeled and
   chopped fine
green onion, chopped

Dissolve jello in 1 cup boiling water. Add onion and let stand until partly set, then fold in rest of ingredients and chill.

Elgin, Man.
Branch No. 216

Shrimp Salad

1 pt. shrimp
1 head lettuce
1 hard boiled egg
mayonnaise
beets
lettuce
celery tips
salt and pepper

Strain shrimp, chop lettuce and slice egg. Place in salad bowl, a layer of shrimp, then a layer of lettuce. Season with salt and pepper. Spread mayonnaise over all. Garnish with sliced beets, lettuce, celery tips and eggs. Chill.

Eastport, Nfld.
Branch No. 41

Crabmeat Salad

1 lb. crabmeat
½ cup mayonnaise
2 tbsp. chopped onion
1 cup chopped celery
2 tbsp. chopped sweet pickles
2 hard cooked eggs, chopped
salt and pepper
lettuce

Remove any shell or cartilage from crabmeat, being careful not to break meat into small pieces. Combine all ingredients except lettuce. Serves 6.

Eastport, Nfld.
Branch No. 41

Spinach Salad

1-10 oz. bag spinach
sliced mushrooms
½ lb. cooked crumbled bacon
1 can mandarin orange pieces
1 large avocado

Marinade:
½ cup olive oil
¼ cup cider vinegar
¼ cup sugar
½ tsp. salt
½ tsp. paprika
¼ tsp. dry mustard
1/8 tsp. pepper
¼ tsp. celery salt
½ medium onion, chopped
   fine

Shake up marinade and let sit for at least one day. Do not refrigerate. Put oranges, avocado, and a little dressing in bottom of bowl. Put spinach and mushrooms on top. Cover with remaining marinade and toss. Serve at once.

McBride, B.C.
Branch No. 75

Jellied Salad

1-3 oz. pkg. lime Jello
1 cup boiling water
1 cup crushed pineapple
1 cup celery, chopped fine
1 pkg. lemon Jello
1 cup boiling water
1-8 oz. pkg. cottage cheese
1 cup whipping cream,
   whipped
2 tbsp. sugar
1 pkg. red Jello

Mix together lime Jello and one cup boiling water. Let set awhile. Add crushed pineapple and celery. Let mixture set until firm. Mix lemon Jello and 1 cup boiling water together. Let cool until it starts to thicken. Mix cottage cheese and whipped cream together with lemon Jello mixture. Spread over first layer and let set. Prepare red Jello according to pkg. directions. Let set a little and spread over top of cheese mixture. Use a 9x10″ pan. Makes a nice colorful Christmas salad.

Riding Mountain, Man.
Branch No. 202

Shrimp Delight

1-2½ oz. pkg. Sherriff seasoned tomato salad jelly powder
1 cup boiling water
½ cup cold water
1 tsp. Worcestershire sauce
1 tsp. horseradish
dash Tabasco sauce
¼ cup whipping cream
1 tsp. finely chopped green
   onion
½ cup cooked shrimp

Dissolve jelly powder in boiling water, add cold water, worcestershire sauce, horseradish and tabasco sauce. Mix with electric beater to dissolve horseradish sauce. Chill. When partially set, beat jelly into whipping cream (unwhipped). Let partially set again, fold in shrimp and onion. Pour into 2-cup jelly mold. Chill until set.

Slave Lake, Alta.
Branch No. 110

Dutch Potato Salad

1 tsp. flour
2 tbsp. brown sugar
½ cup water
¼ cup vinegar
1 cup salad dressing
8 hot cooked potatoes
4 strips bacon, fried and
   crumbled
3 hard boiled eggs
green onion to taste

Combine flour, sugar, water and vinegar in top of double boiler, stir in salad dressing and cook until slightly thickened. Dice potatoes, combine bacon, eggs and onion; add to potatoes. Pour hot dressing mixture over ingredients and mix.

Ignace, Ont.
Branch No. 168

Cucumber Salad

1 cup oil
¼ cup sugar
¼ cup Catalina dressing
¼ cup vinegar
¼ cup water
salt and pepper
1 cucumber, sliced
1 green pepper, sliced
1 onion, sliced

Mix all ingredients except vegetables. Pour over vegetables shortly before serving.

Elkhorn, Man.
Branch No. 58

Tomato Aspic Jelly Salad

1 large pkg. lemon jello
1½ cups boiling water
2¼ cups clamato juice
1 tbsp. vinegar
tabasco sauce to taste
drop of red food coloring
parsley flakes
chopped onion (optional)
Cucumber (optional)

Blend together first six ingredients. Top with parsley flakes.

Swan River, Man.
Branch No. 39

Make Ahead Salad

broccoli
cauliflower
celery
Italian dressing with pimento

Break up vegetables into bite sized pieces, putting equal amounts of all three in a bowl, or vary vegetables to suit your family favorites. Pour Italian dressing over vegetables and marinate overnight.

Strathclair, Man.
Ladies Auxiliary
Branch No. 154

Onion Salad

6 onions
½ cup water
½ cup vinegar
¾ cup sugar
2 tsp. salt
1 cup Miracle Whip
1 tsp. celery seed
salt
pepper

Slice and separate onion rings. Stir together water, vinegar, sugar and salt until dissolved. Pour over onions, stirring occasionally. Drain and combine with remaining ingredients. Chill.

Elkhorn, Man.
Branch No. 58

Sauerkraut Salad

1 qt. sauerkraut, drained
2 cups diced celery
1 cup green pepper, diced
1 medium onion, diced
1 small can pimento, chopped
1 tsp. salt
2 cups sugar
½ cup vinegar

Combine all ingredients; let stand for 24 hours before serving. Yields 10 servings.

Chezzetcook, N.S.
Branch No. 161

Bean Salad

1 can green beans
1 can yellow beans
1 can lima beans
1 can kidney beans, rinsed
1 large Spanish onion, thinly
   sliced
1 large green pepper, thinly
   sliced

Drain beans. Mix ingredients of marinade and stir into bean, onion and pepper mixture. Let marinate at least overnight or until you are ready to serve the next day. Drain and serve.

Marinade:
¾ cup white sugar
½ cup salad oil (not olive oil)
½ cup vinegar
½ tsp. paprika
1 tsp. salt
1 tsp. pepper

Squamish, B.C.
Branch No. 277

Cole Slaw

1 large head cabbage, shredded
2 medium onions, grated
2 carrots, grated
¾ cup sugar

Mix together first three ingredients. Sprinkle with sugar and let stand while making dressing.

Dressing:
1 cup vinegar
2 tsp. celery seed
½ cup sugar
2 tsp. dry mustard
1 tsp. salt
1 cup Mazola oil

Bring to a boil all ingredients except Mazola oil. Add oil and boil ½ minute, no longer. Pour over cabbage mixture while still hot. Stir well and refrigerate. Toss and serve. Keeps well.

Shubenacadie, N.S.
Branch No. 111

14 Day Coleslaw

1 medium cabbage, shredded
1 medium carrot, grated
1 medium onion, chopped fine
1 green pepper, chopped
   (optional)
¾ cup sugar
2 tsp. salt
⅔ cup salad oil
1 cup vinegar
pinch celery seed
¼ tsp. tumeric

Put all vegetables into bowl. Boil together remaining ingredients for one minute. Pour over vegetables and let cool. Place in container with lid and refrigerate. Good for 14 days.

Emo, Ont.
Branch No. 99

Greek Chick Pea Salad

2 tsp. prepared mustard
1½ tsp. salt
1¼ cups olive or vegetable oil
½ cup lemon juice
¼ tsp. pepper
2-20 oz. cans chick peas,
   drained
1 medium red onion, sliced in
   rings
¼ lb. cheese, grated or
   crumbled
2 tbsp. chopped fresh parsley

Combine all ingredients and refrigerate one hour. May be saved for several days if needed. Keeps well. Spoon into lettuce lined bowls.

Edmonton, Alta.
Norwood Legion
Branch No. 178

Macaroni Salad

2 cups uncooked shell macaroni, cook and cool
2 ripe tomatoes, chopped
1 green onion, chopped
½ green pepper, chopped
¼ cucumber, chopped

Mix vegetables with macaroni. Blend dressing well and pour over vegetables and macaroni;

refrigerate. Remove 15 minutes before serving and stir well. Great with barbeques.

Dressing:
⅔ cup sugar
½ cup salad oil
⅓ cup ketchup
¼ cup vinegar
1 tsp. salt
¼ tsp. pepper
1 tsp. paprika

Bow Island, Alta.
Branch No. 197

Rainbow Salad

1 cup shredded cabbage
1 cup chopped green pepper
1 cup grated carrot
1 cup sliced celery
1 cup chopped lettuce
1 cup tomato chunks
1 cup cooked peas
1 cup grated cheese
1 cup chopped cucumber
1 cup sliced onion rings

Combine in a large bowl. Mix dressing and pour over salad mixture. Toss lightly and chill.

Dressing:
½ cup vinegar
1 tsp. sugar
½ tsp. salt
1/8 tsp. pepper

Windsor, N.S.
Ladies Auxiliary
Branch No. 9

Winter Salad

1 cup celery, chopped
1 cup cauliflower (optional)
1 cup onion
1 green and 1 red pepper, or
   just one
6-8 cucumbers, chopped
1½ tsp. salt
1 cup sugar
1 cup vinegar
1 tsp. celery salt

Mix together first six ingredients and let sit for ½ hour. Mix together remaining ingredients, but do not heat. Stir until sugar is dissolved. Add to vegetables and mix well. Store in fridge.

Killarney, Man.
Branch No. 25

Green Onion Salad

1 pkg. lemon jello
1 cup hot water
1 cup cottage cheese
1 cup chopped celery
4 small green onions, chopped
⅔ cup salad dressing

Dissolve jello in hot water; set aside to cool. Combine all ingredients and pour into a 9x9″ dish. Chill until firm. Cut in squares and serve on lettuce leaves. Yields 6 servings.

Roblin, Man.
Ladies Auxiliary
Branch No. 24

Cheese Jello

1 small can crushed pineapple
    and juice
½ cup sugar
1-3 oz. pkg. lemon jello
1 pkg. dream whip
1 cup shredded cheddar cheese

Place pineapple and sugar in saucepan and heat to dissolve sugar. Add lemon jello, stir and pour into serving dish and let partially set. Whip dream whip and fold in jello. Add ¾ cup grated cheddar cheese and top with remaining ¼ cup cheese. Let set overnight.

Waskada, Man.
Branch No. 92

Greek Salad

1 onion, sliced and separated
    into rings
2 tomatoes, sliced into wedges
1 cucumber, sliced
½ cup black olives
1 green pepper, cut into rings
salt
pepper
1 cup crumbled Feta cheese
⅓ cup Herb & Garlic salad
    dressing

Prepare vegetables and place in a bowl. Add cheese and dressing. Toss lightly.

Valemount, B.C.
Branch No. 266

Cherry Coke Jello Salad

1 pkg. cherry jello
1 cup hot water
1 cup Coke
3-4 oz. cream cheese
1 cup crushed pineapple
½ cup pecans

Dissolve jello and cheese in hot water, stir and cool slightly, then add other ingredients. Let set.

Red Lake, Ont.
Ladies Auxiliary
Branch No. 102

Asparagus Salad Mold

1 can asparagus
1 large pkg. cream cheese
1 cup mayonnaise
1 onion, finely chopped
10 stuffed olives, sliced
    (optional)
1 pkg. Knox gelatin
¼ cup water
salt and pepper to taste

Dissolve gelatin in water. Place cream cheese, mayonnaise, onion, asparagus, salt and pepper in blender and chop/blend until mixed. Add gelatin mixture and mix well. Pour in mold to set.

Chester Basin, N.S.
Everett Branch No. 88

Layered Salad

1 head iceberg lettuce, broken
    into bite size pieces
spinach, broken into bite size
    pieces
salt
1 cup frozen peas, thawed
1 lb. bacon, crumbled
2 cups grated cheddar cheese
1½ cups mayonnaise

Layer in order given, spreading mayonnaise over cheese to seal completely. Cover with saran wrap and refrigerate overnight. Toss salad or leave layered to serve.

Grande Prairie, Alta.
Branch No. 54

Macaroni Salad

2 cups macaroni
2 tsp. salt
small piece margarine
½ cup cider vinegar
½ cup sugar
2 medium onions, chopped
½ cup celery, chopped
1 medium green pepper,
    chopped
5 hard boiled eggs, chopped
mayonnaise to taste

Cook macaroni, salt and margarine in boiling water for 7 minutes. Drain thoroughly. When cold add mixture of vinegar and sugar, which has been heated and cooled. Add remaining ingredients.

Grand Manan, N.B.
Branch No. 44

Oriental Rice Salad

1 cup Uncle Ben's long grain
    rice, uncooked
1 pkg. small frozen peas
1½ cups chopped celery
1 green onion

Cook rice and peas. Mix together all ingredients and chill.

Dressing:
½ cup salad oil
2 tbsp. vinegar
3 tbsp. soya sauce
1 tsp. curry powder
½ tsp. salt
½ tsp. celery seed
½ cup white sugar

Pour over rice mixture. Mix well and chill overnight. For layer salad, multiply recipe.

St. Peters, N.S.
Branch No. 47

Cottage Ring

1-3 oz. pkg. lime jello
1 cup hot water
2 tbsp. lemon juice
¼ tsp. salt
1 cup mayonnaise
1 tbsp. chopped green onion
1 cup finely chopped celery
1 cup finely chopped green
  pepper
1 cup creamed cottage cheese

Dissolve jello in hot water. Stir in lemon juice and salt. Chill until thickness of unbeaten egg white. Beat in mayonnaise until blended. Fold in onion, celery, green pepper and cottage cheese. Spoon lightly into oiled quart ring mold. Chill until set.

Pointe du Bois, Man.
Branch No. 70

Berry Salad

1 pkg. strawberry jello
1 cup boiling water
2 cups partridgeberries or
  cranberries
2 medium apples, diced
¾ cup white sugar

Dissolve jello in boiling water and chill until partially set. Mix berries and apples with sugar and stir into jelly. Chill and serve.

Gander, Nfld.
Branch No. 8

Lime Jello Salad

1 pkg. lime jello
1 cup boiling water
12 large marshmallows
1 cup crushed pineapple
½ cup shredded cheese
1 cup whipping cream or
  dream whip
pineapple juice and enough
  water to make ¾ cup

Dissolve jello in boiling water; quickly add marshmallows and stir till dissolved. Add pineapple juice and water to jello mixture. Let this chill till it begins to set. Add drained pineapple and cheese. Whip cream and add. Let set.

Emo, Ont.
Branch No. 99

Taco Salad

1 lb. hamburger
1 can red kidney beans
1 medium head lettuce
4 tomatoes
4 oz. grated yellow cheese
1 pkg. Dorito's taco flavour
  chips
1 large bottle Catalina dressing

Brown meat; add beans and simmer 10 minutes. Drain on paper towels and cool. Cut up lettuce and tomatoes. Add grated cheese and meat. Just before serving toss with crushed or broken taco chips and catalina dressing. Note: You may not require a whole bottle of dressing — add it to your own taste.

Winnipeg, Man.
Kent Memorial Branch No. 119

Orange Pineapple Salad

2-3 oz. pkg. orange jello
1 cup boiling water
1 cup pineapple juice
1 cup crushed pineapple
1 cup cottage cheese
1 tbsp. minced onion
¾ cup Miracle Whip
1 cup chopped celery

Dissolve jello in boiling water. Add cottage cheese and pineapple juice. Mix with miracle whip. When partially set, beat in crushed pineapple, celery and onion.

Waverley, N.S.
Dieppe Branch No. 90

Molded Salad

1 pkg. lemon jello
1 cup boiling water
1 cup pineapple juice
2 tbsp. vinegar
¼ tsp. salt
1 cup ground cabbage
1 cup ground carrots
½ cup crushed pineapple

Dissolve lemon jello in boiling water. Add remaining ingredients and chill until set.

Lawrencetown, N.S.
Ladies Auxiliary
Branch No. 112

Cream Cheese Salad

1½ cups boiling water
1-4 oz. pkg. lemon jello
½ cup mayonnaise
1-4 oz. pkg. cream cheese, cut
  in cubes
1 cup mini-marshmallows
½ cup chopped celery
½ cup crushed pineapple,
  drained
½ cup chopped maraschino
  cherries

Pour boiling water over jello and stir until completely dissolved. Add mayonnaise, marshmallows and cream cheese. Stir until well blended. Chill until mixture is thickened. Beat until smooth and fold in celery, pineapple and cherries. Pour into a 1 qt. mold. Chill until firm.

Grand Forks, B.C.
Branch No. 59

Cherry Salad Supreme

1-3 oz. pkg. raspberry or
  cherry Jello
1-21 oz. can cherry pie filling
1-3 oz. pkg. lemon jello
1-3 oz. pkg. cream cheese
⅓ cup mayonnaise
1-8¾ oz. can or 1 cup crushed
  pineapple
½ cup whipping cream
1 cup mini-marshmallows
2 tbsp. chopped nuts

Dissolve raspberry Jello in 1 cup boiling water. Stir in pie filling. Turn into 9x9x2″ baking pan. Chill till partially set. Dissolve lemon Jello in 1 cup boiling water. Beat together cream cheese and mayonnaise. Gradually add lemon Jello. Stir in undrained pineapple. Whip ½ cup whipping cream. Fold into lemon mixture with marshmallows. Spread on top of cherry layer. Top with chopped nuts. Chill till set. Serves 12.

Elkhorn, Man.
Branch No. 58

Mustard Mold Classique

1 pkg. unflavored gelatin
½ cup cold water
1 cup mayonnaise
¼ cup prepared mustard
¼ tsp. salt
¼ tsp. paprika
½ cup heavy cream, whipped

Soften gelatin in cold water, stir over low heat until dissolved. Cool. Combine mayonnaise, mustard and seasonings. Gradually stir in gelatin. Chill until slightly thickened; fold in whipped cream. Pour into lightly oiled 1 qt. mold. Chill until set. Excellent with ham but goes with almost any meat.

Gull Lake, Sask.
Branch No. 119

Crushed Pineapple Carrot Mold

1-20 oz. can crushed pineapple, drained
pineapple juice and enough water to make 1½ cups syrup
1 pkg. lemon jello
½ cup white sugar
¼ tsp. salt
2 tbsp. lemon juice
1 cup grated carrot
1 pkg. dream whip, whipped
vegetables or other fruit, such as apples, cabbage and olives may be used as an option

Heat pineapple juice to boiling point; add lemon jello, stirring well until dissolved. Add sugar, salt and lemon juice. Chill till slightly thickened. Add pineapple and carrot. Fold in dream whip. Pour into a greased 8″ bowl or 1½ qt. ring mold. Chill until firm. Make a day ahead of serving so it is thoroughly set and easier to unmold. If canned fruit is used, drain well before using.

Gilbert Plains, Man.
Branch No. 98

Coffee Liqueur Mold

1 pkg. unflavored gelatin
¼ cup coffee liqueur
1 cup strong hot coffee
¼ cup sugar
1 cup whipping cream
1 cup chopped pecans
1 cup whipped cream

Soften gelatin in coffee liqueur. Dissolve in hot coffee. Add sugar and stir until dissolved. Cool to lukewarm. Stir in cream. Pour into mold. Chill until set. To serve, turn out of mold onto serving plate. Top with whipped cream and sprinkle with chopped pecans.

Sanford, Man.
Branch No. 171

Summer Salad

1-10 oz. can tomato soup
1-3 oz. pkg. lemon jello
1 cup cottage cheese
1 cup salad dressing
1 cup finely chopped celery
¼ cup grated onion
1 cup finely chopped green pepper
1 cup grated medium cheddar cheese
salt to taste
1 small can chicken, shrimp, crab, tuna or salmon

Mix soup in pot; add jello and stir to dissolve. Cool. Blend cottage cheese and salad dressing; add to soup mixture and stir. Chill till partially set. Fold in vegetables, cheese and choice of meat. Salt to taste. Set in 5 cup ring mold and chill. Rinse out with cold water. Makes 6 to 8 servings.

Lumby, B.C.
Branch No. 167

Pineapple Salad

1 can crushed pineapple, drained
1 pkg. lemon jello
1 tsp. salt
1 cup boiling water
4 oz. cream cheese
1 cup whipped cream or salad dressing
¼ cup diced green pepper
⅓ cup walnuts
⅓ cup diced celery
½ cup grated carrots

Dissolve lemon jello and salt in boiling water. Add reserved pineapple juice and cream cheese. Stir well until dissolved. When cool add whipped cream. Add remaining ingredients and put in mold to set.

Petitcodiac, N.B.
Branch No. 41

Coleslaw Souffle

1-8 oz. can crushed pineapple
¾ cup boiling water
1 cup finely shredded cabbage
½ cup chopped walnuts
1-3 oz. pkg. orange jello
¾ cup mayonnaise
1 cup shredded carrot
½ cup raisins
3 egg whites, beaten stiff

Fold a 22″ piece of aluminum foil in half lengthwise. Tape firmly around a 1 qt. soufflé dish. Drain pineapple, reserving juice. Dissolve jello in boiling water. Add reserved liquid. Beat in mayonnaise. Freeze in loaf pan till firm 1″ from edge but soft in center, about 20 minutes. Beat in large bowl till fluffy. Fold in pineapple, cabbage, carrot, raisins and then egg whites. Pour into prepared dish. Chill till set. Remove foil. Serves 6.

Whitehorse, Yukon
Branch No. 254

Lemon-Lime Jellied Salad Mold

First Layer:
1-3 oz. pkg. lime jello
1½ cups boiling water
1 pkg. gelatin
¼ cup cold water
1 cup crushed pineapple, drained (reserve juice for second layer)

Dissolve lime jello in 1½ cups boiling water. Soften gelatin in ¼ cup cold water and add to lime jello mixture; stirring till dissolved. Cool a while and add crushed pineapple. Pour into mold and allow to set slightly.

Second Layer:
1-3 oz. pkg. lemon jello
reserved pineapple juice and enough boiling water to make 1½ cups syrup
1 pkg. gelatin
¼ cup cold water
8 oz. cream cheese
⅓ cup mayonnaise

Dissolve lemon jello in pineapple juice and boiling water. Soften gelatin in cold water and add to lemon jello mixture. Stir to dissolve and allow to cool. Beat cream cheese till creamy and add mayonnaise, beat well. Beat lemon jello into cream cheese and mayonnaise. Pour at once over first layer. Allow to chill overnight in fridge. Oil mold slightly beforehand for easy removal of jelly.

Ste. Rose, Man.
Branch No. 232

Ambrosia Salad

1-11 oz. can madarin orange segments
1 cup sour cream
1 cup mini-marshmallows
1 cup flaked coconut
1-13 oz. crushed pineapple

Combine ingredients; chill for 24 hours. Lovely set in an orange ring mold.

Prince George, B.C.
Branch No. 43

Pistachio Salad

1-4 oz. pkg. pistachio instant pudding
1-35 oz. container Cool Whip thawed
1-19 oz. can crushed pineapple and juice
1 cup mini-marshmallows
1 can mandarin oranges, drained

Dissolve pudding mix in pineapple and juice. Add marshmallows, oranges and Cool Whip. Mix well. Refrigerate at least one hour. Serves 6 to 10.

Hamiota, Man.
Branch No. 174

Lazy-Day Salad

1 large can crushed pineapple, undrained
1 large can fruit cocktail, drained
2 cans mandarin oranges, drained
1 pkg. vanilla instant pudding mix
1-9 oz. pkg. Cool Whip
½ cup pecans
½ cup coconut

Mix first four ingredients together well and add Cool Whip. Pour in deep dish; sprinkle with nuts and coconut.

Grand Manan, N.B.
Branch No. 44

Beet Salad

6 medium beets, cooked, peeled and sliced
1 large onion, sliced in rings
2 or 3 stalks celery, diced

Marinade:
3 tbsp. cider vinegar
½ tsp. sugar
½ tsp. salt
1/8 tsp. pepper
1/8 tsp. dry mustard
½ tsp. basil
4 tbsp. vegetable oil

Combine all ingredients and refrigerate overnight.

East St. Paul, Man.
Branch No. 215

Four Fruit Jello Salad

2-3 oz. pkg. strawberry jello
1 pt. frozen strawberries
1 medium can crushed pineapple
1 ripe banana, mashed
1 pt. sour cream
1½ cups boiling water

Dissolve jello in boiling water. Add all fruits and juices (no more water). Put half of jello mixture in dish and let set in refrigerator. Cover with sour cream when set and add rest of jello mixture. Refrigerate. Leave the second half of the jello out of fridge till the first half has set.

Elkhorn, Man.
Branch No. 58

Fruit Salad

2-11 oz. cans mandarin orange sections, drained
1-20 oz. can pineapple chunks, drained
2 cups or 1 lb. seedless green grapes, halved
2 cups mini-marshmallows
½ cup flaked coconut (optional)
1 cup commercial sour cream
lettuce leaves
maraschino cherries (optional)

In large mixing bowl combine orange sections, pineapple chunks, grapes, marshmallows and coconut. Stir in sour cream. Cover and refrigerate at least 24 hours. If desired, spoon onto lettuce-lined salad plates and garnish with cherries. Makes 8 to 10 servings.

(Reserve drained syrup and/or juice to use in holiday punches or as part of liquids in salads.)

Brandon, Man.
Wheat City Branch No. 247

Burger Sauce

½ cup sweet pickle juice
1 small onion
2 tbsp. brown sugar
½ cup ketchup
¼ cup green pepper
2 tbsp. dry mustard

Mix all ingredients together in saucepan and boil 5 minutes.

Montreal, Que.
Flanders Branch No. 63

Homemade H.P. Sauce

1 pt. brown vinegar
2 tsp. mustard
2 tsp. white sugar
2 tsp. salt
2 tbsp. molasses
1 tbsp cinnamon
1 tbsp. cloves

Mix all ingredients and boil together for 20 minutes. Bottle.

Rapid City, Man.
Branch No. 49

Sour Cream Mustard Sauce

1 cup sour cream
3 tbsp. prepared mustard
2 tbsp. chopped onion
salt and pepper to taste

Mix ingredients together. Chill.

Elgin, Man.
Elgin Branch No. 216

Sweet Hot Mustard

3 heaping tbsp. flour
1 tsp. salt
dash of pepper
1 tbsp. tumeric
1 tbsp. oil
1 cup white sugar
⅓ cup vinegar
1 small can or ⅓ of large can Keen's dry mustard

Mix until smooth. Keeps very well.

Sanford, Man.
Branch No. 171

Bar-B-Que Sauce

1 cup ketchup
1 cup vinegar
¼ cup brown sugar
¼ tsp. dry mustard
dash of hickory (optional)
2 tbsp. worcestershire sauce
dash tabasco sauce
1 tbsp. soya sauce
1 tbsp. chili powder

Put all ingredients in a pot and bring to a boil. Pour over meat. This is excellent for spareribs and chicken cooked in the oven. This can also be brushed on for barbeque sauce.

Wells, B.C.
Branch No. 128

Plum Pudding Brandy Sauce

¼ cup butter
¼ cup flour
⅔ cup brown sugar, lightly packed
1½ cups milk
¼ cup brandy

Melt butter in saucepan. Mix together flour and sugar and blend into butter. Gradually blend in milk. Cook over medium heat, stirring constantly until thickened. Stir in brandy. Serve hot on steamed pudding. Makes 2 cups.

Montreal, Que.
Maisonneuve Branch No. 66

Sweet and Sour Barbeque Sauce

2 cups tomato juice
½ cup water
⅓ cup brown sugar
¼ cup vinegar
3 tbsp. cornstarch
2 tbsp. soya sauce

Mix all ingredients together and boil until thickened.

Winnipeg, Man.
Ladies Auxiliary
West Kildonan Branch No. 30

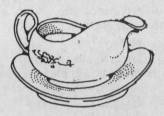

Meaty Spaghetti Sauce

2 tbsp. vegetable oil
1 clove garlic, minced
¾ cup chopped onion
1½ lbs. hamburger
1 can mushroom pieces and stems (optional)
1-12 oz. can tomato paste
3 cups hot water
½ tsp. sugar
½ tsp. oregano
1 tsp. salt
¼ tsp. pepper
spaghetti, cooked and drained
grated parmesan cheese

Heat oil in heavy skillet; cook garlic and onion until soft. Add meat and mushrooms, cook, stirring until meat is crumbly. Mix tomato paste, water, sugar and seasonings, stir into meat. Simmer for 30-40 minutes or until sauce thickens. Serve over hot spaghetti, sprinkle with cheese.

Lundar, Man.
Ladies Auxiliary
Branch No. 185

Sweet and Sour Meatballs Sauce

1½ cups brown sugar
3 tbsp. cornstarch
½ cup water
½-¾ cup vinegar
1 small can pineapple chunks
2 tbsp. soya sauce
salt and pepper to taste

Cook brown sugar, cornstarch, water and vinegar until thick. Add remaining ingredients and mix. Pour over meatballs. Add desired vegetables.

Redwater, Alta.
Ladies Auxiliary
Branch No. 251

Chili Sauce

2 large cans tomatoes
3 onions, chopped
1 green pepper
celery
salt
2 cups brown sugar
1 cup vinegar
1 tsp. cinnamon

Mix tomatoes, brown sugar and vingegar together. Heat and add remaining ingredients. Simmer for couple of hours or until right consistency.

Schreiber, Ont.
Branch No. 109

Chili Sauce

18 large ripe tomatoes
1 green pepper
3 onions
½ bunch celery
1 tbsp. salt
1 cup sugar
2 cups vinegar
1 tsp. cloves
1 tsp. nutmeg
1 tsp. cinnamon

Chop vegetables fine and add remaining ingredients. Boil slowly for 2 hours. Seal.

Napinka, Man.
Napinka Branch No. 89

Freezer Tomato Sauce

20 large tomatoes, chopped
4 onions, chopped
4 large carrots, chopped
½ cup celery, chopped
3 tbsp. sugar
¼ tsp pepper
2 tbsp. salt

Boil tomatoes, onion and carrots for ½ hour, stirring often. Add remaining ingredients and cool. Measure 3 cups at a time and whip in blender one minute. Freeze in cartons. Great for cabbage rolls, sausage, lasagna, meatballs or tomato soup. Spices may be added.

Woodlands, Man.
Branch No. 248

Dressings

Best Ever Cole Slaw Dressing

3 rounded tbsp. Miracle Whip
½ cup vegetable oil
¼ cup vinegar
3 tbsp. sugar

Place all ingredients in a jar or plastic container and shake well. Will keep for weeks in fridge. Shake before using.

Hamiota, Man.
Branch No. 174

Salad Dressing

1 can sweetened condensed
  milk
½ cup vinegar
½ cup oil
1 egg
2 tsp. mustard
1 tsp. salt

Mix ingredients together and beat well. Store in jar in fridge.

Cowansville, Que.
Branch No. 99

Melody Dressing

½ cup salad oil
⅓ cup ketchup
¼ cup vinegar
2 tbsp. lemon juice
⅓ cup sugar
1 tsp. paprika
1 tsp. salt

Measure all ingredients into bottle or jar. Cover tightly and shake well. Chill thoroughly. Shake well before serving. Yields 1¼ cups.

Shubenacadie, N.S.
Branch No. 111

Lemon Dressing

½ cup salad oil
½ cup lemon juice or vinegar
½ tsp. salt
2 tbsp. sugar or ½ tsp. liquid
  sucaryl
dash cayenne pepper

Combine all ingredients and store in bottle. Shake well before using.

Steinbach, Man.
Branch No. 190

Boiled Salad Dressing

2 eggs, well beaten
¾ cup white sugar
½ tsp. salt
dash of pepper
1 cup white vinegar
3 tsp. cornstarch
2 tsp. dry mustard
½ cup cold water
1 tbsp. butter
cold milk

Mix cornstarch and dry mustard with cold water. Add to mixture of well beaten eggs, sugar, salt, pepper and vinegar. Boil until thick and clear. Stir constantly. Remove from heat and add butter. Add cold milk to required thickness.

Morin Heights, Que.
Branch No. 171

Chef's Dressing

⅓ cup tomato juice
⅓ cup oil
¼ cup vinegar
¼ tsp. pepper
½ tsp. oregano
½ tsp. dry mustard
¼ tsp. soya sauce

Combine all ingredients and shake well. (Four calories per tablespoon). Makes one cup.

Winnipeg, Man.
Transcona Branch No. 7

French Dressing

1 small onion
1 can tomato soup
1½ cups salad oil
1½ tbsp. dry mustard
1½ tbsp. worcestershire sauce
1½ cups white sugar
1 cup white vinegar
1 small clove garlic, peeled
1½ tbsp. salt
1 tbsp. paprika

Place all ingredients in a blender. Start on low speed for one minute. Then blend at high speed or liquify one or two minutes. Makes about 48 oz. Pour into glass bottle or jar with a tight lid. Will keep up to three months in refrigerator.

Bathurst, N.B.
Branch No. 18

Salad Dressing

½ cup white sugar
¾ cup Mazola oil
¾ cup apple cider vinegar
¼ tsp. celery salt
¼ tsp. garlic salt
¼ tsp. prepared mustard
1 tsp. ketchup

Mix all ingredients well and store in fridge.

Cowansville, Que.
Branch No. 99

Creamy Mustard Dressing

3 tbsp. prepared mustard
2 tbsp. vinegar
¼ tsp. salt
2 tbsp. sugar
2 tbsp. evaporated milk
1 tbsp. angostura aromatic
    bitters

Combine all ingredients in a bowl. Beat with rotary beater until light and fluffy. Use in any salad calling for dressing. Makes ⅔ cup.

Stony Mountain, Man.
Ladies Auxiliary
Branch No. 142

Cooked Salad Dressing

¼ tsp. salt
2 tbsp. sugar
1 tbsp. flour
¾ tsp. dry mustard
few grains cayenne pepper
2 eggs, slightly beaten
2 tbsp. butter or margarine
¾ cup milk
¼ cup vinegar or lemon juice

Sift dry ingredients, add egg, butter, milk and vinegar. Cook for 3 to 4 minutes or until thick.

Abbotsford, B.C.
Ladies Auxiliary
Branch No. 15

Salad Dressing For Cole Slaw

1 cup mayonnaise
1 cup oil
1 cup vinegar
1 cup sugar
1 tsp. salt

Combine all ingredients and blend well. Store in fridge.

Winnipeg, Man.
Henderson Hwy. Branch No. 215

Meats

Beef

Ground Beef Roast Rolled with Zucchini and Cheese

2 tbsp. salad oil
1 lb. zucchini shredded
   (3 cups)
¼ lb. Swiss cheese shredded
   (1 cup)
¼ cup dried bread crumbs
salt
2 lb. ground beef
1 tsp. thyme leaves
1/8 tsp. pepper
1-8 oz. can tomato sauce
1-8 oz. pkg. sliced bacon
8 small potatoes, peeled, and
   cut in half
¼ cup butter, melted

1. In a saucepan over high heat, in hot oil cook zucchini, stirring quickly and frequently until tender-crisp, about 3 minutes. With slotted spoon, remove zucchini to bowl: to zucchini add cheese, bread crumbs, ½ tsp. salt, mix well, set aside.
2. In bowl mix well ground beef, thyme, pepper, ½ cup tomato sauce and 1½ tsp. salt. On a sheet of waxed paper, about 12 inch long, pat beef mixture into a 10-inch square. Spread zucchini mixture over beef square, leaving 1-inch edge all around.
3. To roll, lift narrow end of waxed paper and begin to roll zucchini-topped beef mixture, jelly-roll fashion, pressing lightly with fingers to start roll. Peel paper back, then continue lifting paper and rolling beef until completely rolled. Place beef roll, seam-side down, on rack in open roasting pan. Spread remaining tomato sauce over roll. Lay bacon slices crosswise on roll, tucking ends under roll. Arrange potatoes around beef roll. With pastry brush, brush potatoes with melted butter. Bake at 350°F. for 1½ hours, turning potatoes occasionally.

Montreal, Que.
Mazeppa Branch No. 183

Macaroni Meat Casserole

½ cup macaroni, cooked in
   salt and cooled
¾ lb. ground meat
1 can tomato soup
8-10 soda crackers, crushed
1 tsp. fat or butter
1 large onion
½ cup grated cheese

Put cooked macaroni in bottom of 1½ qt. casserole. Brown meat in fat. Pour meat over macaroni. Spread finely chopped onion over meat. Cover with tomato soup. Spread cheese over this, then the crumbs. Can add salt, pepper and any spices of your choice.
Bake at 350°F. for one hour.

Hartney, Man.
Branch No. 26

Chinese Hamburger

1 lb. beef hamburger
1 small onion chopped
1 cup celery sliced
Cook until browned. Add:
1 can mushroom soup
¾ cup water
3 tbsp. soya sauce
½ cup raw rice
1 tbsp. brown sugar
1 can bean sprouts
Combine all ingredients, place in 2 qt. casserole. Bake uncovered for 1 hour at 350°F.

Teulon, Man.
Branch No. 166

Best Ever Meat Loaf

2 eggs
2/3 cup milk
2 tsp. salt
¼ tsp. pepper
3 slices bread, crumbled
1 onion, chopped
½ cup shredded raw carrots
1 cup shredded cheddar
   cheese
1½ lbs. ground beef
¼ cup brown sugar
¼ cup ketchup
1 tbsp. prepared mustard

Beat eggs lightly. Add milk, salt, pepper and bread. Mix until bread disintegrated. Add onion, carrot, cheese and beef. Mix well. Put in 9x5″ loaf pan. Combine brown sugar, ketchup and mustard. Spread over loaf. Bake at 350°F. for one hour.

Abbotsford, B.C.
Ladies Auxiliary
Branch No. 15

Hamburger and Bean Sprout Casserole

¾ cup rice
2 cups onions
2 cups celery
1½ lbs. hamburger
Cook rice as directed. Brown hamburger, onions and celery. Drain and mix rice and hamburger mixture in large casserole or 2 small casseroles. Add:
1 can mushroom pieces
¼ cup soya sauce
1 can cream of chicken soup
1 can bean sprouts
Sprinkle 1½ cups chow mein noodles over top and bake 30 minutes at 350°F.

Gilbert Plains, Man.
Ladies Auxiliary
Branch No. 98

Layered Dinner

1 lb. ground beef
3 medium potatoes sliced
3 medium carrots, sliced
½ cup peas
½ cup shredded cabbage
1 can tomato soup
1 medium onion sliced
salt and pepper

Use a large casserole or small roaster and layer in the following way. Half the meat on the bottom, slice potatoes, then the rest of the meat, then carrots, onions, peas and cabbage. Cover with soup. Bake 2 hours in a medium oven or until meat is tender. Uncover and bake another 15 minutes. If liquid reduces, add more tomato juice or water. Serve with hot biscuits and dessert of your choice.

Killarney, Man.
Branch No. 25

Easy Lasagna

1 lb. ground beef
3½ cups canned tomatoes
1-8 oz. can tomato sauce
1 envelope spaghetti sauce
   mix
1 clove garlic, minced
8 oz. lasagna or wide noodles
1-16 oz. pkg. thin sliced
   Mozzarella cheese
½ cup Parmesan cheese
1 cup cream style cottage
   cheese

Brown meat slowly. Spoon off excess fat. Add next 4 ingredients. Simmer, covered, for 40 minutes. Stir occasionally, salt to taste. Cook noodles in boiling salted water until tender, drain. Rinse in cold water. Place half the noodles in an 11x7-inch pan, cover with one third the sauce and half of the Mozzarella cheese. Add half of the cottage cheese. Repeat layers ending with the sauce. Top with Parmesan cheese. Bake at 350°F. for 25 to 30 minutes. Let stand 15 minutes, cut into squares. Serves 6.

Wells, B.C.
Branch No. 128

Mexican Meat Pie

Bottom:
¾ cup flour
½ tsp. salt
2 eggs, beaten
1-8 oz. block Mozzarella
   cheese, grated
⅓ cup milk
1 tbsp. cornmeal

Topping:
½ lb. hamburger
¼ cup onion, chopped
1 tsp. chili powder
1 medium green pepper,
   chopped
4 oz. jar Cheese Whiz
½ cup tomatoes, chopped
   (canned whole tomatoes
   can be used, drained)

Mix together ingredients for bottom. To prepare topping, brown the meat, drain, add green pepper and onion, cook slowly until tender. Add ½ cup Cheese Whiz and chili powder, stir over low heat until cheese is melted, add tomatoes. Combine remainder of Cheese Whiz with eggs, flour, salt and milk, beat until smooth. Pour into 9-inch pie plate and sprinkle a little of the Mozzarella cheese on top; spoon meat mixture over this batter and bake at 400°F. for 25 to 30 minutes.

Hopewell, N.S.
Branch No. 137

Easy Casserole

1 lb. ground beef
1 can beef consommé, un-
   diluted
1 cup rice, cooked
½ cup plum sauce
1 can bean sprouts
1 can mushrooms
1 onion
½ cup green pepper, chopped
salt and pepper

Brown beef in pan with green pepper and onion. Place in casserole dish; add remaining ingredients. Mix well. Bake at 325°F. for 30 minutes.

Antigonish, N.S.
Ladies Auxiliary
Arras Branch No. 59

Baked Chinese Rice

1 lb. hamburger, browned
2 onions, chopped
pepper
1 can mushrooms plus juice
½ cup soya sauce
1 green pepper chopped
¼ cup celery chopped fine
1 can mushroom soup
   undiluted
1 can bean sprouts, drained
1½ cups Minute Rice, un-
   cooked

Mix together. Cover and bake at 350°F. for 1 hour or until done. No added salt.

Salisbury, N.B.
Ladies Auxiliary
Branch No. 31

Round-Up Steak and Rice Casserole

1 lb. beef round steak,
   tenderized, cut in thin
   strips
1 cup uncooked long grain
   rice
¼ cup flour
salt and pepper
¼ tsp. garlic salt
2 tbsp. shortening, melted
1 cup chopped onion
1 cup chopped celery
1-14½ oz. can tomatoes
2 cubes or 2 tsp. liquid OXO
   beef bouillon (2 cups)
1 tsp. salt
1 green pepper, cut in rings

Season steak strips with salt, pepper and garlic salt. Roll in flour. Brown in shortening. Push meat to one side of pan. Add onion and celery. Sauté until tender. Stir in tomatoes and beef bouillon. Bring to a boil. Cover, reduce heat and cook slowly for 30 minutes. Add rice and 1 tsp. salt. Stir well. Place pepper rings on top. Cover and continue cooking for 20 minutes. Makes 4-6 servings.

Domain, Man.
Ladies Auxiliary
Branch No. 208

Veal Stroganoff

1½ lbs. lean stewing veal
2 tbsp. flour
2 tbsp. paprika
2 tbsp. salad oil
1 onion, chopped
1 can consomme
2 tsp. tomato paste
¾ cup sour cream

Cube the veal and toss with flour and paprika. Stir-fry veal and onions quickly in hot oil until lightly colored. Pour in the consomme and cover. Simmer 30 minutes or until tender. Stir in paste mixed with sour cream and reheat without boiling. Taste for seasoning. Serve over hot drained noodles.

Thompson, Man.
Branch No. 244

Beef Stroganoff

3-8 oz. steaks or equivalent
   (cut in small strips)
3 tbsp. oil
1 onion
1 tsp. paprika
1 can mushroom stems and
   pieces
3 tbsp. flour
2 cups hot beef stock
salt and pepper
½-1 cup sour cream
1 tbsp. parsley flakes

Heat oil in frying pan. Sauté meat strips quickly. Set in pan and if wanting steak well done, complete in oven until very tender. When ready add sliced onions to oil and cook until transparent. Add paprika and mushrooms. Sauté 4 minutes. Sprinkle on flour while stirring the vegetables. Cook 2 to 3 minutes. Gradually add beef stock, season and bring liquid to a boil; simmer 3 to 4 minutes. Add beef and gently heat (do not boil). Just before serving, add sour cream and parsley.

Hythe, Alta.
Ladies Auxiliary
Branch No. 93

Swedish Pot Roast

4 lbs. beef pot roast, chuck or
   brisket
1 tsp. nutmeg and cinnamon
½ tsp. ginger
salt and pepper
4 bay leaves
2 tbsp. shortening
2 onions, sliced
1 clove garlic, diced
½ cup brown sugar
½ cup vinegar
½ cup water

Combine nutmeg, cinnamon, ginger, salt and pepper and rub into the meat. Heat cooker with shortening and brown meat well on all sides. Add onion, garlic, brown sugar dissolved in vinegar and water, and bay leaves. Close cover securely. Place pressure regulator on vent pipe and cook 40 minutes with pressure regulator rocking slowly. Let pressure drop on its own accord. If roast is too moist, place uncovered in regular oven for a few minutes.

Cranberry Portage, Man.
Ladies Auxiliary
Branch No. 137

Chow Mein Casserole

1 cup diced onion
1 cup diced celery
1 lb. hamburger
1 cup Minute Rice
1 pkg. Lipton's chicken
   noodle soup
1 can Chow Mein bean
   sprouts
1 can dry noodles

Sauté onions and celery in fry pan. Add hamburger and cook until brown. Add Minute Rice, soup mix, bean sprouts and juice and ½ cup water and half the can of dry noodles. Mix well and turn into casserole dish. Cover with remaining noodles and bake 1 hour at 350°F.

Winnipeg, Man.
Kent Memorial Branch No. 119

Spaghetti Sauce and Beef

In a large pot combine:
1 tbsp. oil or butter
2 medium chopped onions
½ tsp. pepper
1 tsp. minced onion
½ tsp. crushed chili
1 tsp. salt
1 tsp. minced garlic
1 tsp. oregano
Stir in:
1-7½ oz. can tomato paste
Add:
2 cans tomato soup
1-28 oz. can tomatoes, cup up
2 tbsp. sugar
2 bay leaves
1 can drained mushrooms

Simmer over low heat for 2 hours covered. Stir occasionally. Add 2 lbs. ground beef browned. Can be stored in fridge or frozen in portions.

Salisbury, N.B.
Ladies Auxiliary
Branch No. 31

Peppy Stuffed Peppers

4 green peppers
1 lb. ground beef
2 cups cooked rice (⅔ cup
   raw)
¼ cup chopped onion
1½ tsp. salt
1/8 tsp. black pepper
2-8 oz. cans tomato sauce or
   soup

Cut peppers in half lengthwise. Remove seeds and wash. Combine beef, cooked rice, onion, salt, black pepper and ½ can tomato sauce. Pile mixture into peppers and place in a large baking pan. Pour tomato sauce over each pepper. Cover tightly and bake at 350°F. for 1¼ hours or until peppers are tender, basting occasionally. Makes 4-6 servings.

Lunenburg, N.S.
Ladies Auxiliary
Branch No. 23

Beef and Vegetable Casserole

10 oz. frozen lima beans
1½ thinly sliced carrots
1 cup boiling water
1½ lbs. lean ground beef
2 tbsp. chopped onion
1 tbsp. oil
1-10½ oz. can condensed
   cream of mushroom soup
⅓ cup vegetable liquid
1½ tsp. salt
¼ tsp. thyme
6 ¾-inch thick tomato slices
½ tsp. salt
2 tbsp. grated Parmesan
   cheese

In a pot boil 1 cup water. Add lima beans and carrots. Cover and cook for 15 to 20 minutes until tender. Drain; reserve ⅓ cup liquid. In a frying pan brown ground beef and onion in oil. Pour off drippings. Add soup, vegetable liquid, vegetables, salt and thyme. Mix well. Pour into a casserole. Top mixture with tomato slices. Sprinkle with salt and cheese. Bake at 350°F. for 35 to 40 minutes. Serves 6.

Milltown, N.B.
Ladies Auxiliary
Branch No. 48

Healthy Hamburgers

1 lb. ground beef
¼ cup finely chopped celery
¼ cup grated carrots
¼ cup chopped onions
¼ cup parsley
¼ cup wheat germ
1 tsp. salt
1 tsp. Worcestershire sauce
¼ tsp. pepper
1 egg

An interesting hamburger containing celery, carrots and wheat germ. It can be broiled or barbequed over coals.

Cheticamp, N.S.
Ladies Auxiliary
Branch No. 32

Sweet and Sour Meatballs

1 lb. ground beef
2 tbsp. chopped onion
½ cup bread crumbs
1 tbsp. chopped parsley
½ tsp. garlic salt
½ tsp. pepper
1 egg
⅔ cup milk

Mix all together and form in meatballs. Brown meatballs in salad oil, then place them in casserole dish. Sprinkle ½ tsp. curry powder over and 1 can pineapple chunks. Prepare sauce.

Sauce:
¼ cup sugar
1/8 tsp. salt
¼ cup vinegar
1 tbsp. soya sauce
juice from pineapple chunks
1 tbsp. cornstarch

Bring to a boil and pour over meatballs. Place in oven and bake for 30 minutes or more.

Plum Point, Nfld.
Ladies Auxiliary
Branch No. 55

Pepper Steak

2-3 lbs. sirloin tip, serving
   pieces
½ cup chopped onion
2 cloves garlic, diced
1 tbsp. salt
dash pepper
1 beef bouillon cube
1 cup hot water
1-16 oz. can stewed tomatoes
1 green pepper, chopped
3 celery stalks, chopped
   coarsely
1 can whole mushrooms
2 tbsp. soya sauce
2 tbsp. cornstarch
½ cup cold water

Brown meat in hot fat. Put in roaster and add all the vegetables. Cover and bake 1 hour at 350°F. Add soya sauce. Combine cornstarch and cold water. Stir into meat mixture. Cook 10 minutes longer. Serve with rice.

Oak River, Man.
Ladies Auxiliary
Branch No. 150

Vegetable Beef Casserole

1 lb. lean hamburger
1 large onion
1 can peas, reserve juice
1½ cups diced carrots
1½ cups diced turnip
2 cups diced potatoes
1-2 cans tomato soup, as
   desired
salt and pepper

Sauté onion, brown hamburger and set aside. Prepare vegetables and cook in boiling salted water until tender. Drain vegetables and add to meat and onion. Stir in tomato soup. If not enough liquid, use pea juice. Bake at 350°F. for 30 minutes, then raise temperature to 425°F. Cover top with biscuits and bake 8 to 10 minutes.

Biscuits:
2 cups flour
3 tsp. baking powder
1 tsp. salt
¾ cup shortening
1 egg
milk

To flour, baking powder and salt add shortening and work in well. Add egg and a little milk, just enough so that dough can be handled easily. Roll to ½-inch thickness, cut and bake 8 to 10 minutes at 425°F.

Multiply this recipe by 5 and you will have servings for up to 50 people.

Windsor, N.S.
Ladies Auxiliary
Branch No. 9

Sweet and Sour Meat Balls

3 lbs. hamburger, make up
   hamburger as usual
1-10 oz. can tomato sauce
1 small bottle chili sauce
1 bottle water (use bottle
   from chili sauce)
1 small jar grape jelly

In pan add grape jelly and then add the rest of ingredients, then add meatballs.

Winnipeg, Man.
Ladies Auxiliary
Branch No. 115

Pepper Steak

1 lb. round steak
salt and pepper
¼ cup oil
1 green pepper, cut in strips
1 cup celery, cut in pieces
¼ cup chopped onion
clove garlic
1 can consommé soup
   undiluted
2 tbsp. cornstarch
¼ cup water
¼ cup soya sauce
1 can water chestnuts
   (optional)
hot cooked noodles or rice

Cut steak diagonally into thin strips, then cut into 2-inch pieces. Heat oil; add meat, stirring frequently; brown. Add garlic and consommé. Cook over low heat until tender, about 1 hour. 15 minutes before serving add vegetables. Cover and cook over moderate heat until vegetables are crispy. Blend cornstarch, water and soya sauce, add to mixture. Cook and stir, until thickened. Water may be added if you feel sauce is too thick.

Thompson, Man.
Ladies Auxiliary
Branch No. 244

Shipwreck Casserole

1 can tomato soup
2 large onions
1 lb. lean hamburger
1 cup chopped celery
1 can water (use soup can)
2 large potatoes
½ cup uncooked rice
1 cup chopped carrots

In large casserole arrange sliced onion, potatoes, and hamburger. Sprinkle rice over meat, add celery and carrots. Add tomato soup and can of hot water. Season and bake till well done.

Westlock, Alta.
Ladies Auxiliary
Branch No. 97

Sweet and Tender Meatballs

1 lb. ground beef
¼ cup bread crumbs
¼ cup chopped onions
4 tsp. soya sauce
1 egg
garlic salt
dash pepper
2 cups chopped tomatoes,
   fresh or canned
3 tbsp. oil for cooking meat
2 tbsp. vinegar
2 tbsp. brown sugar
2-10 oz. cans mushroom soup

Mix beef, crumbs, onions, egg, garlic salt and pepper. Shape into little balls and cook in oil. Remove from pan as they are cooked. Pour off fat, mix remaining ingredients. Add to meat, cover and let cook slowly for about 20 minutes. Serve on white rice.

Cowansville, Que.
Ladies Auxiliary
Branch No. 99

Quick Chop Suey

2 tbsp. fat
½ lb. ground beef
1 onion
¾ cup sliced celery
1 cup undiluted canned
   consommé soup
1 cup canned bean sprouts
½-10 oz. can sliced mush-
   rooms
1 tbsp. cornstarch
2 tbsp. soya sauce
2 cups hot cooked rice

Melt falt in skillet. Sauté beef, sliced onions and celery until meat browns and vegetables are golden. Add drained bean sprouts, consommé soup and undrained mushrooms. Cover skillet. Simmer 10 minutes. Combine cornstarch and soya sauce. Stir in beef mixture, stirring constantly. Cook until thickened and smooth, about 5 minutes. Serve over hot rice.

Kelwood, Man.
Ladies Auxiliary
Branch No. 50

Spagetti with Meat Sauce

2 tbsp. olive oil
2 garlic cloves, minced
½ cup chopped onion
½ cup chopped celery
¾ cup sliced mushrooms
2 tbsp. chopped parsley
½ cup chopped green pepper
1 lb. ground beef
½ lb. ground pork
1-28 oz. can tomatoes
1-5½ oz. can tomato paste
1 tbsp. salt
1/8 tsp. paprika
1/8 tsp. cayenne
½ tsp. basil
¼ tsp oregano
¼ tsp. pepper
1 bay leaf
16 oz. spaghetti

Sauté vegetables in oil until onion is golden. Add beef and pork and cook until lightly browned. Add remaining ingredients and simmer 2 hours. Cook spaghetti according to directions on pkg. Pour sauce over spaghetti and if desired, sprinkle with Parmesan cheese. Yield 8 servings. Note: If more liquid is needed, add water.

Boiestown, N.B.
Ladies Auxiliary
Normandy Branch No. 78

Bean Casserole

½ lb. bacon, chopped
1 lb. hamburger
½ cup onions
½ cup ketchup

Cook or fry above and then add:

½ cup brown sugar
1 tsp. mustard
2 tsp. vinegar
salt
1-19 oz. can pork and beans
1 can lima beans, drained
1 can kidney beans, undrained

Mix well and put in casserole. Heat in oven at 350°F.

Schreiber, Ont.
Ladies Auxiliary
Branch No. 109

Teriyaki Burgers

(Microwave)

½ cup soya sauce
3 tbsp. sugar
3 green onions, sliced
½ tsp. ground ginger
1/8 tsp. instant minced garlic
   or 1 clove garlic, minced
1 lb. ground beef
1-8¼ oz. can pineapple
   (4 slices)
4 hamburger buns, split and
   toasted

In 2 qt. (8x8) baking dish, combine soya sauce, sugar, onions, ginger and garlic; mix well. Shape beef into 4 patties. Add to soya sauce mixture, turning over to coat. Cook, uncovered 6 minutes or until done, turning once during last half of cooking time. Top with pineapple slice and cook, uncovered for 30 seconds to warm pineapple. Serve on toasted buns.

Ste. Anne, Man.
Ladies Auxiliary
LaVerendrye Branch No. 220

Tasty Stew

1-2 lbs. lean stewing meat, cut
   up
1 can cream of tomato soup
2 tbsp. vinegar
2 tbsp. brown sugar
salt
pepper
onion salt

Place meat in roaster. Cover with tomato soup. Add vinegar, brown sugar, and season to taste. Cover and roast from 2½ to 3 hours at 350°F. This is nice with potatoes, rice or macaroni. A different result can be obtained by covering beef with 1 can cream of mushroom soup. An hour before serving, the juice of 1 can of mushrooms can be added, the mushrooms reserved until about 15 minutes before serving, when they are stirred into the mixture and served when hot.

Piapot, Sask
Ladies Auxiliary
Branch No. 12

Taco Pie

2 lbs. ground beef
2 onions, chopped
1 pkg. taco mix

Fry beef and onions. Add taco mix. Put in well greased 8x12-inch pan. Mix together:

3 eggs
¾ cup Bisquick
1¼ cups milk

Mix well and pour over meat mixture and bake at 375°F. or 25 minutes. Take from oven and put 1½ cups grated Cheddar cheese over top. Return to oven and bake 10 minutes longer.

Stony Mountain, Man.
Ladies Auxiliary
Branch No. 142

Pineapple Meat Balls

1½ lbs. ground beef (750 g)
½ cup bread crumbs (125 ml)
½ cup water (125 ml)
1½ tsp. salt (7 ml)
¼ tsp. pepper (1 ml)
1-14 oz. can pineapple tidbits, reserving syrup
   (398 ml)
½ cup chopped green pepper
   (125 ml) (optional)
1-10 oz. can condensed chick-
   en with rice soup (284 ml)
1 tbsp. soya sauce (15 ml)
½ cup sugar (125 ml)
½ cup pineapple juice
   (125 ml)
½ cup vinegar (125 ml)
3 tbsp. cornstarch (45 ml)

Put first 5 ingredients in bowl. Mix together well and shape into small balls. Brown. Remove to a 2 qt. (2.5 l) casserole. In medium size saucepan, combine pineapple, green pepper, soup, soya sauce, sugar and pineapple juice. Bring to a boil. Stir cornstarch in vinegar. Stir to make smooth. Add to boiling mixture, stirring and cooking until thickened. Pour over meatballs. Cover. Bake at 350°F. (180°C.) for 30 minutes. Serves 6.

Benito, Man.
Ladies Auxiliary
Branch No. 228

Beef and Macaroni Casserole

1 lb. minced beef
1 cup chopped onions
1-28 oz. can tomatoes
1 tsp. salt
1/8 tsp. pepper
2 tsp. Worcestershire sauce
1 cup macaroni (2 cups uncooked)

Cook beef until fat coats pan. Add onions and cook until beef is brown and onions transparent. Stir in tomatoes and seasonings and bring to a boil. Combine with cooked macaroni and turn into greased baking dish. Bake at 350°F. until bubbly, 35-40 minutes. Serves 6. This freezes well.

Mafeking, Man.
Ladies Auxiliary
Branch No. 93

Beef Goulash

½ head cabbage, cut up small
2 onions, cut up small
1 green pepper, cut up small
2 lbs. hamburger
1-10 oz. can tomato soup
1-7 oz. can tomato sauce
1-7 oz. can tomato paste
1-28 oz. can tomatoes
1 can mushroom pieces,
   undrained
¼ cup olive juice
1 tbsp. Worcestershire sauce
3 drops Tabasco sauce

Cook hamburger, add celery, onions and green pepper. Heat all ingredients in pot. Cook over low heat for 4 hours. Cook 1 pkg. egg noodles (medium size). Mix noodles with above mixture. Put in casseroles. Put grated Mozzarella cheese on top. Heat in oven when needed.

Montreal, Que.
Ladies Auxiliary
Flanders Branch No. 63

Appetizer Meatballs in Spicy Sauce

(Microwave)

Can be made one day ahead.

- 1/3 cup brown sugar, firmly packed
- 1-8 oz. can tomato sauce
- 3 tbsp. lemon juice
- 1/8 tsp. garlic salt
- 1/2 cup dry red wine or 1/2 cup water plus 1 tbsp. lemon juice
- 1/3 cup shredded peeled potato (1 small)
- 1 lb. lean ground beef
- 1 small onion, finely minced
- 1 egg
- 1/2 tsp. salt

In saucepan, combine the brown sugar, tomato sauce, lemon juice, garlic, salt and wine. Bring to a boil while stirring. Reduce heat and allow to simmer gently, uncovered, until sauce is thickened (about 20 minutes). Combine shredded potato, meat, onion, egg and salt. Shape into balls the size of a large marble. Arrange on rimmed baking pans. Bake at 500°F. for 4 to 5 minutes or until lightly brown. Remove and add to the prepared sauce (including pan juices). Cool, cover and refrigerate. Heat to serve. Makes 5 dozen.

Murdockville, Que.
Ladies Auxiliary
Branch No. 218

Hamburger Mix

- 5 lbs. hamburger
- 1 pkg. onion soup mix
- 1 pkg. brown gravy mix
- 1 pkg. Sloppy Joe mix
- 2 1/2 cups water
- 2 1/2 cups bread crumbs
- 5 eggs

Mix all together and shape into patties. Place on cookie sheet and freeze. Place patties in plastic bags after frozen.

Shoal Lake, Man.
Ladies Auxiliary
Branch No. 72

Lasagna

- 1 lb. hamburger
- 1/4 tsp. garlic salt or fresh garlic
- 1 small onion, chopped
- 1/2 tsp. pepper
- 1 large can tomatoes
- 1-8 oz. can tomato sauce
- 1 pkg. spaghetti sauce mix
- 1 pt. cottage cheese
- 3/4 cup Parmesan cheese
- 2 eggs

Reserve 1/4 cup Parmesan cheese to sprinkle over top. Mix last 3 ingredients well and set aside. Set aside 8 oz. Mozzarella cheese, 8 or 9 noodles.
Brown hamburger and drain. Add garlic, onion, pepper and tomatoes. Simmer 10 minutes. Add sauce and sauce mix. Simmer 30 minutes. Put in layers in greased pan starting with meat sauce, noodles, cheese mix, Mozzarella cheese and ending with meat sauce. Repeat in this order till all ingredients are used. Sprinkle 1/4 cup Parmesan cheese over top. Bake at 350°F. for 30 minutes or until bubbly and brown.

Bathurst, N.B.
Ladies Auxiliary
Branch No. 18

Cape Breton Meat Pie

- 2 lbs. lean ground beef
- 1 lb. lean ground pork
- salt
- pepper
- poultry seasoning
- 10 medium potatoes

Put meat in pot, cover with water, and simmer 30 minutes. Add spices. Cook and mash potatoes. When above mixture cooks, add potatoes and mix well, as not to be lumpy, fill double crust pie shells. Should make 5 to 7 pies. Bake at 375°F. till crust is golden. Will freeze up to 6 months.

Sydney, N.S.
Ladies Auxiliary
Branch No. 12

Cheesy Beef Pie

- 1 lb. ground beef
- 1/2 cup chopped onion
- 1-8 oz. can tomato sauce
- 1/4 cup snipped parsley
- 1/2 cup canned chopped mushrooms, drained
- 1/4 tsp. dried oregano leaves crushed
- 2 pkgs. refrigerated crescent rolls (8 rolls in each)
- 3 eggs
- 6 slices sharp process American cheese

In skillet brown beef and onion, drain. Stir in next 4 ingredients and 1/8 tsp. pepper; set aside. Unroll one pkg. of rolls. Place the 4 sections of dough together, forming a 12x6-inch rectangle. Seal edges and perforations together. Roll to 12-inch square, fit into 9-inch pie plate, trim. Separate one of the eggs; set aside yolk. Beat egg white with remaining 2 eggs, spread half over dough. Spoon meat into shell. Arrange cheese slices atop; spread remaining egg mixtur over cheese. Mix reserved yolk and 1 tbsp. water, brush lightly on edge of pastry. Roll second pkg. of rolls as before, place atop filling, trim, seal and flute edge. Cut slits for steam to escape. Brush with remaining egg yolk and water mixture. Bake at 350°F. for 50-55 minutes. Cover with foil if pastry gets too brown. Let stand 10 minutes before serving. Serves 6.

Winnipeg, Man.
Ladies Auxiliary
Imperial Veterans in Canada
Branch No. 84

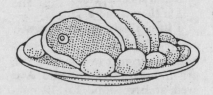

Coal Miner's Pie

1 lb. ground round
2 medium onions, chopped (1 cup)
1-15 oz. can tomato sauce
2 medium sweet green peppers, coarsely chopped
1 cup canned corn, drained or 1 cup frozen kernel corn
1-2 tbsp. chili powder
1¼ tsp. salt
1 tsp. pepper
2 eggs
1 tbsp. vegetable shortening
½ cup buttermilk
¾ cup yellow cornmeal
1 tbsp. all-purpose flour
1 tsp. baking soda

Preheat oven to 350°F. Brown beef and onions in Dutch oven or large kettle, breaking up meat with a wooden spoon, until meat is no longer pink. Stir in tomato sauce, green pepper, corn, chili powder, 1 tsp. of the salt and the pepper. Bring to boiling; lower heat; cover; simmer 15 minutes. Pour meat mixture into ungreased 10-inch deep-dish pie plate. Beat together eggs, shortening and buttermilk in a small bowl for 1 minute. Beat in cornmeal, flour, baking soda and remaining ¼ tsp. salt just until well blended. Spoon over the top of meat; spread evenly to cover entire surface.

Reserve Mines, N.S.
Ladies Auxiliary
Branch No. 2

Savoy Meat Loaf

1 pkg. onion soup mix
1 cup milk
2 slices day-old bread, finely crumbled
6 or 8 slices bacon
1½ lb. ground beef
1 tbsp. finely chopped parsley (optional)

Place soup mix in a large bowl, stir in milk and add bread. Mix well and let stand for 10 minutes. Add meat and parsley, mix well and place in an ungreased shallow baking dish or pie plate. Bake at 325°F. for 30 minutes. Place bacon strips on top and bake until done, about 30 minutes.

Gull Lake, Sask.
Ladies Auxiliary
Branch No. 119

Sweet and Sour Steak

3 tbsp. flour
3 tbsp. oil
¾ cup brown sugar
¾ cup water
2 tbsp. cornstarch
⅓ cup vinegar
⅓ cup ketchup
1 tbsp. soya sauce
3 tbsp. water

Cut and flour steak. Heat oil in pan and brown steak. Mix sugar, vinegar, ketchup, soya sauce and water. Pour over steak. Cover and simmer 1½ hours until tender. Mix cornstarch and 3 tbsp. water and add to sauce. This can also be used for meatballs.

Stonewall, Man.
Ladies Auxiliary
Branch No. 52

Barbequed Steak

steak, cut in serving pieces
salt and pepper
3 tbsp. lard
⅓ cup chopped celery
1 can tomato soup
2 tbsp. brown sugar
2 tbsp. Worcestershire sauce
2 tsp. prepared mustard
½ cup onion
1 small garlic clove
2 tbsp. lemon juice
few drops Tabasco sauce

Sprinkle steak with salt and pepper and brown in melted lard, with onions, celery and garlic. Add all other ingredients. Stir a little and cover. Cook about 1 or 1½ hours, till meat is tender at low heat.

Morris, Man.
Ladies Auxiliary
Branch No. 111

Steak Supper

1½ lb. chuck steak
1 envelope onion soup
4 medium carrots
4 stalks celery
2 or 3 potatoes
2 tbsp. butter
1 tsp. salt

Heat oven to 450°F. Tear off a 2½-foot length of 18-inch foil. Place meat in centre and sprinkle with onion soup mix. Cover with vegetables. Dot with butter and secure to hold juices. Place on baking sheet. Bake for 1-1½ hours.

Stony Mountain, Man.
Ladies Auxiliary
Branch No. 142

Jellied Veal Loaf

2 lbs. veal breast or shoulder
3 cups cold water
2 tbsp. salt
2 tbsp. chopped sweet pickle
2 tbsp. vinegar
6 tbsp. mayonnaise
salt and pepper to taste
1-2 tbsp. gelatin
¼ cup cold water

Cut meat into 1-inch dice, removing fat and gristle. Simmer meat in a covered pan with water and salt for about one hour or until very tender. Drain off broth and chill; there should be 2 cups - if not add cold water. Combine meat with pickle, vinegar, mayonnaise and seasonings. If broth forms a stiff jelly when cold, use 1 tbsp. gelatin, otherwise use 2 tbsp. Soften the gelatin 5 minutes in the ¼ cup cold water, then melt over hot water. Heat broth until just liquid, add melted gelatin, stir thoroughly into meat mixture. Pour into glass pan (8½x4½x2½) which has been rubbed with salad oil and chill until firm. Turn out and slice.

Montreal, Que.
Ladies Auxiliary
Maisonneuve Branch No. 66

Oven Barbequed Steak

3 lb. round steak
2 tbsp. oil
½ cup chopped onion
¾ cup ketchup
½ cup vinegar
¾ cup water
1 tbsp. brown sugar
1 tbsp. prepared mustard
1 tbsp. Worcestershire sauce
½ tsp. salt
1/8 tsp. pepper

Cut steak in serving or bite-size pieces and brown in oil. Transfer steak to casserole dish. Add onion to skillet and brown. Add remaining ingredients. Simmer for 5 minutes. Pour sauce over steak. Cover casserole dish and bake at 350°F. for 1½ to 2 hours or until steak is tender. This recipe makes 10 servings.

Gladstone, Man.
Ladies Auxiliary
Branch No. 110

Steak Supper in Foil

1½ lb. chuck steak, 1 inch thick
1 can cream of mushroom soup
1 envelope onion soup mix
3 medium carrots, quartered
2 stalks celery, cut into 2-inch pieces
3 medium potatoes, pared and quartered
2 tbsp. water

Heat oven to 450°F. Place 24x16-inch piece of aluminum foil in baking pan; place meat in foil. Stir together mushroom soup and dry onion soup mix, spread on meat. Top meat with vegetables, sprinkle water on vegetables. Fold over and seal securely. Cook 1½ hours or until tender.

Hodgson, Man.
Ladies Auxiliary
Branch No. 158

Garlic Sausage

3 lbs. hamburger
1 cup water
2 tbsp. hickory liquid smoke
½ tsp. garlic powder
1/8 tsp. mustard seed
¼ tsp. onion powder
1/8 tsp. celery seed
3 tbsp. Morton's Tender Quick salt (navy blue bag)

Mix all thoroughly with hands. Form into four loaves. Roll in foil and refrigerate for 24 hours or overnight. Prick holes in bottom of foil and bake in broiler pan with a little water at 325°F. for 1½ to 2 hours. Serve hot or cold. Freezes well.

Ste. Anne, Man.
Ladies Auxiliary
LaVerendrye Branch No. 220

Chinese Hash

1 lb. ground beef
2 medium onions, chopped
1 can cream of mushroom soup
1 can cream of chicken soup
1¼ tsp. soya sauce
⅓ oz. can crisp chinese noodles
2 tbsp. salad oil
1 cup celery sliced
1½ cups warm water
½ cup rice
¼ tsp. pepper

Brown meat in salad oil until crumbles. Add onions, celery and soups. Rinse cans with warm water and add to mixture. Stir in uncooked rice, soya sauce and pepper. Turn into greased casserole, cover and bake at 350°F. for 30 minutes. Remove cover and bake 30 minutes longer. Cover with crisp noodles and bake 15 minutes.

Fort McMurray, Alta.
Ladies Auxiliary
Branch No. 165

Beef Roladen-Tenderloin

sliced dill pickle, diagonally sliced
German mustard
chopped onion
mashed capers
water
salt and pepper
bacon
garlic

Flatten beef tenderloin, unroll and spread mustard, onions and capers. Put 3 slices of pickle on each Roladen. Salt and pepper and place ½ or 1 slice bacon on top of pickles. Roll up and put 3 toothpicks through to keep together. Then brown in pan with bit of bacon fat. After the meat is browned, pour water over top and simmer for about 2 to 3 hours. Take out and make a gravy.

Kelowna, B.C.
Ladies Auxiliary
Branch No. 26

Baked Liver and Bacon

4 serving size slices beef liver
salt and pepper to taste
flour for dredging
1 egg, beaten with ¼ cup milk
½ cup fine dry bread crumbs
8 strips bacon

Generously butter a shallow baking pan. Salt and pepper liver slices and dredge lightly with flour. Beat egg with the milk and dip floured slices in egg mixture and then in bread crumbs to coat. Lay liver slices close together in buttered pan and cover all with bacon slices. Bake at 350°F. until bacon is crisp and brown, about 30 minutes. Liver is ready to serve when the bacon is done.

Plumas, Man.
Ladies Auxiliary
Branch No. 189

No Boil Lasagna

1 tbsp. vegetable oil
1 clove garlic, minced
1-10 oz. can sliced mushrooms
1 cup cottage cheese (250 g)
1-10 oz. pkg. frozen chopped
  spinach, thawed (optional)
1 egg, slightly beaten
1-6 oz. pkg. Mozzarella
  cheese
1 medium onion, chopped
1 lb. ground beef
½ cup water
⅓ cup grated Parmesan
  cheese
2 tsp. vegetable oil
¾ pkg. lasagna noodles
  uncooked
2-14 oz. cans tomato sauce
1 tsp. oregano
1 tsp. salt

Sauté onion and garlic in oil. Add ground beef and brown. Remove excess fat. Stir in tomato sauce, mushrooms with their liquid, water and oregano, bring to a boil and remove from heat. Combine cottage cheese, Parmesan cheese, well drained spinach, egg, oil and salt. Spoon ⅓ of sauce into a 9x13-inch baking dish. Cover with ⅓ of lasagna. Spread another ⅓ of sauce over and cover with another ⅓ of lasagna. Spread cheese and spinach mixture over and cover with remaining lasagna and sauce. Top with cheese slices. Cover with foil paper and bake at 375°F. for 45 minutes. Uncover and bake until cheese starts to brown, about 15 minutes.

Whitehorse, Yukon
Ladies Auxiliary
Branch No. 254

Kitchen Sausage

5 lbs. hamburger
100 ml Tender Quick salt
15 ml mustard seed
10 ml black pepper
15 ml garlic salt
5 ml liquid smoke

Mix together and knead 5 minutes. Put into container with a tight fitting lid and store in refrigerator 4 days. Each day take out and knead 5 minutes. On fourth day after kneading, roll into 4 or 5 logs. Bake at 150°F. for 10 hours.

Holland, Man.
Ladies Auxiliary
Victoria Branch No. 121

Mushroom Meatballs

1 can cream of mushroom
  soup
½ cup water
1 egg, slightly beaten
½ tsp. salt

Measure out ¼ cup soup mixture. Combine with:
1 lb. ground beef
½ cup dry bread crumbs
2 tbsp. minced onion
1 tbsp. parsley

Shape into meatballs. Brown in pan with 1 tbsp. shortening. Add remaining soup mixture. Cover and cook over low heat for 15 minues. Stir occasionally. Serves 4.

Armdale, N.S.
Ladies Auxiliary
Halifax County Branch No. 153

Chili Con Carne

2 lbs. hamburger
4 tbsp. butter
4 small onions
2 cups or more tomatoes
2 cans kidney beans
4 stalks celery
1 tsp. salt
1 tsp. or more red pepper
1 tsp. or more chili powder

Melt butter in pan; add hamburger and onion; cook till almost done. Put in kettle or big pot and add tomatoes, beans, celery, salt and pepper. Simmer 1½ hours; add chili powder and simmer 30 minutes longer. Serve hot.

Strathclair, Man.
Ladies Auxiliary
Branch No. 154

Alberta Fillet of Beef en Croute

1¾ cups all-purpose flour
  (425 ml)
¼ tsp. salt (1 ml)
⅓ cup butter (75 ml)
⅓ cup shortening (75 ml)
1 egg yolk
1½ tsp. olive oil (7 ml)
⅓ cup cold water (75 ml)
1-2½ lbs. fillet of beef
  (1,250 kg)
salt and pepper
¼ lb. fresh morils (125 g) or
  2 oz. dried morils (60 g)
  or other mushrooms
¼ lb. liver paté (125 g)
¼ cup minced chives (50 ml)
1 egg, beaten

Prepare pastry by cutting butter and shortening in a mixture of flour and salt. Add the egg yolk, the oil and cold water, mixing with a fork to bind the mixture. Form the dough into a ball and refrigerate until ready to use. Sprinkle the fillet lightly with salt and pepper. Sauté in a little hot oil in skillet without cooking inside of the meat. Cool completely. Chop mushrooms. Combine mushrooms, liver paté and chives. Coat the fillet of beef with this mixture. Roll pastry in a rectangle large enough to cover the fillet completely. Roll pastry around the fillet, placing the seam underneath. Fold the two ends of the pastry underneath. Brush the pastry with a beaten egg. Decorate the top with pastry trimmings cut in attractive designs and brush with beaten egg. Prick pastry to prevent it from cracking during baking. Bake at 375°F. (190°C.) 40 to 50 minutes for rare meat and a little longer for the meat to be well done. Serve cut in ¾-inch (2 cm) slices. 6 servings. To rehydrate the dry mushrooms, cover with hot water and a little vinegar, 1 minute. Wash with hot water 3 or 4 times, press lightly.

Strathmore, Alta.
Ladies Auxiliary
Branch No. 10

Veal Parmigiana

1 egg, fork beaten
¼ tsp. salt
1 tbsp. water
1/8 tsp. pepper
½ cup dry bread crumbs, roll to very fine
¼ cup grated Parmesan cheese
1½ lbs. veal cutlets, 4 chops or round steak
⅓ cup cooking oil
1-7½ oz. can tomato sauce
4 slices Mozzarella cheese

In small bowl combine egg, water, salt and pepper. On large plate mix together crumbs and Parmesan cheese. Cut veal in 4 serving pieces. Dip each piece in egg mixture then in crumb mixture. Fry in oil, heated in fry pan. Brown both sides. Put in large shallow baking dish. Pour tomato sauce over top. Place cheese slice over each piece. Bake covered at 300-350°F. for 35 minutes until tender. Remove cover and continue baking to melt cheese for 10 minutes. Serves 4.

Camrose, Alta.
Ladies Auxiliary
Branch No. 57

Barbequed Short Ribs

3 lbs. beef ribs
1 onion, chopped
¼ cup vinegar
1 tbsp. brown sugar
1 cup ketchup
¼ cup water
1 tsp. prepared mustard
3 tbsp. Worcestershire sauce
½ cup sliced celery
2 tsp. salt

Brown ribs slowly in heavy saucepan or Dutch oven. Add onions and cook 3 minutes. Add remaining ingredients. Cover and simmer in oven about 2 hours. Also, you may use pork chops or pork ribs.

Gladstone, Man.
Ladies Auxiliary
Branch No. 110

Sweet and Sour Shortribs

2 lbs. shortribs
2 tbsp. fat
¾ cup water
2 tbsp. cornstarch
¼ cup brown sugar
1 tsp. salt
1-12 oz. can pineapple chunks drained, reserving syrup
⅓ cup vinegar
1 tbsp. soya sauce
½ cup green pepper slices
¼ cup thinly sliced onions

Brown shortribs in hot fat. Add water, cover and cook slowly until tender, about 1½ to 2 hours, adding more water if necessary. Combine sugar, and cornstarch; add salt, pineapple syrup, vinegar and soya sauce. Cook over low heat until thick, stirring constantly. Pour over ribs, let stand 10 minutes. Add green peppers, onion and pineapple. Cook 5 minutes. Makes 4 servings.

Mission, B.C.
Ladies Auxiliary
Branch No. 57

Orange Style Leg of Lamb

(Microwave)

5-5½ lb. leg of lamb
¼ cup orange juice
½ cup orange marmelade
dash cinnamon
1 tsp. orange peel

Place lamb fat side down in 13½x¾x1¾-inch baking dish. Cook in microwave for 25 minutes. Turn roast over. Cook 20 minutes longer. Drain off excess fat. Combine remaining ingredients in bowl. Spoon orange sauce over lamb. Cook an additional 5 minutes. Let stand 10 minutes before serving. Yields: 6 to 8 servings.

Swan River, Man.
Ladies Auxiliary
Branch No. 39

Zesty Beef Pot Roast

(Prepared in pressure cooker)

3 lbs. short ribs, shoulder, brisket or cross-rib beef roast
1 tsp. salt
¼ tsp. pepper
1 medium onion, chopped
1 lemon sliced
2 tbsp. brown sugar
1 tbsp. Worcestershire sauce
½ tsp. dry mustard
1 clove garlic, crushed
½ cup tomato sauce
2 tbsp. flour
¼ cup water

Heat enough oil in pressure cooker to brown beef well on all sides. Add all other ingredients except flour and water. Close cover securely. Cook 30 to 40 minutes, depending on shape of roast. Let pressure drop. Remove roast from cooker. Remove excess fat from juices. Thicken juices with flour and water mixed, cook until gravy has thickened. Yields 8-10 servings.

15 lbs. of pressure (considered standard)
Rare — 8-10 minutes per lb.
Medium — 10-12 minutes per lb.
Well done — 12-15 minutes per lb.

Roast may be crispied and further browned by placing under broiler for a few minutes before serving.

Elkhorn, Man.
Ladies Auxiliary
Branch No. 58

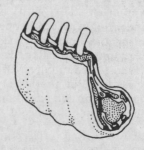

Barbequed Lamb Chops

6-8 lamb chops
¾ cup ketchup
¾ cup water
½ cup chopped onions
2 tbsp. brown sugar
3 tbsp. Worcestershire sauce
½ tsp. salt
dash hot pepper sauce

Arrange chops in shallow baking dish. Combine remaining ingredients and pour over chops. Cover dish with foil and bake at 350°F.

Clarenville, Nfld.
Ladies Auxiliary
Branch No. 27

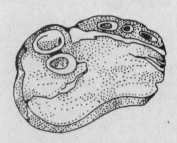

Beefy Pizza

1 lb. ground beef
1 cup soft bread crumbs
1 egg
salt and pepper
½ tsp. oregano
Mozzarella cheese
4 oz. tomato sauce
1 can mushroom pieces, drained
1 small onion, chopped
2 tbsp. green pepper, chopped

Combine beef, bread crumbs, egg, salt, pepper and oregano. Mix well in 9-inch pie pan. Form a beef crust. Lay a couple of slices of Mozzarella cheese over crust. Top with tomato sauce, onion, green pepper and mushrooms and dash of oregano again if you like. Bake at 350°F. for 55 minutes. Drain of excess fat. Put another layer of cheese on top and bake 5 minutes longer to melt the cheese.

Sinclair, Man.
Ladies Auxiliary
Branch No. 243

Luau Short Ribs
"Sweet 'n Sour"

3 lbs. lean beef short ribs
½ cup flour
1 tsp. salt
½ tsp. pepper
1 medium onion, sliced
1 cup hot ketchup
2 tbsp. wine vinegar
2 tbsp. Worcestershire sauce
½ cup honey
¼ cup water

Wipe shortribs with damp paper towel. Mix flour, salt and pepper. Coat ribs with mix. Arrange in large baking dish. Place sliced onion on top. Mix remaining ingredients. Pour over ribs. Cover. Bake at 350°F. for 2 hours or until tender. For crisp ribs, remove cover last 30 minutes. Makes 6 servings.

Montreal, Que.
Ladies Auxiliary
Maisonneuve Branch No. 66

Pork

Hodge Podge
(A dinner of
new vegetables.)

Cut new string beans and carrots into pieces. Cover with boiling salted water. Add cut potatoes; cook 15 minutes. Add shelled peas and cook until tender.
Broad beans, sugar peas, cauliflower should be cooked separately and added to the platter of vegetables.
1 cup finely diced salt pork fried to a golden brown, add 1 cup cream, 1 cup liquid, a little chives, pepper or a dash of paprika. Boil up quickly, dribble over vegetables.

Western Shore, N.S.
Ladies Auxiliary
Branch No. 144

Mustard Glazed Ham

Combine:
½ cup brown sugar
1 tsp. dry mustard
2 tbsp. flour
3 tbsp. vinegar

Spread over ham. Stud with cloves if desired. Bake at 325°F.

Salisbury, N.B.
Ladies Auxiliary
Branch No. 31

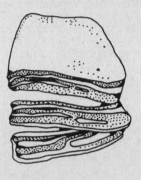

Pork Chops

Seasoned Flour:
2 cups flour
2 tbsp. salt
1 tbsp. celery salt
1 tbsp. black pepper
2 tbsp. dry mustard
4 tbsp. paprika
2 tbsp. garlic powder
1 tsp. ginger
½ tsp. thyme
½ tsp. basil
½ tsp. oregano

Sift together and store in tightly covered jar.

Dredge pork chops in ½ cup seasoned flour (enough for 6 chops). Brown on both sides in frying pan. Arrange in baking dish. Top each chop with a slice of lemon. Combine:
⅔ cup ketchup
⅔ cup water
3 tbsp. brown sugar

Pour over chops. Cover and bake at 350°F. for 30 minutes. Uncover and bake 20 to 30 minutes longer. Add water if necesaary.

Armdale, N.S.
Ladies Auxiliary
Halifax County Branch No. 153

Gala Easter Ham

8-10 lb. ham
1 can sliced pineapple
2 tsp. cornstarch
3 tbsp. brown sugar
3 tbsp. prepared mustard
¼ cup flaked coconut

Place ham, fat side up on rack in shallow pan. Bake at 325°F. for 2½ to 3 hours. Drain and measure juice from pineapple. Add water if necessary to make ¾ cup. Combine juice, cornstarch, brown sugar and mustard in small saucepan, stirring until smooth. Heat to simmering, stirring occasionally. Stud ham with cloves, brush and glaze. Bake 30 minutes longer until glazed. Trim ham with pineapple. Cut remaining pineapple into thin wedges. Add to remaining glaze along with coconut. Serve over sliced ham. The coconut can be omitted.

Sinclair, Man.
Ladies Auxiliary
Branch No. 243

"La Tourtiere"

(Pork Pie?

2 lbs. ground beef
2 lbs. ground pork
1 tsp. salt, to taste
lots of pepper
1 large onion, chopped fine
water
flour
1 tsp. cinnamon
1 shake nutmeg
1 shake cloves

Mix meat, seasonings and onion. Add a wee bit of water, depending on how dry the meat is. Sprinkle a few handfuls of flour to thicken. Add cinnamon, nutmeg and cloves. (Not too much nutmeg or cloves, always more cinnamon.) Simmer until thick so that it will be stiff enough (not too runny). Fill unbaked pastry shells and cover. Bake at 450°F. for 10 minutes. Reduce heat to 350°F. and continue baking until done, at least an hour.

Thompson, Man.
Ladies Auxiliary
Branch No. 244

Orange Barbequed Pork Chops

(Microwave)
6-8 pork chops
1 cup ketchup
½ cup water
2 tbsp. lemon juice
2 tbsp. vinegar
2 tbsp. Worcestershire sauce
1 medium onion, finely chopped
½ cup finely diced celery
2 tbsp. brown sugar
1 tsp. salt
½ tsp. dry mustard
1 orange, thinly sliced

Place pork chops in 2 qt. casserole. Combine rest of ingredients except orange and pour over pork chops. Cover with dish lid and microwave on High for 6 minutes. Baste pork chops. Place orange slices on pork chops. Cover and microwave on High for 6 minutes or until done.

Elgin, Man.
Ladies Auxiliary
Branch No. 216

Bacon and Liver Bake

6 slices bacon
1 cup chopped onion
½ cup flour
1 lb. liver
½ cup fine bread crumbs
1 tbsp. melted butter
1½ cups milk
salt and pepper

Cut bacon in 1-inch pieces and combine with onion in pan. Fry until crisp and tender. Remove from pan. Combine flour, salt and pepper and coat liver with this, reserving remaining mixture. Brown liver in drippings. Place in baking dish. Blend flour in drippings in pan until smooth, add milk and stir. Pour over liver; sprinkle with bacon and onion. Top with buttered crumbs. Bake at 350°F. for 25 minutes.

Valemount, B.C.
Ladies Auxiliary
Branch No. 266

Spanish Pork Chops with Rice

1 tbsp. fat
4 pork loin chops, ¾-inch thick
½ cup uncooked special processed rice
1 cup sliced onions
1¼ cups minced green pepper
½ tsp. salt
¼ tsp. pepper
½ tsp. paprika
1 tsp. sugar
1-28 oz. can tomatoes

Melt fat in skillet, add chops and brown on both sides. Remove chops to a 2 qt. casserole and arrange them around sides of casserole to provide space for rice. Add rice. Add remaining ingredients to pan in which chops were fried. Stir to pick up drippings. Pour over chops. Bake at 400°F. for 45 minutes. (I use ordinary rice, partially cooked.)

Mafeking, Man.
Ladies Auxiliary
Branch No. 93

Newfoundland Jiggs Boiled Dinner

2 lbs. salt beef or spare ribs
6 potatoes
1 medium turnip
6 carrots
1 head cabbage
2 cups split peas

Cut salt beef in 2-inch pieces and soak in cold water overnight. Tie peas in cloth bag and soak also. Drain off water. Bring to a boil and cook slowly for 3 hours or until tender. Clean vegetables. Add turnip, potatoes and carrot 30 minutes before serving dinner. Add cabbage last 15 minutes. Do not overcook. Turn peas pudding into a bowl and mash with butter and pepper.

Clarenville, Nfld.
Ladies Auxiliary
Branch No. 27

Spareribs with Celery Stuffing

1½ lbs. spareribs
½ cup chopped onion
2 cups soft bread crumbs
dash pepper
2 tbsp. butter or drippings
½ cup chopped celery
½ tsp. salt

Brown onions in fat. Add celery, bread crumbs, salt, pepper and ½ cup water. Place dressing in baking pan and cover with seasoned spareribs. Bake uncovered at 350°F. for 1½ to 2 hours.

Ear Falls, Ont.
Ladies Auxiliary
Branch No. 238

Sweet and Sour Ham

½ cup beef broth
1 onion, diced
3 stalks celery, sliced
1 green pepper, sliced
1 cup pineapple chunks
¼ cup sugar
3 tbsp. cornstarch
¼ tsp. ginger
¼ cup pineapple juice
½ cup vinegar
2 tbsp. soya sauce
2 cups cubed ham, cooked pork or chicken
1½ cups sliced mushrooms
1¼ cups sweet mixed pickles, quartered
1 tomato sliced
4 cups hot cooked rice
2 cups shredded Gouda, Swiss or Cheddar cheese

Combine first 5 ingredients in saucepan. Bring to boil, then cover and simmer 5 minutes. Vegetables should still be crisp. Blend next 6 ingredients together until smooth; stir into vegetable mixture. Cook, stirring constantly, until thickened. Add ham, mushrooms, pickles and tomato. Heat through. Combine hot rice and cheese. Serve ham mixture over rice. Makes 6 servings.

Vernon, B.C.
Ladies Auxiliary
Branch No. 25

Newfoundland Potato Pork Cakes

8 large potaties
1 lb. salted fat back pork
2½ cups flour
3 tsp. baking powder

Boil and mash potatoes. Cut pork into pieces and fry. Add the scrunchions to mashed potatoes. Mix in sifted flour and baking powder. Form into cakes. Bake at 350°F. for 30 minutes.

Clarenville, Nfld.
Ladies Auxiliary
Branch No. 27

Sweet and Sour Pork

3 green peppers, cut into pieces
¾ cup oil
1 tsp. salt

Batter:
2 large eggs
1 tsp. salt
1 lb. pork tenderloin or pork butt
⅔ cup chicken bouillon
1-19 oz. can pineapple chunks, drained

Sauce:
5 tsp. cornstarch
¼ cup vinegar
1 cup white sugar
4 tsp. soya sauce
1⅓ cup chicken bouillon

Simmer green pepper for 10 minutes. Heat oil and salt in frying pan.

Cut pork in ½-inch cubes. Prepare batter and drop pork cubes into batter to coat them. Drop into hot fat. Brown on all sides. Pour off fat and drain pork.

In frying pan put in chicken bouillon, drained pineapple chunks, green pepper and pork. Cover and simmer for 10 minutes. Make sauce, add to frying pan, stir until thickened, about 5 minutes. Serves 4-6 people.

Miami, Man.
Ladies Auxiliary
Branch No. 88

Scalloped Potatoes with Vienna Sausage

4 cups sliced raw potatoes
1 can sliced mushrooms
¼ cup flour
4 tbsp. chopped onion
1 cup milk
3 canned tomatoes, cut in half
¼ cup grated cheese
salt and pepper to taste
1-4 oz. can Vienna sausages

Put half of sliced potatoes, sliced sausages and mushrooms in a casserole. Sprinkle with half the flour and half of the onions. Salt and pepper to taste. Repeat with rest of ingredients. Pour milk over all in casserole. Cover and bake at 350°F. for 45 minutes. Remove lid, add tomatoes and cheese. Return to oven and bake uncovered for 30 to 40 minutes.

Winnipeg, Man.
Ladies Auxiliary
Brooklands Weston Branch No. 2

Barbequed Spareribs

3 lb. spareribs or rib ends
1 tbsp. salt
1 tbsp. mixed pickling spice
1 medium onion, sliced
½ cup barbeque sauce
¼ cup corn syrup

Cut ribs into serving size pieces and place in a large kettle. Cover ribs with water, add salt, pickling spice and sliced onions. Heat slowly to boiling, reduce heat, cover, and simmer for 1 hour. Remove kettle from heat and allow ribs to cool in the liquid. When ready, arrange ribs in a single layer on a broiling pan. Combine barbeque sauce and corn syrup in a cup, brush onto ribs. Broil until nicely brown on first side, turn meat and repeat until evenly glazed.

Emo, Ont.
Ladies Auxiliary
Branch No. 99

Apple Stuffed Pork Chops

(Microwave)

1 cup bread crumbs
1 cup pared and cubed cooking apples
2 tbsp. butter
1 tsp. salt
4-6 medium pork chops

In small bowl, combine bread crumbs, apples, butter and salt. Cook 2 to 3 minutes, stirring after every minute. Cut a slit in each pork chop and stuff with bread crumb mixture. Arrange in a 2 qt. glass baking dish. Cook, covered, 16 to 20 minutes, rotating dish ¼ turn halfway through cooking time. Rest, covered, 10 minutes, before serving. 4 to 6 servings.

L'Ardoise, N.S.
Ladies Auxiliary
Branch No. 110

Orange Glazed Pork Loaf

1½ lb. ground pork
1 cup quick-cooking oatmeal
1 egg
1 medium onion, chopped
1 tsp. marjoram
½ tsp. salt
¼ tsp. cloves
¼ tsp. pepper
¼ cup orange juice
2 tbsp. lemon juice
2 tbsp. brown sugar
1 tsp. dry mustard
6 slices orange

Mix together ground pork, oatmeal, egg, onion, marjoram, salt, cloves, pepper, orange juice and lemon juice. Sprinkle brown sugar and mustard on bottom of loaf pan. Top with orange slices. Press ground pork mixture firmly into loaf pan. Bake at 350°F. for 1 hour. Let stand 10 minutes. After removal from oven, invert onto a heated platter. Serve hot or chilled. Makes 6 servings.

Debert, N.S.
Ladies Auxiliary
Branch No. 106

Chinese Oven-Fried Pork Chops

1 egg
3 tbsp. soya sauce
1 tbsp. dry sherry or water
1/8 tsp. ground ginger
½ tsp. garlic powder
seasoned dry bread crumbs
6 lean pork chops

Put a little oil in roaster or broiler pan. Mix first 5 ingredients together in a bowl. Place bread crumbs on a plate or wax paper. Dip pork chops in egg mixture, then press into bread crumbs evenly on both sides. Arrange in single layer in pan. Bake in a slow oven, 300°F. for approx. 20 minutes, or until done. Turn only once.

Hartney, Man.
Ladies Auxiliary
Branch No. 26

Pork Chop 'n Red Cabbage Casserole

4 pork chops
½ cup onions, diced
1 medium or 6 cups chopped red cabbage
6 medium potatoes, diced
1 cup or 2 apples sliced or diced
2 cups boiling water
4 tbsp. vinegar

Place pork chops in frying pan and brown. Sprinkle with salt and pepper. Place in Dutch oven in layers: first cabbage, then potatoes, apple and onions. Spread the 4 pork chops on top and pour the 2 cups of boiling water in frying pan. Bring to a boil, then pour over the mixture in the Dutch oven. Cook on stove at medium temperature for 1 hour or until well done. Now add vinegar, salt and pepper to taste. Mix well — ready to serve.

Oak Lake, Man.
Ladies Auxiliary
Branch No. 79

Individual Tourtieres

1 lb. lean minced pork
¼ cup chopped onion
½ tsp. salt
dash pepper
¼-½ tsp. savory
dash cloves
1 small bay leaf
¼ cup boiling water
pastry for 9-inch, 2 crust pie

Combine pork and seasonings. Add bay leaf and water. Simmer uncovered, stirring occasionally until meat is white, about 20 minutes. Cool and skim off any fat. Line 6 individual pie pans, about 3½″ in diameter, with pastry. Divide cooled meat mixture evenly between 6 pie shells. Cover each with pastry, seal edges and cut small vents so steam can escape, in each. Bake at 425°F. about 25 minutes, or until lightly browned. 6 servings.

This recipe may be made in small tart pans. Shorten the baking time by about 5 minutes. Yield: 12 small tarts.

Montreal, Que.
Ladies Auxiliary
Maisonneuve Branch No. 66

Sausage Surprise

6 slices white bread
1 lb. bulk pork sausage
1 tsp. prepared mustard
4 oz. grated Parmesan cheese (1 cup)
2 eggs
1 cup milk
1 tsp. soya sauce
salt and pepper to taste

Place bread in bottom of greased baking dish. Brown sausage in frying pan and pour off fat. Place sausage over bread and sprinkle with cheese. Combine mustard, eggs (slightly beaten), milk, soya sauce, salt and pepper. Pour over sausage. Bake at 350°F. for 30 minutes.

Strathclair, Man.
Ladies Auxiliary
Branch No. 154

Ham Croquettes

3 tbsp. butter, melted
⅓ cup all-purpose flour
½ tsp. salt
1 cup milk
2 cups coarsely ground
   cooked ham
1 tbsp. finely chopped onion
2 tbsp. prepared mustard
1 egg, beaten
½ cup fine cracker crumbs

Combine melted butter and flour. Add salt and milk. Cook quickly, stirring constantly, till thickened. Cool. Add ham, onion and mustard. Chill. Shape in croquettes (size of breakfast sausage). Dip in beaten egg, then in cracker crumbs. Let stand a few minutes to set. Fry in deep fat (375°F.) 7 to 8 minutes or till brown. Drain on paper towels. Makes 12 to 16 croquettes or 6 generous servings. Any leftover meat can be used if ham is not available. Serve with Pickle Sauce and broiled peach halves or Gauche Sauce.

Pickle Sauce:
   1 cup hot Medium White
      Sauce
   2 hard cooked eggs, chopped

Gauche Sauce:
   1 cup ketchup
   1 tbsp. Worcestershire sauce
   2-3 dashes Tabasco sauce
   1 cup water
   ¼ cup vinegar
   1 tbsp. sugar
   1 tsp. salt
   1 tsp. celery seed
Simmer 30 minutes.

Hazelridge, Man.
Ladies Auxiliary
Branch No. 146

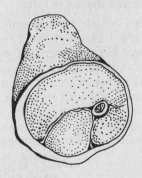

Japanese Pleasure

1½ lbs. lean pork, cut in
   cubes
2 onions, sliced in rings
1 green pepper, sliced
3 carrots, sliced thin
1 garlic clove
½ cup brown sugar
½ cup vinegar
½ cup ketchup
½ cup chili sauce
1 cup water
1 tsp. soya sauce
1 can beef consommé soup
salt to taste

Brown meat in pan, add other ingredients to pan. Simmer for 1 hour on low heat. Just before serving, dissolve 2 tbsp. cornstarch in water and add to mixture to thicken.

Louisbourg, N.S.
Ladies Auxiliary
Branch No. 62

Stuffed Peanut Pork Chops

2 cups soft bread crumbs
¼ cup chopped salted peanuts
2 tbsp. chopped onion
2 tbsp. melted butter or
   margarine
2 tsp. mustard sauce
1-10 oz. can cream of mushroom soup, undiluted
4-1-inch thick rib pork chops,
   slit for stuffing
1 tbsp. shortening or cooking
   oil

Combine the first 5 ingredients. Add 1 tbsp. soup and toss to moisten. Trim fat from chops. Stuff pocket in chops with dressing. Secure with toothpicks. Brown in shortening. Remove from skillet and place in 8-inch square baking dish. Spoon remaining soup over chops. Cover and bake at 350°F. for 30 minutes. Uncover and bake 30 minutes longer. Serves 4.

Melita, Man.
Ladies Auxiliary
Branch No. 127

Barbequed Ribs

10 lb. spareribs or beef short
   ribs
1-14 oz. bottle ketchup
1-12 oz. bottle chili sauce
1 cup chopped onion
1 clove garlic, mashed with
   1 tsp. salt
Juice of 1 lemon
½ cup wine vinegar
1 cup brown sugar
2 tbsp. Worcestershire sauce
1 tsp. dry mustard
few drops Tabasco sauce
1 cup water
1 lemon, sliced thin

Cut ribs into serving portions. Place on a rack in shallow roasting pan. Brown on both sides at 350°F. for about 30 to 45 minutes. Drain excess fat. Season to taste. To prepare sauce, combine ingredients, except sliced lemon, and simmer to 30 minutes. Pour sauce over ribs and bake about 1½ hours or until tender. Baste several times during cooking. Tuck lemon slices between the ribs for the last 15 minutes of baking time.

Hazelridge, Man.
Ladies Auxiliary
Branch No. 146

Barbequed Spareribs

Sauce:
   2 tbsp. butter
   1 onion, chopped
   3 tbsp. sugar
   2 tsp. mustard
   2 tsp. paprika
   ½ tsp. pepper
   1 cup ketchup
   2 tbsp. Worcestershire sauce
   ¼ cup vinegar

Cut ribs into serving size pieces. Bake at 325°F. for about 1 hour. Cook onions in butter until clear; add remaining ingredients and bring to a boil. Drain fat off spareribs and add sauce. Bake approx. 45 minutes longer. Use chicken pieces or chicken wings instead of spareribs, if desired.

Petitcodiac, N.B.
Ladies Auxiliary
Branch No. 41

Nick's Barbeque Spare Ribs

3-5 lbs. spare ribs, cut in
   2-inch pieces
2 cloves garlic, crushed
½ cup liquid honey, not buck
   wheat

Rub spare ribs with crushed garlic. Place in large flat pan and brush with honey. Bake at 375°F. for 10 minutes. Turn over once. Meanwhile make sauce. After 10 minutes are up, strain.

Sauce:

3 tbsp. margarine or bacon
   fat
2 onions chopped
1 bouillon cube dissolved in
1½ cups water
3 tbsp. soya sauce
1 tbsp. Worcestershire sauce
pinch dry mustard
2-3 tbsp. brown sugar to taste
8 tbsp. ketchup
½ tsp. salt
pepper to taste
thyme to taste
savory to taste
sage to taste
cayenne to taste

Combine ingredients and simmer uncovered for 30 minutes. Drain fat from meat in pan. Cover with sauce and bake at 300°F. for one hour. Serves 8.

Sydney, N.S.
Ladies Auxiliary
Branch No. 12

Pork Chop Supreme

4-6 pork chops
1 can mushroom soup
1 cup chopped celery
1 cup sliced carrots
½ cup chopped onion
½ cup water

Brown chops in frying pan. Pour off fat. Mix water with soup and pour over chops. Add vegetables. Cook slowly for one hour.

Elgin, Man.
Ladies Auxiliary
Branch No. 216

Barbeque Pork Chops

6 medium pork chops
1 egg, beaten
bread or cracker crumbs
shortening

Sauce:

1 No. 2 can tomatoes
   (approx. 1½ pt.)
¼ cup vinegar
½ cup brown sugar
¼ tsp. cloves
¼ tsp. allspice

Dip chops in egg, roll in crumbs. Sear light brown in hot fat. Cover with sauce which has been boiled 3 minutes. Cover pan, reduce heat and cook slowly for about 1 hour.

Mission, B.C.
Ladies Auxiliary
Branch No. 57

Country Fried Pork Chops

1 can cream of celery soup
4 pork chops
1 can sliced mushrooms,
   drained
½ cup water
½ tsp. thyme
6 whole small white onions
1 cup sliced carrots

Brown the chops and mushrooms, stir in soup, water and thyme. Add onions and carrots. Cover and cook over low heat for 45 minutes. May be done in casserole in oven. Serve with wide noodles, tossed green salad and hot biscuits.

Hodgson, Man.
Ladies Auxiliary
Branch No. 158

Mardi Gras Dinner

3 tbsp. flour
dash pepper
¾ tsp. salt
¼ cup melted margarine
1 tall can evaporated milk
1½ cups shredded Cheddar
   cheese
2 tbsp. grated Parmesan
   cheese
1⅓ cups Minute Rice
1 tbsp. chopped parsley
dash cayenne
½ tsp. oregano
1⅓ cups water
1-1 lb. can solid pack tomatoes, drained and sliced, or
   2 medium tomatoes, peeled
   and sliced thinly
½ medium onion, thinly
   sliced or chopped
1cup or 1-7 oz. can tuna,
   drained and flaked, or
   any leftover meat
paprika

Stir flour, pepper and ¼ tsp. salt into melted margarine in saucepan; mixing until smooth. Gradually add evaporated milk, stirring constantly over medium heat. Cook and stir until sauce is thickened, then add the cheese. Continue to cook until cheeses melt.

Place Minute Rice, parsley, cayenne, oregano, water and remaining salt in a 7½x11x1¾-inch baking dish. Stir to moisten all rice. Place ⅔ of the tomatoes on the rice. Top with onion and tuna. Spread on cheese sauce. Garnish with remaining tomato. Sprinkle with paprika. Bake at 375°F. for 15 minutes. Makes 6 servings.

Hazelridge, Man.
Ladies Auxiliary
Branch No. 146

Garlic Sausage

**5 lbs. lean pork cut into
   1-inch cubes
6 cloves garlic, crushed
2 tsp. salt
1 tsp. pepper
casings**

Mix well so as the seasoning is very well mixed. Stuff into washed and cleaned casings. Prick the casing with a needle to let out air, tie ends with thread. Let hang overnight before roasting uncovered in a flat plan which has been greased for about 1½ hours in oven.

Montreal, Que.
Ladies Auxiliary
Mazeppa Branch No. 183

Fried Pork

(Shanghai Style)

**4 slices shoulder pork, cut
   ½-¾-inch thick
½ leek
1 thin slice ginger root, peeled
1 tbsp. rice wine (dry white
   wine may be substituted)
4 tbsp. soya sauce
2 tbsp sugar, white or brown
3-4 tbsp. oil, peanut or
   vegetable
cornstarch as required**

Pound meat; first on one side, then on the other with blunt edge of cleaver; this is an ideal tool to use since it tenderizes the meat and also breaks up fibres so that the flavoring can easily penetrate.
Bring flat of cleaver down on leek in one sharp blow; repeat with peeled ginger. This will help release flavor.
Lay pork slices in shallow dish or pan. Place leek and ginger on top. Mix wine, soya sauce, sugar and sprinkle over meat. Let stand 20 to 30 minutes to allow meat to absorb all the flavors.
Heat 3-4 tbsp. oil in wok. Stir-fry the leek and ginger to flavor oil. Coat pork slices with cornstarch. Shake off excess cornstarch and fry pork, stretched

out as flat as possible in flavored oil. Try to do 2 at a time. Fry over high heat until browned on one side, turn and when both sides are browned, lower heat and cover wok. Cook until pork is tender and well browned. Do remaining slices same way.
When all pork is cooked, cut into strips ½-¾-inch wide and arrange on serving dish. The slices are cut with a very sharp cleaver. Cut straight down through the meat. Do not use sawing motion as it will break up meat. Serve with rice and steamed vegetables.

Pender Island, B.C.
Ladies Auxiliary
Branch No. 239

Ham-Potato Bake

**4 cups sliced cooked potatoes
2 medium carrots, shredded
   (1 cup)
1½ cups cubed fully cooked
   ham
1-10¾ oz. can condensed
   cream of mushroom soup
½ cup shredded sharp Ame-
   rican cheese (2 oz.)
¼ cup milk
1 tbsp. instant minced onion
1/8 tsp. pepper
¾ cup soft bread crumbs
   (1 slice)
½ cup shredded sharp Ame-
   rican cheese (2 oz.)
1 tbsp. butter or margarine,
   melted**

Layer half the potatoes and half the carrots in a 2 qt. casserole. Stir together cubed ham, condensed mushroom soup, the ½ cup shredded cheese, milk, minced onion and pepper. Pour half the ham mixture over potatoes and carrots in casserole. Repeat layers. Combine soft bread crumbs, the ½ cup shredded cheese, and melted butter; sprinkle over casserole. Bake, uncovered at 350°F. till heated

through, about 45 minutes. Garnish with parsley sprigs, if desired. Makes 4-6 servings.

Lunenburg, N.S.
Ladies Auxiliary
Branch No. 23

Riblets

**riblets
salt and pepper
1 cup ketchup
1 cup beef bouillon
1 tbsp. garlic powder
¼ cup brown sugar
¼ cup red wine vinegar
½ green pepper cut into
   1-inch pieces
1 carrot, thinly sliced**

Preheat oven to 325°F. In a large skillet over low heat, cook riblets until brown; drain excess fat as necessary. Place browned riblets in a large baking dish, sprinkle with salt and pepper. Combine remaining ingredients in a small saucepan and bring to a boil. Spoon over riblets. Cover and bake 1½ hours, then uncovered for 30 minutes.

New Perlican, Nfld.
Ladies Auxiliary
Branch No. 6

Seven Layer Dinner

Slice the following into a 9-inch casserole:
   **1-inch layer of raw potato,
      sliced thin
   layer of sliced onion
   layer of sliced carrots**
Sprinkle with:
   ¼ cup uncooked rice
Add:
   **1 can of peas and juice
   layer of small sausage**
Cover with:
   **1 can tomato soup, diluted
      with 1 can water**
Bake at 350°F. for 2 hours. Cover casserole for the first hour. Serves 6.

Roblin, Man.
Ladies Auxiliary
Branch No. 237

Spicy Short Ribs

2 tbsp. vegetable oil
2 onions, sliced
1 tbsp. Worcestershire sauce
¼ tsp. cayenne pepper
4 lb. beef short ribs
1 tbsp. dry mustard
¾ cup water
1 tsp. salt
1 tsp. curry powder

Brown short ribs in heavy Dutch oven; stir in onions. In small bowl mix other ingredients, pour over beef. Cook coverd at 350°F. until tender, approx. 2 hours. May also be cooked in Dutch oven on top of stove. Additional cooking time improves flavor. 4-6 servings.

Hopewell, N.S.
Ladies Auxiliary
Branch No. 137

Fast Barbeque Spareribs

4 lbs. spareribs
1 cup sliced onions
1 cup ketchup or tomato sauce
2 tbsp. Worcestershire sauce
¼ cup vinegar
¼ cup brown sugar
2 tsp. prepared mustard
1 tsp. paprika
2 tsp. salt

Brown the spareribs. Combine all other ingredients and pour over the browned spareribs. Bake covered for 1 hour at 375°F., then bake uncovered till sauce thickens.

Montreal, Que.
Ladies Auxiliary
Mazeppa Branch No. 183

Chicken & Turkey

Turkey Loaf

2 cups cooked turkey
2 cups soft bread crumbs
¼ cup celery, chopped very fine
3 egg yolks
⅓ cup sherry wine
2 tbsp. cream
1 tsp. salt
1 tbsp. minced onion

Cut turkey into very small pieces; add bread crumbs and celery. Beat egg yolks, add wine and cream to egg yolks. Add salt and onion and mix all together lightly. Pack into greased loaf pan and bake at 350°F. for 40 minutes. Serve with giblet gravy or mushroom sauce.

Cheticamp, N.S.
Ladies Auxiliary
Branch No. 32

Japanese Chicken Wings
(May be used as appetizers)

3 lbs. chicken wings
1 egg, beaten
1 cup flour
1 cup butter

Cut wings in half. Dip in slightly beaten egg; then flour. Fry in butter until deep brown and crisp. Put in shallow roasting pan and pour sauce over wings. Bake for 30 minutes. Spoon sauce over wings during cooking.

Sauce:
3 tbsp. soya sauce
3 tbsp. water
1 cup white sugar
½ cup vinegar
1 tsp. Accent
½ tsp. salt

Winnipeg, Man.
Ladies Auxiliary
Charleswood Branch No. 100

Skillet Chicken Dinner

1 chicken (2-3 lb.), cut in approx. 8 pieces
¼ cup flour
1 tsp. salt
2 tbsp. vegetable oil
1 cup ketchup
½ cup dry sherry or white wine
¼ cup water
2 tbsp. lemon juice
1 cup sliced onions
1 tbsp. Worcestershire sauce

½ tsp. Tabasco sauce
2 large potatoes, cut in chunks
¾ lb. medium mushrooms
1-10 oz. pkg. frozen peas

Combine flour and salt in small bowl. Dip chicken pieces in flour mixture. Heat oil in large skillet and brown chicken on both sides. Pour off excess fat. In small bowl, combine ketchup, wine, water, lemon juice, onion, Worcestershire and Tabasco sauces; mix well. Pour over chicken; bring to a boil. Reduce heat; cover and simmer 15 minutes. Add potatoes to skillet; baste with pan liquids. Cover and cook 30 minutes longer, basting often till chicken is tender. Add mushrooms and peas. Cook, covered, 5 minutes longer. (Carrots may be used in place of mushrooms.)

Elkhorn, Man.
Ladies Auxiliary
Branch No. 58

Curried Chicken

⅔ cup butter
1 cup honey
½ cup mustard
2 tsp. curry
2 chickens, cut up

Melt and combine first 4 ingredients. Place chicken, meat side down. Bake at 375°F. for 45 minutes. Turn chicken and bake 15 minutes longer.

Domain, Man.
Ladies Auxiliary
Branch No. 208

Scallopine with Orange Sauce

2 chicken breasts, whole
   (approx. 14 oz. each),
   boned, skinned and halved
1 tsp. salt
¼ tsp. pepper
flour
2 large navel oranges
1 tbsp. olive oil
1 tbsp. butter or margarine
1 small minced onion (¼ cup)
2 tsp. tomato paste
1 cup chicken broth
2 tbsp. minced parsley

1. Place chicken breasts between sheets of wax paper and pound firmly with a meat mallet or a rolling pin until they are ¼ inch thick or thinner. Sprinkle with salt and pepper; dip in flour and pat briskly to remove excess flour.
2. Grate rind of one orange; reserve. Cut off all remaining rind and pulp from both oranges. Cut in half, then lengthwise into slices.
3. Heat oil and sauté till golden brown; then remove from pan and keep warm.
4. Add onion to skillet and sauté. Stir in tomato paste, chicken broth and rind. Return scallopine to pan and simmer about 5 minutes.
5. When tender, remove to warm platter. Add orange slices to sauce and heat through. Spoon on scallopines and sprinkle with parsley.

Kelowna, B.C.
Ladies Auxiliary
Branch No. 26

Chinese Chicken Wings

2 lbs. chicken wings (I use more)

Cut off tips of chicken wings and boil these for soup. Cut the rest in half and flour them. Fry till brown in oil or butter. Place chicken in a flat baking dish. Arrange pineapple chunks over

chicken. Bring sauce to a boil and pour over chicken. Bake at 350°F. for approx. 30 minutes.
Sauce:
   ¾ cup honey
   ¼ cup pineapple juice
   ½ cup vinegar
   4 tbsp. ketchup
   1 tbsp. soya sauce
   1½ tsp. salt

Mission, B.C.
Ladies Auxiliary
Branch No. 57

Chicken Broccoli Casserole

fresh broccoli, cut into flowerettes
1 pkg. chicken (we use legs and thighs)
Sauce:
   1 cup Miracle Whip
   2 cans cream of chicken soup
   1½ tsp. curry
   1½ tsp. lemon juice

Place fresh broccoli in bottom of roaster. Lay chicken pieces over top. Spread sauce over top and bake at 350°F. for 45 minutes. (You can double this recipe but you probably wouldn't need to double the sauce.)

Crystal City, Man.
Ladies Auxiliary
Branch No. 35

Celebration Chicken

Lay chicken pieces on tin foil on a cookie sheet or shallow pan. Mix and pour over the following:
   1 envelope onion soup mix
   ½ cup ketchup
   ¼ cup brown sugar
   ¼ cup water

Cover with tin foil and seal edges. Bake at 375°F. for 1 hour or until done. Delicious.

Nipigon, Ont.
Ladies Auxiliary
Branch No. 32

Cocktail Chicken Wings

24 chicken wings
2 cloves garlic
½ tsp. ground ginger
½ cup Regina red cooking wine or very dry red wine
¼ cup soya sauce

Wash and disjoint wings into 3 sections. Discard tips. In a large pan, combine garlic, ginger, wine, soya sauce and chicken parts. Marinate 3-4 hours. Place on broiler pan. Broil till appear dry, 3-5 minutes. Take out and brush with melted butter or margarine. Return to oven for 5 minutes. Turn them over and repeat on other side. May be frozen.

Wetaskiwin, Alta.
Ladies Auxiliary
Branch No. 86

Chicken Pot Pie

2 chicken breasts
1 large can peas
1 large can mixed vegetables
½ cup chopped celery
2½ cups flour
½ cup shortening
2 tbsp. baking powder
½ tsp. salt
milk to moisten

Cube and cook chicken breasts. Make grave with stock. Place in saucepan with peas, mixed vegetables and celery. Cook until gravy thickens and bubbles. Place in large casserole and cover with biscuit dough. Season to taste. Make biscuit dough with last 5 ingredients; with just enough milk to moisten dough. Roll out to cover casserole. Bake, 10 minutes covered, at 400°F., uncover and bake 10 minutes longer.

Rouge River, Que.
Ladies Auxiliary
Branch No. 192

Kentucky Chicken

chicken
salt
flour
2-3 eggs
2-3 tbsp. milk
2 cups fine bread crumbs
½ cup barbeque seasoning

Cut up chicken and sprinkle with salt. Let stand for a couple of hours or overnight. Dip pieces into flour. Beat eggs with milk. Dip chicken pieces into this and roll in mixture of bread crumbs and barbeque seasoning. Deep fry till dark brown and bake at 325°F. till tender. If too dry, add ½ cup water while baking.

Steinbach, Man.
Ladies Auxiliary
Branch No. 190

Chicken and Noodles

1 chicken (3-4 lbs.), cut up
2 stalks celery, with leaves
1 medium onion, sliced
1½ tsp. salt
boiling water
noodles
¼ cup chicken fat, butter or margarine
2 tbsp. flour
1 can mushrooms
1 egg yolk, slightly beaten
3 tbsp. cream
1 tsp. butter or margarine

Place chicken, celery, onion and 1 tsp. salt in a saucepan. Add water to cover. Simmer until tender, about 1½ hours. Remove chicken and strain broth. Chill chicken and broth. Remove skin and bones from chicken. Leave meat in fairly large pieces. Skim fat from broth. Measure 2 tbsp. fat into a saucepan; blend in flour and remaining ½ tsp. salt. Add 1 cup broth. Cook over low heat, stirring until thickened. Brown mushrooms in remaining 2 tbsp. fat. Combine egg yolk and

cream and slowly stir into the sauce. Add chicken and mushrooms and heat to serving temperature. Meanwhile, cook noodles in remaining broth, add more water if necessary. Drain and pour chicken mixture over noodles. This recipe is also good for a maintenance ulcer diet. Yield: 4 to 5 servings.

Cranberry Portage, Man.
Ladies Auxiliary
Branch No. 137

Peachy Chicken

4 lbs. chicken, cut up
1 cup ketchup
½ cup chopped celery
½ cup chopped onion
1 tsp. Worcestershire sauce
1 cup chopped canned peaches
¼ cup peach juice
¼ cup brown sugar
½ cup white vinegar
1½ tsp. soya sauce

Dry chicken. Dip lightly in flour. Brown in oil; drain. Combine all ingredients. Pour over chicken and cover. Simmer 30 minutes. Serve with boiled rice.

New Glasgow, N.S.
Ladies Auxiliary
Normandy Branch No. 34

Chicken and Rice Hot Dish

1 frying chicken, cut in serving size pieces
1 cup uncooked rice, Not Minute Rice
1 can cream of mushroom soup
1 can cream of celery soup
2 cans water
1 envelope Lipton onion soup mix

Lay chicken in bottom of casserole and cover with rice. Add remaining ingredients except onion soup mix. Sprinkle onion soup mix on top. Bake at 350°F. for 2 hours. Season to taste.

Rainy River, Ont.
Ladies Auxiliary
Branch No. 54

Company Chicken

2 cups bread crumbs
¾ cup grated Parmesan cheese
2 or more cloves garlic, crushed
2 tbsp. salt
1/8 tsp. pepper
2 frying chickens, cut up
¼ lb. or more butter or margarine, melted
2 tbsp. butter

Mix crumbs, cheese, garlic, pepper and salt in bowl. Wash chicken and pat dry. Dip in melted butter and coat with mixture. Arrange in roasting pan, making sure that chicken pieces do not overlap each other. Dot with the 2 tbsp. butter. Bake at 350°F. for 1 hour. Do not turn.

Montreal, Que.
Ladies Auxiliary
Mazeppa Branch No. 183

Chicken or Turkey Casserole

2 cups diced cooked chicken or turkey
½ cup white sugar
2 tbsp. cornstarch
1 can pineapple chunks, drained
1 cup hot water
1 chicken bouillon cube
1 tsp. salt
2 tsp. vinegar
2 tsp. soya sauce
1 can mushrooms, drained

Mix pineapple juice, sugar, hot water and cornstarch in double boiler. Add mushrooms, pineapple chunks, salt, vinegar and soya sauce. Cook slightly, add meat. Pour into a casserole dish. Cover with Chow Mein noodles. Bake at 350°F. for 20 minutes.

New Glasglow, N.S.
Ladies Auxiliary
Normandy Branch No. 34

Sweet and Sour Delight

**1 pkg. onion mushroom soup
mix
¼ cup brown sugar (75 ml)
¼ cup vinegar (50 ml)
2 lbs. chicken pieces (1 kg)**

Preheat oven to 350°F.(180°C.) In small bowl, combine soup mix, brown sugar and vinegar; set aside. Place chicken pieces in shallow baking dish and pour sauce over and around. Cover and bake for 1 hour. Mix sauce with pan juices and spoon over chicken on serving platter.

Camrose, Alta.
Ladies Auxiliary
Branch No. 57

Chicken Wings

Sauce:
**½ cup soya sauce
½ cup pineapple juice
touch garlic powder
2 tbsp. brown sugar
½ tsp. ginger**

Prepare sauce and place chicken wings uncooked in sauce and let stand overnight. Bake in sauce at 350°F. for one hour. Turn every 20 minutes while cooking so they will brown evenly.

Joggins, N.S.
Ladies Auxiliary
Branch No. 4

Hawaiian Chicken

**1-8 oz. can crushed pineapple
½ cup ketchup
3 tbsp. brown sugar
3 tbsp. soya sauce
3 tbsp. cornstarch
½ tsp. salt**

Mix all ingredients together and cook 5 minutes. Place chicken in roaster or casserole, pour sauce over and cover. Bake at 350°F. for 1½ hours. Remove lid and bake another 15 minutes. Serve with rice.

Ste. Anne, Man.
Ladies Auxiliary
Branch No. 220

Delicious Chicken

**2 chickens, cut in eighths
1 envelope onion soup mix
1-8 oz. jar apricot jam
1-8 oz. bottle Russian dressing
pepper
garlic powder**

Season chicken with pepper and garlic and place in baking pan. Mix soup mix, jam and dressing together to make a sauce. Pour sauce over chicken and marinate overnight. Bake, uncovered, basting from time to time. Bake at 350°F. for 1-1½ hours.

Winnipeg, Man.
Ladies Auxiliary
General Monash Branch No. 115

Turkey-Chicken A-la-King

**3 cups chopped cooked turkey
or chicken
½ cup chopped green pepper
¼ cup chopped onion
½ cup chopped celery
2-10 oz. cans cream soup
(chicken, mushroom, etc.)
1 small can sliced mushrooms,
drained
1-10 oz. pkg. frozen peas
pimento (optional)**

Combine all ingredients in large pan. Stir to mix well. Cover and cook over medium heat for about 2 hours. Delicious served with toast and a salad.

Ear Falls, Ont.
Ladies Auxiliary
Branch No. 238

Chicken Livers

**1 lb. chicken livers
rinsed and drained well
on absorbent paper**
Sauce:
**2 tbsp. liquid honey
2 tbsp. soya sauce
2 tbsp. white wine
¼ cup Mazola oil
1 clove garlic, crushed**

Pour sauce over chicken livers;

bake at 375°F. for 30 minutes, turning livers once in sauce. Delicious served with fried rice.

Sydney, N.S.
Ladies Auxiliary
Branch No. 128

Chicken Marengo

**approx. 3 lbs. chicken pieces
3 tbsp. shortening or oil
1 can golden mushroom soup
1 can tomato soup
1 medium clove garlic,
minced
1 lb. small white onions,
whole**

Dredge chicken pieces lightly with flour and brown in shortening or oil. Pour off fat. Add remaining ingredients. Cover and simmer or bake in oven at 350°F. for 45 minutes or until chicken is fork tender. Stir occasionally. Uncover and cook until sauce is of desired consistency. A small amount of water may be added if needed. Makes 6 servings.

Melita, Man.
Ladies Auxiliary
Branch No. 127

Chicken Casserole

**1 can Chow Mein noodles
1 can cream of mushroom
soup
1 can mushrooms
1 onion, chopped
1 green pepper, chopped
1 cup celery pieces
2 cups cooked chicken
¼ cup water
salt and pepper**

Mix mushroom soup, mushrooms, onion, green pepper, celery, chicken, water, salt and pepper together. Place in casserole dish and sprinkle with Chow Mein noodles. Bake at 425°F. for approx. 30 minutes.

Yarmouth, N.S.
Ladies Auxiliary
Wedgeport Branch No. 155

Chicken Egg Foo Yong

Combine:
¾ cup finely chopped chicken or turkey
⅓ cup finely chopped celery
¼ cup finely chopped green pepper
¼ cup finely chopped mushrooms
¼ cup finely chopped water chestnuts
½ tsp. salt
dash pepper
Add mixture to:
6 eggs, well beaten
Mix well. Making six patties, pour mixture on well greased griddle. Shape with pancake turner by pushing egg back into patties. When set and brown on one side, turn to other side. Serve with brown sauce. Serves 3.

Brown Sauce:
1 tbsp. butter or margarine, melted
2 tsp. cornstarch
1 tsp. sugar
½ cup water
1½ tbsp. soya sauce

Combine cornstarch and sugar; blend into melted butter. Add water and soya sauce. Cook, stirring constantly, till mixture thickens and is bubbly.

Stewiacke, N.S.
Ladies Auxiliary
Branch No. 70

Honey Curried Chicken

1 chicken, cut up for frying
⅓ cup honey
⅓ cup butter
¼ cup prepared mustard
4 tsp. curry powder

Melt honey and butter together, mix in mustard and curry (mustard and curry can be adjusted to suit taste). Place chicken pieces in casserole, meaty side down. Pour sauce over meat and bake at 375°F. for 30 to 40 minutes. Baste often for last 15 to 20 minutes until sauce has thickened.

Edmonton, Alta.
Ladies Auxiliary
Jasper Place Branch No. 255

Cantonese Chicken

3 lbs. chicken parts
¼ cup vinegar
1 can tomato soup
¼ cup brown sugar
1 tbsp. cooking oil
1 tsp. curry
1 tsp. celery seed
1 tbsp. soya sauce

Mix soya sauce and oil. Spread over chicken. Sprinkle with brown sugar, celery seed and curry. Broil 10 minutes. Mix vinegar and soup; pour over chicken. Bake at 350°F. for 1½ hours. Serve with rice.

Wetaskiwin, Alta.
Ladies Auxiliary
Branch No. 86

Oven Barbequed Chicken Burgers

chicken breasts or thighs
1 tbsp. prepared mustard
lemon juice, to make paste

Buy deboned chicken breasts or debone them yourself. Salt both sides of chicken and arrange in baking dish. Remove skin from chicken; set aside. In a small bowl combine the mustard and lemon juice. Brush half this mixture on top of chicken. Bake 20 minutes in oven preheated to 400°F. When golden brown, turn and brush the other side with the remaining sauce. Bake for about one hour.

Reserve Mines, N.S.
Ladies Auxiliary
Branch No. 2

Chicken Fried Rice

2 cups uncooked rice (not instant)
3½ cups water
½ cup soya sauce
½ cup oil
1 envelope onion soup mix, not mixed
1 onion chopped
1 can mushroom pieces
1 green pepper, chopped
1 celery, chopped
3 cups cooked chicken

Mix all ingredients together. Cook, covered, in casserole at 350°F. for 1½ hours.

Montreal, Que.
Ladies Auxiliary
Flanders Branch No. 63

Chicken Fried Rice

(This is a good dish for leftovers.)

2 tbsp. vegetable oil
2 small onions
1 egg
2 sticks celery
1 can mushrooms or about 6-8 small fresh mushrooms
1 green pepper
(use any or all of these vegetables)
chicken, ham, fish or beef can be used
2 cups or more of boiled rice
soya sauce to taste

Heat oil in a large frying pan. Break egg into pan, do not scramble. Put in chopped onions and celery if it is used. Then add the chopped mushrooms and green pepper. After these are heated through, add the leftover meat. Cook all together. Add rice, which should be quite dry. Add soya sauce to taste and serve hot with soya sauce, sweet and sour sauce or plum sauce.

Milltown, N.B.
Ladies Auxiliary
Branch No. 48

Turkey A-la-King

3 tbsp. Crisco oil
3 tbsp. flour
½ cup turkey stock
1½ cups Pacific milk
2 cups diced cooked turkey
1 cup canned mushrooms
2 tbsp. pimento or green
     pepper
salt and pepper
2 egg yolks

Heat oil, blend in flour and add liquid. Cook, stirring constantly until mixture thickens. Add turkey, mushrooms, chopped pimento and seasonings. Pour some of the mixture over beaten egg yolks. Add to remaining mixture and cook 2 minutes. Serve on toast or hot biscuits.

Emerson, Man.
Ladies Auxiliary
Branch No. 77

Lemon Chicken

chicken breasts from one
     chicken, cut in strips
     against grain, flatten thin
Batter:
     ½ cup flour
     ¼ tsp. salt
     1 egg, separated
     1½ tbsp. oil
     dash cayenne pepper
     ½ cup water

Blend salt, egg yolk, oil, cayenne pepper, flour and water together. Beat egg white and fold into batter.
Heat oil in pan, deep fryer or wok. Dip chicken in batter, then fry until golden in oil. When completed, pour on Lemon Sauce.

Lemon Sauce:
     4 tbsp. cornstarch
     1 cup cold water
     6 tbsp. lemon juice
     1 tbsp. lemon extract
     1½ tbsp. sugar

Mix and heat until thick; add a few slices of lemon and simmer 10 minutes.

Hazelridge, Man.
Ladies Auxiliary
Branch No. 146

Chicken Oriental

(To use up
cooked chicken)

chicken breasts, cut up
1-14 oz. can pineapple chunks
1-10 oz. can mushrooms
2 tbsp. brown sugar
2 tbsp. vinegar
1 tbsp. soya sauce
2 green peppers
2 onions
2 tbsp. cornstarch

Drain pineapple and mushrooms; reserving juice. Combine liquids and add enough water to make 2 cups. Pour over chicken and bring to a boil. Simmer; then stir in brown sugar, vinegar and soya sauce. Cut peppers and onions into rings and add. Simmer until tender. Mix cornstarch with water and cook until thick.

Grandview, Man.
Ladies Auxiliary
Branch No. 14

Barbequed Chicken Casserole

1 frying chicken
½ cup flour
2 tsp. salt
1 tsp. paprika
¼ cup salad oil
½ cup chopped celery
1 onion
1 cup ketchup
2 tbsp. Worcestershire sauce
1 tbsp. brown sugar
pepper
1 cup water

Dip chicken in flour, salt and paprika. Fry until brown and place in casserole. Pour off all oil, but 1 tbsp.; add onion and sauté until brown, add celery, ketchup, Worcestershire sauce, sugar, pepper and water. Thicken with cornstarch if necessary. Pour over chicken and bake until tender at 350°F.

Wawanesa, Man.
Ladies Auxiliary
Branch No. 28

Chicken Wings

chicken wings
barbeque sauce
2 cloves garlic

Marinate chicken wings in barbeque sauce and garlic overnight. Bake on cookie sheet at 325°-350°F., turning every 10-15 minutes until golden brown, approx. 1 hour.

Fort Frances, Ont.
Ladies Auxiliary
Branch No. 29

Soya Ginger Chicken

Broiled or barbequed, this recipe will become a favorite.

⅓ cup soya sauce
2 tbsp. oil
½ tsp. ginger
¼ tsp. pepper or to taste
1 broiler-fryer chicken, cut up
     (approx. 3 lbs.)

Blend soya sauce, oil, ginger and pepper in a large shallow dish or heavy plastic bag. Place chicken in marinade, turning to coat. (If using bag, press out air and seal tightly.) Let stand at least 3 hours or refrigerate overnight. Remove chicken, reserve marinade. Place chicken, skin side down on a greased broiler pan rack. Broil at 400°F. about 6 inches from heat source, basting twice with reserved marinade for 20 minutes, then turn. Broil 15 minutes longer or until tender.
Over Charcoal:
Starting skin side up, grill chicken about 5 inches from white hot coal, turning and basting often with marinade for 50 minutes or until chicken is fork tender and juice runs clear when meat is pricked. Makes 4 servings. 363 calories per serving. (44 g protein, 2 g carbohydrates, 18 g fat, 196 mg cholesterol, 1,7 g iron, 52 mg sodium).

Montreal, Que.
Ladies Auxiliary
Mazeppa Branch No. 183

Chicken Gai Kue

2 or 3 chicken breasts, skinned and deboned
1 clove garlic, minced (optional)
1 slice peeled fresh ginger, minced, or ¼ tsp. ground ginger
1 tbsp. dry sherry (15 ml)
1 tbsp. light soya sauce (15 ml)
1 cup pancake mix (250 ml)
1 cup water (250 ml)
1 tsp. vinegar (5 ml)
3 cups vegetable oil (750 ml)

Flatten meat out and cut into 1-inch cubes. Combine chicken, pieces, garlic and ginger. Add sherry and soya sauce, mix well and let marinate. Mix together pancake mix, water and vinegar. Heat oil to 375°F. for deep frying. Dip each piece of chicken in batter and deep fry till golden brown, approx. 5 minutes, for a batch. Serve with Sweet and Sour Sauce.

Sweet and Sour Sauce:
1 tbsp. cornstarch (15 ml)
½ cup brown sugar (125 ml)
⅓ cup vinegar (75 ml)
⅔ cup water (150 ml)
⅓ cup ketchup (75 ml)
4 tbsp. sesame seeds (60 ml) (optional)

Blend cornstarch and sugar in a saucepan. Stir in vinegar and water. Cook, stirring constantly, until thick and clear. Add ketchup, stirring until well blended. Pour sauce over chicken pieces and sprinkle with sesame seed.

Holland, Man.
Ladies Auxiliary
Victoria Branch No. 121

Easy Chicken Casserole

1 chicken, cut up
1 cup uncooked rice
1 can mushroom soup
1½ cups water
1 envelope onion soup mix

Sprinkle rice in bottom of casserole. Combine mushroom soup and water and pour over rice. Place chicken pieces on top of mixture and sprinkle onion soup mix over. Add salt and pepper to taste. Cover and bake at 350°F. for 2 hours.

Carberry, Man.
Ladies Auxiliary
Branch No. 153

Tater Dip Chicken

1 average size frying chicken, cut into serving size pieces (I use just breasts or wings, or drumsticks)
1 egg
2 tbsp. water
¼ tsp. sage or 1½ tsp. poultry seasoning
¾ tsp. salt
dash pepper
1 cup instant mashed potato flakes
¼ cup butter or margarine

Beat egg slightly; beat in water, salt, pepper and sage. Dip chicken in egg mixture, then coat each with potato flakes. Put butter in large shallow baking dish and melt in oven. Place coated chicken in melted butter in one layer. Bake at 400°F. for 30 minutes, turn pieces over and bake 30 minutes longer, uncovered throughout baking time.

Elkhorn, Man.
Ladies Auxiliary
Branch No. 58

Spanish Chicken
(Fowl)

chicken, cut up
2 cups celery, chopped fine
½ green pepper, chopped fine
2 large onions, chopped fine
1 can tomato soup
1 can water or a little more
salt and pepper to taste
2 cloves garlic

Cut up chicken and fry in fat till nice and brown. Place in bottom of baking dish or roaster. Add remaining ingredients. Bake at 350°F., covered, for 45 minutes, then remove cover and continue baking until tender, basting occasionally.

St. Peters, N.S.
Ladies Auxiliary
Branch No. 47

Fish

How to cook live lobsters

Do not cook lobsters which have ceased moving. Fill a deep container with enough salted water to completely cover the lobster (¼ cup salt for each gallon of water). Bring water to a boil. Grasp each lobster behind the head and plunge it head first into boiling water. Cover container. Start timing when water returns to boil. Reduce heat a little. Simmer 12 to 15 minutes for 1 lb. lobster and add 1 minute longer for each additional ¼ lb. Do not over cook. Serve at once or cool quickly under cold running water.

How to broil live lobsters

Turn live lobster shell side down, split lengthwise and remove intestinal vein and stomach, scoop out greenish tomally and discard the black coral roe. Place open lobster, flesh side up, on a broiler pan. Brush meat with melted butter. Sprinkle with salt, pepper and paprika or buttered bread crumbs. Broil 4 inches from heat for 12 to 15 minutes or until lightly browned. Serve with melted butter and lemon wedges.

Kensington, P.E.I.
Ladies Auxiliary
Branch No. 9

Canned Fish
(Jack, White or Pickerel)

4 tbsp. Aylmer tomato soup
2 tbsp. vegetable oil
2 tbsp. vinegar
1 tsp. salt

Place ingredients in bottom of jar. Cut fillets into 2½-3-inch pieces. Pack into sterilized jars to 1 inch from top. Seal and process at 10 lbs. pressure or for 3 hours in a canner. Halve the ingredients for pint jars, and process 1 hour at 10 lbs. pressure. Do not use a creamed tomato soup.

Cranberry Portage, Man.
Ladies Auxiliary
Branch No. 137

Curried Clams

4 medium onions
2 lbs. hamburger
¾ oz. curry powder
3 cans clams
3 cans mushroom soup
cooked rice

Sauté onions. Add hamburger and cook. Add curry powder and simmer. Add clams, including juice; simmer. Add mushroom soup. Serve on a bed of rice. Salmon may be substituted for clams.

Whycocomagh, N.S.
Ladies Auxiliary
Branch No. 123

Haddock Au Gratin

¼ cup fine dry bread crumbs
¼ cup grated Cheddar cheese
1 lb. haddock fillets
¼ cup mayonnaise

Brush all sides of fillets with mayonnaise and coat with crumbs and cheese. Arrange in single layer in a shallow baking dish. Bake at 375°F. for 20-25 minutes or until golden and fish flakes easily when tested with a fork. 4 servings.

Tantallon, N.S.
Ladies Auxiliary
St. Margaret's Bay Branch No. 116

Walleye Done in Oven

4 walleye fillets
1 green pepper, sliced
salt and pepper to taste
1 onion, sliced
1 can tomatoes

Cut onion in slices and separate rings. Line bottom of cake pan with onion rings and sliced green pepper. Lay fish on top. Pour on tomatoes; add salt and pepper. Bake at 325°F. for 45 minutes, till fish is tender.

Ear Falls, Ont.
Ladies Auxiliary
Branch No. 238

Halibut Steaks with Chinese Sauce

1½ lbs. halibut steaks (cut approx. 1-inch thick)
2 tbsp. dry sherry
2 tbsp. lemon juice
2 tbsp. soya sauce
2 tbsp. salad oil
1 tsp. salt
½ tsp. pepper
½ tsp. ground ginger
4 green onions, cut into pieces

Fill steamer pot with water up to 1½ inches below steamer rack. Bring to rapid boil. Meanwhile wipe fresh halibut with damp cloth. If frozen, do not thaw. Place fish on large piece of double thickness heavy-duty foil. Turn edges of foil up all around fish to contain liquids to be added later. Lay fish on steamer rack over rapidly boiling water. Combine remaining ingredients; pour over fish. Cover tightly. Steam fresh fish 15 minutes; frozen fish, 25 minutes, or until fish flakes easily when fork-tested. Baste fish occasionally with sauce during cooking. Makes 4 servings.

Port Hardy, B.C.
Ladies Auxiliary
Branch No. 237

Crab Au Gratin

Equally good as a first course or an entrée, this gratin takes little time to prepare and is sure to please lovers of seafood.

2 tbsp. butter
2 tbsp. chopped scallion or green onion
1 well-packed cup crab meat, with cartilage removed
salt and pepper
¼ tsp. dried tarragon
⅓ cup dry vermouth
1 tbsp. all-purpose flour
¾ cup 35% cream
½ tsp. tomato paste
lemon juice
¼ cup grated Swiss cheese
1 tbsp. melted butter

Melt butter in a large heavy skillet, add scallion and toss over medium heat for just a minute or so. Add crab, season with salt, pepper and tarragon, sauté briefly, then add vermouth. Increase temperature to high and boil until liquid is almost completely evaporated. Remove pan from heat and set aside.

Mix flour with some of the cream. When smooth, mix in remaining cream, then tomato paste. Mix into crab, place over medium heat and stir several minutes. Season with lemon juice and more salt, pepper and tarragon.

When heated through, place in a shallow, buttered ovenproof casserole and top with cheese and melted butter. Place in a 400°F. oven and bake 15 minutes, or until lightly browned. Serve with a salad and crusty bread or rice. Serves 4.

Port Hardy, B.C.
Ladies Auxiliary
Branch No. 237

Fish Casserole

2 lbs. cod fillets
2 cups bread stuffing
1 can cream of mushroom
   soup
1 cup grated cheese
salt and pepper

Grease 2 qt. casserole with butter. Layer bottom of dish with fish, salt and pepper. Add layer of stuffing and another layer of fish. Add a second layer of stuffing. Pour can of undiluted mushroom soup on top of stuffing. Cover with grated cheese. Bake at 350°F. for 45 minutes or until fish is done. Serve with green vegetables and mashed potatoes.

Wabush, Labrador, Nfld.
Ladies Auxiliary
Grant Crerar Branch No. 57

Fish Chowder

1 lb. fresh haddock fillets
1 medium onion, diced or
   grated
1 tsp. salt
2 cups rich milk
2 cups potatoes, diced
1½ cups boiling water
pinch pepper
1½ tsp. butter

Cook potatoes and onions in water with salt; simmer about 15 minutes; then add fillets cut into bite size pieces. Simmer gently until fish flakes, approx. 10 minutes longer, then add milk and pepper. Reheat until hot, but do not boil. To give more flavor to chowder add a large piece of Dulse when fillets are put in pot. This can be removed before serving if you desire. Add butter before serving. (Dulse can be optional).

Jacquet River, N.B.
Ladies Auxiliary
Durham Branch No. 77

Oysters In a Sea Bed

½ lb. fresh spinach, washed
   and dried
½ envelope onion soup mix
   (mix contents before mea-
   suring)
5 oz. sour cream
1 tsp. flour

Cut spinach into bite size pieces and set aside. Combine remaining ingredients in a large bowl. Add the chopped spinach. Mix and fold until it is very well mixed and packed. Place drained fresh oysters in a buttered casserole, or if you want to be fancy, in the deep side of an oyster shell. Cover with seasoned spinach. Bake at 375°F. for 15 to 20 minutes. Serves 4 to 5 people.

Pender Island, B.C.
Ladies Auxiliary
Branch No. 239

Hot Creamy Tuna Burgers

2 cans tuna
½ cup hamburger relish
1 can cream of chicken soup
1 can cream of mushroom
   soup
2 tbsp. green pepper,
   chopped fine
2 tbsp. onion, chopped fine
dash Tabasco sauce
pepper
18 hamburger buns

Combine all ingredients, season lightly to taste, and spread between buttered buns. Wrap each in foil. Bake at 400°F. for 12 minutes. These make good freezer type sandwiches. Wrap well in foil and freeze until needed. Remove frozen buns and bake at 400°F. for 30 minutes right in the foil. Of course, if you have a microwave, wrap in saran wrap and freeze.

Fort Macleod, Alta.
Ladies Auxiliary
Branch No. 46

Sweet and Sour Pickerel

1 lb. pickerel fillets or cheeks
flour
salt and pepper
1 cup water
¼ cup brown sugar
4 tbsp. vinegar
1 tbsp. soya sauce
1 tbsp. cornstarch
2 tbsp. water

Mix flour with salt and pepper to coat fish. Dredge fish pieces in flour. Brown in hot fat. Add water, brown sugar, vinegar and soya sauce. Season to taste. Add cornstarch and water paste. Simmer till clear.

Steinbach, Man.
Ladies Auxiliary
Branch No. 190

Baked Haddock and Grapefruit

1½ lb. haddock fillets
1 tsp. salt
1/8 tsp. pepper
2 tbsp. grapefruit juice
¾ cup ½-inch soft bread
   cubes
3 tbsp. butter, melted
¼ tsp. leaf thyme
1 grapefruit, sectioned
melted butter

Preheat oven to 400°F. Butter a shallow baking pan, about 12x7x2 inches. Cut fish into serving-size pieces. Sprinkle both sides with salt and pepper, lay in prepared pan in a single layer. Sprinkle with grapefruit juice. Mix bread cubes, butter and thyme and sprinkle over fish. Bake 15 minutes. Lay sections of grapefruit on top of fish. Brush lightly with butter and continue baking 10 minutes longer or until fish flakes easily with a fork. Serve immediately. Serves 4.

Nfld. Provincial Command
Ladies Auxiliary

Clam Casserole

2 cans minced clams
2 eggs, beaten
30 salted saltines
1 can cream of mushroom
  soup
⅔ cup milk
¼ cup melted butter
½ cup lemon juice

Drain clams, but not completely dry, add lemon juice, 1 tsp. Worcestershire sauce and a dash Tabasco sauce. Combine all ingredients, pour into greased casserole. Sprinkle with slivered almonds. Bake at 350°F. for one hour.

Grand Manan, N.B.
Ladies Auxiliary
Branch No. 44

Shrimp Quiche

1-8 oz. pkg. frozen butter
  flake rolls
4 oz. cooked or canned
  shrimp, diced
1 egg
½ cup heavy cream
2 tbsp. minced green onion
½ tsp. salt
¼ tsp. dill
1/8 tsp. cayenne pepper
½ cup shredded Swiss cheese

Separate rolls into 20 pieces, press into sides and bottom of 20 greased muffin pans, divide shrimp evenly in shells, beat remaining ingredients together until well blended. Pour about 2 teaspoons in shells, sprinkle cheese on top. Bake at 350°F. for 20 minutes, or until center appears set. Serve either warm or cold.

Winnipeg, Man.
Ladies Auxiliary
Henderson Highway Branch No. 215

Shake and Bake
(For Fish)

4 cups bread crumbs
1 tbsp. paprika
1 tbsp. salt
½ cup vegetable oil
1 tbsp. celery salt
1 tsp. pepper

Place bread crumbs in blender and make fine. Mix all ingredients together. Coat pieces of fish and fry or microwave.

Pine Falls, Man.
Ladies Auxiliary
Branch No. 64

Curried Shrimp on Steamed Rice

2 lbs. shrimp, fresh or frozen
3 tbsp. butter or margarine
2 small onions, chopped
1 clove garlic, minced
1 tsp. curry powder
½ tsp. salt
1 cup (8 oz.) tomato sauce
1 cup chicken broth
½ cup sliced, blanched
  almonds
3 tbsp. lemon juice
½ cup light cream

Clean shrimp. Cook fresh shrimp in a saucepan in enough boiling water to cover for 5 minutes. Drain. Melt 2 tbsp. of butter in a saucepan, add onion, and garlic. Cook over medium heat for about 3 minutes. Sprinkle curry powder and salt into onion mixture. Blend well. Add tomato sauce, chicken broth (canned, or made with 1 chicken bouillon cube and 1 cup boiling water). Simmer for 30 minutes, stirring occasionally. Meanwhile, melt remaining 1 tbsp. butter in a skillet, add almonds, heat stirring often, until toasty brown. Stir in lemon juice, cream and shrimp into sauce and heat thoroughly. Serve over fluffy steamed rice. Sprinkle with toasted almonds. 3 servings.

Montreal, Que.
Ladies Auxiliary
Mazeppa Branch No. 183

Lobster Casserole

1 cup cream of mushroom
  soup
1 cup cream of celery soup
¼ cup green pepper, chopped
2 tbsp. pimento, chopped
2 cups lobster or 1 can lobster
  or 1 can shrimp or 2 cups
  lobster with ½ cup cheese
  that will melt

Combine above ingredients and add 1 cup noodles, cooked previously for 10-15 minutes. Sprinkle with paprika and bake for 30 minutes at 375°F. Serves 6. If too thin, add more noodles.

Parrsboro, N.S.
Ladies Auxiliary
Branch No. 45

Old-Style Nova Scotia Lobsters

1 lb. lobster or more
½ square butter
½ cup boiling water
1-2 tsp. vinegar
salt and pepper
1 cup cream

Cut lobster meat in pieces and place in frying pan with butter, turning pieces until each is a good red color. Add boiling water, vinegar, salt and pepper; simmer for a few minutes. Add the cream and serve at once in puff pastry shells. Good for Sunday breakfast, luncheon or party dish. Scrumptious.

Antigonish, N.S.
Ladies Auxiliary
Arras Branch No. 59

Salmon Wellington

2 lbs. salmon fillets (divide off about ¼)
⅓ cup cream
salt and pepper
2 tsp. lemon juice

Mince divided off ¼ and blend in salt and pepper. Slice rest of salmon into very thin slices.

½ cup minced onion
1 tbsp. butter

Sauté onion in butter and set aside. Combine:

1 tbsp. flour
1 tbsp. butter

Sauté:

½ cup or 1 can sliced mushrooms
1 tbsp. butter

Add:

½ cup cream

Cook over medium heat until reduced to half. Add flour mixture and simmer 5 minutes. Add lemon juice, salt and pepper. Remove from heat and set aside.

2-7 oz. pkg. puff pastry
5 hard boiled eggs, halved lengthwise
1 beaten egg

Roll out pastry to 12x6 inches. Place on greased cookie sheet. Along centre put half the salmon slices, then the sautéd onions, then ½ mushroom mixture, followed by the rest of the salmon slices, two rows of eggs, remaining mushroom mixture, then the minced salmon. Cover with second layer of pastry. Seal edges of pastry with beaten egg. Seal well. Brush top with rest of egg, slash a few holes in top. Bake at 400°F. for 25 minutes. Serves 8 to 10.

Bowser, B.C.
Ladies Auxiliary
Branch No. 211

Salmon Pinwheels

1-7¾ oz. can salmon
¾ cup grated cheese
2 tbsp. chopped green onion
3 tbsp. chopped stuffed olives
½ tsp. dill weed
1/8 tsp. pepper
2 tsp. lemon juice
¼ cup mayonnaise
1-8 oz. pkg. refrigerated crescent rolls

Drain salmon, reserving juice for sauce. Flake salmon with a fork and combine with remaining ingredients. Pinch sections of rolls together to make one rectangle. Spread with salmon filling and roll up from long side. Cut into 12 pinwheels. Place cut side down on buttered pan or baking dish. Bake at 375°F. for 20 to 25 minutes, until golden brown. Serve with Parsley Sauce.

Parsley Sauce:
2 tbsp. butter
1 tbsp. flour
½ tsp. salt
1/8 tsp. pepper
¼ tsp. dry mustard
reserved salmon juice
1½ cups milk
2 egg yolks, beaten
2 tbsp. chopped fresh parsley

Melt butter; blend in flour and seasonings. Add salmon juice and milk. Cook, stirring constantly until thickened and smooth. Add a small amount of sauce to beaten egg yolks, then add yolk mixture to remaining sauce. Cook and stir till thickened, add parsley and serve over rolls.

I sometime use a rich biscuit dough instead of refrigerated rolls - its cheaper.

Port Hardy, B.C.
Ladies Auxiliary
Branch No. 237

Salmon Oysters

1 pt. canned salmon or fresh cooked (should be sockeye or similar)
2 eggs
1 tbsp. finely minced onion
½ cup flour (may use ½ flour and ½ crushed crackers)
1 tsp. baking powder
salt and pepper to taste

Drain juice from salmon and retain. Mince salmon, removing dark skin, add well beaten eggs and retained salmon juice, flour, salt, pepper and baking powder. Mix well and drop by spoonful (or chill and shape into oblong oyster shapes) into hot fat. Turn to brown both sides.

Deliciously different! Try them served with french fries, cole slaw and Tartar sauce. They are also delicious as appetizers.

Qualicum Beach, B.C.
Ladies Auxiliary
Branch No. 76

Fish Casserole

1 can celery soup
½ cup milk
salt and pepper
Worcestershire sauce
½ pkg. noodles
1 can tuna or salmon
½ cup margarine, melted
grated cheese

Use cooked sea shell noodles. In large bowl mix celery soup and milk. Add salt, pepper, Worcestershire sauce. Add noodles and tuna to mixture. Butter casserole dish. Add mixture and top with fine bread crumbs. Melt ¼ cup margarine and drizzle over bread crumbs. Sprinkle with grated sharp cheese. Bake uncovered at 350°F. for one hour. Any type of flaked fish may be used.

Whycocomagh, N.S.
Ladies Auxiliary
Branch No. 123

Oriental Fish Fillets

2 lbs. fish fillets
1 cup orange juice
2 tbsp. ketchup
1 tbsp. chopped parsley
dash garlic salt
1/2 tsp. pepper
1/2 tsp. dried oregano
2 tbsp. soya sauce
2 tbsp. melted butter
1 tbsp. lemon juice

Place fillets in shallow baking pan. Combine remaining ingredients and pour over fish. Bake at 450°F. for 15 minutes. Serves 4-6.

Nfld. Provincial Command
Ladies Auxiliary

Nova Scotia's Crab Delight

2 cups cooked rice
2 cans cheddar cheese soup
dash salt
1 can asparagus pieces
2-5 oz. cans crabmeat
2 tbsp. butter
bread crumbs or crackers

Heat soup. Add crabmeat and mix well. Place rice, asparagus and crab mixture in casserole, in that order. Top with bread crumbs and melted butter. Bake at 375°F. for 30 minutes or until bubbly hot.

Halifax, N.S.
Ladies Auxiliary
Scotia Branch No. 25

Seafood Casserole

1/2 cup chopped celery
1/4 cup chopped onion
2 tbsp. chopped green pepper
2 tbsp. butter or margarine
1 can cheddar cheese soup
1/4 cup water
2 cups cooked fish or seafood
1 tsp. lemon juice
2 tbsp. buttered bread crumbs

Cook celery, onion and pepper in butter until tender. Add re-maining ingredients. Pour into a 1 qt. casserole. Bake at 350°F. for 25 minutes. Stir. Top with buttered bread crumbs and bake 5 minutes longer.

Sioux Lookout, Ont.
Ladies Auxiliary
Branch No. 78

Baked Digby Scallops

bread crumbs
scallops
salt and pepper
parsley
margarine
wine and cheese (optional)

Breads crumbs:
In a saucepan, add 3-4 tbsp. margarine, break up 3-4 slices of bread. Stir over medium heat till bread is covered with margarine. Put some crumbs on top of each serving.
Rinse scallops, cut big ones if desired. Place 5-7 in individual scallop shells, and 1 tbsp. or more of margarine, salt and pepper to taste. Place some bread crumbs on top and sprinkle with parsley flakes. Bake at 450°F. for 30 minutes or longer if scallops are frozen. May also be cooked under broiler till crumbs are lightly browned.

Digby, N.S.
Ladies Auxiliary
Branch No. 20

Fish Batter

1 cup flour
1 cup beer
1 egg
1 tbsp. oil
1 tsp. baking soda
1 tsp. salt
1 tbsp. sugar

Mix dry ingredients. Add beer; beating well, then egg and oil. Dip fish pieces in flour first, then into batter. Deep fry. (Do not use Labatt's beer.)

Cranberry Portage, Man.
Ladies Auxiliary
Branch No. 137

Cook's Choice Seafood Deluxe

1/2 cup chopped celery
2 cups thick white sauce
1/2 cup cubed cheddar cheese
1/2 cup sliced mushrooms,
   well drained
1 tbsp. onion flakes or
   3 green onions, chopped
2 tsp. parsley
1/2 tsp. dry mustard
dash black pepper
3 hard boiled eggs, sliced
12-16 oz. frozen fish fillets,
   cut up in 1/2-inch pieces,
   thawed and pressed dry
   with paper towel
1/2 cup cracker crumbs
2 tbsp. melted butter
2 tbsp. grated Parmesan
   cheese
   (May use instead of fish, or
   in combination 6-12 oz.
   small shrimp or crabmeat,
   thawed and pressed dry.)

Cook celery until tender in butter to be used for white sauce. Remove and prepare white sauce, add cheddar cheese, stir until melted. Fold in celery, mushrooms, onion flakes, parsley, mustard, pepper, eggs and fish. Pour into 1 qt. casserole dish or individual shell bakers. Combine butter, crumbs, and Parmesan cheese. Spread evenly over fish mixture. Bake at 350°F. for 30 minutes. Makes 4 servings.

Hodgson, Man.
Ladies Auxiliary
Branch No. 158

Fisherman's Luck

1 lb. halibut fillet
1 lb. scallops
1 large can lobster or crab meat
1⅓ cups cooked rice
½ cup flour
2 cans oysters
1 qt. milk
1 can mushroom soup
6 tbsp. butter

Cook halibut and scallops in milk, slowly, for 8 minutes. Drain and reserve milk for sauce. Blend flour and butter, add milk; gradually add soup and juice from lobsters and oysters. Stir constantly over medium heat until thickened. Butter large casserole and layer sauce, then rice, then fish. Sprinkle with buttered crumbs on top. Bake at 350°F. for one hour.

Lower Sackville, N.S.
Ladies Auxiliary
Calais Branch No. 162

Fish Cakes

1 lb. salt codfish (fresh fish may be used with the addition of 1 tsp. salt to cooking water)
2 cups sliced potatoes
2 tbsp. butter
2 eggs, slightly beaten
¼ cup milk
¼ tsp. pepper
dash nutmeg (optional)
1 stalk celery, finely diced
1 small onion, finely diced

Soak or scald codfish; drain and shred. Add potatoes and cover with boiling water. Cook until very tender. Drain and mash. Add butter, eggs, celery, onion, milk, pepper and nutmeg. Beat until light and fluffy. Chill. Shape into balls and flatten. Fry until brown on either side. Frying temperature (375° to 385°F.)

Chezzetcook, N.S.
Ladies Auxiliary
Branch No. 161

Poached Salmon Steaks

1 tbsp. lemon juice or white vinegar
1 tsp. salt
2 onion slices
parsley
4 cups water
4 salmon steaks, fresh or frozen

Place all ingredients except salmon in a large skillet. Bring to a boil. Carefully add salmon steaks in a single layer. Bring again to a boil. Cover and simmer 6 to 8 minutes. Remove steaks with slotted spoon to hot platter. Serve with sauce if desired.

Sooke, B.C.
Ladies Auxiliary
Branch No. 54

Wild Game Meats

Savoury Moose Steaks

1½ lbs. moose steak, 1-inch thick
1 tbsp. dry mustard
4 tbsp. cornstarch
½ tsp. salt
1/8 tsp. pepper
2 tbsp. fat
1 cup sliced onion
1 diced carrot
1½ cups canned tomatoes

Cut nicks around steak, mix mustard, cornstarch, salt and pepper; rub into steak on both sides, pound into steaks on both sides. Melt falt in pan, sear steaks on both sides and transfer to greased casserole. Cover with onions, carrots and tomatoes. Cover and bake at 350°F. for 1½ hours or until meat is very tender. Serve with oven brown potatoes. Serves 4. Very good.

Hodgson, Man.
Ladies Auxiliary
Branch No. 158

Moose Stew

moose meat
water
onions
tomato soup
carrots
potatoes
macaroni

Cut up moose meat into bite size pieces and brown. Add the remaining ingredients and simmer together at least one hour or till meat is tender. Just before serving, add flour to thicken. (If using bull moose, simmer longer as the meat is tougher.)

Whitehorse, Yukon
Ladies Auxiliary
Branch No. 254

Venison and Vegetable Stew

6 tbsp. salad oil
3 lbs. venison chuck or rump, cut into 1½-inch cubes, no fat
1 cup chopped onion
1 cup chopped celery
2 tbsp. finely chopped parsley
1 clove garlic, finely chopped
1-8 oz. can tomato sauce
2 beef bouillon cubes
1½ tbsp. salt
¼ tsp. pepper
6 potatoes, diced
6 carrots, diced

In Dutch oven, heat oil, brown venison cubes well on all sides. Remove and set aside. Add chopped onions and celery to Dutch oven and sauté until tender, about 10 minutes. Return venison to pan. Add parsley, garlic, tomato sauce, bouillon cubes, salt, pepper and 2 cups water. Bring to boiling. Reduce heat and simmer covered for 1¼ hours. Add vegetables, and simmer, covered, 1 hour longer or until tender. Remove from heat. Mix flour with 2 tbsp. cold water and stir into stew. Makes 6 servings.

Foxwarren, Man.
Ladies Auxiliary
Branch No. 152

Venison Swiss Steak

**2 lbs. round steak, cut 1-2
   inches thick
3 large onions
1½ cups water or tomatoes
salt
pepper
flour**

Roll meat in flour, then pound in. Season with salt and pepper. Brown both sides slowly in a heavy skillet, add water or tomatoes and sliced onions. Cover tightly and cook slowly on top of stove, or in oven at 325°F. for 1½ to 2 hours or until tender, remove meat and thicken gravy.

Boiestown, N.B.
Ladies Auxiliary
Normandy Branch No. 79

Roast Wild Duck

**3 or 4 wild ducks
quartered apples
sliced orange
onion slices
celery leaves**

Stuff ducks with apple, orange, onion and celery. Place on rack in roasting pan. Roast, uncovered, at 425°F. Baste several times with hot water, then with pan juices or wine until well done, about 1-1½ hours, depending on size of ducks. Remove from oven and discard stuffing. Serve with Mushroom-Wild Rice Stuffing.

**Mushroom-
Wild Rice Stuffing:
  ½ lb. sliced mushrooms or
    ½ can buttom mushrooms
  ¼ cup butter or margarine
  ¼ cup chopped onion
  1 tbsp. chopped parsley
  ½ cup chopped celery
  2 cups cooked wild rice or
    1-2¾ oz. pkg. instant wild
    rice, cooked
  ¾ tsp. salt
  dash pepper**

Sauté mushrooms 5 minutes in melted butter. Add onion, pars-

ley and celery. Cook 3 minutes longer. Add cooked wild rice, salt and pepper. Heat thoroughly. Serve on platter, under duck pieces.

Bellevue, Alta.
Ladies Auxiliary
Branch No. 19

Moose Chop Suey

**2 lbs. moose meat, cut into
  small pieces
4 tsp. soya sauce
1 green pepper, chopped
1 onion, chopped
1 cup water
2 tsp. fat or oil
1 can mushrooms and sauce
1 stalk celery, chopped
1 can bean sprouts
2 tsp. Worcestershire sauce**

Heat fat in frying pan. Add onion and brown meat. Cook in water until tender. Add chopped vegetables and gravy browning. If necessary, thicken with flour and water cornstarch. Serve over hot rice.

Stephenville Crossing, Nfld.
Ladies Auxiliary
Branch No. 44

Barbequed Caribou or Moose Ribs

**3 lbs. ribs, cut in pieces
1 cup ketchup
2 tbsp. vinegar
2 tbsp. brown sugar
1 tsp. salt
¼ salt pork, diced
1 tbsp. prepared mustard
2 tbsp. lemon juice
1 onion, chopped
¼ tsp. pepper**

Brown ribs in salt pork. Place in casserole and cover with barbeque sauce. Bake at 325°F. for 2½ hours. Baste sauce over ribs frequently. Delicious served with rice.

Stephenville Crossing, Nfld.
Ladies Auxiliary
Branch No. 44

Moose Cabbage Rolls

**1 onion, chopped
1 lb. ground lean moose meat
salt and pepper to taste
1 onion, grated
½ cup cooked rice
2 cups canned tomatoes,
  crushed
2 tsp. vinegar
2 tbsp. sugar
¼ tsp. chili powder
8 large cabbage leaves**

Soften cabbage leaves in boiling water. Brown meat and onion in pan, season with salt and pepper, add cooked rice; mix well. Place a large spoonful on cabbage leaf, roll. Place them in a pot with rolled edge down or fastened with toothpicks, add remaining ingredients and a little water, simmer or bake 1½ to 2 hours.

Happy Valley, Labrador, Nfld.
Ladies Auxiliary
Branch No. 51

Baked Turr

**2 cups bread crumbs
½ tsp. savoury
½ tsp. salt
1 small onion, chopped
¼ tsp. pepper
1 tbsp. shortening**

Clean birds and drain well, then dress. The above is enough for one turr. Place dressed bird in roaster and sprinkle lightly with salt. Bake for one hour. Prick skin with fork so fat will drain off. Return bird to oven, putting a ¼ lb. salt pork around and over the bird, and bake until pork is brown. Add 4 or 5 cups hot water, 1 large onion and 1 tsp. salt. Bake until tender and brown. Baste or turn often.

**Gravy:
2-3 tbsp. flour
5 tbsp. cold water**

Mix well. Add to liquid in roasting pan after the bird is cooked. Boil for 2 minutes.

Clarenville, Nfld.
Ladies Auxiliary
Branch No. 27

Turr Hearts and Livers

1 lb. turr hearts and livers
1 onion
fat pork, diced
1 cup water

Brown hearts and livers in fat pork. Add onion and water; cover and cook for 20 minutes. Thicken gravy if desired. Serve on toast, rice or with potatoes.

Catalina, Nfld.
Ladies Auxiliary
Branch No. 16

Baked Rabbit in Buttermilk

1 rabbit, cut up
2 cups buttermilk
paprika
2 tbsp. melted butter
4 strips bacon
2 cups bread crumbs
salt and pepper

Place rabbit in small roaster or casserole dish. Combine butter and bread crumbs; spread over rabbit and add seasoning. Cover with buttermilk, top with bacon strips and bake at 350°F. for 2 hours or until meat is tender.

Hopewell, N.S.
Ladies Auxiliary
Branch No. 137

Moose or Deer Meat Loaf

1 medium onion, chopped fine
3 tbsp. lard
3 lbs. ground moose or deer meat
2 cups bread crumbs
1 cup tomato juice
1 tsp. paprika
1 tsp. pepper
1 tsp. salt

Simmer onion in lard. Mix together all ingredients and put in a greased loaf pan. Pour ¼ cup tomato juice over meat in pan and spread even on top. Bake at 350°F. for 1 hour.

Bellevue, Alta.
Ladies Auxiliary
Branch No. 19

Roast Venison

4 lb. venison roast
2 tbsp. flour
2 cloves garlic, minced
2 tbsp. brown sugar
1 tsp. prepared mustard
1 tbsp. Worcestershire sauce
¼ cup vinegar or lemon juice
1 large onion, sliced
1-14½ oz. can tomatoes

Allow fresh or frozen venison to stand overnight in Marinade in fridge. Season with salt, roll in flour and brown in hot skillet. Place in crock-pot cooker and add remaining ingredients. Cover and cook on Low 10 to 12 hours.

Marinade:
½ cup vinegar
2 cloves garlic, minced
2 tbso. salt
cold water to cover game

Mix ingredients together in bowl just large enough to cover game with water, soak frozen or fresh game overnight in fridge. No need to stir this marinade. Use for red meat or game birds.

Cartwright, Man.
Ladies Auxiliary
Branch No. 86

Marinated Venison Roast

5-6 lb. venison roast
6-8 carrots, cut up
1 cup onions
4 parsley roots, cut up
3 bay leaves
2 tsp. spice peppers, whole

Boil carrots, onion, parsley, bay leaves and peppers for 30 minutes in a little water. Combine:
2 cups white vinegar
4 cups water
2 tbsp. salt

Add the cooked vegetables and bring to a boil. Pour over the meat, cover and let cool. Put in the fridge for 2 or 3 days. Turn meat every day. Drain. Place meat in a roaster. Arrange vege-tables around, add a little water and roast till done. Remove vegetables; put through colander or blender. Put in saucepan, add 2 tbsp. sugar. Mix 1 cup sour cream with flour and add to vegetable mixture and cook to make a nice thick gravy. Pour over sliced meat. Serve with bread dumplings, rice or riced potatoes.

Bellevue, Alta.
Ladies Auxiliary
Branch No. 19

Roast Antelope

Wipe roast with a damp cloth. Rub with a cut clove of garlic and butter or margarine. Sprinkle with salt and a little cayenne pepper. Place the roast, skin side down, on rack in roaster. Cover with slices of fat side bacon. Roast at 300°F. allowing 35 to 40 minutes per lb. Serve with orange sauce.

Tangerine Sauce:
juice from 11 oz. can manda-rin orange sections, and enough water to make 1 cup liquid
1 tbsp. cornstarch
½ tsp. marjoram
dash salt
1-6 oz. can frozen concentra-ted tangerine juice
mandarin orange sections
1 tbsp. chopped candied ginger

Place liquid in saucepan. Mix cornstarch, marjoram and salt, stir into liquid in pan. Add frozen juice. Stir-cook until sauce thickens. Add mandarin orange sections and candied ginger. Simmer for 2 minutes.

Bellevue, Alta.
Ladies Auxiliary
Branch No. 19

Beaver Tails

This tid-bit of the old-time trappers will be tasted by few of the younger generation, more's the pity.

Broil over hot coals for a few minutes (or in hot oven). The rough, scaly hide will blister and come off, leaving the tail clean, white and solid. Then roast or boil until tender. This is considered very strengthening food (use only young beaver). For a treat, cool, souse in vinegar, add raw onion rings, salt and pepper to taste.

Steinbach, Man.
Ladies Auxiliary
Branch No. 190

Gaspe Sipate

**1 recipe not-too-rich pie
  pastry
1 small rabbit
3 partridges or rock cornish
  hens
1 lb. meat balls
1 lb. salt pork
onions
sliced potatoes
marjoram
thyme
poultry seasoning
bouillon cubes or powder
water**

Line iron oven with pie pastry, rolled ¼ to ½ inch thick. Cover pastry with a layer of salt pork, cubed. Follow this with a layer of rabbit, meat balls and seasoning. Follow with a layer of sliced potatoes. Repeat layers and end with salt pork on top. Mix bouillon with water — enough to fill oven ¾ full. Bake uncovered at 400°F. for 20 minutes. Add top layer of pastry, place cover on oven and return to oven at a reduced temperature of 275°F. Bake for 4-5 hours or until meat is tender. (Note: use raw meat and potatoes.)

New Richmond, Que.
Ladies Auxiliary
Bay Chaleurs Branch No. 172

Barbequed Rabbit

**2 rabbits, cut up
½ tsp. salt
½ cup flour
pork fat or oil**
**Sauce:
2 tbsp. brown sugar
1 tsp. dry mustard
2 tbsp. Worcestershire sauce
¼ cup vinegar
1 cup tomato juice
1 tbsp. paprika
1 tsp. salt
¼ cup ketchup
1 onion, chopped**

Dredge rabbit with flour and brown in fat. Place in large casserole. Combine all ingredients of sauce and pour over rabbit. Cover and bake at 325°F. for 2 hours. Baste frequently.

Carbonear, Nfld.
Ladies Auxiliary
Branch No. 23

Simmered Rabbit

**2 small rabbits, cut in serving-
  size pieces
1 cup vinegar
12 oz. beer
2 large onions, sliced
1 tbsp. mixed pickling spice
1 tsp. salt
1/8 tsp. pepper
¼ cup flour
¼ cup fat
1 tbsp. sugar**

Marinate rabbit pieces in the combined vinegar, beer, onions, pickling spice, salt and pepper in a covered crock. Cover and place in refrigerator for 1 or 2 days, turning meat several times. To cook: Dry rabbit pieces with paper towel. Dip in flour and brown on all sides in fat in Dutch oven or deep frying pan. Pour off fat. Strain marinade, add sugar and pour over meat. Bring to boiling point. Cover and simmer over low heat for 40 minutes or until rabbit is tender. Thicken gravy if desired.

Bellevue, Alta.
Ladies Auxiliary
Branch No. 19

Stewed Wild Rabbit

Cut rabbit into pieces. Place in marinade and let stand overnight in refrigerator.

**Marinade:
1½ qts. water
½ cup vinegar
1 onion
1 tsp. mixed pickling spice
1 tbsp. salt**

Remove from marinade and place rabbit pieces into roasting pan. Add:

**1 diced onion
1 cup water
1/8 tsp. pickling spice
5 strips bacon**

Place in oven and bake at 325°F. for about 1 hour, then add:

**1 cup carrots
1 stalk diced celery
4 potatoes
4 cups water
salt**

Spread vegetables all around the meat. Add water and salt and continue baking until meat and vegetables are tender.

Hodgson, Man.
Ladies Auxiliary
Branch No. 158

Vegetables, Rice, Eggs & Cheese

Boston Baked Beans

1 lb. dried pea beans
1 medium onion
½ cup molasses
½ tsp. dry mustard
¼ cup brown sugar, firmly
   packed
1 tsp. salt
¼ lb. lean salt pork, diced

Pick over beans and rinse. Place in a large bowl. Add water to cover and let stand overnight; drain. Combine beans and onion in a large saucepan; add water to cover. Heat to boiling. Cover and simmer 45 minutes or until skins of beans burst when you blow on several in a spoon. Drain liquid into a small bowl. Measure 1 cup of bean liquid and combine with molasses, mustard, brown sugar and salt. Layer half of the salt pork and all of the beans into a 8 cup bean pot. Pour molasses mixture over top and cover with remaining liquid. Top with remaining salt pork. Cover and bake at 300°F. for 4 hours. Uncover and bake one hour longer. After 2 hours of baking check beans. If they seem to be dry add more liquid.

Port Rexton, Nfld.
Branch No. 20

Cream Style Corn
(for freezing)

10 cups corn, cut off of cob
1½-2 cups water
¼ cup sugar
1 tbsp. salt
2 tbsp. butter

Mix and cook in oven at 325°F. or 350°F. till bubbly. Stir often. Cool and put in freezer bags. Freeze.

Miami, Man.
Ladies Auxiliary
Branch No. 88

Wild Rice

Preparing wild rice — Quick-Soak Method. Wash required amount of wild rice under cold, flowing water. Stir rice into 3 time the amount of boiling water (1 cup rice requires 3 cups boiling water). Parboil for 5 minutes only. Remove from heat. Let soak in same water (covered) for one hour. Drain, wash and cook as directed in recipe.

Chicken and Rice Casserole

1 cup wild rice
½ tsp. salt
1 medium onion
2 or 3 stalks celery
1 medium green pepper
1 cup fresh mushrooms, sliced
   or 1-10 oz. can
¼ cup soya sauce
2 chicken bouillon cubes
1½ cup water, chicken or
   meat stock

Dissolve bouillon cubes in water. Use amount desired of boned chicken, beef or pork pieces. Use quick-soak method to prepare rice, then boil in salted water until tender, about 30 minutes. Drain and rinse. In frying pan sauté onion, celery, green pepper (all of which are chopped fine) and sliced mushrooms. Place this mixture in casserole dish; add chopped cooked chicken and cooked rice. Add soya sauce to chicken stock and pour over all ingredients in casserole. Bake covered at 350°F. until moisture is absorbed, about 2 hours. Serves 8.

Steinbach, Man.
Branch No. 190

Never Fail Cheese Souffle

1⅓ cups milk
3 tbsp. soft butter or margarine
5 tbsp. flour
½ tsp. salt
dash pepper
⅓ cup grated cheese
4 eggs

Combine milk, butter, flour and seasonings to make a white sauce. Add cheese. Whisk sauce until smooth and thick. Cool slightly, add well beaten egg yolks. Gently fold in well beaten egg whites. Pour into a greased 2 qt. baking dish. Set in a pan of hot water and bake 40 to 50 minutes at 350°F. Serve immediately. Mix with some bacon and ripe tomatoes.

Teulon, Man.
Branch No. 166

Spanish Rice

3 tbsp. bacon fat
1 cup uncooked rice
¾ cup chopped onion
½ cup chopped green pepper
½ cup chopped celery
1-14oz. or 19 oz. can tomatoes
1 cup water
1 tsp. salt
1 tsp. chili powder

Heat 2 tbsp. fat in frying pan. Add rice, stirring frequently until rice is lightly browned. Add remaining bacon fat. Stir in onion, green pepper and celery; sauté until tender, about 5 minutes. Stir in tomatoes, water, salt and chili powder. Bring to a full boil, reduce heat and cover. Simmer 20 minutes or until tender. If rice is not tender add ¾ cup more water and simmer a bit longer until tender.

Winnipeg, Man.
Ladies Auxiliary
Transcona Branch No. 7

Zucchini Patties

3 cups coarsely shredded
   zucchini
2 eggs, beaten
1 cup shredded cheese
½ cup onion, chopped
1 cup Biscuit Mix

Combine all ingredients and
form into patties. Fry slowly in
a little oil or butter.

Pine Falls, Man.
Ladies Auxiliary
Branch No. 64

Baked Potato Boats

(Microwave)

4 potatoes (approx. 7 oz. each)
2 tbsp. butter
1 cup milk
salt and pepper
½ cup shredded sharp cheese
paprika

Select four uniform, medium
sized baking potatoes and scrub
well. Pierce each potato all the
way through with a large fork.
Arrange potatoes on paper
towel, leaving about 1″ space
between potatoes. Bake in microwave oven on high for 10 to
15 minutes. Turn potatoes halfway through cooking time. Tip:
If potatoes feel slightly firm
after cooking, allow a few
minutes standing time. Potatoes
will finish cooking on their
own. Let stand a few minutes to
cool. Cut thin slice through skin
from top of each potato. Scoop
out potato from skins, leaving
thin, unbroken shell from each
potato. Mash potatoes, stir in
butter, milk, salt and pepper.
Whip until potato mixture is
light and fluffy. Lightly spoon
potato mixture back into shells.
Top each potato with cheese.
Sprinkle with paprika. Place
potatoes in a circle on paper
plate. Cook in microwave oven
for 5 minutes. Tip: If desired,
stuffed potatoes may be prepared ahead and refrigerated.
Heat in microwave oven 6 to 7
minutes.

Elgin, Man.
Elgin Branch No. 216

Broccoli Casserole

2-10 oz. pkg. broccoli, drain
2 tbsp. butter
2 tbsp. flour
½ tsp. salt
dash pepper
1 cup milk
4 oz. cream cheese
1 cup shredded cheddar cheese
1 cup bread crumbs
2 tbsp. butter, melted

Melt butter in saucepan; add
flour, salt and pepper. Add
milk and stir until bubbly. Reduce heat. Blend in cream
cheese. Stir until smooth. Place
broccoli in baking dish. Pour
sauce over and mix lightly. Top
with cheddar cheese and bread
crumbs which have been tossed
in the melted butter. Bake at
350°F. for 40 to 45 minutes.
Serves 6.

Elgin, Man.
Ladies Auxiliary
Branch No. 216

Asparagus and Cheese Puff

4 slices white bread
2 tbsp. butter
¼ cup finely chopped onion
1 can asparagus spears
4 slices Swiss cheese
3 eggs
½ tsp. salt
¼ tsp. pepper
½ tsp. curry powder
1 cup milk
½ cup light cream

Trim crust from bread and cut
in half. Generously butter
8x8x2″ pan. Arrange bread and
sprinkle onions over. Arrange
asparagus over bread. Top with
cheese. Beat eggs with remaining ingredients. Pour over bread
and asparagus. Bake at 450°F.
for 20 minutes or until puffed
and firm. Cut in squares and
serve with a crisp salad. Great
for ladies' luncheon!

Winnipeg, Man.
Ladies Auxiliary
St. Vital Branch No. 16

Curried Spaghetti

1 cup chopped onion
3 tbsp. butter or margarine
2 tsp. curry powder
3½ cups chicken broth
½ cup water
8 oz. uncooked spaghetti,
   broken in half
1 medium green pepper, diced
1-5 oz. can pimentos, drained
   and chopped

In 4 qt. pot, sauté onion in butter until golden. Stir in curry
powder, broth and water. Heat
to boiling. Add uncooked spaghetti so that liquid continues to
boil. Cover. Simmer about 7
minutes or until spaghetti is just
tender enough to swirl. Do not
overcook. Stir occasionally. Stir
in green pepper and pimentos.
Remove from heat. Cool uncovered for 15 minutes or
quick-cool mixture by placing
pot in sink or large pan filled
with cold water. Ladle into freezer containers and cover. Label
and freeze up to three months.
To serve: Dip one container
spaghetti mixture in hot water 2
to 3 minutes (until mixture can
be easily turned into saucepan).
For a 1 qt. container, add 2
tbsp. water. Cover and cook
over low heat about 40 minutes.
For pt. container, add 1 tbsp.
water. Cover and cook over low
heat about 20 minutes. Stir
occasionally. Serve immediately. Serving suggestion: Arrange
warm hard cooked egg halves
over spaghetti. Salted peanuts
and coconut are good accom-
paniments.

Stony Mountain, Man.
Ladies Auxiliary
Branch No. 142

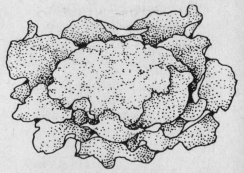

Acorn Squash 'N Apples

(Microwave)

2 acorn or butternut squash
salt
2 medium apples, peeled and
   sliced
8 tbsp. brown sugar
4 tbsp. butter or margarine
cinnamon

Leave squash whole and cook 8 to 10 minutes or until they feel soft to the touch. Let stand 5 minutes. Cut in half and remove seeds. Place cut side up in shallow baking dish. Sprinkle with salt. Fill with apples, 1 tbsp. butter and a dash of cinnamon. Cook, covered with wax paper for 4 to 5 minutes or until apples are tender.

Ste. Anne, Man.
La Verendrye Branch No. 220

Potato Puffs

½ cup flour
1½ tsp. baking powder
¼ tsp. salt
1 cup mashed potatoes
2 eggs

Mix flour, baking powder and salt together. Blend in to mashed potatoes. Mix again and add beaten eggs. Stir thoroughly. Drop by spoonfuls into hot grease. Fry until golden brown on both sides.

Winnipeg Beach, Man.
Ladies Auxiliary
Branch No. 61

Birds' Nest

eggs
1 pt. sauerkraut (scald if very
   salty and pour off water)

Amount of sauerkraut and eggs used will vary with number of diners. Fry sauerkraut until tender, stirring occasionally. Make indentations and put in eggs (without shell). Cook until done. Serve with bread or potatoes.

Mahone Bay, N.S.
Branch No. 49

Baked Onions in Tomato Juice

(Microwave)

12 small onions (approx.
   1½ lbs.)
¼ cup tomato juice
salt
pepper
½ tsp. Worcestershire Sauce
2 tbsp. chopped fresh parsley
2 tbsp. butter

Place peeled onion in greased casserole. Combine tomato juice with seasonings and pour over onions. Dot with butter and cover. Microwave on High for 3 minutes and then on medium for about 10 minutes. Stir occasionally during cooking. Note: If fresh parsley is not available, a small amount of dried may be used.

Bowsman, Man.
Ladies Auxiliary
Branch No. 51

Turnip Puff

3 cups hot mashed turnip
2 tbsp. butter
2 eggs, beaten
3 tbsp. flour
1 tbsp. brown sugar
1 tsp. baking powder
1 tsp. salt
pepper to taste
nutmeg to taste
1 tbsp. melted butter
¼ cup bread crumbs

Coat bread crumbs with melted butter. Grease 1½ qt. casserole. Preheat oven to 375°F. Combine turnip, butter and egg, beating thoroughly. Add flour, sugar, baking powder, salt, pepper and nutmeg. Mix until well blended. Put in casserole. Top with buttered bread crumbs. Bake for 25 minutes. Serves 6 to 8.

Elkhorn, Man.
Branch No. 58

Chinese Green Vegetables

1 head cauliflower, broken
   into flowerettes
1 bunch broccoli, broken into
   flowerettes
1 carrot, sliced diagonally
celery, cut in 1 to 2″ diagonal
   slices
1 large Spanish onion
1 or 2 cans whole mushrooms
2 green peppers, cut into large
   pieces

Blanch cauliflower, broccoli and carrot in boiling water, drain. Heat small quantity oil in large skillet or wok. Add vegetables and stir fry in heated oil about 30 minutes. Add ¼-½ cup soya sauce, 1½ tsp. lemon juice or vinegar.

Hartney, Man.
Branch No. 26

Pan Cabbage

1 tsp. butter
2 cups shredded cabbage
1 cup grated carrots
1 large onion, sliced
¼ tsp. salt
¼ tsp. pepper
1 cup boiling water

Melt butter in pan, add onion and cook over low heat until soft. Add cabbage and carrots; pour boiling water over vegetables. Cover and simmer slowly for 15 minutes.

Selkirk, Man.
Ladies Auxiliary
Branch No. 42

Mushroom Rice

1 cup long grain rice
1 can mushroom stems and
   pieces
¼ cup oil
½ pkg. onion soup mix
2 cups water

Mix together in casserole and bake at 350°F. for one hour. Add more liquid if needed.

Morden, Man.
Branch No. 11

Cheese Star Casserole

6 slices bread
1 lb. Velveeta cheese
2½ cups cooked mixed vegetables
2 tbsp. butter
2 tbsp. flour
2 cups milk
salt and pepper to taste

Make 3 cheese sandwiches, trim crusts and cut in half diagonally. Make cream sauce using butter, flour and milk. Stir in ¾ lb. of the Velveeta cheese (or whatever is left after making the sandwiches). When melted, add the vegetables. Pour half of sauce into a casserole. Arrange sandwiches in sauce, points up. Add remaining sauce. Bake at 350°F. for 30 minutes. Serves 6.

Thunder Bay, Ont.
Ortona Branch No. 113

Sweet Potatoes and Pears Caramel

2 lbs. sweet potatoes, cooked and peeled
1-29 oz. can pear halves, drained
¼ cup butter or margarine, melted
½ tsp. salt
¼ tsp. cinnamon
¼ tsp. nutmeg
½ cup brown sugar, packed
4 oz. shredded coconut

About 1½ hours before serving preheat oven to 350°F. With sharp knife slice sweet potatoes lengthwise into ½" thick pieces. In large bowl gently toss sweet potatoes with next five ingredients until well mixed. Grease casserole dish. Spoon mixture into greased 12x8" casserole dish, evenly sprinkle with brown sugar, then coconut. Bake 30 minutes, or until hot and bubbly.

Montreal, Que.
Mazeppa Branch No. 183

Summer Squash Casserole

2 lbs. squash, 6 cups cooked and mashed
¼ cup chopped onion
1 cup cream of chicken soup
1 cup shredded carrot
1-8 oz. pkg. McLarens stuffing mix
½ cup melted margarine
1 small carton sour cream

Cook squash and chopped onion in salt and water for 5 minutes; mash. Combine soup and one carton sour cream, margarine, carrot and onion. Mix and spread half of stuffing in pyrex square dish. Spoon mixture on top and sprinkle remaining stuffing on top. Bake at 350°F. for 20 to 25 minutes.

Hantsport, N.S.
Lucknow Branch No. 109

Scalloped Tomatoes

1-19 oz. can tomatoes
1 large onion, chopped
1 tbsp. sugar
½ tsp. salt
½ tsp. pepper
1 tbsp. chopped parsley
1/8 tsp. thyme
1/8 tsp. rosemary
1/8 tsp. oregano
1 cup rather dry bread cubes
1 tbsp. melted butter
¼ cup grated cheddar cheese
2 tbsp. parmesan cheese, grated

Combine tomatoes, onion, sugar and seasonings in baking dish. Toss bread cubes with butter and cheese; sprinkle over tomatoes. Bake at 350°F. for 15 to 20 minutes or until topping is lightly browned. Makes 6 servings.

West Pubnico, N.S.
Ladies Auxiliary
Branch No. 66

Magic Quiche

½ lb. cooked crumbled bacon
4 oz. shredded Swiss cheese
½ cup chopped onion
1 can corn kernels, drained
4 eggs
¼ tsp. salt
1/8 tsp. pepper
1/8 tsp. nutmeg
2 cups milk
½ cup Tea Bisquick

Grease quiche pan or large pie plate. Spread bacon, cheese, corn and onion in bottom of pan. Blend remaining ingredients at high speed for one minute and pour over first mixture. Bake at 350°F. for 55 minutes. Cool 5 minutes before cutting.

Schreiber, Ont.
Ladies Auxiliary
Branch No. 109

Cabbage Rolls

2 medium or 3 small cabbages
1½ cups rice, partly cooked
½ lb. (generous) ground beef, cooked and drained
¼ lb. chopped bacon, cooked and drained
1 medium onion. chopped and cooked in bacon fat
1 tsp. salt
½ tsp pepper or to taste
1 tbsp. sugar (optional)
tomato juice, sauerkraut juice and a small amount of sauerkraut, or tomato soup and tomato sauce can be used to cover

Wilt cabbage in boiling water. Combine meat, rice, onion, salt and pepper. Roll meat mixture in cabbage leaves and secure. Add liquid and cook for one hour or until cabbage and rice are tender.

Slave Lake, Alta.
Branch No. 110

Veal Wild Rice

2 lbs. boneless veal cubes
1 medium onion, chopped
1-6 oz. pkg. wild and white
  rice mixture
1-10½ oz. can condensed golden mushroom soup
1 cup or 2 stalks celery,
  chopped
1-8½ oz. can water chestnuts,
  undrained and sliced
⅓ cup or 2½ oz. jar mush-
  rooms, undrained
1 tbsp. soya sauce
1½ cups water

Combine all ingredients in 2 qt. casserole and mix well. Cook, covered, for 30 minutes or until wild rice is tender, stirring once.

Ste. Anne, Man.
La Verendrye Branch No. 220

Hodge Podge

Here's a favorite in the early summer when the vegetables are young and you are anxious to sample the produce from your garden. If you want to reduce the calorie content, use half milk and half cream. The salt pork can be replaced with margarine, but then it wouldn't be the traditional Maritime Special, would it?

yellow beans
carrots
potatoes
peas
cauliflower
1 cup vegetable stock
1 cup table cream
chives
parsley

Wash and trim vegetables, there is no need to peel them. Cook beans, carrots and potatoes together in boiling salt water. Cook the peas and cauliflower separately. Fry the salt pork until golden brown. Add cream and vegetable stock. Season with chives or chopped green onion and parsley. Bring to a boil quickly and mix into vegetables just before serving.

Campobello, N.B.
Branch No. 83

Scalloped Potatoes

1 can cream of celery soup
½ cup milk
Worcestershire Sauce
salt
pepper
4 cups potatoes, sliced thin
½ cup onions
1 cup shredded sharp cheese
1 tbsp. butter

Combine celery soup, milk, Worcestershire Sauce, salt and pepper. Layer potatoes, onion and cheese in a casserole. Pour liquid over. Bake covered at 375°F. for one hour, and uncovered for 15 minutes.

Montreal, Que.
Flanders Branch No. 63

Baked Macaroni and Cheese

25 ml margarine
25 ml flour
2 ml salt
0.5 ml pepper
350 ml milk
250 ml grated cheddar cheese
1 ml Worcestershire Sauce
1 ml prepared mustard
250 ml macaroni
75 ml buttered bread crumbs
25 ml grated cheddar cheese

Melt butter, blend in flour and seasonings. Add milk, and cook, stirring constantly until thickened. Remove from heat. Add 250 ml grated cheese, Worcestershire Sauce and mustard. Stir until smooth. Cook macaroni in 1.25 L boiling water and 5 ml salt. Cook at full boil uncovered, stirring occasionally until tender but firm, 7 to 9 minutes. Drain. Rinse with hot water and drain again. Add to sauce and pour into a 1 qt. baking dish. Mix bread crumbs and 25 ml grated cheese together and sprinkle on top. Bake at 200°C. (400°F.) for about 20 minutes. Makes 3 servings.

Catalina, Nfld.
Branch No. 16

Rice and Zucchini Casserole

2 cups cooked rice
2 onions, sliced
2 cans mushroom soup
6 small zucchini, sliced
½ lb. sharp cheese, grated

Cook onion and zucchini over low heat until soft with butter in frying pan. Cover and stir occasionally. Put layer of rice, layer of vegetable mix, some cheese and part of soup. Repeat layer. Bake at 350°F. for 45 minutes.

La Sooke, B.C.
Branch No. 54

Devilled Eggs

12 hard boiled eggs, cut
  lengthwise
½ tsp. salt
1/8 tsp. white pepper
1½ tsp. prepared mustard
3 tbsp. mayonnaise
1 tbsp. vinegar (sweet pickle
  vinegar if available)
3 drops Tabasco Sauce

Remove egg yolks to a bowl. Arrange whites on a tray and sprinkle lightly with salt. Mash yolks thoroughly and add remaining ingredients. Blend together thoroughly. Fill cavities of whites with spoon or pastry bag. Sprinkle with paprika. Chill thoroughly.

Chemainus, B.C.
Ladies Auxiliary
Branch No. 191

Creamy Beets

¼ cup sour cream
1½ tbsp. prepared horse-
  radish
1 tsp. dill
1-16 oz. jar sliced pickle beets
  well drained
½ cup thinly sliced green
  onions

Combine sour cream, horseradish and dill in mixing bowl. Add pickled beets and onion. Toss gently. Makes 2 cups.

Montreal, Que.
Mazeppa Branch No. 183

Egg Batter For Fish, Vegetables Or Fruit

1 cup flour
½ tsp. salt
2 eggs, separated
3 tbsp. vegetable oil
dash cayenne pepper
1 cup water or beer
fish, vegetables or seafood
   (oyster, squid, mussels,
   etc.) for deep frying
fruit (thick slices of unpeeled,
   cored apple sprinkled with
   cinnamon or nutmeg;
   bananas, strawberries, etc.)

Mix together flour and salt. In smaller bowl whisk egg yolks, oil and pepper and add to flour mixture. Gradually whisk in water; mixing until smooth batter is obtained. Beat egg whites until stiff and fold into batter just before serving. Heat oil and deep fry any combination of fish, vegetables, seafood or fruit, completely covered at 375°F. (190°C.) until puffed and golden. Drain and serve with rice or fruit as a dessert. Allow approx. 8 pieces per person. Makes 4 to 6 servings.
(Tip for batter frying. Dredge all vegetables, etc. in flour and shake off excess before dipping in batter. Batter will adhere to above better. Let batter drain a bit so you don't have too much on each piece.)

Pender Island, B.C.
Branch No. 239

Curried Rice

1 cup Minute Rice
3 tbsp. butter
¼ tsp curry powder
2½ cups beef broth
½ tsp. salt

Combine all ingredients in a casserole. Cover and bake at 350°F. for 50 minutes.

Catalina, Nfld.
Branch No. 16

Hamburger Quiche

1-9″ unbaked pie shell
¾ cup hamburger meat,
   browned and drained
¼ cup mayonnaise
¾ cup milk
3 eggs
1 tbsp. cornstarch
1½ cups cubed cheddar
   cheese, or a mixture of
   cheddar and mozzarella
dash pepper
½ cup green onions

Put meat in shell, then cheese and green onions. Dash pepper. Mix together mayonnaise, milk, eggs and cornstarch. Blend well and pour egg mixture over ingredients in pie shell. Bake at 400°F. for 35 to 40 minutes or until knife inserted comes out clean.(Hamburger may be substituted with crisp bacon or chopped cooked ham, and green pepper and onion may be used instead of green onion).

Gander, Nfld.
Branch No. 8

Perogie Puffs

2 cups creamed cottage cheese
4 cups flour
1 tsp. baking soda
1 tsp. salt
¼ cup vegetable oil
1 cup warm water
2 eggs

Press cottage cheese through potato ricer or sieve. Add to flour, baking soda and salt. Rub well together. Mix oil, water and beaten eggs and add to flour mixture. Knead and add more flour if needed to make rather a sticky dough (not dry). Pinch off piece of dough, flatten in palm of your hand and fill with mixture of mashed potato, Cheez Whiz, bacon pieces (if desired), salt and pepper to taste. Deep fry until brown. These freeze well.

Steinbach, Man.
Branch No. 190

Saucy Vegetables

Sauce:
1 can chicken broth
2 tbsp. cornstarch
1 tbsp. soya sauce
¼ tsp. ground ginger

Vegetables:
5 cups of prepared vegetables such as: frozen broccoli spears, frozen peas, thinly sliced carrots and diagonally sliced celery

To make sauce, combine first four ingredients and bring to a boil. Simmer until thickened. Serve over cooked vegetables; or put all ingredients together and bring to a boil. Turn heat down, cover, and simmer 10 minutes or until vegetables are tender-crisp. Serves 4 to 5.

Plum Point, Nfld.
Branch No. 55

Pyrohy

1 cup cold instant mashed
   potatoes
3 cups flour
1 tsp. salt
1 tsp. cream of tartar
3 eggs
¼ cup oil
¼ cup warm water
2 heaping tbsp. Cheez Whiz
   (optional)

Place in large bowl and whip with fork, then with hands. Knead well. Let stand ½ hour or overnight if desired. Roll thin and fill with your favorite filling. Our favorite is equal parts mashed potatoes and dry curd cottage cheese with about a cup of cheddar cheese curds. Salt and pepper to taste.

Peace River, Alta.
Branch No. 62

Deluxe Potatoes

2 lbs. frozen hashbrowns
1 cup diced onion
1-10 oz. can cream of chicken
soup
1-500 g. carton sour cream
½ cup margarine
8 oz. sharp cheese, grated
salt and pepper to taste

Thaw potatoes for 30 minutes. Mix all ingredients and pour into 9x13″ pan. Top with Cornflake crumbs. Bake at 350°F. for one hour.

Emo, Ont.
Ladies Auxiliary
Branch No. 99

Vegetable Pie

2 cups chopped broccoli
½ cup chopped onion
⅓ cup chopped green pepper
1 cup shredded cheese
1½ cups milk
¾ cup Bisquick
3 beaten eggs
1 tsp. salt
¼ tsp. pepper

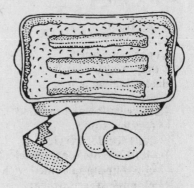

Cook broccoli in salted water, drain and chop. Mix vegetables and cheese in greased pie plate. Beat remaining ingredients till smooth and pour over the vegetables. Bake at 400°F. for about 40 minutes, or until brown and centre is set.

Schreiber, Ont.
Ladies Auxiliary
Branch No. 109

Additional Recipes

_____
_____
_____
_____
_____
_____
_____
_____
_____
_____
_____
_____
_____
_____
_____
_____

Cakes, Frostings, Cookies, Squares & Desserts

Cakes Frostings

Honey Cake

4 eggs
¾ cup sugar
1 cup oil
½ cup orange juice
½ cup Coke or strong tea
2 tsp. cinnamon
1 tsp. allspice
1 cup honey
2½ cups flour
½ tsp. baking soda
pinch salt
3 tsp. baking powder

Mix all ingredients well. Put mixture into an ungreased pan and bake at 350°F. for 55 to 60 minutes.

Wainwright, Alta.
Ladies Auxiliary
Worthington Branch No. 29

Watergate Cake

1 Duncan Hines white cake mix, without the pudding in the mix
1-106 g pkg. pistachio instant pudding
3 eggs
1 cup oil
1 cup 7-up
½ cup walnuts

Combine all ingredients except walnuts and beat together. Add walnuts last. Bake at 350°F. for 40 to 60 minutes in a large pan. For glass pan, bake at 325°F.

Icing:
2 pkgs. Dream Whip
1 pkg. pistachio instant pudding
1½ cups milk
½ cup walnuts

Combine all ingredients except walnuts and beat till thick. Add walnuts. Keep in fridge.

Plumas, Man.
Ladies Auxiliary
Branch No. 189

Blueberry Cake

½ cup butter or margarine
1 cup sugar
2 eggs
¾ cup milk
2 cups flour
2 tsp. baking powder
¼ tsp. salt
½ tsp. lemon or vanilla
1 cup blueberries

Mix all ingredients, adding blueberries last. Sprinkle with ¾ cup brown sugar, mixed with 1 tsp. cinnamon and bake. Or omit sugar topping and put Fluffy Frosting on cool cake.

Fluffy Frosting:
1 egg white
¾ cup sugar
1 tsp. vanilla
¼ tsp. cream of tartar

Mix to peak. Add ¼ cup boiling water and mix again to peak.

Chezzetcook. N.S.
Ladies Auxiliary
Branch No. 161

Best Ever Orange Cake

6 egg whites (¾ cup)
1¾ cups sifted all-purpose flour (sift before measuring)
½ tsp. salt
1½ cups white sugar
6 egg yolks
6 tbsp. fresh orange juice
1 tbsp. grated orange peel

confectioners sugar

Let egg whites warm to room temperature in large bowl, about 1 hour. Sift flour and salt together; set aside. Beat egg whites till foamy with electric mixer on medium speed. Gradually beat in ½ cup sugar, 2 tbsp. at a time. Continue beating until stiff peaks form. In a small bowl, with same beater, beat yolks until thick and lemon colored, about 3 minutes. Gradually add the 1 cup sugar. Add flour to yolk mixture at low speed, alternating with orange juice, beginning and ending with flour. Add orange peel. Using whisk and under and over movement, add yolk mixture to egg whites, folding just enough to blend. Pour into an ungreased 9½ to 10-inch pan. Bake 35 to 40 minutes until done but testing by gently touching. Invert and cool one hour. Loosen from pan. Sift confectioners sugar on top. To cut cake, use knife with serrated edge. Delicious.

Sanford, Man.
Ladies Auxiliary
Branch No. 171

Rhubarb Cake

Base:
1½ cups flour
3 tbsp. sugar
¾ cup margarine

Press above ingredients into a 9x13-inch pan. Bake at 350°F. for 15 minutes. Cool base and cover with filling. Mix together:

5 cups rhubarb, chopped
¾ cup milk
1¼ cups white sugar
4 egg yolks, beaten (reserve egg whites)
1 tsp. vanilla
3 tbsp. flour

Bake filling on base for 45 minutes. Remove from oven and top with meringue. Return to oven for 18 minutes.

Basic Meringue:
4 egg whites
6 tbsp. sugar

Beat egg whites and sugar together until very stiff and foamy.

Sanford, Man.
Ladies Auxiliary
Branch No. 171

Dutch Apple Cake

Batter:
- 1 cup flour
- 1½ tsp. baking powder
- ½ tsp. salt
- 4 tbsp. sugar
- ¼ cup margarine
- 1 egg
- ¼ cup milk

Topping:
- 3 cups sliced apples
- 1 tsp. cinnamon
- ¼ tsp. nutmeg
- ½ cup brown sugar
- 3 tbsp. melted margarine

Sift together dry ingredients; cut in margarine, add beaten egg and milk. Spread dough in an oiled 9x9-inch cake pan. Arrange sliced apples in rows over top of dough. Mix the sugar, spices and margarine until crumbly and sprinkle over apple slices. Bake at 350°F. for 30 minutes. Serve warm with ice cream or cheese. I use my own Heyer apples when fresh or frozen.

Roblin, Man.
Ladies Auxiliary
Branch No. 24

Apple Cherry Cake

- 1 cup white sugar
- 3 eggs
- ¾ cup oil
- ½ cup orange juice
- 2 cups flour
- 1 tsp. vanilla
- 1 tsp. baking powder
- 1 tsp. almond extract
- 4 apples, peeled and thinly sliced
- 1-20 oz. can cherry pie filling

Mix sugar, eggs, oil, orange juice and flavoring. Add dry ingredients and mix well. Place half of the batter in a 9x12 pan. Slice apples over this. Spoon on pie filling. Cover with remaining batter. Sprinkle sugar and a little cinnamon on top of cake. Bake at 350°F. for 1 hour.

Mafeking, Man.
Ladies Auxiliary
Branch No. 93

Gingerbread

- 2⅓ cups flour
- 2 tsp. baking soda
- ½ tsp. baking powder
- ⅓ tsp. salt
- ⅓ tsp. cloves
- 1½ tsp. cinnamon
- 2 tsp. ginger
- ½ tsp. nutmeg
- ¾ cup brown sugar
- ¾ cup molasses
- 2 eggs
- 1 cup boiling water
- 1 cup raisins
- ¾ cup shortening, melted after measuring

Prepare 9x13-inch pan. Sift together dry ingredients. Combine molasses and sugar in large bowl; add shortening, mixing well. Add eggs and beat well. Add dry ingredients and raisins. Add boiling water and beat well. Bake at 325-350°F. for approx. 1 hour. Delicious served with whipped cream, ice cream or lemon sauce.

Chester Basin, N.S.
Ladies Auxiliary
Everett Branch No. 88

Confetti Cake

- 1 cup salad oil
- 1 tsp. vanilla
- 3 tbsp. hot water
- 3 egg yolks
- 1½ cups white sugar
- 1 cup shredded raw carrots
- 1 cup shredded raw beets
- ½ cup chopped nuts (optional)
- 2 cup sifted flour
- 2 tsp. baking powder
- ½ tsp. salt
- 3 egg whites

Mix together first 5 ingredients. Sift together flour and baking powder. Add remaining ingredients, except egg whites. Mix well and fold in stiffly beaten egg whites. Bake in a greased 9x13-inch pan at 350°F. for approx. 45 minutes.

Hartney, Man.
Ladies Auxiliary
Branch No. 26

Pineapple Refrigerator Cake

- 24-30 graham wafers, crushed
- 4 tbsp. melted butter
- 1½ cups icing sugar
- ½ cup butter
- 1 egg
- 1 cup whipping cream

Mix graham wafer crumbs and melted butter together. Press ¾ of mixture into pan. Cream together icing sugar, butter and egg. Whip the whipping cream. On top of crumb mixture, add a layer of sugar mixture, a layer of whipped cream, a layer of crushed pineapple and remaining graham wafer crumb mixture. Refrigerate for 24 hours before serving.

Sicamous, B.C.
Ladies Auxiliary
Branch No. 99

Cherry Pound Cake

- 1 cup butter
- 1-8 oz. pkg. cream cheese
- 1½ cups sugar
- 1½ tsp. vanilla
- 4 eggs
- 2 cups flour
- ¼ cup flour
- 1 cup cherries, drained
- 3 tsp. baking powder
- ½ cup chopped pecans (optional)

Grease and flour an 8-inch tube pan. Combine the ¼ cup flour with cherries. Blend butter, sugar, cream cheese and vanilla together. Add eggs, one at a time; beating well. Gradually add baking powder and 2 cups flour. Fold floured cherries into batter. Sprinkle nuts in pan with batter. Bake at 325°F. for 1 hour, 20 minutes. Cool 5 minutes and remove from pan.

Waverley, N.S.
Ladies Auxiliary
Dieppe Branch No. 90

Queen Elizabeth Cake

1 cup dates
1 tsp. baking soda
1 cup boiling water

Cut dates to small pieces. Add baking soda and water. Squash and cool. Mix together:

¼ cup margarine
1 cup sugar
1 egg
1½ cups flour
dash salt
1 tsp. vanilla
½ cup walnuts (optional)

Mix together and add date mixture. Bake at 350°F. for 30 minutes or till cake is done in center.

Icing:

7 tbsp. brown sugar
¾ cup coconut
4 tbsp. margarine
3 tbsp. Carnation milk

Boil for 1 minute, stirring often. Pour over warm cake and return to oven and lightly brown top on high. This makes a delicious topping and icing can be doubled.

Terrace Bay, Ont.
Ladies Auxiliary
Branch No. 223

Almond Cake

1 cup butter
¾ cup sugar
1 egg
½ cup almond paste
1 tsp. almond extract
2 cups sifted flour
¼ cup sliced almonds

Preheat oven to 350°F. Cream butter and sugar. Separate egg, beat yolk into butter mixture, add almond paste and flavouring. Add flour, mix well. Press into an ungreased 9x9-inch pan. Beat egg white until frothy. Add almonds. Spread over cake. Bake 30 minutes or until golden brown. Cool.

Winnipeg, Man.
Ladies Auxiliary
Imperial Veterans in Canada
Branch No. 84

Pumpkin Spice Cake

2 cups flour
1 tsp. salt
2 tsp. baking powder
¼ tsp. baking soda
1 tsp. ginger
½ tsp. nutmeg
½ tsp. cinnamon
¼ tsp. cloves
1½ cups brown sugar
½ cup soft margarine
¾ cup cooked pumpkin
¼ cup milk
2 eggs

Mix ingredients. Turn batter into a greased 13x9x2-inch pan. Bake at 350°F. for 35-40 minutes. Cool in pan and ice.

Salisbury, N.B.
Ladies Auxiliary
Branch No. 31

Gingerbread Apricot Upside-Down Cake

2 tbsp. butter
½ cup brown sugar, firmly packed
1 can apricot halves, drained
1 pkg. gingerbread mix or a batch of your own homemade gingerbread
whipped cream

Melt butter on top of stove in a 9-inch cake pan. Remove from heat, and spread brown sugar evenly over the pan, pressing it into the butter. Place a layer of apricot halves on top of the sugar. Prepare gingerbread batter and pour into the pan over the apricots. Bake for about 30 minutes, or until the cake is done, at 350°F. Remove from oven and while still warm, turn out on a large plate so that the topping comes easily out of the pan. Serve garnished with whipped cream. You may replace the apricots with peach halves or pineapple rings.

Yarmouth, N.S.
Ladies Auxiliary
Branch No. 61

Banana Cake

½ cup butter
1 cup sugar
2 eggs, beaten
1 tsp. baking soda
4 tsp. boiling water
1 cup mashed bananas
2 cups sifted pastry flour
1 tsp. baking powder
½ tsp. salt
1 cup chopped nuts
1 tsp. vanilla

Cream butter and sugar; add beaten eggs. Dissolve baking soda in boiling water and add mashed bananas. Sift together flour, baking powder and salt. (Add alternately with banana mixture.) Add nuts and vanilla last. Bake at 350°F. for 40 minues in a greased 8-inch square pan.

Boiestown, N.B.
Ladies Auxiliary
Normandy Branch No. 78

Date Almond Cake

Part I:

½ cup butter
2 egg yolks
1 tsp. baking powder
½ cup white sugar
1½ cups flour
1 tsp. vanilla

Part II:

1 cup chopped dates and raisins
½ cup water

Part III:

2 egg whites
chopped almonds or walnuts
1 cup brown sugar

Mix Part I and spread on greased pan. Cook together ingredients in Part II till thick. When nearly cool, spread over first part. Beat egg whites from Part III until stiff. Slowly beat in brown sugar. Cover cake with this and sprinkle with chopped almonds. Bake at 325°-350°F. for 30 to 35 minutes.

Domain, Man.
Ladies Auxiliary
Branch No. 208

Anna's Blueberry Cake

½ cup butter
1 cup sugar
2 eggs
1 cup milk
2½ cups flour (scant)
1 tsp. baking soda
2 tsp. cream of tartar
1 tsp. salt
1 pint blueberries

Use ½ cup of the flour to coat the blueberries. Combine all ingredients except blueberries, adding these the last. Bake at 350°F. until done. Test with a toothpick.

Grand Harbour, N.B.
Ladies Auxiliary
Grand Manan Branch No. 44

Dream Cheese Cake

¼ cup butter
1 cup graham crumbs
   (16 large crackers)
1 tsp. cream of tartar
6 eggs, separated
19 oz. cream cheese
3 tbsp. flour
½ tsp. salt
1 pint sour dairy cream
1 tsp. vanilla

Have all ingredients at room temperature. Butter generously a 9″ round springform pan. Mix butter and crumbs. Reserve ¼ cup crumbs and press remainder in pan. Add cream of tartar to egg whites and beat till foamy. Add 3 tbsp. sugar and beat till stiff. Beat cheese till soft. Mix 1½ cups sugar, flour and salt. Blend into cheese. Add egg yolks, one at a time, beating thoroughly. Add sour cream and vanilla. Blend in egg whites and pour into pan. Sprinkle with reserved ¼ cup crumbs. Bake at 325° for 1¼ hours or till firm. Turn off heat and open oven door, leave in for 10 minutes longer. Remove from oven and let stand on rack away from drafts till cool. Chill.

Montreal, Que.
Ladies Auxiliary
Mazeppa Branch No. 183

Puffed Wheat Cake

⅓ cup butter and margarine
½ cup honey and syrup
1 cup brown sugar
1 tbsp. cocoa
1 tsp. vanilla
8 cups puffed wheat

Melt butter in saucepan; add sugar, syrup, cocoa and vanilla. When this bubbles remove from heat and pour over puffed wheat. Press down with wet hands (when hands are wet, puffed wheat will not stick).

Steinbach, Man.
Ladies Auxiliary
Steinbach Branch No. 190

Banana Cake

2¼ cups flour
1⅔ cups white sugar
1¼ tsp. baking powder
1¼ tsp. baking soda
1 tsp. salt
⅔ cup shortening
⅔ cup buttermilk or sour
   milk
3 eggs
1¼ cups mashed ripe bananas
⅔ cup fine chopped nuts

Beat together eggs, shortening and sugar. Sift together flour, baking powder, baking soda and salt. Combine all ingredients and beat 3 minutes on high speed. Grease and flour pan. Bake at 350°F. for 45 to 50 minutes. Makes a big cake.

Kelwood, Man.
Ladies Auxiliary
Branch No. 50

Lemon Cake

1 pkg. lemon Jello
1 cup hot water
1 lemon cake mix
¾ cup cooking oil
4 eggs
1 tsp. lemon juice
Glaze:
   2 cups icing sugar
   4 tbsp. Real Lemon juice

Mix Jello and hot water; cool.

Mix oil, cake mix and eggs. Beat till smooth. Then add lemon juice and Jello.

Bake at 350°F. for 35 to 40 minutes. After removing from oven, immediately punch holes in cake with a big fork. Pour glaze and spread over cake.

Fort Frances, Ont.
Ladies Auxiliary
Branch No. 29

Pumpkin Cupcakes

½ cup butter or margarine
1⅓ cups sugar
2 eggs, beaten until frothy
1 cup mashed, cooked, unseasoned pumpkin or winter squash
2¼ cups sifted all-purpose flour
3 tsp. baking powder
½ tsp. baking soda
½ tsp. salt
¾ tsp. ground ginger
½ tsp. ground cinnamon
½ tsp. ground nutmeg
¾ cup milk
¾ cup coarsely chopped pecans or walnuts

Cream butter and sugar until light, beat in eggs; then mix in pumpkin. Sift flour with baking powder, baking soda, salt and spices; add to creamed mixture alternately with milk, beginning and ending with dry ingredients. Mix in nuts.

Spoon into well-greased muffin tins, filling each about ¾ full. Bake at 375°F. for 25 to 30 minutes or until cupcakes begin to pull from sides of muffin tin and tops are springy to the touch. Cool cakes upright in their pans or wire racks for 5 minutes, then remove and cook to room temperature before serving. Frost or not, as you wish.

New Glasgow, N.S.
Ladies Auxiliary
Normandy Branch No. 34

Polka-Dater Cake

1 cup boiling water
1¼ cups chopped dates
1 cup butter
1¼ cups white sugar
1 tsp. vanilla
2 eggs
1¾ cups flour
1½ tsp. baking soda
½ cup chocolate chips
½ cup chocolate chips
½ cup chopped walnuts

Pour boiling water over dates. Mash, and allow to cool. Cream butter, sugar and vanilla. Beat in eggs. Sift together flour and baking soda; add to date mixture. Add ½ cup chocolate chips. Spread in a 15x10x1″ pan. Top with ½ cup chocolate chips and walnuts, just sprinkle them over the top. Bake at 350°F. for 35 minutes or until done.

Winnipeg, Man.
Ladies Auxiliary
Brooklands-Weston Branch No. 2

Lazy Daisy Cake

1 cup dates, cut fine
1 cup boiling water
Pour boiling water over dates and let stand till cool. Mix:
½ cup butter
1 egg, well beaten
1 cup white sugar
1½ cups flour
1 small tsp. baking soda
1 tsp. baking powder
1 tsp. vanilla
Topping:
¾ cup brown sugar
3 tbsp. butter
3 tbsp. cream
¼ cup walnuts
¼ cup coconut

Bake cake at 350°F. for 25 minutes. Boil topping mixture for 2 minutes. Spread on baked cake and return to oven. Brown 5 minutes.

Howick, Que.
Ladies Auxiliary
Howick Branch No. 123

Bangbelly

A Traditional
Christmas Eve Dish

3 cups cooked rice
1 cup flour
1 cup molasses
2 cups raisins
1¼ cups salt pork, cubed
1½ tsp. baking soda
1 tsp. baking powder
1 tsp. cinnamon
½ tsp. allspice
¼ tsp. cloves
¼ tsp. mixed spice

Allow rice to cool and add salt pork and molasses. Sift together flour and spices. Add raisins, mixing all ingredients together. Pour into 9″x9″ greased pans. Bake at 350°F. for 1¼ hours.

Springdale, Nfld.
Ladies Auxiliary
Branch No. 40

Poppy Seed Sponge Cake

1 cup boiling water
¼ cup poppy seeds
Soak 30 minutes to cool, stirring occasionally. Add this mixture to:
1 Duncan Hines Deluxe II Lemon cake mix
1-4 serving size Jello instant lemon pudding powder
4 eggs
½ cup cooking oil

Blend all ingredients, including poppy seed mixture; and mix 2 minutes at medium speed. Grease Bundt or Angel Food pan with oil and bake at 350°F. for 45 minutes. Unmold. Cover with the following glaze.

Glaze:
4 tbsp. lemon juice
⅓ cup icing sugar
Mix and brush on hot cake.

Langruth, Man.
Ladies Auxiliary
Branch No. 162

Harvey Wallbanger Cake

1 pkg. yellow cake mix
1 pkg. instant vanilla pudding
1 cup cooking oil
4 eggs
¼ cup vodka
¼ cup Galliano
¾ cup orange juice

Combine all ingredients and beat 4 minutes. Pour into a greased and floured Bundt pan. Bake at 350°F. for 45 to 50 minutes. Dust with sugar or frost with a thin orange glaze.

Hartney, Man.
Ladies Auxiliary
Branch No. 26

Strawberry Angel Cake

1 Angel Food cake, cut in 3 layers
2 egg whites
½ cup sugar
½ cup frozen strawberries

Beat egg whites till stiff, add sugar and strawberries. Fill cake with strawberry ice cream between layers. Ice with egg whites and strawberry mixture. Put in freezer and use as required.

Deloraine, Man.
Ladies Auxiliary
Branch No. 83

Sunshine Cake

(uncooked)

1 pkg. graham wafers, whole
½ cup brown sugar
2 cups chopped dates
¾ cup water

Combine sugar, dates and water. Cook for about 12 minutes. Place a layer of wafers, then date mixture in pan. Layer alternately until dates and wafers are all used. Spread with your favorite icing and refrigerate overnight. Cut in slices and serve.

Maple Creek, Sask.
Ladies Auxiliary
Branch No. 75

Cookie Sheet Cake

1 cup brown sugar
2 eggs
½ cup margarine
1½ cups flour
½ tsp. baking soda
½ tsp. baking powder
1 tsp. vanilla
1 cup raisins
¾ cup water
1 tsp. instant coffee
1 tsp. cinnamon

Boil together the raisins, water, instant coffe and cinnamon for 2 minutes; cool. Drain and reserve liquid. Add liquid alternately with flour, adding raisins last. Put in well-greased cookie sheet. Bake at 370°F. for 20 minutes. Ice with butter icing.

Lac du Bonnet, Man.
Ladies Auxiliary
Branch No. 164

Matrimonial Cake

1 lb. dates
2 cups cold water
cinnamon or nutmeg
Topping:
2 cups flour
½ lb. margarine
1 tsp. baking soda
2 cups rolled oats
1 cup brown sugar
½ tsp. salt

Boil dates until soft. Thicken with a small amount of cornstarch. Flavor with cinnamon or nutmeg.
Rub margarine, rolled oats, sugar and flour until crumbly. (Mix salt and baking soda with flour). Place half of mixture in a greased pan. Spread on date filling. Top with remaining mixture. Bake at 325°F. for 30 minutes. Pie fillings such as cherry, lemon or blueberry are also good.

Dominion City, Man.
Ladies Auxiliary
Roseau Valley Branch No. 160

Graham Wafer Cake

½ cup shortening
1 cup sugar
1 egg
2 cups graham wafer crumbs
1 cup milk
1 tsp. vanilla
1 cup coconut
½ tsp. salt

Cream shortening and sugar. Add egg and beat in dry ingredients alternately with milk. Bake in a greased and floured cake pan at 350°F. for 35 to 40 minutes or until cake springs back in the middle. This is a delicious moist cake.

Plum Point, Nfld.
Ladies Auxiliary
Branch No. 55

Good Neighbor Cake

1 cup rolled oats
1 cup boiling water
Let stand while rest of cake is being mixed.
1½ cups brown sugar
¼ cup margarine or butter
2 eggs
1½ tsp. vanilla
½ cup raisins
¼ cup chopped nuts
¼ tsp. nutmeg
1 tsp. cinnamon
1 cup flour
1 tsp. baking soda
½ tsp. baking powder

Mix ingredients together well. Add oat mixture and blend together well. Place in a greased 9x9" pan. Bake at 350°F. for 40 to 45 minutes or until done.

Icing:
1 cup brown sugar
1 tsp. margarine or butter
5 tbsp. milk
icing sugar
Boil sugar, margarine and milk together for 3 minutes. Remove from heat and add enough icing sugar for a spreading consistency.

Teulon, Man.
Ladies Auxiliary
Branch No. 166

Bourbon Pecan Cake

2 cups whole candied cherries
2 cups white seedless raisins
2 cups bourbon
2 cups butter or margarine
2 cups sugar
2 cups dark brown sugar, firmly packed
8 eggs, separated
5 cups flour
4 cups pecan halves
1½ tsp. salt
2 tsp. ground nutmeg

Combine cherries, raisins and bourbon in large bowl. Cover tightly and let stand overnight in fridge. Drain fruit and reserve bourbon. Place butter in large bowl and beat at medium speed till soft and fluffy. Add sugars gradually, beating on medium speed until well blended. Add egg yolks until well blended. Combine ½ cup flour with pecans. Sift remaining flour with baking powder, salt and nutmeg. Add 2 cups of flour mixture to the creamed mixture and mix thoroughly. Add reserved bourbon and remainder of flour mixture alternately ending with flour. Beat well after each addition. Beat egg whites until stiff but not dry; fold gently into cake batter. Add drained fruits and floured pecans, blend thoroughly. Grease cake pans, line with greased wax paper and flour. Pour cake batter to within one inch of top. Bake at 275°F. for 2-2½ hours, cool 2 to 3 hours, remove wax paper. Wrap in saturated bourbon cheese cloth and aluminum foil. Store in fridge for several weeks.

Houston, B.C.
Ladies Auxiliary
Branch No. 249

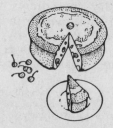

Eva's Blueberry Corn Cake

1 cup cornmeal
1 cup sifted all-purpose flour
¾ cup white sugar
½ tsp. salt
4 tsp. baking powder
1 egg
1 cup milk
¼ cup margarine
2 cups blueberries, fresh or
   frozen

Prepare a 9x13" pan. Measure dry ingredients. Add milk to cornmeal and let stand 10 to 15 minutes. Beat egg and add to creamed sugar and margarine mixture. Add flour and milk mixture alternately, beating well. Fold in blueberries. Bake at 325°F. for about 30 minutes or until golden brown. Serve hot with butter or lemon sauce. (For variery omit blueberries and use only ½ cup sugar. This is the "old-fashioned" corn cake.)

Chester Basin, N.S.
Ladies Auxiliary
Everett Branch No. 88

Sultana Cake

½ lb. butter
1 cup white sugar
3 eggs
2 cups all-purpose flour
½ tsp. baking powder
3 tbsp. milk
2 tsp. vanilla extract
1 tsp. lemon extract
1 lb. raisins

Soak raisins in boiling water until plump, then drain well. Cream butter and sugar till creamy. Add eggs and liquid. Beat in dry ingredients till smooth and creamy. Stir in raisins by hand. Put in loaf pan lined with well-greased layer of brown paper. Bake at 325°F. until done.

Lower Sackville, N.S.
Ladies Auxiliary
Calais Branch No. 162

Pumpkin Cake

2 cups sugar
⅔ cup Mazola oil
4 eggs
2 cups pumpkin
2 cups flour
1 cup nuts
1 tsp. cinnamon
½ tsp. cloves
2 tsp. baking powder
1 tsp. salt
1 cup chocolate chips
½ cup all bran

Bake in Angel Food pan at 350°F., testing for doneness with toothpick method.

Grand Harbour, N.B.
Ladies Auxiliary
Grand Manan Branch No. 44

Tomato Soup Cake

1 cup white sugar
½ cup butter
1 egg
1-10 oz. can tomato soup
1½ cups flour
1 cup raisins
½ cup walnuts
½ tsp. cinnamon
½ tsp. ginger
2 tsp. baking soda

Mix well. Bake at 350°F. for 40 minutes.

Digby, N.S.
Ladies Auxiliary
Branch No. 20

Blueberry Tea Cake

5 tbsp. shortening
1 cup sugar
2 eggs
3 tsp. baking powder
⅔ cup milk
1¾ cups flour
½ cup blueberries

Cream shortening, sugar and eggs; add flour and baking powder. Mix in the milk and stir well. Add blueberries, rolled in a little of the sugar and flour. Bake at 325°F. for 25 minutes.

New Perlican, Nfld.
Ladies Auxiliary
Branch No. 6

Tomato Soup Cake

2 tbsp. shortening
1½ cups white sugar
1 egg
1 can tomato soup
1 tsp. baking soda
1 tsp. cinnamon
1 tsp. nutmeg
½ tsp. cloves
1½ cups flour
1 cup raisins
1 cup chopped walnuts

Cream shortening and sugar together. Add egg, then soup with soda mixed into it. Add dry ingredients, then raisins and nuts. Bake in a greased tube pan at 350°F.

Morin Heights, Que.
Ladies Auxiliary
Branch No. 171

"Prairie Sunrise" Cake

½ cup butter or margarine
1½ cups white sugar
grated rind of ½ an orange
1 egg
1 egg yolk
2½ cups flour
¼ tsp. salt
4 tsp. baking powder
1 cup milk

Divide batter into two parts. To half the batter add 3 tbsp. cocoa and put in tube pan as marble cake. Bake at 350°F. for one hour. Make thin icing flavored with orange.

Stewiacke, N.S.
Ladies Auxiliary
Branch No. 70

Date Orange Cake

½ cup butter
1 cup fine sugar
1 egg
½ tsp. baking powder
2 cups flour
1 cup sour milk
1 tsp. baking soda
1 tbsp. warm water
½ or 1 cup chopped dates
½ cup grated orange rind
nuts (optional)

Dissolve baking soda in warm water. Combine all ingredients and bake at 350°F. for 30 minutes or until done.

Icing:
Juice of 1 orange
½ cup brown sugar

Pour icing over cake while cake is still warm.

Deloraine, Man.
Ladies Auxiliary
Branch No. 83

Pig Eating Good Cake

1 pkg. Duncan Hines yellow
cake mix
4 eggs
1 can mandarin oranges,
undrained
½ cup oil

Mix together and bake in large pan. Make frosting ahead of time and store in fridge until cake has cooled.

Frosting:
1 large Cool Whip
1 pkg. vanilla instant pudding
1 large can crushed pineapple, drained

Mix together all ingredients. This can be put on cake and left in fridge. Serve and cut individually as desired.

Grand Harbour, N.B.
Ladies Auxiliary
Grand Manan Branch No. 44

Holiday Ring Cake

1 cup butter, room temperature
1-8 oz. pkg. cream cheese, softened
1½ cups white sugar
1 tsp. vanilla
2 tsp. grated lemon rind (optional)
4 eggs
1¾ cups flour
1½ tsp. baking powder
½ cup seedless raisins
½ cup golden raisins
½ cup mixed candied fruit or peel
½ cup maraschino or candied cherries
½ cup chopped nuts
½ cup flour

Cream butter and cream cheese with electric mixer. Add sugar and cream well. Beat in vanilla and lemon rind. Add eggs, one at a time, beating well after each addition. Sift flour with baking powder and blend in. Combine fruit and nuts, toss with ¼ cup of the flour. Stir into batter. Pour into greased and floured 10-inch Bundt or tube pan. Bake at 300°F. for 70 to 80 minutes, or until toothpick inserted in center comes out clean. Cool in pan for about 10 minutes, then turn out on wire rack to cool completely.

Waverley, N.S.
Ladies Auxiliary
Dieppe Branch No. 90

Walnut Cake

½ cup shortening
1½ cups white sugar
4 egg whites
¾ cup milk
1 tsp. vanilla
1 cup chopped walnuts
½ tsp. salt
1⅔ cups flour
1 tsp. baking powder

Mix salt, flour and baking powder together in a bowl. Cream shortening and sugar. Add walnuts, milk and vanilla. Add

flour mixture. Beat egg whites until stiff and fold in batter. Bake at 350°F. for one hour in a funnel pan.

Donkin, N.S.
Ladies Auxiliary
Branch No. 5

Orange Cake

½ cup butter
1 cup white sugar
2 eggs
2 tbsp. orange rind
¼ cup orange juice and pulp
2¼ cups sifted flour
½ tsp. salt
2 tsp. baking powder
¾ tsp. baking soda
5/8 cup sour milk or buttermilk
⅓ cup chopped raisins or currants
⅓ cup chopped nutmeats

Cream butter until it is soft and creamy. Gradually add sugar and beat until mixture is light and fluffy. Beat eggs with rotary beater until foamy and add gradually to fat-sugar mixture, beating thoroughly. Add grated orange rind and juice and beat until well blended. Mix flour, salt, baking powder and baking soda and sift 4 or 5 times. Add dry ingredients alternately with milk, making 3 or 4 additions, beginning and ending with dry ingredients. Stir gently and quickly until batter is well blended, but do not overmix. Fold in fruit and nuts and spread carefully into a well greased 8 or 9 inch square cake pan. Bake at 350°F. for 40 to 50 minutes before removing from pan. Cool and serve plain or spread with orange flavored icing.

Grand Forks, B.C.
Ladies Auxiliary
Branch No. 59

Birthday Cake

1 cup shortening
2 cups white sugar
¾ cup boiling water
Mix well and add the following:
3 eggs
3 cups flour
Add 1 egg, then stir, add 1 cup flour, then stir. Repeat for remaining 2 eggs and 2 cups flour.
1 tsp. vanilla
2 tsp. baking powder
¾ cup milk

Mix well. Bake at 350°F. for 1-1½ hours. Makes a large cake.

Havelock, N.B.
Ladies Auxiliary
Branch No. 86

Pineapple Cake

¾ cup margarine
1 cup white sugar
3 eggs
½ each green and red cherries, floured
1-20 oz. can crushed pineapple, drained
1 lb. light raisins, floured
2½ cups flour
2 tsp. baking powder
½ tsp. salt

Mix in order given. Bake at 300°F. for 2 hours in round pans.

Sydney, N.S.
Ladies Auxiliary
Branch No. 128

Raw Apple Cake

½ cup butter or margarine
1 cup white sugar
1 egg, beaten
½ cup cold strong coffee
½ cup grated apple, not fine
½ cup raisins
¼ tsp. nutmeg
½ tsp. cinnamon
1 tsp. baking soda
½ cup nuts
1½ cups flour

Mix as for cake. Bake at 350°F. for 45 minutes. Ice with butter icing which has been flavored with coffee. Use a 7x11-inch pan.

Selkirk, Man.
Ladies Auxiliary
Branch No. 42

Eggless, Milkless Butterless Cake

(Vintage WWI)

1 cup water
2 cups raisins
1 tsp. cinnamon
½ tsp. cloves
1 cup brown sugar
⅓ cup lard
¼ tsp. nutmeg
¼ tsp. salt
Place all ingredients in a saucepan and mix. Place on heat and bring to a boil. Cook 3 minutes. Allow to cool, then add:
2 cups flour
1 tsp. baking soda
½ tsp. baking powder
Flour, baking soda and baking powder should all be sifted together. Place in a greased loaf pan and bake at 350°F. for one hour.

Murdochville, Que.
Ladies Auxiliary
Branch No. 218

Wind Cake

1½ cups flour
1 tsp. baking powder
½ tsp. salt
3 egg yolks
¾ cup cold water
1¼ cups white sugar
3 egg whites
1½ tsp. vanilla

Preheat oven to 325°F. Sift together flour, baking powder and salt. Beat egg yolks till frothy in a large bowl. Add water, beat till bowl is nearly full of liquid and bubbles are small. (About 5 minutes at high speed). Add sugar slowly, beating after each addition. Add sifted ingredients slowly, beating constantly. Beat egg whites till stiff, but not dry. Add to batter then add vanilla. Fold in gently and pour into a 10-inch tube pan. Bake about 50 minutes.

Riding Mountain, Man.
Ladies Auxiliary
Branch No. 202

Bundt Apple Cake

1 cup oil
1½ cups sugar
3 cups flour
2½ tsp. vanilla
4 eggs
¼ cup orange juice
3 tsp. baking powder
½ tsp. salt
Filling:
5 or more apples, diced
2 tsp. cinnamon
5 tbsp. white sugar

Put half of batter in greased Bundt pan. Add the apple mixture, then rest of batter. Bake at 350°F. for 45 to 55 minutes.

Winnipeg, Man.
Ladies Auxiliary
General Monash BranchNo. 115

Vegetable Cake

1 cup vegetable oil
3 egg yolks
1½ cups white sugar
3 tbsp. boiling water
vanilla
Beat with electric mixer. Beat well and add:
1 cup raw carrots, grated
1 cup raw beets, grated
2 cups flour
2 tsp. baking powder
1 tsp. salt
1 tsp. cinnamon
½ cup nuts (optional)
Blend together well and add:
3 egg whites, beaten stiff
Pour batter into a 9x12 or 9x15-inch pan. Bake at 350°F. for 45 minutes. Cover with icing.
Icing:
4 oz. or 250 g. cream cheese
1 tsp. vanilla
3 tbsp. butter
1⅓ cups icing sugar (as needed)
Beat together for 3 minutes and spread over cake. Will ice a 9x12 or 9x15 cake.

Minto, Man.
Ladies Auxiliary
Branch No. 201

Banana Gumdrop Cake

1¾ cups flour
½ tsp. baking soda
1½ tsp. baking powder
¾ tsp. salt
½ cup gumdrops, cut small
1 egg, beaten
¼ cup oil
½ cup sugar
1 cup mashed bananas
½ cup milk
2 tsp. grated orange rind

Mix together the first four ingredients in bowl. Stir in gumdrop pieces. Combine remaining ingredients. Stir into dry mixture until blended. Bake in a greased loaf pan at 350°F. for about 50 minutes.

Gladstone, Man.
Ladies Auxiliary
Branch No. 110

Marble Cake

1 cup or ½ lb. margarine
2 cups sugar
4 eggs, separated
2 tsp. vanilla
3 cups all-purpose flour
3 tsp. baking powder
¼ tsp. salt
1 cup milk or juice
½ cup canned chocolate syrup
¼ cup creme de cacao liqueur

Cream margarine and sugar until light and fluffy. Add egg yolks, one at a time, beating well after each addition. Stir in vanilla. Add sifted dry ingredients alternately with liquid, beginning and ending with dry. Beat egg whites till stiff, and fold into batter. Pour half the batter into a second bowl. Add syrup and liqueur. Spoon both batters into prepared tube pan, alternating layers of white and dark. Draw a knife through batter several times to marbelize. Bake at 350°F. for one hour.

Montreal, Que.
Ladies Auxiliary
Mazeppa Branch No. 183

Peach Cake

1 cup butter
1½ cups white sugar
3 eggs
1-19 oz. can peaches, drained
2 tsp. vanilla
3 cups flour
1 tsp. baking powder
½ tsp. salt
2 cups raisins
1½ cups cherries, cut up
1 cup coconut

Cream butter and sugar. Add eggs, one at a time. Beat well after each. Add drained peaches and vanilla. Add flour, baking powder and salt, sifted together. Add fruit. Mix raisins and cherries with a little of the 3 cups flour to prevent sinking. Bake at 275°F. for one hour, raise temperature to 300°F. and continue baking one hour longer.

Louisbourg, N.S.
Ladies Auxiliary
Branch No. 62

Dark Chocolate Cake

2 cups sugar
1¾ cups all-purpose flour
¾ cup Hershey's cocoa
2 tsp. baking soda
1 tsp. baking powder
½ tsp. salt
2 eggs
1 cup buttermilk or sour milk
1 cup strong black coffee
½ cup vegetable oil
1 tsp. vanilla

Combine first six ingredients in a large mixing bowl. Add remaining ingredients and beat at medium speed for 2 minutes. Batter will be thin. Pour into a greased and floured 13x9x2-inch pan. Bake at 350°F. for 35 to 40 minutes.

Salisbury, N.B.
Ladies Auxiliary
Branch No. 31

Jelly Roll

3 eggs, beaten
1 cup white sugar
3 tbsp. milk
1 scant cup flour
2 tsp. baking powder
¼ tsp. salt
1 tsp. vanilla or lemon extract

Mix and pour into wax paper lined 9x13-inch pan and bake at 400°F. for about 12 minutes. When done, turn onto a dish cloth sprinkled with icing sugar and trim the long edges of roll. Spead with jam or lemon pie filling. Roll in cloth and leave until set. Remove cloth and slice.

New Glasgow, N.S.
Ladies Auxiliary
Normany Branch No. 34

Marshmallow Chocolate Cake

¼ lb. miniature marshmallows
2 squares unsweetened chocolate
½ cup hot water
1½ cups sifted flour
1 tsp. baking soda
1 tsp. salt
2 eggs, beaten
1 cup white sugar
1 cup sour cream
1 tsp. vanilla

Melt marshmallows and chocolate, add hot water, stir to a smooth paste. Cool. Sift flour, baking soda and salt, twice. Beat eggs, add sugar, whip until creamy. Add sour cream, stir till smooth. Fold in flour mixture gradually. Carefully fold in marshmallow and chocolate paste. Add vanilla. Turn batter into 8-inch layer cake pans. Bake at 375°F. for 30 to 35 minutes.

Fairview, Alta.
Ladies Auxiliary
Branch No. 84

Chocolate Cherry Refrigerator Cake

1 pkg. cherry Jello (4 serving size)
1 pkg. chocolate cake mix
1 envelope whipped topping mix
1 pkg. chocolate instant pudding (4 serving size)
1½ cups cold milk

Dissolve Jello in ¾ cup boiling water, add ½ cup cold water. Set aside. Mix and bake cake in a 13x9x2-inch pan. Cool 20 to 25 minutes. Poke deep holes about 1 inch apart in cake with large meat fork. Pour Jello mixture in holes. Refrigerate while preparing topping. In chilled bowl, blend and whip topping. Mix instant pudding and cold milk until stiff, 3 to 8 minutes. Combine whipped topping and pudding. Frost and store cake in refrigerator.

Elgin, Man.
Ladies Auxiliary
Branch No. 216

Mix-Easy Chocolate Cake

⅓ cup vegetable oil
2 squares (2 oz.) Baker's unsweetened chocolate
¾ cup water
1 cup sugar
1 egg
1¼ cups all-purpose flour
½ tsp. salt
½ tsp. baking soda
1 tsp. vanilla
1-6 oz. pkg. semi-sweet chocolate chips
⅓ cup chopped nuts

Heat oil and chocolate in 8-inch square pan, at 350°F. for about 4 minutes. Add water, sugar, egg, flour, salt, baking soda and vanilla. Beat with fork until smooth, about 2 minutes. Spread evenly in pan. Sprinkle with chocolate chips and chopped nuts. Bake at 350°F. for 40 minutes or until cake tester inserted in middle comes out clean.

Frobisher, Sask.
Ladies Auxiliary
Branch No. 343

Easy Mix Chocolate Cake

2 cups sugar
2¼ cups flour
½ cup cocoa
1½ tsp. baking soda
1½ tsp. baking powder
¾ tsp. salt
¾ cup oil
3 eggs, unbeaten
1½ tsp. vanilla
1½ cups milk

Mix dry ingredients in bowl. Make a well in centre of mixture. Put remaining ingredients into well in dry mixture. Beat well with beater or spoon. Pour into a well greased 9x13-inch pan and bake for 35 to 40 minutes.

Piney, Man.
Ladies Auxiliary
Branch No. 176

Chocolate Poppy Seed Bundt Cake

1 cup buttermilk
½ cup poppy seeds
½ cup butter
½ cup Crisco shortening
1½ cups sugar
4 eggs, separated
2½ cups flour
1 tsp. baking soda
2 tsp. baking powder
1 tsp. vanilla
1-6 oz. pkg. chocolate chips
1 tbsp. sugar
1 tbsp. cinnamon

Cream butter, Crisco and sugar. Add egg yolks. Blend well. Sift in dry ingredients. Add vanilla and poppy seeds. Beat egg whites until stiff and fold into batter. Place half of batter in well greased Bundt pan or tube pan. Add chips, sprinkle with sugar and cinnamon. Add remaining batter. Bake at 350°F. for one hour.

Gilbert Plains, Man.
Ladies Auxiliary
Branch No. 98

Date and Walnut Cake

1 lb. dates
1 cup walnuts
1 cup white sugar
1 cup butter or margarine
2 eggs
1½ cups flour
1 tsp. baking soda
1 tsp. vanilla
1 cup water

Cream butter and sugar, add eggs. Pour in cold water, then add flour, baking soda, vanilla chopped dates and walnuts. Pour in layer pans. Bake at 350°F. for one hour. This is an old recipe, but a very nice moist cake.

Woodlands, Man.
Ladies Auxiliary
Branch No. 248

Chocolate Chip Cake

Topping:
½ cup soft butter
2 tbsp. brown sugar
⅔ cup chopped walnuts

Mix until crumbly and spoon into well greased and floured 10-inch flutted pan. Chill.

Batter:
2¾ cups flour
2 tsp. baking powder
1 tsp. salt
1 tbsp. vinegar
milk
1 tsp. vanilla
1 cup soft butter
1 cup brown sugar
4 eggs
1-12 oz. pkg. chocolate chips

Combine dry ingredients in sifter and set aside. Cream butter, sugar and vanilla until fluffy. Add milk and flour mixture alternately with butter mixture; fold in chips. Pour in pan over topping. Cook at 375°F. for one hour. Loosen edges of cake and invert.

Penticton, B.C.
Ladies Auxiliary
Branch No. 40

Chocolate Cake
(large)

1 cup butter or margarine (250 ml)
2 cups white sugar (500 ml)
4 eggs
8 tbsp. cocoa (120 ml)
2 tbsp. vanilla (30 ml)
1 cup milk (250 ml)
3 cups flour (750 ml)
2 tsp. baking powder (10 ml)
1½ cups hot water
2 tsp. baking soda

Add baking soda to hot water and set aside. Mix together remaining ingredients, then add the hot water. Add the cocoa to the hot water also. Bake in a moderate oven. Makes a large cake.

Strathmore, Alta.
Ladies Auxiliary
Branch No. 10

Carrot Cake

1½ cups oil
2 cups sugar
4 eggs
2 cups flour
2 tsp. baking soda
2 tsp. baking powder
½ tsp. cloves
½ tsp. nutmeg
4 tsp. cinnamon
1 tsp. salt
3 cups grated carrots

Beat oil and sugar well. Add eggs, one at a time, beating well after each addition. Add dry ingredients. Fold in carrots. Bake in a greased funnel pan at 350°F. for one hour.

Icing
¼ cup butter
4 oz. cream cheese
1 tsp. vanilla
1 cup icing sugar

Cream butter and cream cheese, add vanilla and icing sugar. Put on cake after it is cold.

Milltown, Bay D'Espoir, Nfld.
Ladies Auxiliary
Centennial Branch No. 61

Lazy Black Forest Cake

1 chocolate cake mix
½ cup brandy
1 can cherry pie filling

Mix cake. Add brandy to cherry pie filling. Place half of cake mix in 9x12-inch pan and put cherry pie filling over cake mix. Add remaining cake mix. Bake. Ice with whipped cream 3 hours before serving.

Slave Lake, Alta.
Ladies Auxiliary
Branch No. 110

Black Forest Cake

Chocolate Sponge Cake:
6 eggs
¾ cup sugar
1 tsp. vanilla
1 cup flour
1 tsp. baking powder
3 tbsp. Nestles Quick

Beat egg whites until stiff and set aside. Beat egg yolks with water, sugar and vanilla until creamy. Fold in sifted flour, baking powder and Nestles Quick. Fold in egg whites. Bake in spring form pan at 350°F. for 30 to 35 minutes. Cool for about 2 hours. Drain 2-16 oz. cans of red pitted cherries and soak in ¼ cup of Kirsch water. Let stand 2 hours.
Cut cake in two layers. Cover bottom half with cherries. Save 14-16 cherries for garnish. Sprinkle cherry juice and Kirsch water over both layers.
Beat 2-½ pints whipping cream. Add 3 tbsp. sugar and 1 envelope gelatin. Spread ¾ of whipped cream over cherries. Cover with top layer of cake.
Put 4 tbsp. whipped cream in piping bag and set aside. Spread remaining whipped cream over top and sides of cake. Sprinkle with chocolate shavings. Pipe small rosettes around edges and garnish with cherries. Refrigerate for several hours.

Red Rock, Ont.
Ladies Auxiliary
Branch No. 226

Coconut Cake

1 cup shredded coconut
1 cup milk
2 cups white sugar
¾ cup butter
1 tsp. vanilla
3 eggs, beaten
2½ cups flour
1 tsp. salt
1 tsp. baking powder
½ cup maraschino cherries (optional)

Soak coconut in milk for 10 minutes. Cream sugar and shortening together. Add vanilla and eggs. Sift dry ingredients together and add alternately with coconut mixture. Bake in tube pan at 325°F. for 50 minutes.

Joggins, N.S.
Ladies Auxiliary
Branch No. 4

Carrot Cake

1½ cups brown sugar
¾ cup plus 2 tbsp. vegetable oil
1 tsp. salt
1 tbsp. cinnamon
4 beaten eggs
2 tsp. baking soda
2 cups grated carrots
1½ cups whole wheat flour
1 tsp. nutmeg

Combine sugar, eggs, oil and carrots; add sifted dry ingredients; mix well. Grease and flour tube pan and bake at 350°F. for one hour. Cool on rack 20 minutes before removing from pan.

Frosting (optional)
3 oz. cream cheese
Juice of 1 orange
grated rind of ½ orange

Soften cream cheese and combine with orange juice and rind. Spread on cake and garnish with mandarin orange slices.

Hopewell, N.S.
Ladies Auxiliary
Branch No. 137

Never Fail Chocolate Cake

3 cups flour
1 tsp. salt
2 tsp. baking soda
2 cups sugar
6 tbsp. cocoa
10 tbsp. oil
2 tbsp. vinegar
2 tsp. vanilla
2 cups cold water

Mix dry ingredients together in bowl, make three holes and put oil in one, vinegar in another and vanilla in the last one. Pour cold water over all of it and stir. Bake at 350° to 375°F. for one hour.

Vavenby and District, B.C.
Ladies Auxiliary
Branch No. 259

Tropical Fruit Cake

1 cup butter
1 cup white sugar
2 eggs, well beaten
1 tbsp. glycerine
1 tsp. almond extract
1 tsp. vanilla extract
1 tsp. lemon extract
1½ tsp. salt
½ cup milk

Mix first nine ingredients in given order. Mix the following in a large pan. The fruit and nuts are all left whole, except the pineapple.
¼ lb. walnuts
¼ lb. brazil nuts
¼ lb. filberts
¼ lb. pecans
8 oz. red maraschino cherries, well drained
8 oz. green maraschino cherries, well drained
2 cups white raisins
3 slices glazed pineapple (one each of green, red and yellow)
Sift together:
2 cups white all-purpose flour
1 tsp. baking powder
Sift flour and baking powder over fruits and nuts and add to first mixture. Bake at 250°F. for 2 to 2½ hours. Bake in a well lined pan (about 10x10) or a large tube pan. The glycerine softens the nuts, so you can cut through them without any trouble.

Campobello, N.B.
Ladies Auxiliary
Branch No. 83

Hot Milk Sponge Cake

This almost-sponge cake is an easily remembered recipe, made with readily available ingredients. It freezes to perfection, so keep a few handy.

2 eggs
1 cup sugar
1 tsp. vanilla
1 cup all-purpose flour
1/8 tsp. salt
3 tbsp. butter
1 tsp. baking powder
½ cup boiling milk

If using rotary beater, beat eggs well, then add sugar and vanilla and continue beating about 5 minutes until very light. With an electric mixer, place unbeaten eggs, sugar and vanilla in bowl and beat 5 to 7 minutes at high speed. Success depends on sugar being well dissolved. Blend flour, salt, baking powder, then add all at once to eggs and just mix. Melt butter in boiling milk, pour over all at once and beat just enough to mix. Pour into a well greased 8x8-inch cake pan and bake at 350°F. for 30 minutes or until golden brown.

Icing for Sponge Cake
4 tbsp. butter or margarine
3 tbsp. canned milk or cream
1 cup brown sugar
1 cup coconut

Blend over low heat until sugar is dissolved. Spread on cake and put in oven for just a minute.

The Pas, Man.
Ladies Auxiliary
Branch No. 19

Prize Winning Carrot Cake

(Chatelaine
2nd Prize Winner)

4 egg yolks, reserve whites
1 cup Mazola oil
1 cup white sugar
1 tsp. vanilla
1¾ cups flour
2 cups finely grated carrots
1 cup raisins
1 cup almonds
2 tsp. baking powder
¼ tsp. baking soda
¼ tsp. salt
beaten egg whites

Beat egg yolks, add sugar and beat well. Add oil, grated carrots, vanilla and salt. Beat well. Add flour, baking powder, and baking soda. Mix until smooth, then add raisins and almonds. Blend in stiffly beaten egg whites. Bake in Angel Food pan at 375°F. for one hour. Remove cake and spread with topping.

Topping:
2 tbsp. butter
½ cup brown sugar
¼ cup finely chopped nuts
2 tbsp. milk

Return to cake and bake 15 minutes.

Montreal, Que.
Ladies Auxiliary
Mazeppa Branch No. 183

Miracle Whip Chocolate Cake

1 cup Miracle Whip
1 cup cold water
1 cup white sugar
1 tsp. vanilla
2 cups flour
½ cup cocoa
1 tsp. baking soda
2 tsp. baking powder
1 tsp. salt

Mix dry ingredients together, then add Miracle Whip and cold water. Pour into a 8x12-inch pan. Bake at 350°F. for 35 minutes.

Oxford, N.S.
Ladies Auxiliary
Oxford Branch No. 36

Zucchini Chocolate Cake

2½ cups flour
½ cup cocoa
1½ tsp. baking soda
1½ tsp. baking powder
1 tsp. salt
2 tsp. cinnamon
¾ cup oil
1 cup brown sugar
1 cup white sugar
2 tsp. vanilla
2 cups grated zucchini (peeled or unpeeled, take out seeds)
½ cup milk
3 eggs
1 cup chopped nuts (optional)
3 tsp. orange peel (optional)

Blend dry ingredients. Grease Bundt cake pan. Beat oil, sugar and eggs. Add vanilla and zucchini. Add dry ingredients alternately with milk. Bake at 350°F. for one hour.

Kelwood, Man.
Ladies Auxiliary
Branch No. 50

Fast 'n Fabulous Fruitcake

2½ cups flour
1 tsp. baking soda
2 eggs, slightly beaten
1-28 oz. jar or 3 cups mincemeat
1 can Eagle Brand sweetened condensed milk
2 cups mixed candied fruit
1 cup walnuts, chopped

Preheat oven to 300°F. Grease a 9-inch tube pan, line with wax paper and grease again. Sift together flour and baking soda and set aside. In larger bowl, combine eggs, mincemeat, milk, fruit and nuts. Add dry ingredients and blend well.
Pour into prepared pan. Bake 1 hour and 50 minutes or until cake tests done. Cool 15 minutes. Turn out of pan and remove wax paper. Garnish with glazed cherries, if desired.

Sydney, N.S.
Ladies Auxiliary
Branch No. 12

Dark Fruit Cake

¾ cup white sugar
1 cup molasses
4 eggs
1 cup shortening
1 lb. raisins
1 lb. dates
1 lb. currants
1 cup mixed peel
¼ lb. chopped walnuts
1 cup milk
1 tsp. cloves
1 tsp. cassia
1 tsp. allspice
vanilla extract
lemon extract
2 tsp. baking soda
1 tsp. salt
flour

Cream sugar, molasses and shortening together. Mix together the fruit and add to first mixture. Add baking soda and salt to milk. Add milk and spices. Add remaining ingredients and stir well. Add flour until quite stiff. Fill baking pans half full. Bake until done, abour 2 hours in a moderate oven.

Caledonia, N.S.
Ladies Auxiliary
A.L. Patterson Branch No. 87

Chocolate Cake

½ cup rolled oats
1 cup boiling water
½ cup butter or margarine
1½ cups brown sugar
¼ tsp. salt
2 eggs
2 tbsp. cocoa
1 tsp. vanilla
1 cup flour
1 tsp. baking soda
1 tsp. baking powder

Pour boiling water over rolled oats, put in butter and sugar. Beat eggs and add. Add dry ingredients and mix well. Bake at 325°F. for 45 minutes. Cake is done when toothpick inserted in centre comes out dry.

Tantallon, N.S.
Ladies Auxiliary
St. Margaret's Bay Branch No. 116

Light Fruit Cake

10 large eggs
4 cups white sugar
3 cups melted butter (1½ lbs.)
4 cups fresh or frozen orange juice
2 cups milk
¾ tsp. cinnamon
¾ tsp. allspice
2 tsp. soda
8 cups flour
3 lbs. bleached sultanas
2 lbs. currants
½ lb. glazed cherries
1½ lb. glazed pineapple
1 lb. walnuts
1 lb. blanched almonds

Blend butter, sugar and add beaten eggs. Add fruit and milk. Mix 2 cups flour over fruit to coat. Bake at 325°F. for 3 hours, or less for small cakes.

Oak Lake, Man.
Ladies Auxiliary

Bishop's Bread
(Economy Fruit Cake)

1½ cups flour
1 tsp. baking powder
pinch salt
4 eggs, well beaten
1 small can crushed pineapple and juice
½ cup margarine
scant cup sugar

Cream margarine and sugar well. Add beaten eggs and pineapple and juice. Blend well. Add flour, baking powder and salt; blend well. The following can be added to the batter:
small container glazed mixed peel or fruit and ½ cup raisins
or
½ cup coconut; ½ cup walnuts or chopped cherries
or
½ cup chopped dates

Pour batter in greased loaf pan and bake at 275° to 300°F. for 1 to 2 hours, or until tester comes out clean. This recipe is easily doubled. Keeps well, and also freezes well.

Oak Lake, Man.
Ladies Auxiliary
Branch No. 79

Tutti Frutti Cake

8 oz. prunes
1¾ cups seedless raisins
4 oz. pkg. cut citron
2 tsp. cinnamon
½ tsp. cloves
1 cup prune cooking liquid
1 cup liquid honey
1 cup sugar
1 cup coarsely broken walnuts
1½ tsp. salt
2 cups water
1-8 oz. pkg. cut mixed candied fruit
½ cup sliced candied cherries
1 tsp. mace
½ tsp. allspice
½ cup orange juice
1 cup soft shortening
4 eggs
5 cups sifted all-purpose flour
1¼ tsp. baking soda

Put prunes in medium saucepan and add water. Bring to a boil, turn down heat, cover and simmer until prunes are tender, about 30 minutes. Drain and cool both prunes and cooking liquid. Measure out 1 cup cooking liquid called for in recipe. Cut up prunes, discarding pits. Combine cut prunes with raisins, citron, mixed fruit, cherries, spices, prune liquid, orange juice and honey in a large bowl. Mix to blend well and let stand at room temperature 2 hours.

Heat oven to 300°F. Grease 3 9x5x3-inch loaf pans and line with greased heavy brown paper.

Beat shortening and sugar together well. Add eggs, one at a time, and beat well after each addition. Add this mixture to fruit mixture along with walnuts. Sift dry ingredients together and add. Blend well. Spoon batter evenly into 3 prepared pans. Bake 1½ to 1¾ hours or until a toothpick inserted in centre of cakes comes out clean. Lift out of pans and cook on racks. Strip off paper when cool and wrap cakes in heavy aluminum foil. Best if allowed to mellow a few days before cutting. Note: This is a medium fruit cake with just enough fruit to make it interesting. It's not too rich to serve with tea at any time of year.

Chatequguay, Que.
Ladies Auxiliary
Chateauguay Branch No. 108

Friendship Cake

1½ cups apricot brandy
7½ cups white sugar
1 qt. sliced canned peaches with syrup
1-19 oz. can pineapple chunks with syrup
3-9 oz. jars maraschino cherries, drained and halved
4 boxes white or yellow supermoist cake mix with pudding in the mix
16 eggs
1½ cups oil
4 cups chopped nuts

Put apricot brandy, 2½ cups sugar and the peaches in a gallon jar (no lid). Combine. Stir daily for 10 days. Keep at room temperature. Cover jar with saran wrap. Don't cover tight, as mixture ferments and must be able to breath. 10th day: Add 2½ cups white sugar, pineapple and juice. Stir daily for 10 days. 20th day: Add 2½ cups white sugar, maraschino cherries. Stir once a day for 10 days. 30th day: Make cake. Drain juice from fruit and reserve juice.

Use 2 boxes of cake mix to flour the fruit. Make a batter with the remaining 2 boxes of cake mix, beaten eggs and oil; add the fruit and nuts. Put in loaf pans and bake at 350°F. (or a little lower) for 60 to 75 minutes. Do not open oven while baking.

The reserved juice can be divided in equal portions of 1½ cups each. Use this culture to give to your friends as a starter for their cakes, hence the name friendship cake. (Culture instead of brandy). Makes 5-7 loaves. Freezes well.

Cumberland, B.C.
Ladies Auxiliary
Branch No. 28

Coffee Fruit Cake

1 cup shortening
2 cups brown sugar
4 eggs
1 cup strong coffee
1 tsp. baking soda
1 cup molasses
4 cups flour
1 tsp. salt
1 tsp. cloves
1 tsp. nutmeg
2 tsp. cinnamon
1 lb. currants
1 lb. raisins
½ cup red cherries
½ cup green cherries

Cream sugar and shortening together. Add eggs, one at a time, blending in thoroughly. Stir in coffee. Add baking soda mixed with molasses. Mix and sift flour, salt and spices. Add enough of the flour mixture to keep it from sticking together. Add the remainder to the first mixture. Add fruit and mix thoroughly. Line bottom of a large pan with several layers of greased brown paper and grease sides of pan. Pour in the cake batter and bake at 250°F. for 2 to 3 hours. A small pan of water in the oven helps to keep the cake from burning during the long cooking.

Lockeport, N.S.
Ladies Auxiliary
Branch No. 80

Brown Sugar Frosting

½ cup brown sugar
4 tbsp. cream
3 tbsp. margarine
1⅔ cups icing sugar
1 tsp. vanilla
2 tbsp. peanut butter (optional)

Boil together first three ingredients; then add remaining ingredients.

Perth Andover, N.B.
Ladies Auxiliary
Branch No. 36

Banana Carrot Cake

½ cup butter or margarine
2 eggs
1 tsp. baking soda
¼ tsp. salt
1 cup grated carrot
¾ cup light brown sugar, firmly packed
2 cups unsifted all-purpose flour
½ tsp. baking powder
1 cup mashed ripe bananas (3 medium size)
½ cup dark raisins
½ tsp. cinnamon
confectioner's sugar (optional)

Grease a 9-inch square baking pan and set aside. Cream butter and sugar until light and fluffy in a large bowl. In small bowl, mix together flour, baking soda, baking powder, cinnamon and salt. Blend in flour mixture alternately with mashed bananas beginning and ending with dry ingredients. Fold in carrot and raisins. Turn into prepared baking pan. Bake at 350°F. for about 45 minutes or until cake tester inserted in center comes out clean. Cool 10 minutes and turn out of pan and cool completely. Sprinkle with confectioner's sugar, if desired.

Whitehorse, Yukon
Ladies Auxiliary
Branch No. 254

No Cook Icing

1 cup white sugar
1 unbeaten egg white
1 tsp. vanilla
¼ tsp. cream of tartar
½ cup boiling water

Beat all ingredients together until stiff. This recipe makes enough icing for a large angel or chiffon cake. It is like a boiled icing, and never fails.

Ear Falls, Ont.
Ladies Auxiliary
Branch No. 238

Wedding Cake
(Three Layers)

12 eggs
1 lb. butter
1½ cups brown sugar
1¼ cups white sugar
1 tsp. vanilla
1 tsp. lemon extract
½ lb. cherries
3 lbs. raisins
½ lb. almonds
¼ lb. walnuts
½ lb. peel or glazed fruit
1 lb. dates
1 lb. currants
1 tsp. salt
1 tsp. mace
2 tsp. cinnamon
¼ tsp. nutmeg
1 tsp. baking soda
2 tsp. cream of tartar
5 cups white flour

Prepare 3 deep cake pans by lining with brown paper; grease well. Mix fruit with 1 cup of the flour. Cream butter, sugar, eggs and add remaining ingredients. Add to the fruit mixture; mix well. Bake for several hours (depending on size of cake pan). Test with straw.

Penticton, B.C.
Ladies Auxiliary
Branch No. 40

Creamy White Frosting

2 tbsp. cold water
4½ tbsp. white sugar
2½ cups icing sugar
⅔ cup shortening
1 tsp. vanilla
salt
1 egg

Mix cold water and sugar. Heat to dissolve sugar. Place icing sugar, egg and shortening in bowl and beat. Add first mixture and vanilla. Beat. Store in refrigerator. May be kept for 2 to 3 months.

Salisbury, N.B.
Ladies Auxiliary
Branch No. 31

Orange Icing

¼ cup soft margarine
1 tbsp. grated orange rind
1 egg yolk
2 tsp. orange juice
1½-2 cups icing sugar

Beat until smooth and fluffy. Use just enough icing sugar to make a good spreading consistency. Spread on cooled cake.

Hartney, Man.
Ladies Auxiliary
Branch No. 26

Peppermint Icing

2½ tbsp. flour
½ cup milk
½ cup sugar
½ cup soft margarine or butter
1 tsp. peppermint extract
2-3 drops desired food coloring (optional)

Combine flour and milk in a small saucepan. Cook over medium heat until mixture is very thick, stirring constantly. Cool. In small mixing bowl, beat sugar and butter at high speed until light and fluffy , about 3 minutes. Gradually add flour mixture and continue beating at high speed 3 minutes until it is the consistency of whipped cream. Blend in flavoring and food coloring.

Saskatoon, Sask.
Ladies Auxiliary
L.A. Nutana Branch No. 362

Bubbly Icing

½ cup melted butter
1 cup brown sugar
4 tsp. evaporated milk
1 cup corn flakes
¾ cup coconut

Mix and spread on cake when baked. Place in oven until bubbly.

Oak Lake, Man.
Ladies Auxiliary
Branch No. 79

Yukon Whipped Cream

2 egg whites
½ cup icing sugar
1 cup grated apple
¼ cup icing sugar
1 tsp. lemon juice

Beat egg whites until stiff; adding ½ cup icing sugar while beating. Add grated apple and ¼ cup icing sugar alternately as the beating continues. Flavor with lemon juice. Chill. Use as a topping for pumpkin or chocolate pie or fruit salad.

Whitehorse, Yukon
Ladies Auxiliary
Branch No. 254

Nestle's Quik Frosting

1½ cups Nestle's Quik
¼ cup margarine
⅓ cup boiling water
2½ cups icing sugar

Cream first three ingredients. Gradually add icing sugar. Covers a large layer cake. Keeps well. A superb chocolate icing. Leftovers keep well in fridge. Sets firm, not messy.

Winnipeg, Man.
Ladies Auxiliary
Branch No. 1

Seven Minute Frosting

2 unbeaten egg whites
1½ cups sugar
5 tbsp. cold water
¼ tsp. cream of tartar
1½ tsp. corn syrup
1 tsp. vanilla

Beat ingredients until well blended. Place in top of double boiler and beat constantly with a rotary beater or electric hand mixer for 7 minutes. Remove from heat and add vanilla. Continue beating until icing is of right consistency to spread. For variety tint with food coloring and decorate with coconut.

Salisbury, N.B.
Ladies Auxiliary
Branch No. 31

Icing

1 envelope Dream Whip
1 pkg. instant pudding, any flavor
1⅓ cups milk

Beat all together until thick.

Minto, Man.
Ladies Auxiliary
Minto Branch No. 201

Almond Paste

2 cups almonds
2½ cups icing sugar
1 egg yolk
1 tbsp. rose water

Put almonds through chopper. Add almond flavoring, egg yolk, rosewater and icing sugar. Knead until well mixed.

Crystal City, Man.
Ladies Auxiliary
Branch No. 35

Soft Icing

3 cups icing sugar
2 egg whites
½ cup sugar
¼ cup water
1⅓ cups Crisco shortening
1 tsp. almond extract
1 tsp. vanilla extract
2 cups icing sugar

Beat icing sugar and egg whites together until blended. Bring sugar and water to a boil. Stir while boiling for 1 minute. Add to the above mixture while still hot. Cool thoroughly. Add remaining ingredients. Beat until light and fluffy. Store in an airtight container. Will keep for weeks in the fridge. Use as you want.

Stettler, Alta.
Ladies Auxiliary
Branch No. 59

Cookies

Fruit Balls

1 cup chopped dates
1 cup chopped walnuts
1 cup shredded coconut
1 cup white sugar
2 egg whites
1 tsp. vanilla
1 tsp. almond extract

Beat egg whites until stiff. Add sugar, then fruit and other ingredients. Drop from spoon onto greased pan. Bake in moderate oven for 15 minutes. While warm, roll into balls and sprinkle with sugar.

Channel, Nfld.
Ladies Auxiliary
Channel Branch No. 11

Ting-a-Lings

6 oz. Vankirk chipits
6 oz. butterscotch chipits
1 cup chow mein noodles
1 cup peanuts

Melt chipits over hot water. Stir in remaining ingredients. Drop onto wax paper and let set. Store in covered dish in fridge or deep freeze.

Napinka, Man.
Ladies Auxiliary
Branch No. 89

Crackerjack Cookies

1 cup margarine
1 cup brown sugar
1 cup white sugar
2 eggs
1½ tsp. vanilla
1½ cups flour
1½ tsp. baking powder
1 tsp. baking soda
2 cups oatmeal
1 cup coconut
2 cups rice krispies

Sift together flour, baking powder and baking soda. Mix together the margarine, sugars, eggs and vanilla. Add flour mixture; then add remaining ingredients. Drop on greased cookie sheet and bake at 350°F. for 10 to 12 minutes.

Fort Frances, Ont.
Ladies Auxiliary
Branch No. 29

Jumbo Raisin Cookies

2 cups raisins
1 cup water
1 cup shortening
2 cups white sugar
3 eggs
1 tsp. vanilla
3½-4 cups flour
1 tsp. baking powder
1 tsp. baking soda
2 tsp. salt
1½ tsp. cinnamon
½ tsp. nutmeg
½ tsp. allspice

Bring water to a boil; add raisins and boil 5 minutes. Cream shortening, sugar, eggs and vanilla. Add cooled raisin mixture and the remaining ingredients. Drop by teaspoonful onto cookie sheet and bake at 350°F. for approx. 12 minutes.

New Glasgow, N.S.
Ladies Auxiliary
Normandy Branch No. 34

Sugar Cookies

1 cup white sugar
1 cup brown sugar
1 cup shortening and butter
2 eggs, beaten
½ cup milk
1 tsp. vanilla
pinch salt
pinch nutmeg
4 tbsp. hot water
flour
2 tsp. cream of tartar
1 tsp. baking soda

Sift together flour, cream of tartar and baking soda. Cream sugar and butter; add eggs, milk, vanilla, nutmeg, salt and water, mixing after each. Add flour mixture, using just enough flour to make a soft dough that is just stiff enough to roll. Bake at 400°F. for 10 to 12 minutes. Makes 5 dozen.

St. Andrews, N.B.
Ladies Auxiliary
Passamaquoddy Branch No. 8

Pumpkin Cookies

1½ cups pumpkin
1½ cups sugar
2 eggs
¾ cup salad oil
1 tsp. vanilla
1½ tbsp. milk
3 cups flour
1½ tsp. baking soda
1 tsp. salt
1-12 oz. pkg. chocolate chips

Mix in order given and drop by spoonfuls onto cookie sheet. Bake at 350°F.

Grand Harbour, N.B.
Ladies Auxiliary
Grand Manan Branch No. 44

Date Balls

1½ cups chopped dates
1 cup white sugar
2 eggs
1 cup rice krispies
½ cup walnuts
vanilla
coconut

Cook dates, sugar and eggs in saucepan until thickened, about 5 minutes, stirring constantly. Add remaining ingredients and cool. Form into balls and roll in coconut.

San Clara, Man.
Ladies Auxiliary
Branch No. 237

Butterscotch No-Bakes

1½ cups sugar
½ cup margarine
⅔ cup evaporated milk
1 cup butterscotch chips
3½ cups rolled oats
½ cup coconut

Combine sugar, margarine and milk in saucepan. Bring to a boil and boil 1 minute, stirring constantly. Remove from heat and add chips. Stir till blended, add rolled oats and coconut. Mix, then cool 5-10 minutes, drop by teaspoonful onto wax paper.

Spirit River, Alta.
Ladies Auxiliary
Branch No. 72

Coconut Crisp Cookies

2 cups brown sugar
1 cup shortening
2 eggs
1 tsp. baking powder
½ tsp. baking soda
2 cups flour
2 cups oatmeal
2 cups coconut

Cream sugar and shortening. Add eggs, then dry ingredients. Roll mixture into small balls, press down with fork. Bake at 400°F. for 10 to 12 minutes.

Sperling, Man.
Ladies Auxiliary
Branch No. 155

Yuletide Jumbles

½ cup butter
1 cup brown sugar
2 eggs
2 cups flour
¾ tsp. baking soda
½ tsp. salt
¼ cup milk
1 tsp. vanilla
¾ cup nuts
1 cup mixed fruit
½ cup chopped cherries

Mix and sift flour, baking soda and salt. Cream butter. Add sugar, vanilla and eggs. Add flour alternately with milk. Add floured fruit and nuts. Drop from spoon onto greased pan. Bake at 325°F. for 15 minutes.

Winnipeg, Man.
Ladies Auxiliary
West Kildonan Branch No. 30

Ice Cream Cone Cakes

favorite cake recipe or cake mix
flat-bottom ice cream cones

Fill ice-cream cones ¾ full and place on cookie sheet. Bake at 350°F. for 15 to 20 minutes. Ice with your favorite frosting. These are ideal at a children's party or in the lunch box. Yield: 20 to 22 cones.

Hazelridge, Man.
Ladies Auxiliary
Branch No. 146

Jam-Jams

2 eggs
1 cup brown sugar
¼ tsp. salt
1 cup shortening
6 tbsp. syrup
2 tsp. baking soda
1 tsp. lemon or vanilla extract

Cream shortening and sugar. Add beaten eggs. Add flour to make a stiff dough. Roll thin and cut. Bake at 350°F. till done. Put together with desired filling while warm.

Pipestone, Man.
Ladies Auxiliary
Branch No. 230

Potato Chip Cookies

½ cup white sugar
1½ cups flour
1 cup margarine
1 tsp. vanilla
½ cup crushed potato chips, plain
½ cup chopped walnuts

Cream sugar, flour and margarine together. Add remaining ingredients. Drop by spoonful onto greased cookie sheet. Bake at 350°F. til golden brown.

Russell, Man.
Ladies Auxiliary
Branch No. 159

Ginger Cookies

¾ cup shortening or margarine
1 cup white sugar
1 egg
¼ cup molasses
2 cups flour
1 tsp. ginger
1 tsp. cinnamon
¼ tsp. salt
1 large tsp. baking soda

Combine all ingredients. Roll into small balls, then roll in some white sugar. Do not press or flatten. Bake in moderate oven until done.

Miami, Man.
Ladies Auxiliary
Branch No. 88

Lemonade Cookies

3 cups sifted flour
1 tsp. baking soda
2 eggs
1 cup soft butter or margarine
1 cup sugar
1-6 oz. can frozen lemonade concentrate, thawed

Preheat oven to 400°F. Place eggs, butter, sugar and half of the lemonade concentrate in blender. Mix well. Add flour and baking soda. Drop on ungreased cookie sheet. Bake about 8 minutes. Brush baked cookies with remaining lemonade. Sprinkle with white sugar if desired.

Argyle, Man.
Ladies Auxiliary
Brandt Argyle Branch No. 222

Blender Cookies

2 cups flour
1 tsp. baking powder
¼ cup apple juice or milk
1 egg
½ cup soft shortening
½ tsp. salt
1 tsp. cinnamon
1 tsp. ground cloves
½ tsp. nutmeg
1⅓ cups brown sugar
2 medium apples, cored and cut in 1-inch pieces
1 cup currants
1 cup nuts

Preheat oven to 400°F. Grease cookie sheets. Sift flour and baking powder. Put apple juice, egg, shortening, salt, spices and brown sugar into blender. Cover and process at high speed until smooth. Stop blender and add apples, currants and nuts. Cover and process at high speed only until nuts are chopped. Empty into flour mixture. Mix well. Drop by teaspoonful. Bake 5 to 7 minutes. While hot, spread with vanilla glaze. To make vanilla glaze, mix icing sugar and water.

Squamish, B.C.
Ladies Auxiliary
Branch No. 277

Butter Buds

1 cup butter, margarine or shortening
2 cups brown sugar
2 eggs
2½ cups flour
1 tsp. baking powder
1 tsp. vanilla

Roll in balls and flatten with fork. Nuts or raisins may be added if desired, also a sprinkling of spice if shortening is used. Bake 12 minutes.

Waskada, Man.
Ladies Auxiliary
Branch No. 92

Oatmeal Cookies

½ cup margarine
1¼ cups sugar
2 eggs
6 tbsp. molasses (almost ½ cup)
1¾ cups whole wheat flour
1 tsp. baking soda
1 tsp. baking powder
1 tsp. cinnamon
2 cups rolled oats
1 cup raisins

Cream margarine and sugar. Add eggs and molasses and beat until fluffy. Stir in remaining ingredients. Drop by tablespoon onto lightly greased cookie sheet. Bake at 325°F. for 10 to 12 minutes. Makes 5½ dozen.

Maple Creek, Sask.
Ladies Auxiliary
Branch No. 75

Lemon Treats

7/8 cup butter
1½ cups sugar
2 eggs
pinch of salt
grated rind and juice of one lemon
1 cup shredded coconut
2 cups flour
1 tsp. baking soda

Mix and let stand for 2 hours. Roll in little balls or drop from teaspoons on cookie sheet. Bake at 325°F. for 15 or 20 minutes.

Saskatoon, Sask.
Ladies Auxiliary
L.A. Nutana Branch No. 362

Nancy's Surprise Cookies with Jam or Jelly

1 cup shortening
1 cup brown sugar, packed
1 cup molasses
2 eggs
5 cups sifted flour
½ tsp. salt
1 tsp. baking soda
1 tsp. cinnamon
1 tsp. ginger

Cream shortening, sugar and molasses. Beat in eggs. Sift in flour, salt, baking soda and spices. Mix, chill overnight and roll thin. Cut into 2-inch circles. Place half on baking sheet. Spoon ½·tsp. jam or jelly in centre of each round. Cover with other round. Press edges together. Bake at 350°F. for 12 to 15 minutes.

Squamish, B.C.
Ladies Auxiliary
Branch No. 266

Tender Crisp Cookies

1 cup margarine or butter
¾ cup brown sugar
¾ cup white sugar
2 eggs, beaten
1 tbsp. hot water
1 tsp. vanilla
1½ cups all-purpose flour
1 tsp. salt
1 tsp. baking soda
2 cups oatmeal
1 cup raisins or walnuts
1 cup chocolate chips

Cream margarine, add sugar and cream well. Add beaten eggs, hot water and vanilla, mix well. Add sifted flour, salt and baking soda. Mix. Add oatmeal, raisins or walnuts, and chocolate chips. Mix well. Drop by teaspoonful onto a greased cookie sheet. Bake at 350°F. for 12 to 15 minutes. Yield: approx. 6 dozen.

Russell, Man.
Ladies Auxiliary
Branch No. 159

Chestnut Cookies

½ cup butter
½ cup lard or margarine
½ cup white sugar
½ cup brown sugar
1 egg
pinch salt
2 cups flour or less
1 tsp. baking soda
2 tsp. cream of tartar
2 cups rice krispies

Mix well, then roll into balls and press with fork. Bake at 350°F. for 10 minutes. Yields: 3 to 4 dozen.

Kenton, Man.
Ladies Auxiliary
Branch No. 118

Butterscotch Cookies

½ cup lard
½ cup brown sugar
1-3 oz. butterscotch pudding
1 egg
1½ cups flour
1 tsp. baking soda
1 tsp. cream of tartar

Combine all ingredients. Roll in balls and flatten with a fork. Bake at 350°F.

Keewatin, Ont.
Ladies Auxiliary
Branch No. 13

Magic Six-Way Cookies

1⅓ cups Eagle Brand milk
½ cup peanut butter
your choice of the following
   six ingredients:
   2 cups raisins
   2 cups cornflakes
   3 cups shredded coconut
   2 cups bran flakes
   1 cup nuts, chopped
   2 cups dates, chopped

Mix together milk and peanut butter. Add your choice of ingredients and mix well. Drop on greased cookie sheet and bake at 350°F. for 12 minutes.

Valemount, B.C.
Ladies Auxiliary
Branch No. 266

Mom's Raisin Cookies

1 cup brown sugar
1 egg
1 tbsp. sour milk
1 tbsp. baking powder
½ cup butter or lard
½ tsp. baking soda
1 cup raisins
1½ cups flour
¼ tsp. nutmeg
¼ tsp. ginger
¼ tsp. cinnamon
1 tsp. vanilla

Mix sugar, butter and egg. Add the flour and raisins, then the spices. Mix baking powder with the flour. Mix well. Drop by teaspoon on cookie sheet and bake at 350°F. for about 15 minutes.

Slave Lake, Alta.
Ladies Auxiliary
Branch No. 110

Cherry Bars

Base:
   1½ cups flour
   ¼ cup icing sugar
   ½ cup butter
Topping:
   2 eggs
   1 cup brown sugar
   1 cup coconut
   1 cup cherries
   ½ tsp. almond flavoring

Measure flour into bowl. Add icing sugar and stir well to blend. Blend in butter with fingertips until mixture is very fine and mealy. Pat firmly into bottom of lightly greased 7x11-inch pan. Bake at 350°F. for 8 minutes. Remove from oven. Beat eggs well; add brown sugar and beat until well mixed. Stir in cherries, coconut and almond flavoring. Spread mixture evenly over partially baked base. Bake at 350°F. for about 30 minutes, or until golden brown. When cool, cut in bars.

Emo, Ont.
Ladies Auxiliary
Branch No. 99

Dad's Cookies

1 cup white sugar
½ cup brown sugar
1 cup butter or margarine
1 egg
1 tsp. vanilla
1 tsp. baking powder
1 tsp. baking soda
1¼ cups oatmeal
1½ cups flour
¾ cup coconut

Cream butter and sugar. Add egg. Add oatmeal, flour, baking powder and baking soda. Mix and shape into rolls. Put in fridge. When firm, slice and bake at 400°F. for 8 to 10 minutes.

Fort Assiniboine, Alta.
Ladies Auxiliary
Branch No. 210

Good Short Bread

2 cups flour
1 cup butter, margarine can be used, but butter is better
½ cup brown sugar

Mix flour and sugar, add butter. Mix by hand. When smooth, roll out on floured board and cut with floured cutter. Bake at 400°F. for 10 minutes.

Foxwarren, Man.
Ladies Auxiliary
Branch No. 152

Ginger Snaps

¾ cup shortening
¼ cup molasses
2 cups flour
1 cup white sugar
2 eggs
¼ tsp. salt
2 tsp. baking soda
1 tsp. cloves
1 tsp. cinnamon
1 tsp. ginger

Cream shortening, molasses, sugar and egg. Add dry ingredients. Mix well. Roll in a ball. Dip in sugar. Place 2 inches apart on cookie sheet. Bake at 350°F. for 12 to 15 minutes.

Justice, Man.
Ladies Auxiliary
Branch No. 233

Jelly Cookies

1 cup margarine
1½ cups brown sugar
1 egg
1 tsp. vanilla
½ tsp. salt
1 tsp. baking soda
¼ cup boiling water
3 cups flour
1 cup oatmeal

Dissolve baking soda in boiling water. Combine ingredients in order given. Roll in balls. Make a dent in centre and fill with jelly. Bake at 400°F. for 8 to 10 minutes.

Petitcodiac, N.B.
Ladies Auxiliary
Branch No. 41

Peanut Butter Cookies

½ cup white sugar
½ cup brown sugar
¾ cup melted butter or margarine
¾ cup peanut butter
1 egg
½ tsp. salt
1 tsp. baking soda
1¾ cups flour

Roll in balls. Flatten with fork. Bake at 300°F.

Salisbury, N.B.
Ladies Auxiliary
Branch No. 31

Gingersnaps

1 cup shortening or butter
1 cup molasses
1 tsp. baking soda
3 cups flour
1 tsp. salt
2 tsp. ginger
1 tsp. vanilla

Bring molasses to a boil, add baking soda. Pour over shortening and blend well. Add vanilla. Add dry ingredients. Chill until dough will slice thinly. Bake at 350°F. for 8 to 10 minutes.

Bathurst, N.B.
Ladies Auxiliary
Branch No. 18

Chocolate Marshmallow Roll

6 squares semi-sweet chocolate
2 tbsp. butter
1 cup icing sugar
1 egg
30 marshmallows, cut
1 tsp. vanilla
¼ tsp. salt
1 cup chopped nuts

Melt chocolate squares and butter over warm water. Mix together remaining ingredients. Add melted chocolate to second mixture. Shape into a roll. Roll in chopped nuts. Wrap in wax paper and keep in fridge.

Winnipeg, Man.
Ladies Auxiliary
Kent Memorial Branch No. 119

English Drop Cookies

2 cups brown sugar
1 cup margarine
1 cup cold coffee
2 eggs, unbeaten
1 tsp. baking soda
1 tsp. baking powder
3⅓ cups sifted flour
½ tsp. salt
1 tsp. cinnamon
1 tsp. nutmeg

Combine and add one or any combination of the following:
1 cup raisins and 1 cup chopped nuts,
or 1 cup chopped dates
or mixed fruit and peel
or 1 cup chocolate chips
or ½ cup coconut

Blend together in order till smooth. Drop by spoonfuls onto greased pan. Bake at 400°F. for 12 minutes. Makes about 5 dozen. Cookies taste better if allowed to set in refrigerator a few hours or overnight before baking.

Great Village, N.S.
Ladies Auxiliary
Mayflower Branch No. 72

Cherry Balls

½ cup margarine
graham crumbs
1½ cups icing sugar
½ tsp. almond extract
1½ cups coconut

Cream margarine. Add icing sugar, almond extract and coconut. Wrap a small amount of this mixture around a cherry and roll in graham cracker crumbs.

New Glasgow, N.S.
Ladies Auxiliary
Normandy Branch No. 34

Ginger Creams

½ cup shortening
1 cup white sugar
1 egg
1 cup molasses
4 cups flour
½ tsp. salt
1 cup hot water
2 tsp. baking soda
2 tsp. allspice

Cream shortening and sugar; add egg and beat well. Combine liquids and baking soda; then add to creamed mixture alternately with flour. Drop by teaspoonful onto greased cookie sheet and bake at 400°F. for 8 minutes. Frost with icing sugar while still warm.

Winnipeg, Man.
Ladies Auxiliary
Brooklands Weston Branch No. 2

Mincemeat Cookies

½ cup shortening
1 cup sugar
2 eggs
2 cups mincemeat
2½ cups flour
2 tsp. baking powder
¼ tsp. salt

Combine all ingredients. Drop onto greased cookie sheet. Bake at 375°F. for 12 minutes.

Sydney, N.S.
Ladies Auxiliary
Branch No. 12

Fattimand

6 egg yolks
6 tbsp. sugar
6 tbsp. sweet milk
1 tbsp. melted butter
¼ tsp. cardamon
1/8 tsp. salt
2 cups flour

Use enough flour to roll out. Beat eggs lightly; add sugar and mix well. Add remaining ingredients. Roll dough in thin sheets and cut into strips. Deep fry until golden brown. Drain on paper towel and sprinkle with icing sugar while still warm.

Murdockville, Que.
Ladies Auxiliary
Branch No. 218

Shortbread

½ cup butter
½ cup icing sugar
¼ cup rice flour
1½ cups flour

Combine ingredients and work with the hands. Pat out small pieces at a time to cut. Bake at 350°F. for about 15 minutes. Recipe can be doubled.

Emo, Ont.
Ladies Auxiliary
Branch No. 99

Ragged Jacks Cookies

2 cups oatmeal
½ cup butter or margarine
1 egg
1 cup flour
½ cup raisins
1 cup brown sugar
1½ tsp. baking powder
vanilla to taste

Combine ingredients. Drop by spoonful onto greased pan. Bake at 350°F. for 10 minutes. For Christmas, add: nuts, fruit, cherries, etc. Press the cookies down with bottom of a glass to give a flat cookie.

Cartwright, Man.
Ladies Auxiliary
Cartwright-Mather Branch No. 86

Icebox Cookies

1 cup margarine
1 cup brown sugar
1 tsp. vanilla
1 tsp. baking soda
1 cup white sugar
2 eggs
3 cups flour
½ tsp. salt
1 cup walnuts, mixed fruits, or raisins

Cream butter, add sugar, eggs and vanilla. Beat well. Add flour, baking soda and salt to first mixture. Add the walnuts or fruits. Form into long rolls. Put in freezer to freeze. Slice thin. Bake at 350°F. until light brown.

Shoal Lake, Man.
Ladies Auxiliary
Branch No. 72

Grandmother's Oatmeal Cookies

2 cups flour
2 cups oatmeal
½ lb. shortening
1 cup brown sugar
1 level tsp. baking soda
1 level tsp. baking powder
½ tsp. salt

Mix as for pastry. Add enough sour cream to roll out. Bake at 350°F.

Kelwood, Man.
Ladies Auxiliary
Branch No. 50

Whipped Shortbread

1 cup soft butter
½ cup icing sugar
¼ cup cornstarch
1½ cups flour

Preheat oven to 325°F. Sift dry ingredients over butter. Whip at low speed until blended, then on high speed until mixture is like whipped cream. Drop by small teaspoon on baking sheet. Dot with a cherry. Bake for 20 minutes, watching carefully.

Winnipeg Beach, Man.
Ladies Auxiliary
Branch No. 61

Christmas Shortbreads

1 cup butter
¼ cup sugar
2 ccups flour
1½ cups coconut
⅔ cup red and green maraschino cherries
¼ cup golden raisins
⅓ cup chopped walnuts or almonds
1 can sweetened condensed milk

Cream butter and sugar together. Blend in flour until mixture resembles coarse crumbs. Pat dough evenly into a greased 9-inch square pan. Bake at 350°F. for 20 minutes. Combine remaining ingredients. Spread evenly on shortbread. Bake an additional 35 minutes or until golden brown.

Waverley, N.S.
Ladies Auxiliary
Dieppe Branch No. 90

Mum's Murchers

½ cup margarine
½ cup shortening
1 cup white sugar
1 cup brown sugar
2 cups rolled oats
¾ cup dessicated unsweetened coconut
2 eggs
1 tsp. baking powder
½ tsp. baking soda
½ tsp. salt
1 tsp. vanilla
½-1 cup raisins, prunes, nuts, etc.
½ cup wheat germ
1½ cups unsifted flour

Cream shortening and margarine and then the rest in order given. Drop by teaspoonful, but don't crowd. Bake at 350°F. for 10 minutes. Watch, as they burn easily.

Strathclair, Man.
Ladies Auxiliary
Branch No. 154

Monster Cookies

6 eggs
2 cups brown sugar
2 cups white sugar
1 tbsp. vanilla
½ lb. butter
3 cups peanut butter
1 tbsp. syrup
9 cups oatmeal
½ cup chocolate chipits
1 cup smarties
4 tsp. baking soda
1 tsp. salt

Combine all ingredients and drop by teaspoonful onto greased cookie sheet. Bake at 350°F. for 10 minutes.

Minnedosa, Man.
Ladies Auxiliary
Branch N. 138

Peppernut Cookies
(Holland)

2 cups white sugar
2 cups syrup
1 lb. margarine
1 tbsp. star of anise spice
1 tsp. cloves
1 tsp. baking soda
2 eggs
½ cup sour milk
8 cups flour

Mix first four ingredients in a pot and cook on top of stove for 2 minutes. Cool; add remaining ingredients, mixing together well. Put dough in freezer and chill for one hour (or until you find dough easy to roll). Shape in logs of ½ to ¾ inches in thickness and about 10 inches long. Roll logs in wax paper and put back in freezer overnight. Slice cookie dough ¼ inch thick. Place on greased cookie sheet. Bake at 350°F. for 10 minutes.
Note: For Christmas finely chopped fruit may be added. Makes dozens of tiny cookies the size of a quarter. Kids love them. They freeze well.

Provost, Alta.
Ladies Auxiliary
Chaplain Provost Branch No. 85

Oatmeal Cookies

½ cup shortening
½ cup brown sugar
½ cup sugar
1 egg
1 tbsp. water
½ tsp. vanilla
¾ cup flour
½ tsp. baking soda
½ tsp. salt
1½ cups rolled oats
1¼ cups chocolate chips or
1 pkg. desiccated coconut or 1 cup peanut butter or 1 cup raisins

Cream shortening and sugar. Stir in beaten egg, water and vanilla. Add sifted dry ingredients, rolled oats and chocolate chips. Drop from a teaspoon onto greased baking sheets. Bake at 375°F. for 10 to 15 minutes.

Halifax, N.S.
Ladies Auxiliary
Scotia Branch No. 25

Mocha Mousse

1-7 oz. pkg. Christies chocolate wafers
¼ cup margarine
1 cup boiling water
4 tsp. instant coffee powder
1-11 oz. pkg. large marshmallows
1 pint whipping cream or
½ pint whipping cream and 1 pkg. Dream Whip

Crush chocolate wafers and mix with melted butter. Save ½ cup for top. Press remainder in bottom of 9x13-inch cake pan.
Melt marshmallows and instant coffee in boiling water in top of double boiler or in microwave oven. Stir until melted. Refrigerate for approximately one hour or until slightly thickened. Whip the cream (whip cream and Dream Whip separately, then fold together). Fold into marshmallow-coffee mixture. Pour over crumbs. Sprinkle remainder of crumbs on top. Chill.

Stettler, Alta.
Ladies Auxiliary
Branch No. 59

Peanut Clusters

1-350 g pkg. chocolate chips
1-350 g pkg. butterscotch
  chips
4 tbsp. peanut butter
¼ bar parafin wax
4 cups peanuts

Melt chips and peanut butter in microwave dish. Melt wax separately. Mix together. Pour over peanuts and blend. Drop in desired size on wax paper. Makes 5 to 7 dozen.

Pipestone, Man.
Ladies Auxiliary
Pipestone Branch No. 230

Banana Oatmeal Macaroons

½ cup white sugar
½ cup brown sugar
½ cup melted margarine
½ cup coconut
1 mashed banana
1 egg, beaten
½ tsp. baking soda
½ tsp. salt
½ tsp. vanilla
¾ cup flour
1½ cups oatmeal

Combine ingredients in order given. Drop from teaspoon onto greased cookie sheet. Bake at 325°F. for 10 to 12 minutes. Let cool 2 to 3 minutes before removing from cookie sheet.

Digby, N.S.
Ladies Auxiliary
Branch No. 22

Easy Layered Chocolate Coconut Cookies

½ cup butter
1½ cups Graham cracker
  crumbs
1-3½ oz. can flaked coconut
1-6 oz. pkg. semi-sweet chocolate chips
1 cup chopped nuts
1 cup or 1-14 oz. can sweetened condensed milk

Melt butter in 13x9x2-inch baking pan while preheating oven to 375°F. Layer each remaining ingredient over butter. Do not mix. Bake 25 minutes. Cool pan on rack. Cut in small squares. Yields: 48 squares.

Campobello, N.B.
Ladies Auxiliary
Branch No. 83

Coffee Oatmeal Cookies

2½ cups flour
½ tsp. salt
2 tsp. baking powder
¼ tsp. baking soda
2½ cups rolled oats
¾ cup shortening
2 cups brown sugar
½ cup cold coffee

Mix flour, salt, baking powder and baking soda; add rolled oats. Cream shortening with sugar, add dry ingredients and coffee alternately. Drop by tablespoon on a greased baking sheet. Flatten until 1/8 inch thick. Bake at 400°F. for 10 minutes.

Howick, Que.
Ladies Auxiliary
Howick Branch No. 123

All Bran Chocolate Cookies

1 cup all bran
1 cup sour milk
½ cup shortening
1 cup white sugar
2 eggs
1½ cups flour
3 tsp. baking powder
½ tsp. baking soda
½ tsp. salt
½ cup cocoa
½ tsp. vanilla

Soak bran in sour milk. Cream shortening and sugar. Add eggs, bran mixture and dry ingredients. Drop by spoonfuls on cookie sheet. Bake in moderate oven.

Joggins, N.S.
Ladies Auxiliary
Branch No. 4

Specalaas

(Cinnamon
Icebox Cookies)

1½ cups butter or margarine
  or ½ lard may be used
2 cups brown sugar, packed
4 cups flour
3 eggs
2 tsp. cinnamon
1 tsp. baking soda

Combine all ingredients together well. More flour may be needed. Roll into 2 large or 3 smaller rolls. Refrigerate overnight and cut into ½-inch slices to bake. Space fairly far apart as these cookies spread out. Bake at 350°F. for 10 to 15 minutes or until golden brown. This may also be frozen and rolls brought out to bake when needed. This is a Belgian recipe.

Deloraine, Man.
Ladies Auxiliary
Branch No. 83

Raisin Cookies

2 cups raisins
1½ cups boiling water
2 cups white sugar
1 cup shortening
3 eggs
4 cups flour
2 tsp. salt
1½ tsp. cinnamon
½ tsp. allspice
1 tsp. baking soda
1 tsp. baking powder
½ tsp. nutmeg

Combine raisins and boiling water in saucepan. Let boil 5 minutes and cool. Cream sugar, and shortening together, add eggs and beat well. Blend into raisin/water mixture. Sift together remaining ingredients. Blend flour and raisin/water mixtures together and drop by teaspoon onto baking sheet. Bake at 400°F. for 10 to 12 minutes.

Murdockville, Que.
Ladies Auxiliary
Branch No. 218

Frosted Strawberries

⅔ cup or ½-15 oz. can Eagle Brand milk
2½ cups or 1-8 oz. pkg. desiccated coconut
1-3 oz. pkg. strawberry Jello
½ cup finely ground blanched almonds
½ tsp. almond extract
red food coloring
½ cup sifted icing sugar
cream
green food coloring

Blend together milk, coconut, ½ pkg. of strawberry Jello, almonds, almond extract and sufficient red food coloring to tint to a strawberry shade. Blend well and mold into the shape of a strawberry. Place remaining ½ pkg. of Jello in flat dish and roll each strawberry in it. Place on wax paper and chill.

Combine icing sugar, enough cream to make a stiff icing and green food coloring. Make leaf for each strawberry. Makes 25 to 30 good size strawberries.

Oak River, Man.
Ladies Auxiliary
Branch No. 150

Kookie Brittle

1 cup margarine
1 cup sugar
2 cups flour
1 cup walnuts
1 cup chocolate chips
1½ tsp. vanilla
1 tsp. salt

Preheat oven to 375°F. Combine margarine, vanilla and salt in bowl. Gradually add in sugar, add flour, then chocolate chips and walnuts. Mixture is rather dry at this stage. Sprinkle a few drops of water over, just enough to bind together. Press evenly in a 15x10x1-inch cookie sheet. Bake for 30 minutes until golden brown. This kookie is a hard crunchy type and looks good if broken like candy. Do not use currants or raisins in this recipe.

Terrace Bay, Ont.
Ladies Auxiliary
Branch No. 223

Smartie Cookies

1 cup shortening
1 cup brown sugar
½ cup white sugar
2 eggs
2 tsp. vanilla
2¼ cups flour
1 tsp. baking soda
pinch of salt
1 cup smarties or chocolate chips

Blend shortening and sugar in a large bowl. Beat in vanilla and eggs. Mix dry ingredients. Combine all ingredients and smarties. Drop from teaspoon to cookie sheet. Stick a few smarties on top of each. Bake at 350°F. for about 10 minutes. Nice for Christmas or children's party.

Steinbach, Man.
Ladies Auxiliary
Branch No. 190

Brown sugar Cookies

½ cup shortening
1 cup brown sugar, lightly packed
2 eggs, beaten
½ tsp. vanilla
1½ cups pre-sifted flour
1 tsp. baking powder
1 tsp. baking soda
½ tsp. salt
⅓ cup sour milk
¾ cup raisins or chopped dates
½ cup chopped nuts

Preheat oven to 350°F. Cream sugar and shortening together. Add eggs and vanilla, and beat until light and fluffy. Blend or sift together dry ingredients. Add to creamed mixture alternately with sour milk. Fold in raisins and nuts. Drop from teaspoon onto greased baking sheets. Bake in oven preheated to 350°F. for about 12 minutes. Yields: 4 dozen cookies.

Yarmouth, N.S.
Ladies Auxiliary
Branch No. 61

Applesauce Cookies

½ cup butter
½ cup white sugar
½ cup brown sugar, firmly packed
1 egg, beaten
1 cup sour applesauce (no sugar added)
1½ cups all-purpose flour
½ cup whole wheat flour
2 tbsp. wheat germ
pinch of salt
½ tsp. baking soda
½ tsp. nutmeg
¼ tsp. ground cloves
1 tsp. cinnamon
½ cup cherries, chopped
¾ cup raisins
½ cup walnuts, chopped

Cream butter and sugar together, add beaten egg and blend well. Add applesauce. Keep out 2 tbsp. of flour to dust fruits and nuts, and mix remaining flour with the rest of dry ingredients. Add to the creamed mixture, then fruits and nuts. Drop by teaspoonful onto a greased cookie sheet. Bake at 375°F. for 8 to 10 minutes or until done. These cookies keep moist for days when stored in an airtight container. Yield: about 3 dozen cookies. They are very nutritious, and make a nice snack or for school lunches.

Canning, N.S.
Ladies Auxiliary
Habitant Branch No. 73

Bird's Nests

1 cup butter or margarine
½ cup brown sugar
2 egg yolks
2 cups flour
1 tsp. vanilla
2 egg whites
coconut

Cream butter, sugar and egg yolks. Add flour and vanilla. Shape into balls. Dip in slightly beaten egg whites and roll in coconut. Press in the centre with finger. Bake and then fill centre with jelly or jam before cool.

Shubenacadie, N.S.
Ladies Auxiliary
Branch No. 111

No Bake Chocolate Macaroons

½ cup butter or margarine
1 cup brown sugar
1 cup white sugar
½ cup milk
3 cups quick-cooking rolled oats
1 cup shredded coconut
1 tsp. salt
6 tbsp. cocoa
1 tsp. vanilla

Combine butter, sugar and milk in saucepan. Boil for exactly 3 minutes and add remaining ingredients. Blend lightly and drop by teaspoon on wax paper or aluminum foil. Chill. Store in a covered container in a cool place.

Hantsport, N.S.
Ladies Auxiliary
Lucknow Branch No. 109

Quick Drops

1 cup chocolate chips
3 tbsp. butter
¼ cup icing sugar
2 cups coconut

Melt chocolate chips and butter over hot water. Blend in icing sugar. Then add coconut. Drop by teaspoon onto wax paper. Chill.

Port Rexton, Nfld.
Ladies Auxiliary
Branch No. 20

Snowballs

1 cup peanut butter
1 cup icing sugar
1 cup Rice Krispies
½ cup chopped walnuts
1 tbsp. butter

Cream peanut butter and icing sugar until smooth. Add Rice Krispies, butter and walnuts and stir. Shape into balls. Mix 2 tbsp. water and 1 cup icing sugar and dip balls into icing sugar mixture. Roll balls in coconut or more chopped nuts. Place in fridge for 15 minutes before serving.

Montreal, Que.
Ladies Auxiliary
Maisonneuve Branch No. 66

Gold Nuggets
(Cookies)

1-4 oz. pkg. cream cheese
½ cup margarine
½ cup sugar
1 tbsp. grated lemon rind
2 tsp. lemon juice
1 cup flour
2 tsp. baking powder
¼ tsp. salt
¾ cup finely crushed corn flakes crumbs or ground almonds

Beat cheese, butter, and sugar until fluffy. Stir in lemon rind and juice. Sift together flour, baking powder, and salt; add to cream cheese mixture and blend until smooth. Chill at least one hour. Shape into balls and roll in corn flake crumbs. Place on ungreased cookie sheet, 2 inches apart. Bake at 350°F. for 12 to 15 minutes. Do not brown. If storing, refrigerate.

Bow Island, Alta.
Ladies Auxiliary
Branch No. 197

No Bake Crisps

⅔ cup peanut butter
½ cup brown sugar
⅔ cup corn syrup
2½ cups Corn Flakes
1 cup flaked coconut
½ cup chopped peanuts or other nuts

Place peanut butter, sugar and corn syrup in heavy saucepan. Cook over low heat until sugar is dissolved, stirring constantly. Stir in Corn Flakes, coconuts and peanuts. Line cookie sheet with wax paper. Drop by teaspoon onto wax paper. Chill until set. Makes 3 dozen.

Winnipeg, Man.
Ladies Auxiliary
West Kildonan Branch No. 30

Slices & Squares

Chewy Cherry Square

1 cup coconut
¾ cup chopped walnuts
½ cup wheat germ
1-10 oz. can condensed milk
¼ cup brown sugar
2 tbsp. melted margarine
¼ cup flour
1-19 oz. can cherry pie filling

Crust:
¾ cup butter or margarine
½ cup brown sugar
1½ cups flour

Rub butter, brown sugar and flour together until crumbly. Pat into a 9x13-inch pan. Bake at 350°F. for 15 minutes, or until golden brown.

Combine coconut, walnuts, wheat germ, flour, sugar and margarine in a small bowl. Set aside. Spread pie filling over crust. Pour condensed milk over the pie filling. Spread coconut mixture over milk. Bake at 350°F. for 35 to 45 minutes or until light brown. Cool before cutting. Store in refrigerator.

Thompson, Man.
Ladies Auxiliary
Branch No. 244

Cherry Bars

1 cup brown sugar
½ cup butter or margarine
2 cups flour
1 cup seedless raisins
½-6 oz. jar cherries, chopped
½ cup coconut
½ cup chopped walnuts
1 can Eagle Brand milk

Mix together the brown sugar, butter and flour. Pack in bottom of 9x12-inch pan. Pour boiling water over raisins and drain off water. Spread ingredients over flour mixture evenly in order given. Bake at 300°F. for 45 minutes or till golden brown. Cut in bars or little squares. Great for teas or even nice for Christmas.

Houston, B.C.
Ladies Auxiliary
Branch No. 249

Lemon Squares

1 cup oatmeal
1 cup flour
½ cup coconut
½ cup coarsely chopped
    walnuts
½ cup brown sugar, firmly
    packed
1 tsp. baking powder
½ cup melted butter
1 can Eagle Brand milk
½ cup lemon juice

Preheat oven to 350°F. (325°F. for glass dish). Mix oatmeal, flour, coconut, sugar, nuts, baking powder and butter to form crumbs.

Combine lemon juice and milk in another bowl. Pat half of crumb mixture in a 9x9-inch pan. Spread milk mixture on top and spread rest of crumb mixture on top. Bake 25 to 30 minutes, or until browned. Cool completely before cutting.

Holland, Man.
Ladies Auxiliary
Branch No. 121

Cherry and Date Slice

Bottom:
1 cup flour
½ cup butter or margarine
2 tbsp. sugar

Cut like pastry; pat into pan and bake until golden brown. Let cool.

Topping:
2 eggs, beaten well
1 cup brown sugar
½ cup coconut
½ cup walnuts, crushed
½ cup maraschino cherries,
    sliced
2 tbsp. flour
1 tsp. baking powder
½ cup dates, cut up
1 tsp. vanilla

Mix topping and pour over bottom evenly. Bake until topping is done, approx. 30 to 40 minutes at 275°F. Use a 9x9-inch pan.

Winnipeg Beach, Man.
Ladies Auxiliary
Branch No. 61

English Toffee Bars

1 cup butter
1 cup sugar
1 egg yolk
2 cups all-purpose flour
1 tsp. ground cinnamon
1 egg white, slightly beaten
1 cup chopped pecans
2 oz. semi-sweet chocolate,
    melted

Cream butter; add sugar gradually, beating until fluffy. Beat in egg yolk. Sift flour and cinnamon. Gradually add to creamed mixture, beating until blended. Turn into a greased 15x10x1-inch jelly roll pan, pressing evenly. Brush top with egg white and sprinkle with pecans and press lightly into dough. Bake at 275°F. for one hour. While still hot, cut into 1½-inch squares. Drizzle with melted chocolate. Cool on wire rack. Makes 5 to 6 dozen.

Eastport, Nfld.
Ladies Auxiliary
Eastport Branch No. 41

Sour Cream Raisin Bars

2 cups raisins
1 cup butter
1 cup brown sugar
1 tsp. baking soda
1¾ cups oatmeal
1¾ cups flour
3 egg yolks, beaten
2½ tsp. cornstarch
1 cup white sugar
1½ cups sour cream

Cook raisins for 10 minutes and drain. Mix butter, brown sugar, baking soda, oatmeal and flour together. Put half of the mixture in bottom of a 9x13-inch greased pan and bake at 350°F. for 7 minutes. Combine remaining ingredients. Cook until thick, add drained raisins and 1 tsp. vanilla. Pour over crust. Top with remaining mix. Bake at 350°F. for 30 minutes. Rich and delicious!

Emo, Ont.
Ladies Auxiliary
Branch No. 99

Apricot Smooth

2½ cups graham wafer
    crumbs
½ cup butter or margarine
1 tbsp. white sugar
Topping:
½ cup margarine
2 eggs, beaten
1½ cups icing sugar, or
    enough to make a thick
    spreadable mixture
almond and vanilla extract to
    taste
3 cans or jars Apricot Baby
    Food
1 or 2 pkgs. whipped topping

Mix together graham wafer crumbs, butter and sugar. Save ½ cup mixture for top of cake. Pat the remainder into a 9x12-inch pan and bake until light brown. Let cool. Combine margarine, eggs and icing sugar. Beat until smooth and spread over top of cake. Spread Apricot Baby Food evenly over icing layer. Whip 1 or 2 pkgs. of topping according to directions and spread on top of cake. Sprinkle wafer mixture over top. Refrigerate.

Minto, Man.
Ladies Auxiliary
Branch No. 201

Peach Squares

½ cup butter
¾ cup white sugar
1 egg, unbeaten
1 cup coconut
1 medium can peaches,
    drained and mashed
graham wafers
Dream Whip

Cream butter, sugar and egg. Add coconut and peaches. Line pan with graham wafers. Cover with filling and top with another layer of wafers. Cover with Dream Whip. Refrigerate.

Deer Lake, Nfld.
Ladies Auxiliary
Branch No. 3

Marshmallow Squares

½ cup peanut butter
2-6 oz. pkg. butterscotch chips
½ cup butter
1 pkg. colored marshmallows

Melt peanut butter, butterscotch chips and butter. Cool slightly, then add marshmallows. Pour into a 9x13-inch pan. Let set.

Salisbury, N.B.
Ladies Auxiliary
Branch No. 31

New York Slice

Layer One:
2 cups graham crumbs
½ cup margarine
¼ cup white sugar
1 egg
¼ cup cocoa
1 cup coconut
½ cup chopped nuts
Layer Two:
¼ cup butter or margarine
3 tbsp. milk
2 tbsp. vanilla custard or
    pudding powder
2 cups sifted icing sugar
Layer Three:
4 squares (ozs.) semi-sweet
    chocolate
2 tbsp. butter

Combine ½ cup margarine, egg cocoa and sugar in heavy saucepan. Cook and stir until mixture is slightly thickened. Combine crumbs, coconut and nuts with the chocolate mixture, blend well. Press into a 9-inch square pan. Cream together ¼ cup butter, milk, custard powder and icing sugar. Spread over mixture in pan. Chill thoroughly. Melt the chocolate with butter and blend well. Spread chocolate over chilled mixture in pan. Allow to stand until chocolate is just set. Cut in small squares, then store in refrigerator.

Nipigon, Ont.
Ladies Auxiliary
Branch No. 32

Farmers Brownies

¼ cup cocoa
1 cup hot water
¾ cup butter
1 cup brown sugar
1 cup white sugar
2 eggs
2½ cups flour
1 tsp. baking powder
1 tsp. baking soda
½ cup sour milk
1 tsp. vanilla
pinch of salt

Mix cocoa in hot water. Add butter and stir to melt. Add sugar and eggs; then dry ingredients with sour milk and vanilla. Stir with spoon only till blended. Spread on large greased cookie sheet. Sprinkle with 1 cup chocolate chips and 1 cup nuts. Bake at 350°F. for 20 minutes.

Frobisher, Sask.
Ladies Auxiliary
Frobisher Branch No. 343

Bikini Squares

½ cup butter
½ cup white sugar
3 tbsp. cocoa or 1 square
    chocolate
1 egg, well beaten
2 cups graham wafer crumbs
1 cup coconut
1 tsp. vanilla
¼ cup butter
2 tsp. instant vanilla pudding
3 tbsp. hot water

Melt butter, sugar and cocoa. Add well beaten egg, graham wafer crumbs, coconut and vanilla. Press mixture into square pan and cool for 10 minutes. Mix remaining ingredients and make a smooth paste. Spread over mixture. Melt 2 squares semi-sweet chocolate and 2 tbsp. butter. Spread over top. Refrigerate and serve. Warning: Too many of these and you can forget your bikini.

Trenton, N.S.
Ladies Auxiliary
Branch No. 29

Chocolate Squares

First Mixture:
3 tbsp. white sugar
¼ cup cocoa
¾ cup flour
½ cup butter
pinch of salt

Cream butter; add sugar and dry ingredients. Blend into stiff dough. Press into bottom of baking pan. Bake at 325°F. for 15 minutes.

Second Mixture:
1½ cups brown sugar
1 cup chopped walnuts
1 tsp. baking powder
½ cup coconut
3 tbsp. flour
2 eggs, well beaten
1 tsp. vanilla

Beat eggs, sugar, flour, baking powder and other ingredients together. Put on top of first mixture. Bake at 350°F. for 25 minutes. Ice with thin chocolate icing. Use a 9x9-inch square pan.

Debert, N.S.
Ladies Auxiliary
Debert Branch No. 106

Butter Tart Square

1¼ cups flour
¼ cup brown sugar
½ cup butter
1 egg
⅓ cup butter
1 cup brown sugar
2 tbsp. cornstarch
1 tsp. vanilla
1 tbsp. flour
½ cup raisins

Combine first three ingredients and press into 9-inch square pan. Bake at 350°F. for 15 minutes. Remove from oven and spread on topping mixture. For topping, mix together remaining ingredients. Return to oven and bake for 20 to 30 minutes or until golden brown.

Drumheller, Alta.
Ladies Auxiliary
Branch No. 22

Pumpkin Bars

1 cup oil
2 cups white sugar
1-14 oz. can pumpkin
4 eggs
2 cups flour
2 tsp. baking powder
1 tsp. baking soda
½ tsp. salt
2 tsp. cinnamon
1 cup raisins

Combine oil, sugar, eggs and pumpkin in a large bowl. Beat well. Mix dry ingredients together. Add ¾ of the flour mixture. Flour raisins with the other ¼, add and beat well. Spread in a well greased and floured jelly roll pan, about 9x13. Bake at 350°F. for 30 minutes. Cool. Ice.

Icing:
3 oz. cream cheese, (room temperature)
1 tsp. vanilla
¼ cup soft margarine
2 tsp. milk or cream
2½ cups icing sugar (approx.)

Beat until smooth. May be garnished with chopped nuts, if you wish.

Peace River, Alta.
Ladies Auxiliary
Branch No. 62

Petite Cherry Cheesecakes

2-8 oz. pkgs. cream cheese, softened
¾ cup sugar
2 eggs
1-21 oz. can cherry pie filling
1 tbsp. lemon juice
1 tsp. vanilla
36 vanilla wafers

Beat cream cheese, sugar, eggs, lemon juice and vanilla till light and fluffy. Line small muffin pans with paper baking cups and place a vanilla wafer in each cup. Fill the cups ⅔ full with cream cheese mixture. Bake at 375°F. for 15 to 20 minutes or till set. Top each with 1 tbsp. pie filling. Chill. Yields: 3 dozen.

Lac du Bonnet, Man.
Ladies Auxiliary
Branch No. 164

Peppermint Marshmallow Squares

½ cup butter
½ cup sugar
¼ cup cocoa
1 egg, beaten
1 tsp. vanilla
2½ cups vanilla wafer crumbs

Melt butter. Add sugar, cocoa and eggs. Cook, stirring constantly until boiling. Turn heat to medium and boil gently for 1 minute, stirring. Remove from heat and stir in vanilla and vanilla wafer crumbs. Turn into a buttered 8x8x2-inch pan. Spread evenly. Chill while preparing marshmallows.

Marshmallows:
1 cup sugar
¼ tsp. salt
1 cup icing sugar
¼ tsp. peppermint extract
½ tsp. butter
1 envelope or 1 tbsp. unflavored gelatin
1 cup cold water
green food coloring
1 tbsp. chocolate chips

Combine sugar, gelatin and salt in saucepan. Stir in water. Bring to a boil and boil gently for 10 minutes. Turn into bowl. Cool, do not chill. Add icing sugar, few drops of green food coloring and peppermint extract. Beat until very thick, like a soft marshmallow, about 5 minutes. Pour over base.

Topping:
Combine chocolate chips and butter in a small dish and set into simmering water. Remove from water when half melted, stir until smooth. Drizzle from tip of spoon in lines one inch apart on mallow. Draw knife through lines to form pattern. Chill and cut.

Thompson, Man.
Ladies Auxiliary
Branch No. 244

Jam Feather Squares

4 tbsp. butter
½ cup white sugar
3 egg yolks
3 tbsp. milk
1 tsp. baking powder
1 tsp. cornstarch
1 cup flour
½ tsp. salt
1 tsp. vanilla

Cream butter, sugar, egg yolks and milk. Sift dry ingredients. Mix with butter mixture. Bake at 400°F. until light brown. Spread with any kind jam. Cover with the following meringue.

Meringue:
3 egg whites
¼ cup brown sugar

Beat egg whites stiff, adding sugar, a little at a time. Bake.

Cheticamp, N.S.
Ladies Auxiliary
Branch No. 32

Chocolate Whipped Cream Squares

Bottom Layer:
½ cup butter or margarine
2 tbsp. icing sugar
1 cup flour

Combine and press into bottom of 8x8-inch pan. Bake at 350°F. for 15 minutes.

Top layer:
½ cup butter
⅔ cup white sugar
2 squares unsweetened chocolate
2 eggs
1 tsp. vanilla

Cream butter and sugar and add melted chocolate and vanilla. Beat in eggs, one at a time. Beat until fluffy, for 10 minutes. Spread over bottom layer. Top with a layer of Dream Whip. Refrigerate one hour.

Sydney, N.S.
Ladies Auxiliary
Branch No. 12

Blueberry Squares

3 tbsp. butter
¼ cup sugar
1 egg yolk
1 tsp. vanilla
1 tsp. baking powder
¾ cup flour
¼ tsp. salt
¼ cup milk

Mix as cake. Spread in an 8x8-inch pan.

Topping:
1 egg white
¼ cup brown sugar
1 cup blueberries

Beat egg white stiff. Add brown sugar and beat until fluffy. Fold in 1 cup blueberries. Bake at 350°F. for 30 minutes.

Sydney, N.S.
Ladies Auxiliary
Branch No. 128

Carmel Cake Squares

1 cup margarine or butter
1½ cups flour
1 cup white sugar
2 eggs
3 tbsp. cocoa

Combine and spread on cookie sheet. Bake at 350°F. for 15 minutes.

Middle:
1½ cups margarine
4 tbsp. flour
2 cups brown sugar
1 can condensed milk
4 tbsp. light corn syrup

Heat till dissolved. Pour over bottom layer, put back in oven for 15 minutes. Cool before putting top layer on.

Top:
6 oz. chocolate chips
2 tbsp. butter

Melt chocolate chips and butter. Spread when cake is cool. Keep in fridge or you can freeze. Put on big enough cookie sheet or it will spill over.

Grande Prairie, Alta.
Ladies Auxiliary
Branch No. 54

No Bake Mincemeat Mallow Cheese Cake

1 cup vanilla wafer crumbs
¼ cup margarine, melted
1¾ cups mincemeat
4 cups mini marshmallows
½ pint heavy cream, whipped
⅓ cup orange juice
2-8 oz. pkgs. cream cheese, softened
2 tsp. grated orange rind

Combine crumbs and margarine. Press onto bottom of a 9-inch springform pan. Chill. Spread mincemeat over crust. Melt marshmallows with orange juice in double boiler. Stir until smooth. Chill until thickened. Combine softened cream cheese and orange rind, beating until well blended and fluffy. Whip in marshmallow mixture; then fold in whipped cream. Pour over mincemeat. Chill until firm. Garnish with additional mincemeat and chopped candied fruit to form a wreath, if desired. Makes 10-12 servings.

Drayton Valley, Alta.
Ladies Auxiliary
Branch No. 269

Kris Kringles

6 oz. semi-sweet chocolate
⅓ cup peanut butter
1 tbsp. butter
1½ cups icing sugar
¼ tsp. salt
⅓ cup liquid coffee
1 egg
3 cups unsalted soda biscuits, crumbled
1 tsp. vanilla

Melt first six ingredients in double boiler. Cool. Add remaining ingredients. Cool and shape into rolls. Makes a nice dainty and keeps well.

Keewatin, Ont.
Ladies Auxiliary
Branch No. 13

Strawberry Swirl

1 cup graham cracker crumbs
1 tbsp. sugar
¼ cup butter or margarine, melted
2 cups fresh or frozen strawberries, cut up
2 tbsp. sugar
1-3 oz. pkg. strawberry Jello
1 cup boiling water
½ lb. marshmallows
½ cup milk
1 cup whipping cream, whipped

Mix crumbs, butter and sugar. Press into a 9x13-inch pan. Chill. Sprinkle 2. tbsp. sugar over strawberries and let stand 30 minutes. Dissolve Jello in boiling water. Drain strawberries and reserve juice. Add enough water to juice to make 1 cup and add to Jello mixture. Chill till partially set. Combine marshmallows and milk. Heat and stir till marshmallows melt. Cool thoroughly. Fold in whipped cream. Add strawberries to gelatine, then swirl in marshmallow mixture. Pour over crust and chill till set. Cut in squares to serve. Good.

Piapot, Sask.
Ladies Auxiliary
Piapot Branch No. 12

Cherry Slice

2½ cups graham wafer crumbs
½ cup butter
½ cup brown sugar
½ pkg. mini marshmallows
1 cup Dream Whip
1-15 oz. can cherry pie filling

Combine first three ingredients and press half in pan. Mix marshmallows and Dream Whip and spread on first mixture. Put cherry pie filling on top and add remaining crumbs. Refrigerate.

Lacombe, Alta.
Ladies Auxiliary
Branch No. 79

Cheese Cherry Squares

2 cups crushed graham
   crackers or cracker crumbs
1 tbsp. flour
1 tsp. sugar
½ cup margarine

Mix until mixture is like corn-meal. Use ¾ of mixture to line bottom of 8x8-inch pan.

Filling:
1 cup white sugar
2 eggs, beaten
1-8 oz. pkg. cream cheese
½ cup chopped cherries or
   other dried fruit
1 tsp. vanilla

Pour over cracker mixture. Sprinkle remaining crackers over filling. Bake for 30 minutes or until filling is set. Cool and cut into squares.

Louisbourg, N.S.
Ladies Auxiliary
Branch No. 62

Lemon Squares

2 cups flour
½ cup icing sugar
1 cup margarine or butter
¼ cup flour
2 cups sugar
1 tsp. baking powder
4 eggs
4½ tbsp. lemon juice
1 tbsp. lemon rind

Combine first three ingredients and blend with a pastry blender. Press into a 9x13-inch pan and bake at 325°F. for 20 to 25 minutes. Combine flour, sugar and baking powder in a small bowl. When crust is baked, remove from oven. Beat together the eggs, lemon juice and lemon rind until frothy; then add flour/sugar mixture and blend. Pour over crust and bake at 325°F. for 20 to 25 minutes. Cool and cut into squares.

Edmonton, Alta.
Ladies Auxiliary
Jasper Place Branch No. 255

Aloha Slice

Base:
1 cup flour
1 tsp. baking powder
⅓ cup butter
1 cup brown sugar
½ cup coconut
½ cup rolled oats

Mix together and press into a 9x9-inch pan.

Topping:
½ cup oil
½ cup brown sugar
2 eggs
½ cup chopped nuts
½ cup raisins
½ cup chopped cherries
1 cup crushed pineapple,
   drained

Combine and spread over the base mixture. Bake at 325°F. for 30 to 35 minutes. Cut while still warm.

Wawanesa, Man.
Ladies Auxiliary
Branch No. 28

Dundee Bars

½ cup butter
½ cup white sugar
2 eggs
1 tsp. vanilla
2 tbsp. lemon juice
1 tbsp. lemon or orange rind
1½ cups flour
pinch of salt
1 tsp. baking powder
½ cup minced fruit
½ cup golden raisins

Combine butter, sugar, eggs, vanilla and lemon juice. Beat until fluffy, about 3 minutes. Add remaining ingredients. Grease pan well and flour. Bake at 325°F. until golden brown. Don't overbake. While still warm, glaze with the following.

Glaze:
¼ cup icing sugar
2 tbsp. lemon juice

Cool completely before cutting.

Sparwood, B.C.
Ladies Auxiliary
Michel Natal Branch No. 81

Coconut Slice

½ cup butter or margarine,
   melted
1 egg, beaten
1 cup brown sugar
⅓ cup milk
1 cup graham crumbs
1 cup fine coconut
graham wafers

Grease 8x8-inch pan with butter and line with graham wafers. Bring butter, egg, brown sugar and milk to a boil. Remove from heat and add remaining ingredients. Mix well and spread over wafers in pan. Cover with more wafers and ice as you wish. Keep refrigerated.

Spirit River, Alta.
Ladies Auxiliary
Branch No. 72

Pecan Cheesecake Bars

Crust:
⅓ cup margarine
⅓ cup brown sugar
1 cup flour
½ cup finely chopped pecans

Combine all ingredients and press into pan. Bake at 350°F. for 12 minutes.

Cheesecake Layer:
1-8 oz. pkg. cream cheese
¼ cup white sugar
1 egg
2 tbsp. milk
½ tsp. vanilla
1 tbsp. lemon juice

Mix together well and spread on crust.

Topping:
2 eggs
¼ cup brown sugar
¾ cup corn syrup
3 tbsp. flour
¼ tsp. salt
1 tsp. vanilla
¾ cup chopped pecans

Beat eggs and add other ingredients. Spread on cheese layer. Bake at 350°F. for 25 minutes. Cool and cut in bars. Freezes very well.

Langruth, Man.
Ladies Auxiliary
Branch No. 162

Petite Blackbottoms

Topping:
  1-8 oz. pkg. cream cheese
  1 egg, beaten
  1/3 cup sugar
  1/8 tsp. salt
  1-6 oz. pkg. chocolate chips

Soften and cube cream cheese. Beat well with mixer. Add egg, sugar and salt. Stir in chocolate chips and set aside.

Batter:
  1 1/2 cups flour
  1 cup sugar
  1/4 cup cocoa
  1 tsp. baking soda
  1/2 tsp. salt
  1 tsp. vanilla
  1 cup water
  1/3 cup oil
  1 tbsp. vinegar

Sift together dry ingredients. Add liquid ingredients and beat well. Using a small cupcake tin, line with cupcake papers. Fill each cup half full with batter. Top with 1 tsp. of topping. Bake at 350°F. for 20 minutes. Yields: 48.

Oak River, Man.
Ladies Auxiliary
Branch No. 150

Butter Tart Bars

  1/2 cup margarine
  1/3 cup brown sugar
  1 1/4 cups all-purpose flour

Combine ingredients and crumble well. Press into ungreased 9x9-inch pan. Bake at 350°F. for 5 minutes.

Top Layer:
  3 eggs
  1 cup brown sugar, packed
  2 tbsp. all-purpose flour
  3/4 tsp. baking powder
  1/4 tsp. salt
  1 1/2 cups chopped raisins
  1/2 cup chopped nuts

Beat eggs and sugar together until light and thick. Add remaining ingredients. Stir and spread over bottom layer. Bake at 350°F. for 30 minutes.

Vegreville, Alta.
Ladies Auxiliary
Branch No. 39

Caramel Toffee Squares

Base:
  1/2 cup plus 2 tsp. butter
  1/4 cup white sugar
  1 1/4 cups flour

Mix well and press into a 9x9-inch pan. Bake at 350°F. for 20 minutes. Cool.

Second Layer:
  1/2 cup brown sugar
  1/2 cup butter
  2 tbsp. corn syrup
  1/2 cup sweetened condensed milk

Combine in saucepan and bring to a boil. Boil 5 minutes. Remove from heat, beat and pour over first layer. I usually use a double boiler as this burns easily if not stirred. Refrigerate until set.

Top Layer:
  1-12 oz. pkg. semi-sweet chocolate chips
  2 tsp. butter
  1 oz. milk

Melt chocolate chips over low heat until they are soft. Pour over second layer. If this is too thick, add a little more butter. Chill and cut into 36 squares.

Tantallon, N.S.
Ladies Auxiliary
St. Margaret's Bay Branch No. 116

Quick Snack

  14 double or 28 single graham wafers, crushed
  1 cup brown sugar
  2 tsp. baking powder
  1 cup chopped dates
  1 cup chopped walnuts
  4 eggs, well beaten

Mix dry ingredients together. Add the well beaten eggs. Stir until moistened. Pour into a 5x7-inch pan. Bake at 350°F. for 25 minutes or longer. Do not bake too long or it will be too dry. This is a very tasty snack, and you do not need icing unless you desire or want a sweeter snack.

Drayton Valley, Alta.
Ladies Auxiliary
Branch No. 269

Apple Bars

Oat Mixture:
  1 3/4 cups rolled oats
  1 1/2 cups sifted vitamin-enriched flour
  3/4 cup butter
  1/4 tsp. baking soda
  1 cup brown sugar

Filling:
  2 1/2 cups sliced apples
  2 tbsp. butter
  1/2 cup sugar
  3/4 tsp. cinnamon

Preheat oven to 375°F. Lightly grease a 9-inch square pan. Prepare oat mixture. Pat half the mixture into the pan. Arrange sliced apples over crumb mixture. Dot with butter and sprinkle with sugar mixed with cinnamon. Cover with remaining crumb mixture. Bake 40 to 45 minutes. Cut in squares or bars. Yield: 16 bars.

Roblin, Man.
Ladies Auxiliary
Branch No. 24

Carrot Bars

  1 1/4 cups cooking oil
  2 cups white sugar
  4 eggs, well beaten
  2 cups flour
  1/2 tsp. salt
  2 tsp. baking soda
  3 tsp. cinnamon
  3 cups ground carrots

Combine cooking oil and sugar. Mix well. Add well beaten eggs. Sift together dry ingredients. Add to sugar and oil mixture and mix well. Fold in carrots. Grease and flour a 15x10x1-inch pan. Bake at 350°F. for 30 minutes. Cool.

Icing:
  1-4 oz. pkg. cream cheese
  2 tbsp soft butter
  1 3/4 cups icing sugar
  1 tsp. vanilla

Mix well and spread on cool cake.

Abbey, Sask.
Ladies Auxiliary
Branch No. 222

Fruit Slice

1½ cups flour
1 tsp. baking powder
½ tsp. baking soda
¼ tsp. salt
1 cup butter
1 cup brown sugar
1½ cups oatmeal
1 can peach pie filling or
   other filling
3 tbsp. white sugar

Sift flour, baking powder, baking soda and salt together. Rub in butter. Add sugar and oatmeal. Mix well. Spread half of crumbs in shallow 8x14-inch greased pan. Pat to make smooth. Cover with peach pie filling. Sprinkle with white sugar. Cover with remaining crumbs. Pat to make smooth. Bake at 325°F. for 30 to 35 minutes, or until lightly browned. Cut in squares and allow to cool in pan.

Emerson, Man.
Ladies Auxiliary
Branch No. 77

Banana Cherry Slice

Base:
  ½ cup butter
  3 tbsp. white sugar
  1½ cups flour
Make into crumbs and pat into a 8x8-inch pan. Bake at 325°F. for 25 minutes. Let cool.

Filling:
  25 marshmallows
  1 mashed banana
  15 maraschino cherries,
    drained and cut up
Melt marshmallows. Add remaining ingredients and blend well. Spread over cool base.

Icing:
  ½ cup creamed butter
  ¾ cup icing sugar
  1 tsp. vanilla
  2 tbsp. cold milk
  2 tbsp. boiling water
Beat all together. When ready, spread on cool cake.

Selkirk, Man.
Ladies Auxiliary
Branch No. 42

Date Almond Squares

Base:
  6 tbsp. butter or margarine
  ½ cup white sugar
  2 egg yolks
  1 tsp. vanilla
  1½ cups flour
  1 tsp. baking powder
  ¼ tsp. salt
Top:
  1½ cups chopped dates
  ¾ cup water
  2 egg whites
  1 cup brown sugar
  ½ cup blanched almonds

Cream butter; blend in sugar; add egg yolks and vanilla. Sift flour with baking powder and salt. Mix together and press into 8x12-inch pan. Cook dates and water together until thick, cool and spread on uncooked bottom crust. Beat egg whites until stiff. Add brown sugar and beat until sugar is blended in. Spread over dates and sprinkle with shaved almonds. Bake at 350°F. for 35 to 40 minutes.

Argyle, Man.
Ladies Auxiliary
Brant Argyle Branch No. 222

Party Chews

Bottom:
  ½ cup butter or margarine
  1 cup flour
  ½ cup brown sugar
Mix well and pat into a 9x9-inch pan. Bake at 350°F. for 15 minutes.

Top Layer:
  2 eggs
  small cup brown sugar
  ½ tsp. vanilla
  ¼ tsp. salt
  1 cup coconut
  1 cup Rice Krispies
  small cup nuts
Beat eggs; add sugar, vanilla, salt, coconut, Rice Krispies and nuts. Mix well. Spread on bottom crust. Bake at 350°F. for 20 to 25 minutes.

Kensington, P.E.I.
Ladies Auxiliary
Branch No. 9

Mandarin Orange Squares

1 cup flour
1 cup brown sugar
1 tbsp. baking soda
1 egg
½ tsp. salt

Mix dry ingredients. Beat egg and add small can mandarin oranges and juice. Put in greased 8x8-inch pan. Bake at 350°F. for 30 minutes.

Topping:
  2 tbsp. butter, melted
  2 tbsp. milk
  scant ¾ cup brown sugar
Pour over cake and put back in oven till bubbles form. Serve hot with ice cream.

Ontario Provincial Command
Ladies Auxiliary

Apple Bars

Dough:
  2½ cups flour
  1 tsp. salt
  1 cup margarine
  1 egg yolk and milk to make
    ⅓ cup liquid or a little more
Sift flour and salt together. Mash margarine into flour, till about the size of large peas. Pour liquid into the mixture and mix till it clings together. Divide in half and roll half to fit 12x17-inch cookie sheet with built up sides. Sprinkle with 2 handfuls of Corn Flakes.

Filling:
  8-10 apples, sliced
  1 cup sugar
  1 tsp. cinnamon
Mix together and place on bottom layer. Place on top crust, seal edge like apple pie, brush with egg white. Bake at 350°F. for 50 or 60 minutes. Remove from oven. Glaze.

Glaze:
  1 cup icing sugar
  2 tbsp. water
  1 tsp. vanilla
When cool, cut in squares.

Fort Macleod, Alta.
Ladies Auxiliary
Branch No. 46

Christmas Squares

½ cup margarine
1 cup brown sugar
1 cup mincemeat
2 eggs
1 tsp. rum or rum extract
½ cup flour
½ tsp. baking powder
½ cup chopped nuts
salt

Cream margarine and sugar together. Blend in mincemeat, eggs and flavoring. Add dry ingredients. Mix well and add nuts. Turn into a 9x13-inch greased and floured pan. Bake at 350°F. for 40 to 45 minutes. Top with butter icing and decorate with halves of red and green cherries.

Rouge River, Que.
Ladies Auxiliary
Branch No. 192

Chocolate Chip Bars

1¼ cups flour
¾ tsp. baking soda
½ tsp. salt

Mix and set aside. Combine:

1¼ cups or 8 oz. dates, cut up
¾ cup brown sugar
½ cup butter
½ cup water

in saucepan. Cook until dates soften. Stir in 1 cup (6 oz.) chocolate chips (semi-sweet) and blend in 2 eggs. Mix well. Add dry ingredients alternately with ½ cup orange juice and ½ cup milk. Blend thoroughly and add 1 cup chopped walnuts. Spread in a greased 15x10-inch jelly roll pan (or if you prefer a cake, bake in greased 9x13-inch pan.)

Orange Frosting:

1½ cups icing sugar
2 tbsp. butter
2 tsp. grated orange rind
2-3 tbsp. orange juice

Combine icing sugar, butter and orange rind. Blend in orange juice. Add more icing sugar if needed.

Rainy River, Ont.
Ladies Auxiliary
Branch No. 54

Chocolate Chip and Walnut Squares

½ cup butter or margarine
1½ cups graham wafers
1 cup shredded coconut
1 small pkg. chocolate chips
1 can sweetened condensed milk
1 cup chopped nuts

Preheat oven to 350°F. Use a 9x13-inch pan. Do not stir this mixture. Melt butter in baking pan. Spread graham wafer crumbs evenly over butter. Place an even layer of coconut. Sprinkle chocolate chips over coconut. Pour sweetened condensed milk over and top with chopped nuts. Do not stir. Bake 35 to 40 minutes. Cool completely before slicing. Delicious.

Edmonton, Alta.
Ladies Auxiliary
Norwood Branch No. 178

Mardi Gras Bars

Pastry:

1¼ cups flour
¼ tsp. salt
⅔ cup brown sugar
¼ cup butter
2 egg yolks
½ tsp. vanilla

Blend together flour and salt. Cream together remaining ingredients; blend in dry ingredients. Press into bottom of 9-inch square pan. Bake in preheated 350°F. oven for 15 minutes.

Topping:

2 egg whites
2 tbsp. flour
½ cup chocolate sundae topping
½ cup coconut
½ cup chopped maraschino cherries
½ cup chopped nuts

Beat egg whites to form stiff peaks. Blend in flour and chocolate sundae topping. Stir in remaining ingredients. Spread over baked crust. Return to oven and bake an additional 18 to 20 minutes. Cool and cut into bars. Makes 24 bars.

Waverley, N.S.
Ladies Auxiliary
Dieppe Branch No. 90

Orange Squares

Base:

1 cup margarine
2 cups flour
pinch salt
1 tsp. baking powder
¾ cup white sugar
2 cups coconut

Mix as for pie crust. Press into pan, reserving half for top.

Filling:

1½ cups white sugar
3 heaping tbsp. custard powder
juice of 2 oranges
1½ cups boiling water
pinch salt

Cook until thick, then add 1½ tbsp. butter. Spread over base and cover with reserved topping. Bake in oven until brown.

Joggins, N.S.
Ladies Auxiliary
Branch No. 4

Chocolate Chip Party Bars

Base:

¼ cup margarine
1 cup brown sugar
1 cup flour
1 tsp. baking powder
½ cup coconut
½ cup rolled oats

Topping:

2 eggs
½ cup brown sugar
¼ cup margarine, melted
1 tbsp. flour
pinch of salt
1-8 oz. pkg. chocolate chips
few nuts

Mix together base and press into a 9x9-inch pan. Blend together topping ingredients and spread over base. Bake at 350°F. for 35 minutes.

Kensington, P.E.I.
Ladies Auxiliary
Branch No. 9

Pineapple Tart Cake

½ cup butter
1 cup flour
1 can crushed pineapple
½ cup sugar
3 level tbsp. cornstarch
1 lump butter
Meringue:
  2 egg whites
  ⅓ cup sugar
  1 cup coconut
  ½ tsp. baking powder

Rub butter and flour together. Press into pan and bake at 350°F. for 5 minutes. Cook and thicken pineapple and sugar with cornstarch. Add butter and spread on crust. Cover with meringue. Continue baking until light brown.

Saskatoon, Sask.
Ladies Auxiliary
Nutana Branch No. 362

Icelandic Vinertarta

1 cup butter or margarine
1½ cups white sugar
3 large eggs
2 tbsp. cream or canned milk
4 cups flour
1 tsp. baking powder
1 tbsp. almond extract
1 tsp. cardamon seed
Filling:
  1 lb. prunes
  1 cup brown sugar
  1 tsp. cinnamon
  ½ cup water that prunes have boiled in

Combine ingredients for the filling and bring to a boil. Cook for a few minutes, then add 1 tsp. vanilla. Roll pastry and cut 5 (or 7) rounds or squares (depending on how large you make them). Bake in moderate oven until lightly brown.
When cool, spread with filling. Continue until all rounds or squares are used. Ice if desired.

Gilbert Plains, Man.
Ladies Auxiliary
Branch No. 98

Arrowroot Squares

30 Arrowroot cookies, broken into pieces, do not crush
½ cup butter, melted
8 tbsp. white sugar
8 tbsp. cocoa
2 eggs, well beaten
1 tsp. vanilla

Cook all ingredients except cookie pieces, together in a double boiler until thick (about 5 to 10 minutes). Pour mixture over cookies. Mix well. Put in an 8x8-inch greased pan and pat down well. Cover with topping.

Topping:
  1½ cups icing sugar
  1 tbsp. butter
  1 tsp. vanilla
  3 tbsp. cocoa
  pinch salt
  milk

Store in fridge until set, then cut in squares. Store in fridge.

Western Shore, N.S.
Ladies Auxiliary
Branch No. 144

Chocolate Fingers

4 cups rolled oats
1 cup fine coconut
½ cup milk
1 cup margarine or butter
1 cup sugar
½ tsp. vanilla
1/8 tsp. salt
1-12 oz. pkg. chocolate chips
½ bar parafin wax

Combine margarine, sugar, vanilla and milk in a saucepan. Bring to a boil over medium heat, about 5 minutes. In another bowl, combine rolled oats, coconut and salt. Mix well. Add syrup mixture. Press into a 9x13-inch greased pan. Place in freezer to harden. Then cut into finger size bars. Melt chocolate chips and wax in double boiler and dip bars. Refrigerate.

Wetaskiwin, Alta.
Ladies Auxiliary
Branch No. 86

Peanut Crunch

1 cup Rice Krispies
½ cup corn syrup
¼ cup melted margarine
2 tbsp. vanilla instant pudding powder
3 tbsp. margarine
1 cup crushed Corn Flakes
½ cup brown sugar
3 tbsp. milk
3 squares semi-sweet chocolate
1 cup peanut butter
2 cups icing sugar

Mix Rice Krispies and Corn Flakes, stir well. Combine brown sugar, corn syrup and peanut butter in saucepan and heat till sugar dissolves. Mix with cereal. Line a 9x13-inch buttered pan with this mixture. Chill. Mix together melted margarine, pudding powder and milk. Blend in icing sugar and spread over cereal layer. Melt 3 tbsp. margarine and 3 squares chocolate. Spread over other layers. Chill and cut into small pieces. Store in fridge.

Whitehorse, Yukon
Ladies Auxiliary
Branch No. 254

Krispie Squares

2 pkgs. butterscotch chips
2 pkgs. chocolate chips
1 cup peanut butter
7 cups Rice Krispies
2 tbsp. water or more
1 cup icing sugar
4 tbsp. margarine

Melt butterscotch chips with peanut butter over low heat. Remove and add Rice Krispies. Spread half of mixture in 8x10-inch pan. Melt chocolate chips, margarine, icing sugar and water over low heat. Spread over mixture in pan. Add remaining butterscotch mixture. Cool in fridge but cut before completely hard.

Grand Harbour, N.B.
Ladies Auxiliary
Grand Manan Branch No. 44

Lemon Crumbles

1 lemon pie filling
1¾ cups soda crackers
1½ cups coconut
¾ cup flour
1 cup butter or margarine
¾ cup white sugar
pinch of salt
2 tsp. baking powder

Combine flour and baking powder, rub in butter. Add soda cracker crumbs, sugar and coconut. Spread half of mixture in greased pan. Cover with lemon pie filling. Spread remaining crumbs on top. Bake at 325°F. for 30 minutes or till brown.

Armdale, N.S.
Ladies Auxiliary
Halifax County Branch No. 153

Gumdrop Bars

⅓ cup soft shortening
1 cup brown sugar
1 egg
2 tsp. vanilla
½ tsp. almond extract
1⅓ cups all-purpose flour, sifted
1 tsp. baking powder
½ tsp. salt
1 tsp. cinnamon
¼ tsp. evaporated milk
1 cup gumdrops, cut up
½ cup walnuts

Heat oven to 350°F. Grease a 9-inch square pan. Beat shortening, sugar, egg and vanilla together until fluffy. Sift dry ingredients together and add to creamed mixture along with milk. Add gumdrops, walnuts, and blend well. Bake about 40 minutes. Cool in pan for 5 minutes. Top with icing below.

Icing:
1 cup sifted icing sugar
½ tsp. vanilla
4 tsp. milk

Combine ingredients and spread over bars. Cool to luke warm. Cut in bars.

Jacquet River, N.B.
Ladies Auxiliary
Durham Branch No. 77

Apple Brownies

½ cup melted butter or shortening
3 medium or large apples
1 cup sugar
1 egg
½ cup walnuts (optional)
1 cup flour
½ tsp. baking powder

½ tsp. baking soda
¼ tsp. salt
1 tsp. cinnamon

Mix butter and sugar, add egg. Beat well. Stir in apples which have been pared, cored and cut in thin slices or strips. Mix and sift dry ingredients and blend with apple mixture. Bake in a 9x9-inch pan at 350°F. for 40 to 50 minutes.   Serve plain or with ice cream. There is no chocolate in this recipe.

St. Andrews, N.B.
Ladies Auxiliary
Passamaquoddy Branch No. 8

Cranberry Squares

½ cup soft butter
1 cup sifted flour
2 tbsp. icing sugar
2 eggs
1 cup white sugar
⅓ cup flour
¼ tsp. salt
1 tsp. baking powder
1 tsp. almond extract
½ cup chopped raisins
½ cup desiccated coconut
½ cup chopped almonds
⅔ cup cranberry sauce

Mix first three ingredients together and spread in the bottom of a greased 8-inch square pan. Beat eggs thoroughly and add sugar, sifted dry ingredients and flavoring. Stir in remaining ingredients.   Spread   mixture evenly over the crust. Bake at 350°F. for 40 minutes. Cool and frost with lemon flavored butter icing. Cut in squares.

Hazelridge, Man.
Ladies Auxiliary
Hazelridge Branch No. 146

Reese's Bars

2½ cups graham cracker crumbs
1 cup peanut butter
1 cup melted margarine or butter
1-12 oz. pkg. chocolate chips, melted
2¾ cups icing sugar

Melt chips in double boiler and set aside. Mix other ingredients. Press firmly into an ungreased 9x13-inch pan. Pour melted chips over top and spread. Refrigerate. Cut before cool.

Stanstead, Que.
Ladies Auxiliary
Branch No. 5

Drizzled Chocolate Mint Bars

1 cup chocolate mint chips (250 ml)
¼ cup margarine (50 ml)
¼ cup icing sugar (50 ml)
1 egg
1½ cups graham wafer crumbs (375 ml)
½ cup chopped walnuts (125 ml)
¼ cup margarine (50 ml)
2 cups icing sugar (500 ml)
2 tbsp. milk (30 ml)
green food coloring (optional)

Melt chips and ¼ cup margarine over hot water. Reserve ¼ cup for top. Add ¼ cup icing sugar and egg to remaining melted chips. Stir in wafer crumbs and nuts. Press evenly on bottom of 8-inch square pan. Chill. Cream ¼ cup margarine, 2 cups icing sugar and milk until fluffy. Add green food coloring. Spread evenly over base in pan. Drizzle or spread reserved melted chips over top. Chill until firm. Cut into bars. Makes about 3 dozen.

Red Deer, Alta.
Ladies Auxiliary
Branch No. 35

Pineapple Brownies

1½ cups flour
1 tsp. baking powder
½ tsp. salt
½ tsp. cinnamon
1 tsp. vanilla
1 cup crushed pineapple
¾ cup margarine
1½ cups white sugar
3 eggs
2 squares chocolate, melted
½ cup walnuts

Cream margarine and sugar. Add eggs, then dry ingredients. Add vanilla. Divide batter, adding drained pineapple to one part and chocolate and nuts to the other. Put half of dark on bottom, all white in center and top with remaining dark. Use 9x9-inch pan. Bake at 350°F. for 30 minutes. Ice with chocolate icing.

Digby, N.S.
Ladies Auxiliary
Branch No. 22

Fudgy Cream Cheese Brownies

Chocolate Batter:
½ cup flour
½ tsp. baking powder
¼ tsp. salt
4 squares semi-sweet
  chocolate
3 tbsp. butter
2 eggs
¾ cup white sugar
Cream Cheese Batter:
1-4 oz. pkg. cream cheese
2 tbsp. butter
½ tsp. vanilla
¼ cup white sugar
1 egg

Mix both batters, using separate bowls. Pour half the chocolate batter into a greased 8x8-inch pan. Spoon cream cheese batter on top, then remaining chocolate batter. Swirl with a knife to make marbled effect. Bake at 350°F. for about 35 minutes. Frost if you wish.

New Richmond, Que.
Ladies Auxiliary
Bay Chaleurs Branch No. 172

Peanut Butter Fudge Slice

½ cup margarine
½ cup peanut butter
1½ cups white sugar
2 squares unsweetened chocolate
2 cups all-purpose flour
3 eggs
1½ tsp. vanilla
1½ tsp. baking soda
¾ tsp. salt
1½ cups cold water

Cream margarine, peanut butter and sugar until fluffy. Add eggs, one at a time. Stir in melted chocolate and vanilla. Sift flour, baking soda and salt; add to creamed mixture alternately with water. Pour into prepared pan. Bake at 350°F. for 1 hour and 10 minutes. Spread with prepared topping.

Topping:
¼ cup margarine
¼ cup peanut butter
½ tsp. salt
2½ cups icing sugar
5-6 tbsp. milk
Beat until light and fluffy. Spread over mixture in pan.

Pipestone, Man.
Ladies Auxiliary
Pipestone Branch No. 230

Walnut Slice

Shortbread Base:
1 cup flour
½ cup butter
1 tbsp. icing sugar
Mix as for pastry and pat into a 8x8-inch pan.

Filling:
2 eggs
1 cup brown sugar
4 level tbsp. flour
1 tsp. baking powder
¼ tsp. salt
1 cup chopped walnuts
½ cup coconut

Beat eggs until light. Add remaining ingredients and mix. Pour on top of shortbread base. Bake at 350°F. for 35 minutes.

Wawanesa, Man.
Ladies Auxiliary
Branch No. 28

Peanut Butter Ribbons

1 cup sifted flour
½ tsp. baking soda
½ cup shortening
¾ cup brown sugar, packed
½ cup peanut butter
½ cup water
1 cup uncooked rolled oats
1-8 oz. pkg. chocolate chips

Sift flour and baking soda into a large bowl. Add shortening, sugar, peanut butter and water. Beat until smooth and creamy, then blend in rolled oats. Spread half the mixture into a greased 8-inch square pan. Cover with melted chocolate chips and top with remaining dough mixture. Bake at 350°F. for 30 to 35 minutes. Cool slightly and cut into bars. Yield: approx. 24 bars.

New Glasgow, N.S.
Ladies Auxiliary
Normany Branch No. 34

Cranberry Oatmeal Squares

1 tbsp. cornstarch
½ cup cold water
2 cups cranberries
¼ cup raisins
1 cup sugar
1 tsp. vanilla
½ cup butter
1 cup oatmeal
¼ cup wheat germ
½ cup flour or whole wheat
  flour
¾ cup brown sugar
¼ cup coconut

Dissolve cornstarch in cold water. Add cranberries, raisins, sugar and vanilla; cook until thick. Combine remaining ingredients in a separate bowl and spread half of mixture in pan. Spread with cranberry mixture and top with remainder of dry mixture. Bake at 350°F. for 30 minutes.

Grand Harbour, N.B.
Ladies Auxiliary
Grand Manan Branch No. 44

Valley Apple Squares

1/3 cup butter
2 tbsp. brown sugar
1 cup flour

Make up as for pastry and spread in bottom of an 8x8-inch pan.

Filling:

1/2 cup sugar
1 large apple, sliced thin
1 egg
juice and rind of 1 lemon
1 tsp. butter

Combine all ingredients and cook over low heat until soft. Cool and spread on base.

Topping:

3/4 cup sugar
1 tbsp. butter
1 egg
1 1/4 cups coconut

Mix in order given and spread on filling. Bake in one operation at 350°F. for about 30 minutes or until golden brown.

New Ross, N.S.
Ladies Auxiliary
New Ross Branch No. 79

Molasses Fruit Bars

3/4 cup shortening
1 1/2 cups sugar
2 eggs
2 tsp. baking soda
3 1/4 cups flour
2 tsp. baking powder
1/2 tsp. cinnamon
1/2 tsp. nutmeg
1/2 tsp. cloves
3/4 tsp. salt
2 cups white raisins
1/2 cup molasses

Cream shortening and sugar; add egg, then dry ingredients with molasses. Roll into 12 long rolls (1/2x13" rolls) and place 3 on a cookie sheet. Bake at 350°F. for 15 minutes only for chewy bars. If desired, drizzle with thin icing (icing sugar and water). Slice at an angle into bars while still warm.

Piney, Man.
Ladies Auxiliary
Branch No. 176

Sputnik's Contribution

(An unbaked slice)

3 cups graham wafer crumbs
3 cups small marshmallows
4 oz. glazed or maraschino cherries
1/2 cup walnuts
1 cup coconut
1 can Eagle Brand milk

Mix till moist and pat into a cake pan and ice with the following:

1/4 cup butter or margarine
1/4 cup milk
1 cup brown sugar

Boil for three mintues, then beat till quite thick and spread over above. Store in refrigerator.

Pipestone, Man.
Ladies Auxiliary
Pipestone Branch No. 230

Date Squares

1 cup sifted flour
1 tsp. baking soda
1 cup brown sugar, packed
2 cups rolled oats
3/4 cup soft butter or shortening

Sift flour, baking soda and brown sugar together. Add rolled oats and soft butter; combine thoroughly. Spread half of this mixture onto a greased and lightly floured 10-inch pan. Pat together well.

Filling:

2 cups chopped dates
1/3 cup brown sugar, packed
1 1/4 cups water
1 tbsp. flour
1 tsp. vanilla

Combine dates, brown sugar, water and flour and cook until thickened, stirring constantly. Cool and add vanilla. Spread filling evenly over pastry mixture; cover with remaining pastry and pat together. Bake at 375°F. for 20 minutes. Cut in squares when cool.

Winnipeg, Man.
Ladies Auxiliary
General Sir Sam Steele Branch No. 117

Rocky Roads

1-6 oz. pkg. butterscotch chips
1/2 cup butter
1 cup icing sugar
2 cups mini marshmallows, colored
1 egg
whole graham wafers
grated coconut

Combine butterscotch chips, butter, egg and icing sugar and melt over low heat. When melted, set aside to cool slightly. Line a 8-inch pan with graham wafer. When mixture cools, stir in 2 cups marshmallows and pour over graham wafers; sprinkle coconut on top.

Penticton, B.C.
Ladies Auxiliary
Branch No. 40

Desserts
Steamed Pudding

1 loaf white bread crumbs
1/2 lb. brown sugar
1/2 tsp. salt
1/2 tsp. cloves
1/2 tsp. cinnamon
1/2 tps. nutmeg
1/2 lb. suet
1/2 lb. currants
1/2 lb. seeded raisins
1/2 lb. seedless raisins
1/2 lb. citron peel
1 cup grated carrots
4 eggs, well beaten
1 cup fruit juice
1 cup milk
1 cup cold coffee
1 small tsp. baking soda
1/2 cup flour to dredge fruit

Combine all ingredients and steam 3 hours.

Pudding Sauce:

1 cup brown sugar
1/2 cup butter
2 egg whites
1 cup whipped cream
vanilla

Boil brown sugar and butter together. Pour over egg whites, which are beaten stiff. Cool and add whipped cream and vanilla.

Oak River, Man.
Ladies Auxiliary
Branch No. 150

Trifle

(This trifle recipe is ideal for catering.)

    white cake
    1 can fruit cocktail, reserve
        cherries
    1 pkg. Jello, any flavor
    juice from fruit cocktail and
        enough water to make
        liquid for Jello
    1-3 cup vanilla instant
        pudding
    whipped cream

Cut up cake to fill bowl half full. Drain fruit cocktail, reserving juice. Sprinkle fruit over cake in bowl. Make Jello, using reserved juice from fruit cocktail as part of liquid. Mix the vanilla pudding and pour over cake mixture. When set, cover with whipped cream and garnish with cherries.

Redwater, Alta.
Ladies Auxiliary
Redwater Branch No. 251

Trifle

    ½ pkg. pudding cake mix
    1 large can fruit cocktail,
        drained
    1 small can mandarin
        oranges, drained
    1 small bottle red maraschino
        cherries, drained
    1 small bottle green maraschi-
        no cherries, drained
    1 pkg. lemon pie filling mix
        (to make one pie)
    ½ pt. whipping cream

Bake the cake and cool. Cut to size of bottom of bowl or cube and place in bowl. Pour on fruit cocktail, then mandarin oranges and cherries, saving a few cherries for top, if desired. Make lemon pie filling and let cool slightly; then pour over the fruit. Whip cream and pour on top. Arrange remaining cherries on top.

Chezzetcook, N.S.
Ladies Auxiliary
Branch No. 161

Pistachio Dessert

Base:
    1 cup flour
    1 cup chopped nuts (pecans
        or almonds are best)
    ½ cup soft butter
Combine all ingredients and press into a 9x13-inch pan. Bake at 375°F. for 15 minutes. Cool.

Center:
    1 cup icing sugar
    1-8 oz. pkg. cream cheese
    1 cup Cool Whip (use a large
        container, reserving some
        for top)
Blend together and over top of base. Refrigerate till set.

Topping:
    2 pkgs. pistachio instant pud-
        ding
    3 cups cold milk
Mix together and spread over cheese mixture. Spread with remainder of Cool Whip and refrigerate. Note: 1 can of drained pineapple may be added to topping mixture.

Carman, Man.
Ladies Auxiliary
Branch No. 18

Pistachio Freezer Cake

(dessert)

    2 pkgs. chocolate wafers,
        crushed
    ½ cup butter, melted after
        measuring
    2 pkgs. pistachio instant
        pudding
    ½ gallon vanilla ice cream
    1 large container Cool Whip

Mix wafer crumbs and butter. Pat into a 9x13-inch pan. Save 1 cup for topping. Mix together pudding, ice cream and Cool Whip. Spread over crumb mixture in pan and top with remaining crumbs. Freeze. Keeps well for 3 weeks. Take out 10 minutes before serving.

Riding Mountain, Man.
Ladies Auxiliary
Branch No. 202

Frozen Pumpkin Dessert

    2½ cups Rice Krispies
    ¾ cup sugar
    ½ cup butter, melted
    1 qt. vanilla ice cream
    1 cup canned pumpkin
    ¾ cup sugar
    ¼ tsp. cinnamon
    ¼ tsp. nutmeg
    1 pkg. Dream Whip or 2 cups
        of whipped topping

Crush Rice Krispies. Mix with sugar and melted butter. Press firmly into a 9x13-inch pan. Chill. Place softened ice cream over the crust. Freeze. Mix pumpkin, spices and sugar together. Fold in Dream Whip. Spread over ice cream layer. Freeze. Cut and serve with additional ice cream if desired. Serves 12 to 15.

Brandon, Man.
Ladies Auxiliary
Wheat City Branch No. 247

Cheese Cake Special

    22 graham wafers, crushed
    ½ cup sugar
    ½ cup butter
Melt butter and combine crushed wafers and sugar. Use ¾ of the mixture for a base, reserving the other ¼ for topping.

    1 small Jello powder, any
        flavor
    1 cup boiling water
    1 large can evaporated milk
    1 cup sugar
    1-8 oz. pkg. cream cheese
    2 tsp. vanilla
Dissolve Jello in boiling water and chill. Chill evaporated milk and beat, add to partially set Jello. Blend cream cheese with sugar and vanilla. Add to Jello mixture. Pour over crumb base and sprinkle with remaining crumbs. Let chill till set.

100 Mile House, B.C.
Ladies Auxiliary
Branch No. 260

Coconut Cream Squares

Bottom:
1 cup graham wafer crumbs
¼ cup butter
¼ cup brown sugar
Combine and press into pan. Bake at 375°F. for 8 minutes.

Topping:
1 pkg. coconut cream pie filling
Dream Whip
Make pie filling and spread over bottom. Top with Dream Whip.

Sydney, N.S.
Ladies Auxiliary
Branch No. 128

Pumpkin Cake Roll

3 eggs
⅔ cups mashed pumpkin
¾ cup flour
2 tsp. cinnamon
1 tsp. baking powder
½ tsp. nutmeg
1 cup finely cut walnuts
powdered sugar
1 cup white sugar
1 tsp. lemon juice
1 tsp. ginger
½ tsp. salt
Filling:
1 cup powdered sugar
½ tsp. vanilla
2-3 oz. pkgs. cream cheese
4 tbsp. butter or margarine

Beat eggs for 5 minutes; gradually beat in sugar. Add pumpkin and lemon. Stir flour, baking powder, cinnamon, ginger, nutmeg and salt. Fold into pumpkin mixture. Put into greased 15x10x1-inch pan. Top with walnuts. Bake at 375°F. for 15 minutes. Turn out on towel sprinkled with sugar. Roll towel and cake together, cool. For filling: Combine sugar, cream cheese, butter and vanilla. Spread over cake. Roll and chill. Yield: 8 servings.

Emerson, Man.
Ladies Auxiliary
Branch No. 77

Vanilla Chocolate Velvet Dessert
(Very good)

Base:
1 cup flour
½ cup margarine or butter
1 cup chopped walnuts
Combine all ingredients and spread in large size cookie sheet. Bake at 350°F. for 20 minutes. Cool.

1-16 oz. pkg. cream cheese
½ cup icing sugar
small container of Cool Whip
1 pkg. vanilla instant pudding
1 pkg. chocolate instant pudding
3 cups milk
small container of Cool Whip

Blend cream cheese with icing sugar and spread over base. Cover with 1 container Cool Whip. Mix vanilla pudding with 1½ cups milk. Mix chocolate pudding with 1½ cups milk. Let pudding thicken. Pour vanilla pudding over Cool Whip, then a layer of chocolate pudding. Cover with another container of Cool Whip. Keep in fridge overnight before serving. Even better if frozen and then brought out before ready to serve. Keeps frozen well.

Russell, Man.
Ladies Auxiliary
Branch No. 159

Figgy Duff

½ cup butter
2 cups flour
1 egg
¾ cup sugar
2 tsp. baking powder
½ cup milk or water
1 cup raisins
pinch of salt

Combine dry ingredients and add milk and egg. Place in cloth bag and boil for 1 hour in pot of water. Ingredients can also be steamed in a pudding mold. To make a plain duff follow same recipe but omit raisins.

Springdale, Nfld.
Ladies Auxiliary
Branch No. 40

Pumpkin Torte

Serves 10 to 12

2 cups graham cracker crumbs
⅓ cup sugar
½ cup melted butter
2 eggs
¾ cup brown sugar, packed
1-8 oz. pkg. cream cheese, softened

Combine cracker crumbs, white sugar and butter. Press crumbs in bottom of 9x13-inch baking pan. Beat eggs and add brown sugar; mix well and blend in the softened cream cheese. Cream well and spoon over the crumbs. Bake at 350°F. for 20 minutes. Cool. Spoon the following pumpkin topping over the cooled cheese layer and set several hours or overnight.

Pumpkin Topping:
2 cups canned pumpkin
½ cup sugar
2 tsp. cinnamon
½ tsp. salt
3 egg yolks
½ cup milk
1 envelope unflavored gelatin
¼ cup water
3 egg whites
¼ cup sugar

Combine pumpkin, ½ cup sugar, cinnamon, salt and egg yolks in a saucepan. Stir in milk and bring to a boil (mixture will plop). Cook, stirring until slightly thickend, about one minute. Remove from heat and stir in gelatin which has been moistened in the water. Cool to room temperature. Beat egg whites to soft peaks and add ¼ cup sugar. Beat stiff and fold into the cooled pumpkin mixture.

Grand Forks, B.C.
Ladies Auxiliary
Branch No. 59

Chocolate Mincemeat Bars

**2 cups flour
2 tsp. baking soda
1 cup sugar
½ cup shortening
3 eggs
1-12 oz. pkg. chocolate chips
1¾ cups mincemeat**

Sift flour and baking soda together; set aside. Combine sugar and shortening, beating till creamy. Add eggs, one at a time, beating after each addition. Continue beating until light. Stir in flour mixture and chocolate chips and mincemeat. Spread in greased 15x10x1-inch pan. Bake at 375°F. for 30 minutes. Cut into bars. Makes nearly 5 dozen if cut small.

Murdockville, Que.
Ladies Auxiliary
Branch No. 218

Spotted Dick

(English)

**2 cups flour
4 level tsp. baking powder
½ cup margarine
water to make a stiff dough
1 cups raisins**

Blanch raisins in boiling water for a few minutes; set aside. Flake margarine into flour and baking powder. Add raisins and water, mixing to stiff consistency. Lay out rectangular cloth (tea towel), dust with flour. Shape dough into long roll. Wrap in towel. Tie ends, put into large pot of rapidly boiling water. Boil one hour, covered. To serve, slice. Serve with either a sprinkle of sugar, syrup or a custard sauce. Recipe may be doubled. Check constantly when cooking that water does not boil dry. Variation: omit raisins. Roll dough into rectangular. Spread with jam. Roll jelly roll fashion and cook as above.

Evansburg, Alta.
Ladies Auxiliary
Branch No. 196

Blueberry Steam Pudding

**½ cup shortening
½ cup brown sugar
1 egg
1 cup flour
2 tsp. baking powder
1 tsp. vanilla
pinch of salt
½ cup blueberries
½ cup milk**

Cream shortening, sugar and egg together. Add remaining ingredients and mix well. Pour into a well greased pudding bowl. Steam for 1½ hours.

Port Rexton, Nfld.
Ladies Auxiliary
Branch No. 20

Blueberry Delight

Base:
**2 cups wafer crumbs
½ cup melted margarine**
Mix together and press into pan. Chill.

Filling:
**1-8 oz. pkg. cream cheese
½ cup white sugar
2 eggs, beaten
½ tsp. vanilla**
Beat together and spread over base. Bake at 350°F. for 20 minutes. Cool. Spread 1 can of blueberry pie filling over top. Top with whipped cream or Dream Whip.

Selkirk, Man.
Ladies Auxiliary
Branch No. 42

Nova Scotia Blueberry Grunt

**1 qt. blueberries
½ cup sugar or more to taste
½ cup water
2 cups flour
4 tsp. baking powder
1 tsp. sugar
1 tbsp. butter
1 tbsp. shortening
milk**

Boil blueberries, sugar and water in a large saucepan, till there is lots of juice. Sift together flour, baking powder and sugar. Cut in butter and shortening. Add sufficient milk to make a soft dough like biscuit dough. Drop by tablespoon over berries. Cover tightly and cook 15 minutes. Serve with cream. Delicious.

Antigonish, N.S.
Ladies Auxiliary
Arras Branch No. 59

Blueberry Buckle

**½ cup shortening
½ cup sugar
1 egg, beaten
2 cups flour
2½ tsp. baking powder
¼ tsp. salt
½ cup milk**

Combine to make a stiff dough and spread in a greased casserole. Spread with 3 cups blueberries (other fruit may also be used). Crumble the following over top:
**½ cup brown sugar
½ cup flour
½ tsp. cinnamon
¼ cup butter**
Bake at 350°F. for 45 to 50 minutes. Cut in squares and serve warm. Top with ice cream if desired.

Caledonia, N.S.
Ladies Auxiliary
A.L. Patterson Branch No. 87

Float Pudding

**1 cup flour
½ cup white sugar
salt
½ cup raisins, dates or sliced apples
2 tsp. baking powder
½ cup sweet milk**
Mix together and put into buttered dish.

Sauce:
**1 cup brown sugar
butter (size of an egg)
3 cups boiling water
1 tsp. vanilla**
Dissolve and pour over batter, but do not mix. Bake at 350°F. for 30 to 45 minutes.

Red Lake, Ont.
Ladies Auxiliary
Branch No. 102

Quick Easy Dessert

(No cooking)

- ½ box graham wafers, crushed
- ¼ cup plus 1 tbsp. melted butter or margarine
- ¼ cup brown sugar
- ½ pkg. colored mini marshmallows
- ½ can (or whole, if desired) pie filling of your choice
- ½ pt. whipped cream or 1 envelope Dream Whip

Mix crumbs, melted butter and brown sugar. Press half of mixture into an 8x8-inch square pan. Beat cream until stiff; add marshmallows and spread half of mixture over crumbs in pan, then cover with pie filling, balance of whipped cream mixture, then sprinkle with other half of crumbs on top. Chill in fridge a few hours or overnight. Can be frozen for future use.

Evansburg, Alta.
Ladies Auxiliary
Branch No. 196

Old-Fashioned Molasses Pudding

- 1 cup molasses
- ½ cup sugar
- 1 tsp. cinnamon
- 1 tsp. cloves
- 1 tsp. spice
- ½ cup hot water
- 1 tsp. baking soda
- ½ cup butter, melted
- ½ lb. raisins
- 3 cups sifted flour
- ½ tsp. salt

Combine molasses, sugar and spices. Dissolve baking soda in hot water; then add to molasses mixture. Add melted butter and raisins. Mix well. Add sifted flour and salt, a little at a time. Pour into pudding bag or greased mould and steam 2 to 2½ hours. (Cover mould tightly).

Wabush, Labrador
Ladies Auxiliary
Grant Crerar Branch No. 57

Butter Brickle Dessert

- 2 cups flour
- ½ cup oatmeal
- ½ cup margarine
- ½ cup brown sugar
- 1 cup chopped pecans
- 1 jar Kraft caramel sauce
- 1 pt. vanilla ice cream

Melt margarine; add flour, oatmeal, brown sugar and pecans. Pat thin on cookie sheet and bake at 400°F. for 15 minutes. Crumble while hot and spread half on bottom of a 9x13-inch pan. Drizzle half jar of caramel sauce over crumbs, then spread ice cream over top. Cover with remaining crumbs, then sauce. Freeze.

Grandview, Man.
Ladies Auxiliary
Branch No. 14

Steamed Cranberry Pudding

- 2 tsp. baking soda
- ½ cup molasses
- ½ cup boiling water
- 1 cup cranberries, fresh or frozen
- 1⅓ cups flour
- 1 tsp. baking powder

Add baking soda to molasses, then stir in the boiling water and put into large bowl. Sift flour and baking powder. Combine with molasses mixture. Coat cranberries with a bit of flour, so they will not sink to bottom and mix into butter. Steam for 1½ hours in a well greased quart mould. I use a tomato juice can covered with foil.

Cream Sauce for Pudding:
- ½ cup sugar
- ½ cup whipping cream
- ¼ cup butter

Mix and stir together. Cook over boiling water for 15 minutes.

Bridgetown, N.S.
Ladies Auxiliary
Branch No. 33

Apple Torte

Base:
- ½ cup margarine
- ⅓ cup sugar
- ¼ tsp. vanilla
- 1 cup flour

Mix together and pat into bottom of 8x8-inch pan.

Filling:
- 1-8 oz. pkg. cream cheese
- 1 egg
- ¼ cup sugar
- ½ tsp. vanilla

Cream together and spread over bottom layer.

Topping:
- 1 can apple pie filling cinnamon

Cover with apple pie filling and sprinkle with cinnamon. Bake at 400°F. for 10 minutes; reduce heat to 375°F. and continue baking for 25 minutes.

Note: Apple topping can be made from fresh apples as follows: In flat saucepan, boil ¾ cup water with ⅔ cup sugar for 5 minutes. Add 1 tbsp. lemon juice and four large apples that have been peeled, cored and sliced. Simmer until apples are soft, stirring frequently. When apples are cooked, thicken with cornstarch dissolved in cold water.

For a large apple torte I double the recipe for the base and filling and bake an additional 10 minutes at 375°F.

Wedgeport, N.S.
Ladies Auxiliary
Branch No. 155

Berry Rice
(A cool summer dessert)

1 cup whipping cream or
  1 pkg. Dream Whip
¼ cup sugar
1 cup cold cooked rice
1-12 oz. pkg. frozen raspberries or other small fruits

Whip cream until stiff. Stir in sugar. Fold carefully into rice. Drain thawed berries, reserving syrup, and place in a glass dish. Pour rice mixture on top and chill. Serve thickened syrup as sauce.

Rapid City, Man.
Ladies Auxiliary
Branch No. 49

Rice Pudding

½ cup rice (not instant)
¾ cup raisins
4 tbsp. sugar
sprinkle of salt

Place in casserole and add 4 cups milk. Sprinkle with nutmeg. Bake at 325°F. for 1½ to 2 hours. Stir occasionally.

Fairview, Alta.
Ladies Auxiliary
Branch No. 84

Spiced Bread Crumb Pudding

1 cup dry bread crumbs
1 cup sour milk
¼ cup shortening
½ cup sugar
2 tbsp. molasses
½ cup flour
½ tsp. cinnamon
¼ tsp. cloves
1 tsp. baking soda
¾ cup raisins

Soak bread crumbs in sour milk for a few minutes. Cream shortening and sugar. Add remaining ingredients; then bread crumbs and milk. Mix together well. Pour into greased casserole. Bake at 350°F. for 45 minutes. Serve hot or cold and top with ice cream if desired.

Carman, Man.
Ladies Auxiliary
Branch No. 18

Petite Cherry Cheese Cake

2-8 oz. pkgs. cream cheese,
  softened
¾ cup sugar
2 eggs
1 tbsp. lemon juice
1 tsp. vanilla
24 vanilla wafers
1 can cherry pie filling or
  other fruit topping

Beat cream cheese, sugar, eggs, lemon juice and vanilla until light and fluffy. Line small muffin pans with paper baking cups. Place a vanilla wafer in the bottom of each cup. Fill cups ⅔ full of cream cheese mixture. Bake at 375°F. for 15 to 20 minutes or until set. Top each with about 1 tbsp. of fruit topping. Chill.

Valemount, B.C.
Ladies Auxiliary
Branch No. 266

Cherry Slip

2½ cups wafer crumbs
½ cup butter or margarine,
  melted
3 tbsp. white sugar
1 pt. cream
4 tbsp. icing sugar
1 tsp. vanilla
1 can cherry or blueberry pie
  filling
1 small pkg. mini marsh-
  mallows

Combine wafer crumbs, butter and white sugar. Press into a 8x9-inch pan, reserving ¼ cup for topping. Whip the cream, add icing sugar and vanilla. Add mini-marshmallows to pie filling. Put half of whipped cream on crumb mixture in pan. Add pie filling mixture, top with remaining whipped cream and sprinkle with balance of crumbs. Keep refrigerated. Cut in squares and serve. A very nice dessert.

Grande Prairie, Alta.
Ladies Auxiliary
Branch No. 54

Apple Nut Pudding

2 eggs, beaten
1 cup white sugar
¾ cup flour
½ tsp. salt
1 tsp. baking powder
½ tsp. cinnamon
½ tsp. nutmeg
1 tsp. almond extract
1½ cups raw apples, diced
¾ cup chopped walnuts

Beat eggs until fluffy; gradually add white sugar. Sift together dry ingredients and fold into egg mixture. Add remaining ingredients. Pour batter into 8x12-inch pan and bake at 350°F. for 40 minutes. Serve hot or cold with whipped cream.

Bathurst, N.B.
Ladies Auxiliary
Branch No. 18

Sex in a Bowl

¾ cup finely chopped
  almonds
1 cup flour
½ cup margarine
1-8 oz. pkg. cream cheese
1 cup icing sugar
1 pkg. vanilla instant pudding
1½ cups milk
1 pkg. chocolate instant
  pudding
1½ cups milk
1 large container Cool Whip

Combine almonds, flour and margarine. Press into 9x13-inch pan. Bake at 350°F. for 20 minutes. Cool. Mix cream cheese and icing sugar together until creamy, then spread on cooled base. Beat together vanilla pudding with milk. Let stand 2 minutes, then spread on top of cream cheese layer. Beat together chocolate pudding and milk. Let stand 2 minutes, spread over vanilla layer. Let stand 15 minutes. Top with Cool Whip.

Whitehorse, Yukon
Ladies Auxiliary
Branch No. 254

Chocolate Log
(Excellent dessert)

5 eggs, separated
2 tbsp. cocoa
½ cup icing sugar
2 tbsp. flour
Dream Whip

Beat egg whites until very stiff. Beat egg yolks until lemon color. Add icing sugar; beat again. Combine flour and cocoa; add to egg yolks and sugar. Combine egg yolk mixture with egg whites; beat 4 to 5 minutes on high speed. Pour into a 9x13-inch cake pan lined with wax paper. Bake at 400°F. for 10 to 12 minutes. Turn out on icing sugared tea towel. Peel off wax paper and roll while still warm. When cool, whip Dream Whip and spread on cake. Roll up again. Ice.

Icing:

1 pkg. chocolate instant
** pudding**
1 pkg. Dream Whip
1½ cups cold milk

Combine and spread over roll. Leftover icing may be frozen for further use.

Dominion City, Man.
Ladies Auxiliary
Roseau Valley Branch No. 160

Chocolate Cinnamon Roll

1 cup whipping cream
½ tsp. cinnamon
1-8 oz. pkg. thin chocolate
** wafers**

Beat cream and cinnamon until stiff. Cover each wafer with 1 tbsp. whipped cream mixture and stack into 3 piles of about 10 wafers each. Lay stacks end to end on a cookie sheet, joining ends with cream mixture. Frost roll with remaining cream. Cover with plastic wrap and chill overnight. Cut diagonally into ½-inch slices and serve. This makes a tasty light dessert.

Snow Lake, Man.
Ladies Auxiliary
Branch No. 241

Pumpkin Marshmallow Dessert

1-28 oz. can pumpkin
1 pkg. large marshmallows
pinch of nutmeg
pinch of cinnamon
pinch of allspice
pinch of ginger
1 tsp. vanilla

Melt marshmallows and pumpkin in double boiler. Add spices and vanilla. Cool. Line 8x13-inch pan with graham wafers. When pumpkin is cool, fold in 1½ pkgs. beaten Dream Whip. Put 2 pkgs. of beaten Dream Whip on top of dessert. Sprinkle graham crumbs on top. Chill overnight. This will cut up quite nicely into squares.

Swan River, Man.
Ladies Auxiliary
Branch No. 39

Yaroslawa's Cheese Cake

1½ cups vanilla wafers
2 tbsp. butter
2 tbsp. sugar

Mix together and pat into round cake pan.

1½ lbs. cottage cheese
½ lb. cream cheese
1 cup white sugar
5 egg yolks, save the whites
2 cups sour cream
1 tsp. vanilla
1 tsp. lemon juice
4 tbsp. flour

Stir cheese to soften. Add sugar, then cream well. Add unbeaten egg yolks; stir enough to blend. Stir in sour cream, vanilla, lemon juice and flour. Then fold in egg whites. Pour mixture into crumb lined pan. Bake at 300°F. for one hour. Turn oven off and let cake remain in oven 1 hour with oven door closed and 30 minutes with door open.

Montreal, Que.
Ladies Auxiliary
Mazeppa Branch No. 183

Pineapple Cheese Cake

1-8 oz. pkg. cream cheese
1-8 oz. pkg. and 1 extra pkg.
** Dream Whip (5 pkgs.)**
2 cups cold milk
1 pkg. pineapple Jello
½ cup pineapple juice or
** water (I drain the juice**
** from the crushed pine-**
** apple)**
¼ cup sugar
1-14 oz. can crushed pine-
** apple**

Mix Dream Whip (5 pkgs.) with milk. Mix cream cheese with sugar. Make Jello with juice and set in fridge until soupy; then add Jello and pineapple to cream cheese. Hastily fold in the Dream Whip. Pour over wafer crust and let set in fridge. The crust is just a regular graham wafer and margarine crust like you use for pies.

Peace River, Alta.
Ladies Auxiliary
Branch No. 62

Honeycomb Pudding

½ cup sugar
½ cup butter
1 cup milk
½ cup flour
4 eggs
1 tsp. baking soda
1 cup molasses

Beat together sugar, butter, milk and flour. Add the well beaten eggs. Stir baking soda into molasses until it foams, then add to the mixture. Steam in mold for 1½ hours. Serve with hard sauce.

Hard Sauce:

½ cup butter
1 cup icing sugar
1 tsp. vanilla or sherry

Beat all together with electric mixer.

Lunenburg, N.S.
Ladies Auxiliary
Branch No. 23

Duff
(Christmas Pudding)

1½ cups brown sugar, packed
2 large tbsp. shortening
3 eggs
1 cup sour cream
1 cup milk
½ cup molasses
4 cups flour
2 tsp. baking soda
1 tsp. cream of tartar
1 tsp. cinnamon
1 tsp. nutmeg or mace
¼ tsp. ground cloves
raisins, candied peel and nuts
   to suit taste

Combine all ingredients and steam 3 hours. Serve warm with Lemon Sauce.

Lunenburg, N.S.
Ladies Auxiliary
Branch No. 23

Strawberry Ribbon Cake
(6 to 8 servings)

⅓ cup white sugar
1¼ cups fine graham wafer
   crumbs
⅓ cup melted butter
1-3 oz. pkg. strawberry Jello
¼ cup sugar
1¼ cups boiling water
1-10 oz. pkg. frozen strawberries or 1½ cups fresh
   strawberries, crushed
1 tbsp. lemon juice
½ pt. or 1¼ cups whipping
   cream
1-8 oz. pkg. soft cream cheese
½ cup icing sugar
pinch of salt
1 tsp. vanilla

Crust: Combine sugar and wafer crumbs. Drizzle with melted butter and combine thoroughly. Press mixture evenly in the bottom of a 9-inch square cake pan. Chill thoroughly.
Strawberry Layer: Combine Jello and sugar and dissolve in boiling water. Stir in strawberries and lemon juice. Chill until softly set.
Cheese Layer: Beat whipping cream or Dream Whip until stiff. Cream the cheese. Beat in icing sugar, salt and vanilla and part of the whipped cream. Fold in remaining whipped cream.
To assemble: Spread half the cream cheese mixture over the crumb base. Cover with half the Jello mixture. Repeat with remaining cream cheese mixture and top with Jello mixture. Chill for several hours, until firm. Cut in squares and serve.

Pointe du Bois, Man.
Ladies Auxiliary
Branch No. 70

Fruit Cocktail Dessert

1-19 oz. can fruit cocktail,
   undrained
1-19 oz. can crushed pineapple, undrained
1 pkg. pistachio pudding
2 tbsp. Cool Whip or
   whipped topping

Combine fruit and pudding. Let set until thickened. Fold in Cool Whip. Let set in fridge for a couple of hours, or if in a hurry, put in freezer for 5 minutes or so. A lovely light dessert that can be ready in a short time.

Lawrencetown, N.S.
Ladies Auxiliary
Branch No. 112

Carmel Dumpling

1½ cups brown sugar
2 tbsp. butter
1 cup hot water
1 tsp. vanilla
½ cup white sugar
2 tbsp. butter
½ cup milk
1 tsp. baking powder
dash of salt
1 cup flour

Combine brown sugar, 2 tbsp. butter, water and vanilla. Boil. Mix together remaining ingredients. Drop by teaspoonful onto boiling mixture and bake until light brown at 350°F. for 30 minutes. Serve warm with whipped cream or ice cream.

Wolfville, N.S.
Ladies Auxiliary
Branch No. 74

Honeycomb Mould

1 pkg. fruit Jello
2 cups milk
1 egg
1 tsp. sugar

Separate egg and beat white until firm and stiff. Pour milk and egg yolk with Jello into saucepan. Heat until mixture starts to rise in pan. Remove immediately, add beaten egg white and mix well. Chill.

Rouge River, Que.
Ladies Auxiliary
Branch No. 192

Crown Jewel Dessert

1-3 oz. pkg. orange Jello
1-3 oz. pkg. cherry Jello
1-3 oz. pkg. lime Jello
3 cups boiling water
2 cups cold water
1 cup pineapple juice
¼ cup sugar
1-3 pz. pkg. lemon Jello
1½ cups graham wafer
   crumbs
⅓ cup melted butter or
   margarine
2 envelopes Dream whip or
   2 cups whipped cream

First Step: Prepare the 3 flavors of Jello separately, using 1 cup of boiling water and ½ cup cold water for each. Pour each flavor into a 8-inch square pan. Chill until firm or overnight.
Second Step: Mix pineapple juice and sugar. Heat until sugar is dissolved. Remove from heat. Dissolve lemon Jello in hot juice; then add ½ cup cold water. Chill until slightly thickened. Meanwhile, mix crumbs and butter, press into 9x13-inch pan.
Third Step: Cut the firm Jello into ½-inch cubes. Then prepare whipped topping as directed; blend with lemon Jello. Fold in Jello cubes. Pour into pan. Chill at least 5 hours or overnight. Cut and serve.

Cranberry Portage, Man.
Ladies Auxiliary
Branch No. 137

Triple Treat Jello

1-3 oz. pkg. lime Jello
1-3 oz. pkg. lemon Jello
1-3 oz. pkg. raspberry Jello
1 cup cold water
3 cups hot water
1 cup crushed pears
2-8 oz. pkgs. cream cheese
½ bag mini-marshmallows
½ pt. whipping cream
½ cup mayonnaise

Bottom: Mix lime Jello, 1 cup hot water and 1 cup crushed pears. Mix well and pour in 9x12-inch pan and let set.
Centre: Melt cream cheese and marshmallows. Cool. Whip cream and mix with mayonnaise and add to above mixture. Mix lemon Jello and cool. Combine all these ingredients together. Add to bottom layer.
Top: Mix raspberry Jello, 1 cup hot water and the cold water. Pour over the centre layer. Allow to set.

Melita, Man.
Ladies Auxiliary
Branch No. 127

Mocha Delight

1-7 oz. pkg. chocolate wafers
½ cup melted butter
1 cup boiling water
4 tsp. instant coffee
1-11 oz. pkg. large plain marshmallows
2 cups whipped cream or prepared Dream Whip

Crush wafers; combine with melted butter and pat into a 9x13-inch pan. Reserve ½ cup for top. Combine boiling water, coffee and marshmallows in double boiler. Melt, then chill in fridge for one hour. Fold in whipped cream. Spread over base. Sprinkle the remaining crumbs over top. Chill 3 to 4 hours or overnight.

Ste. Rose, Man.
Ladies Auxiliary
Ste. Rose Branch No. 232

Apple Raisin Dessert

¼ cup butter or margarine
¾ cup white sugar
½ tsp. cinnamon
¼ tsp. nutmeg
1 tsp. grated lemon rind
½ cup raisins
2 cups peeled, sliced apples
⅓ cup butter or shortening
⅔ cup white sugar
2 eggs, well beaten
½ tsp. vanilla
1⅓ cups all-purpose flour
½ tsp. salt
3 tsp. baking powder
⅔ cup milk

Preheat oven to 350°F. Melt butter in 8-inch square pan. Combine sugar, cinnamon, nutmeg and lemon rind. Sprinkle half of mixture over melted butter, then half of raisins, cover with apples, remaining raisins and sugar mixture. Cream butter with sugar until fluffy. Add eggs and vanilla ad beat thoroughly. Add sifted dry ingredients alternately with the milk, mix well. Pour over apples and bake 40 to 50 minutes. Turn out on serving plate immediately. Serve with whipped cream or apple flavored sauce.

Wolfville, N.S.
Ladies Auxiliary
Branch No. 74

Apple Flavored Sauce

⅓ cup butter
¾ cup brown sugar
3 tbsp. cornstarch
pinch of salt
2½ cups or 1 can apple juice

Melt butter, sugar, cornstarch and salt. Cook till mixture is slightly browned, add apple juice gradually and cook, stirring constantly till sauce thickens, then cook 5 minutes more. Serve over warm apple raisins dessert. Serves 6 or 8.

Wolfville, N.S.
Ladies Auxiliary
Branch No. 74

Fresh Apple Kuchen

2 cups unsifted all-purpose flour
¾ cup sugar
½ tsp. salt
¼ tsp. baking powder
½ cup butter or margarine
1 lb. cooking apples
½ tsp. cinnamon
¼ tsp. nutmeg
2 egg yolks
1 cup heavy cream

Combine flour, 2 tbsp. sugar, salt and baking powder in medium bowl. Cut in butter with pastry blender until mixture resembles coarse crumbs. Turn into 9-inch round cake pan, pat firmly against bottom and sides of pan. Preheat oven to 400°F. Wash, pare and core apples. Cut into ½-inch thick wedges; arrange in pastry lined pan. Combine remaining sugar with cinnamon and nutmeg; sprinkle over apples. Bake 15 minutes. Beat eggs with cream; pour over apples. Bake 30 minutes longer, or until top is golden brown. Place pan on wire rack; let stand 10 minutes. Serve warm or cold.

Bowser, B.C.
Ladies Auxiliary
Branch No. 211

Apple Caramel

6 cooking apples, pared, cored and halved
½ cup margarine
1 cup brown sugar
½ cup pastry flour
¼ tsp. salt
1 cup chopped nuts

Arrange apple halves on flat baking dish. Cream margarine; mix in flour, salt and sugar; then add nuts. Spread over the apples and bake at 375°F. for 35 minutes. Serve hot with cream.

Winnipeg, Man.
Ladies Auxiliary
Brooklands Weston Branch No. 2

Little Green Apples

6 firm medium size apples
1 pkg. lime Jello
1 small pkg. cream cheese
1 small pkg. cream or topping

Preheat oven to 325°F. Peel and core apples and place one in each section of a six-cup muffin tin. Dissolve Jello in one cup hot water, then pour over apples. Bake for 10 minutes, then turn each apple over and bake 15 minutes, watching carefully not to overbake. Remove from oven, and cool in pans. Chill in refrigerator. Soften cream cheese with 1 tsp. milk, then gently fill cavity of apples. Top with whipped cream or topping.

Caledonia, N.S.
Ladies Auxiliary
A.L. Patterson Branch No. 87

Cool Fruit Delight

1 cup graham cracker crumbs
4 tbsp. margarine, melted
¼ cup sugar
1-10 oz. bag mini-marsh-
  mallows, white or colored
1-28 oz. can fruit cocktail,
  drained
1-20 oz. container sour cream
maraschino cherries and mint
  leaves (optional)

To prepare crust, combine graham cracker crumbs and sugar; add melted margarine and press mixture into bottom of springform pan (about 9½-inch). Combine mini-marshmallows, fruit cocktail and sour cream; blend well (delicately) and pour over crust. Chill several hours, or overnight. Optional: garnish top of pie with maraschino cherries and mint leaves. Serves 12.

Montreal, Que.
Ladies Auxiliary
Maisonneuve Branch No. 66

Mom's Apple Pudding

2 cups water
1½ cups brown sugar
2 cups flour
4 tsp. baking powder
2 tbsp. white sugar
½ tsp. salt
3 tbsp. shortening
½ cup milk
1 egg, beaten
sliced apples, apple sauce or
  pie filling
cinnamon
sugar

Boil water and brown sugar together for a few minutes and set aside. Sift together dry ingredients. Cut shortening into dry mixture. Mix milk and beaten egg into dry ingredients. Roll dough ½ inch thick. Spread with apples. Sprinkle with cinnamon and sugar. Roll in a long roll. Cut in 2-inch thick slices. Place cut side down in 9x13-inch cake pan and pour hot syrup between rolls. Bake at 350° to 375°F. for 30 to 45 minutes, or until nicely browned. Serve hot or cold with cream, whipped cream or ice cream.

Kenton, Man.
Ladies Auxiliary
Woodworth Branch No. 118

Apple Pudding

unpeeled, sliced apples
sugar
cinnamon
1½ cups flour
½ cup butter
½ cup white sugar
pinch of salt

Slice apples into greased dish or deep pie plate. Sprinkle with sugar and cinnamon. Mix remaining ingredients. Rub together like pie crust and cover apples with these crumbs. Bake in a moderate oven for 20 to 25 minutes. Serve with cream or ice cream.

Brandon, Man.
Ladies Auxiliary
Wheat City Branch No. 247

Banana Dessert

2 cups graham wafers
⅔ cup melted butter
2 sticks or 1 cup butter,
  softened
2 eggs
2 cups icing sugar
1 tsp. vanilla
3 large bananas, sliced and
  dipped in pineapple juice
1 can crushed pineapple,
  drained, reserve juice for
  dipping bananas
1 large container whipping
  cream or substitute
nuts
cherries

Combine graham wafers and melted butter, press into bottom of a 9x13-inch pan. Beat softened butter, eggs, icing sugar and vanilla until firm. Spread over first layer in bottom of pan. Spread sliced and dipped bananas evenly over second layer. Cover with crushed pineapple; then cover with whipped cream. Sprinkle with nuts and cherries. Place in fridge for several hours.

Ontario Command
Ladies Auxiliary

Cherry Square Dessert

2 eggs
¾ cup white sugar
½ cup Mazola oil
1 tsp. vanilla
1½ cups flour
2 tsp. baking powder
¼ tsp. salt
1 can cherry pie filling

Combine all ingredients except cherry pie filling. Grease a 9x15-inch pan. Pour the stiff batter into pan and spread evenly. Spoon on cherry pie filling in blobs on top of the batter. Bake at 350°F. for 45 to 60 minutes or until the cherries sink into the batter and batter turns a golden brown. Serve in 2-inch squares topped with whipped cream.

Lower Sackville, N.S.
Ladies Auxiliary
Calais Branch No. 162

Banana Fluff

1 egg
1 cup white sugar
1 cup milk
1 tbsp. gelatin
¼ cup cold milk
1-1½ cups whipping cream
1½ cups graham wafer
   crumbs
¼ cup melted butter
sliced bananas

Beat egg, add sugar and milk. Cook in double boiler till slightly thickened. Add gelatin softened in cold milk and cool till it begins to thicken. Fold in whipped cream. Moisten graham wafer crumbs with melted butter. Press into 9x9-inch pan, saving some for top. Spread a layer of sliced bananas over crumbs. Add half of custard mixture. Spread another layer of sliced bananas and top with remainder of custard. Sprinkle reserved crumbs over top. Refrigerate.

Cypress River, Man.
Ladies Auxiliary
Branch No. 188

Cherry Delight

graham wafer pie crust
1 pkg. vanilla pudding and
   pie filling
1½ cups milk
1 can cherry pie filling
1 envelope Dream whip
1-1½ cups mini-marsh-
   mallows

Make graham wafer pie crust according to directions on box. Press into the bottom of an 8-inch pyrex pan, reserving 2 or 3 tbsp. of mixture for top of dessert. Bake until lightly brown and cool. (Baking may be omitted). Make up vanilla pudding, using 1½ cups of milk, instead of 2 cups as called for. Spread on crumb mixture. Cool. Cover with cherry pie filling. Whip Dream Whip; add mini-marshmallows and spread over cherries. Sprinkle with reserved crumbs. Cool in fridge at least 8 hours.

St. Paul, Alta.
Ladies Auxiliary
Branch No. 100

Lemon Cake Pudding

¼ cup sifted flour
1 cup sugar
¼ tsp. salt
1½ tsp. grated lemon rind
¼ cup lemon juice
2 egg yolks, beaten
1 cup milk
2 egg whites, beaten stiff

Place flour, sugar and salt in bowl. Add rest of ingredients, but fold in egg whites, beaten stiff. Pour into 1½ qt. casserole. Set in pan of hot water. Bake in moderate oven for 45 to 50 minutes. Serve warm or cold.

Mission, B.C.
Ladies Auxiliary
Branch No. 57

Lemon Delight

(For banquets)
Yield: 30 pieces

3 cups graham wafer crumbs
¾ cup melted butter
3 tbsp. brown sugar

Mix together. Save ¼ cup to sprinkle on top. Pat the rest smoothly in 15x18-inch pan.

Filling:

1-6 oz. lemon Jello
2 cups boiling water
2 cups canned Alpha or Carnation canned milk, not 2%
¼ cup lemon juice or
   Realemon
½ tsp. grated lemon rind
¾ cup sugar

Stir Jello and boiling water until completely dissolved. Let set until it just begins to thicken. Meanwhile whip the milk; lemon juice and lemon rind; add sugar and slightly thickened Jello. Continue beating until nice and fluffy. Pour over crumbs in pan and level out. Sprinkle reserved crumbs on top and refrigerate overnight if possible (no less than 8 hours). A nice light dessert.

Stettler, Alta.
Ladies Auxiliary
Branch No. 59

Pineapple Meringue Cake

½ cup butter
½ cup sugar
4 egg yolks
½ cup cake flour
4 tbsp. milk
1 tsp. baking powder
2 tbsp. cake flour
¼ tsp. salt

Cream butter and sugar. Separate eggs, add well beaten egg yolks and mix well. Add sifted cake flour alternately with milk. Sift remaining 2 tbsp. flour with baking powder and salt and add, mixing well. Pour into 2 8-inch round cake pans.

Meringue Topping:

4 egg whites
¾ cup sugar
1 tsp. vanilla
¾ cup chopped nutmeats

Beat egg whites till stiff. Add a light sifting of the sugar and fold in, adding sugar gradually. It should hold a point when beater is drawn up. Add vanilla and spread meringue on each of the unbaked layers. Sprinkle the chopped nuts on top. Bake at 325° to 350°F. for 20 to 25 minutes. Allow to cool and remove from pan.

Pineapple Filling:

1 cup whipping cream
1½ tbsp. powdered sugar
1 cup crushed pineapple,
   drained
¼ tsp. vanilla

Place one layer, meringue side down on a cake plate. Whip cream, add powdered sugar, pineapple and vanilla. Spread filling on first layer. Place other side on pineapple, meringue side up.

Fort Macleod, Alta.
Ladies Auxiliary
Branch No. 46

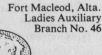
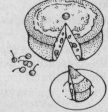

Pineapple Dessert

Crust:
  1½ cups graham wafer
    crumbs
  ½ cup melted butter
  ½ cup brown sugar

Mix and press into a 9x14-inch pan.

Filling:
  2 cups milk
  ¼ cup ice cream
  1 pkg. vanilla instant pudding
  2 envelopes Dream Whip
  1 can crushed pineapple,
    undrained

Combine all ingredients except pineapple in a large bowl and mix. Beat with an electric beater until thick. Fold in pineapple and juice. Pour over crust and top with a few crumbs. Refrigerate. Best after it has been made a day or two.

Pilot Mound, Man.
Ladies Auxiliary
Branch No. 62

Raspberry Dessert

  20 graham wafers
  ¼ cup sugar
  ¼ cup butter

Blend as for pie crust. Reserve ¼ cup for top. Line bottom of square pan with remaining mixture.

Filling:
  1 pkg. raspberry Jello
  1 cup boiling water
  1 pkg. frozen raspberries

Dissolve Jello in boiling water. Add frozen raspberries and let stand till it starts to set. Pour on top of graham crust.

Topping:
  20 marshmallows
  ½ cup milk
  1 cup cream

Melt marshmallows and milk in double boiler. Let cool. Whip cream and add to cooled marshmallows. Mix. Spread on Jello layer. Sprinkle crumbs on top.

Lundar, Man.
Ladies Auxiliary
Lundar Branch No. 185

Pineapple Delight

First Layer:
  125 ml butter, softened
  625 ml graham wafer crumbs

Combine butter and crumbs. Press into a 33x21x5 cm pan. Bake at 160°C. for 15 minutes and let cool.

Second Layer:
  125 ml butter, softened
  2 eggs
  5 ml vanilla
  375 ml sifted icing sugar

Beat butter until light and fluffy. Add eggs, one at a time, beating until smooth. Add vanilla. Gradually add icing sugar, beat until light in texture. Spread on first layer.

Third Layer:
  250 ml whipping cream
  50 ml granulated sugar
  1-398 ml can crushed pineapple, drained
  125 ml flaked almonds, toasted

Whip cream and sugar together until stiff peaks form. Fold in well drained pineapple. Spread on second layer. Top with toasted almonds. Cover and chill overnight. Yields: 12 to 16 servings.

Pointe du Bois, Man.
Ladies Auxiliary
Branch No. 70

Rhubarb Crisp

  4 cups diced rhubarb
  1/8 tsp. salt
  ½ cup white sugar
  1 tsp. grated orange rind

Sprinkle rhubarb with salt and let stand 20 minutes. Sprinkle with sugar and orange rind; set aside. Cream together:

  ¼ cup shortening
  ½ cup white sugar
  ½ tsp. vanilla
  1 egg, unbeaten
  1 cup sifted pastry flour
  ¼ tsp. salt
  1½ tsp. baking powder

Drop by spoonfuls on top of rhubarb. Bake at 350°F. for 35 to 40 minutes.

Canning, N.S.
Ladies Auxiliary
Branch No. 73

Springtime Pudding

  3 cups diced rhubarb
  1 cup sugar, divided in 2
  3 cups bread cubes
  ½ cup milk
  ¼ cup butter or margarine
  2 eggs
  1 tsp. vanilla

Preheat oven to 350°F. Grease a shallow dish. Mix rhubarb with ½ cup sugar and set aside. Cut up bread crumbs and sprinkle with milk. Cream butter, add ½ cup sugar. Add eggs, one at a time, beating well. Stir in vanilla. Stir in soaked bread crumbs and rhubarb. Put in prepared dish. Bake 40 to 45 minutes or until set. Serve with cream.

Teulon, Man.
Ladies Auxiliary
Teulon Branch No. 166

Meringue Topped Rhubarb

  2 cups flour
  2 tbsp. sugar
  ½ cup butter
  pinch of salt
  5-6 cups rhubarb, cut fine
  6 egg yolks
  1 cup cream
  2 cups sugar
  ¼ tsp. salt
  ¼ cup flour

Blend 2 cups flour, 2 tbsp. sugar, butter and pinch of salt. Put in lightly greased pan. Bake at 350°F. for 15 minutes. Beat egg yolks slightly; add remaining ingredients and pour over baked layer. Bake 45 minutes longer. Add meringue topping and bake another 15 minutes.

Topping:
  6 egg whites
  ¾ cup sugar
  1 tbsp. vanilla
  ¼ tsp. salt

Beat egg whites; add sugar, one tbsp. at a time. Add vanilla and salt.

Boissevain, Man.
Ladies Auxiliary
Branch No. 10

Strawberry Bavarian Cream

1-16 oz. pkg. frozen sliced strawberries
½ tbsp. lemon juice
2 envelopes unflavored gelatin
¾ cup hot milk
2 egg yolks
1 cup heavy whipping cream

Remove fruit from freezer, open pkg. and cut into 12 cubes. Put hot milk, lemon juice and gelatin into blender. Cover and blend on high speed to count of 40. With blades spinning, remove inner lid and add egg yolks and cream. Then quickly begin to add frozen fruit squares, one at a time. As mixture begins to set, push frozen fruit squares down into mixture with a long thin spatula. That's it. Spoon into sherbet dishes. Garnish as you wish with whipped cream and/or fresh fresh fruit. I find I like to add about 2 tbsp. of sugar unless the fruit is already very sweet. Preparation time: 7 minutes. Serves 6 generously.

Mc Bride, B.C.
Ladies Auxiliary
Branch No. 75

Lemon Luscious

1 cup flour
½ cup butter or margarine
1 cup chopped walnuts
1-8 oz. pkg. cream cheese
3 cups milk
½ cup sugar
1 container Cool Whip
2 pkgs. lemon instant pudding

Base: Mix flour and butter until creamy, add chopped walnuts. Spread in pan and bake at 350°F. for 10 minutes. Cool.
First Filling: Mix cream cheese and sugar; then fold in 1 cup Cool Whip. Spread on base.
Second Filling: Mix instant pudding with milk and spread on first filling.
Topping: Spread remaining Cool Whip over all and refrigerate.

West Pubnico, N.S.
Ladies Auxiliary
Branch No. 66

Strawberry Ribbon Dessert

Crust:
⅓ cup sugar
⅓ cup butter, melted
1¼ cups graham wafer crumbs

Combine sugar, wafer crumbs and melted butter. Press evenly into 8 or 9-inch pan. Chill thoroughly.

Strawberry Layer:
1-3 oz. pkg. strawberry Jello
1-10 oz. pkg. frozen strawberries or 1½ cups crushed fresh strawberries
¼ cup sugar
1¼ cups boiling water
1 tbsp. lemon juice

Combine Jello and sugar. Dissolve in boiling water. Stir in strawberries and lemon juice. Chill until set softly.

Cheese Layer:
1¼ cups whipping cream
½ cup icing sugar
1 tsp. vanilla
1-8 oz. pkg. cream cheese
1/8 tsp. salt

Beat whipping cream until stiff. Cream cheese, beat in icing sugar, salt and vanilla and whipped cream.

To assemble: Spread half of cream cheese mixture over crumb base. Cover with half Jello mixture. Repeat in layers. Chill and cut in squares.

San Clara, Man.
Ladies Auxiliary
Branch No. 237

Mandarin Orange Dessert

1 pkg. orange Jello
1 1/8 cups boiling water
1 tbsp. lemon juice
1 pt. vanilla ice cream
1 can mandarin oranges, drained

Dissolve Jello in boiling water and lemon juice. Add ice cream. When starting to set, add mandarin oranges. Pour into mold.

Kelowna, B.C.
Ladies Auxiliary
Branch No. 26

Cinnamon Pineapple Meringe Torte

Base:
½ cup butter
½ cup sugar
4 egg yolks, save whites
6 tbsp. milk
1 cup flour
1 tsp. baking powder

Cream butter and sugar well, add beaten egg yolks, milk and flour sifted with baking powder. Mix well. Pour into a 9x12-inch greased pan. Bake at 350°F. for 15 minutes or until golden brown.

Filling:
1-19 oz. can crushed pineapple, undrained
2 tbsp. cornstarch
½ cup sugar

Combine and boil until thick, stirring often so as not to scorch. Cool and spread on cake when baked.

Topping:
½ cup sugar
½ tsp. cinnamon
egg whites

Mix sugar and cinnamon. Beat egg whites until fairly stiff and add sugar mixture. Beat until it holds a peak. Spread meringue over cake topped with pineapple. Return to oven and bake until meringue turns light brown. Cut in pieces, 1x2½ inches.

Montreal, Que.
Ladies Auxiliary
Mazeppa Branch No. 183

Strawberry Chiffon Dessert

1½ cups graham cracker crumbs
¼ cup butter or margarine
1-3 oz. pkg. strawberry Jello
¾ cup boiling water
1 can sweetened condensed milk
⅓ cup lemon juice, bottled or fresh
1-15 oz. pkg. frozen strawberries, thawed
3 cups mini-marshmallows
½ pt. whipping cream or Dream Whip

Melt butter, combine with graham crumbs and pat firmly on the bottom of a 9x9-inch pan. Dissolve Jello in boiling water in a large bowl. Stir in marshmallows, milk, lemon juice and strawberries. Fold in whipping cream. Pour into prepared pan onto crumb crust. Chill 2 hours.

Foxwarren, Man.
Ladies Auxiliary
Branch No. 152

Strawberry Almond Flan

½ cup butter, softened
1 cup flour
½ cup finely chopped almonds
3 tbsp. sugar
1-3 oz. pkg. cream cheese
1 cup whipping cream
1 pkg. vanilla pudding and pie filling
1 tsp. almond extract
1½ cups milk
strawberries for garnish

Cream butter until fluffy, beat in flour, almonds and sugar. Put in bottom of an 8-inch springform pan. Bake at 350°F. for 25 minutes. Cool. Beat cream cheese with ¼ cup sugar, until smooth. Whip cream, fold half into cheese mixture. Pour into crust. Chill. Prepare pudding mix, adding almond extract. Cool. Carefully spread on top of cream cheese mixture. Pipe remaining whipped cream on top for decoration. Garnish with strawberries.

Teulon, Man.
Ladies Auxiliary
Teulon Branch No. 166

Additional Recipes

_____
_____
_____
_____
_____
_____
_____
_____
_____
_____

Pies & Pastry

Peaches and Cream Pie

Crust:
- ¾ cup flour
- 1 tsp. baking powder
- ½ tsp. salt
- 1 pkg. vanilla pudding (not instant)
- 1 egg
- ½ cup milk
- 1 can sliced peaches

Topping:
- 8 oz. soft cream cheese
- ½ cup sugar
- 3 tbsp. peach juice
- 1 tbsp sugar
- ½ tsp. cinnamon

Combine ingredients for pie crust and beat for 2 minutes. Pour into a deep 10″ pie plate. Drain sliced peaches (reserving the juice) and arrange slices on the pie crust. Blend cream cheese, ½ cup sugar and peach juice. Beat 2 minutes and spoon on the pie crust. Top with mixture of 1 tbsp. sugar and cinnamon. Bake at 350°F. for 30 minutes.

Pine Falls, Man.
Ladies Auxiliary
Branch No. 64

Lassy Tart

Line an 8″ pie plate with pastry. Prepare pastry strips for the top.

Filling:
- 1 egg
- 1 cup soft bread crumbs
- 1 cup molasses

Beat the egg; add molasses and beat well. Stir in bread crumbs. Pour into unbaked pie crust. Top with strips of pastry and bake at 400°F. for 20 minutes.

Stephenville Crossing, Nfld.
Branch No. 44

Japanese Fruit Pie

- 1 cup butter
- 2 cups sugar
- 4 eggs
- 1 cup chopped pecans or walnuts
- 1 cup coconut
- 1 cup raisins
- 1 tbsp. vanilla
- 1 tbsp. vinegar
- 1-9″ unbaked pie shell

Preheat oven to 350°F. Melt butter, add sugar in large bowl. Beat eggs well and add to mixture. Stir in nuts, coconut, raisins, vanilla and vinegar. Pour into pie shell (do not overfill). Bake 45 minutes.

Thunder Bay, Ont.
Ortona Branch No. 113

Strawberry Dream Pie

- 1-3 oz. pkg. strawberry Jello
- 1 pkg. (4 portions) vanilla pudding and pie filling
- 2 cups water
- 1 tsp. lemon juice
- 1½ cups prepared Dream Whip, whipped
- 1 cup sliced strawberries
- 1-9″ baked pie shell, cooled

Combine Jello, pudding mix, water and lemon juice in saucepan. Cook and stir over medium heat until mixture comes to a boil. Pour into a bowl and chill until thickened. Fold in whipped topping, blending well. Stir in strawberries. Pour into pie shell and chill until set. Garnish with additional whipped topping and strawberries.

Slave Lake, Alta.
Ladies Auxiliary
Branch No. 110

Raspberry or Strawberry Pie

Crust:
- 1 cup flour
- 1 tbsp. sugar
- ½ tsp. salt
- ½ cup salad oil
- 1 tbsp. milk

Mix together and line pie plate. Bake 10 minutes at 400°F. When cool, fill with fresh berries. (May use your own pie crust recipe.)

Topping:
- 1 cup water
- 1 cup sugar
- 3 tbsp. cornstarch
- 1 pkg. Jello (raspberry for raspberry pie and Strawberry for strawberry pie)

Mix together all ingredients and boil until thickened. Cool and pour over prepared pie. Serve with whipped cream or topping. Delicious!

Salmo, B.C.
Branch No. 217

Sour Cream Raisin Pie

- 1 cup sour cream
- 1 cup brown sugar
- 2 egg yolks
- ½ cup raisins
- 1 tsp. cinnamon
- 1 tsp. baking soda
- 1 cooked pie shell
- 2 egg whites
- ¼ cup sugar

Boil first 5 ingredients till thick, then add baking soda. Pour into cooked pie shell. Beat egg whites till very stiff. Add sugar and beat. Top raisin mixture with this. Brown in oven.

Benito, Man.
Ladies Auxiliary
Branch No. 228

Angel Pie

5 eggs
1½ cups sugar
1 tsp. cream of tartar
2 lemons, grated
¾ qt. real cream
2 tbsp. icing sugar
¾ cup coconut

Step one: Separate egg whites in bowl. Put egg yolks in double boiler and set aside. Beat egg whites till stiff and add cream of tartar, beat again; then add 1 cup sugar and beat. Put in 9x13″ pan. Bake at 200°F. for 1 hour. Cool. Step two: Cook egg yolks with ½ cup sugar and grated lemons and juice till slightly thickened. Remove from heat and cool. Whip the cream with icing sugar till stiff. Spread half on egg white layer, then lemon mixture, then another layer of whipped cream. Top with unsweetened coconut. May be frozen.

Wetaskiwin, Alta.
Branch No. 86

Cheese Pie

½ cup butter or margarine
2 eggs
1½ cups flour
½ tsp. salt
¼ cup sugar
¾ cup milk
1 tsp. baking powder

Cream butter and sugar; add eggs and mix well. Sift in dry ingredients alternately with milk. Grease pan and spread half of batter in pan. Put in filling and top with remaining batter. Bake at 350°F. 45 minutes or until golden.

Filling:
1-12 oz. pkg. dry cottage cheese
1-8 oz. pkg. creamed cottage cheese
1 egg
salt and pepper to taste

Serve hot with sour cream and strawberries.

Winnipeg, Man.
Ladies Auxiliary
General Monash Branch No. 115

Sugar Pie

2½ cups brown sugar
¾ cup oatmeal
1 egg
1¼ cups milk
2 tbsp. soft butter
½ tsp. vanilla

Combine all ingredients and pour into a 9″ uncooked pie shell. Bake at 350°F. for 30 minutes. If using pyrex pie plate, bake at 325°F. for 30 minutes.

Cowansville, Que.
Branch No. 99

Manitoba Blueberry Pie

1 cup blueberries
1 cup water
1 cup sugar
3 tbsp. cornstarch
1 tbsp. butter
3 cups chilled raw berries

Boil 1 cup blueberries, water and sugar in saucepan. Thicken with cornstarch. Remove from heat and add butter. Let melt. Add raw berries and pour into a baked pie shell. Serve with whipped cream.

Napinka, Man.
Branch No. 89

Perfect Pumpkin Pie

1 cup brown sugar
½ tsp. cloves
½ tsp. allspice
½ tsp. nutmeg
½ tsp. ginger
½ tsp. salt
1½ tsp. cinnamon
2 large eggs, slightly beaten
1½ cups cooked pumpkin
1 large can Alpha evaporated milk
1-9″ unbaked pie crust

Blend sugar, spices and salt together. Add eggs, pumpkin and milk. Mix well. Pour into pie shell. Bake at 425°F. for 15 minutes; reduce heat to 350°F. and continue baking 40 minutes longer. Cool.

Oak River, Man.
Branch No. 150

Dutch Apple Pie

2 lbs. apples
1 tbsp. lemon juice
1 cup sugar
3 tbsp. flour
½ tsp. nutmeg
½ tsp. cloves
¼ tsp. allspice
½ cup heavy cream
pastry for 1-9″ pie crust
1 egg yolk
1 tbsp. water
1 tsp. sugar
cinnamon

Preheat oven to 400°F. Lightly grease a 1½ qt. casserole. Peel and core apples. Slice thinly. Place slices in a large bowl and sprinkle with lemon juice. In a small bowl, combine sugar, flour and spices. Pour over apples. Toss gently to coat all slices. Add cream, mix well. Turn into prepared casserole. On lightly floured surface roll out pastry to a 9½″ circle over top of casserole. Make several cuts for vents. Brush with egg yolk beaten with water. Sprinkle with sugar and cinnamon.

Murdochville, Que.
Branch No. 218

Deep Apple or Peach Pie

1 tbsp. butter or margarine
½ cup brown sugar
cinnamon
slices of tart apple or 1-2 cans of sliced peaches
brown sugar

Spread butter over bottom of glass baking dish. Add brown sugar and cinnamon; stir smoothly. Roll out pie crust and lay over mixture and press around sides of dish. Fill with slices of apple or peach, whichever desired. Sprinkle brown sugar over fruit. Cover with top crust which has cut outs in centre. Bake. Nice to serve hot.

Piapot, Sask.
Branch No. 12

Peanut Butter Cream Pie

¼ cup butter
1¼ cups graham crumbs
     crumbs

Filling:
4 oz. cream cheese
⅓ cup peanut butter
1 cup icing sugar
½ cup milk
1-500 ml container Cool Whip
crushed salted peanuts

Melt butter, add graham cracker crumbs. Put into 8x8" pie pan. Cool. Blend cream cheese and peanut butter. Add icing sugar and milk. Mix well. Blend in Cool Whip and spread over crumbs. Top with crushed salted peanuts. Freeze 12 to 24 hours

Rainy River, Ont.
Branch No. 54

Sour Cream Apple Pie with Crumble Crust

1-9" unbaked pie shell
1 egg
½ cup sour cream
½ tsp. vanilla
pinch nutmeg
1-19 oz. can apple pie filling

Preheat oven to 425°F. Whisk egg, sour cream, vanilla and nutmeg together. Stir in can of apple pie filling. Turn into unbaked pie shell.

Topping:
½ cup brown sugar
½ cup flour
½ cup cold butter

Stir together brown sugar and flour. Cut in butter until pebbly. Sprinkle evenly over top of pie filling. Bake on bottom shelf of preheated oven for 10 minutes. Reduce heat to 350°F. and continue baking for 15 to 20 minutes, until centre of pie filling seems set when slightly jiggled. About 482 calories per serving.

Rapid City, Man.
Branch No. 49

Apple Crumb Pie

⅔ cup sugar
2 tbsp. flour
¾ tsp. ground cinnamon
6-8 tart apples, pared, cored
     and sliced (6 cups)
1-9" unbaked pie shell
½ cup flour
¼ cup sugar
¼ cup butter

Combine first 3 ingredients; stir into apples. Turn into pastry shell. Combine remaining flour and sugar; cut in butter till crumbly. Sprinkle over apples. Bake at 400°F. for 45 to 50 minutes or till done. If pie browns too quickly, cover edge with foil.

Stanstead, Que.
Stanstead Frontier Branch No. 5

Macaroons

8 oz. self-raising flour
½ tsp. salt
2 oz. lard
2 oz. margarine
8 tsp. cold water

Mix flour and salt in bowl. Rub in lard and margarine. Using a knife to cut and stir, mix with cold water to form a stiff paste. Turn dough onto floured board and roll out thinly. Line 12 muffin tins.

Filling:
2 oz. fine sugar
2 oz. ground almonds
1 egg
raspberry jam

Mix almonds and sugar with sufficient beaten egg to make soft mixture. Place a little jam in each pastry lined muffin tin, then one teaspoonful of almond mixture. Sprinkle lightly with fine sugar. Make thin strips of pastry from cuttings and lay across tops at right angles. Bake in moderately hot oven for 20 minutes or till golden brown.

Sparwood, B.C.
Michel Natal Branch No. 81

Never Fail Lemon Pie

1¼ cups sugar
6 tbsp. cornstarch
2 cups cold water
⅓ cup lemon juice
3 eggs, separated
3 tbsp. butter or margarine
1½ tsp. lemon extract
2 tsp. vanilla

Mix sugar and cornstarch together in top of double boiler. Add water. Combine egg yolks with juice and beat. Add to rest of mixture. Cook in double boiler until thick and add margarine.

Never Fail Meringue:
1 tbsp. cornstarch
2 tbsp. cold water
½ cup boiling water
3 egg whites
6 tbsp. sugar
2 tsp. vanilla
pinch salt

Blend cornstarch and cold water in saucepan. Add boiling water and cook, stirring until clear and thick. Cool. With electric beater beat egg whites until foamy. Gradually add sugar and beat until stiff, but not dry. Turn mixer to low speed. Add salt and vanilla. Gradually beat in cooled cornstarch mixture. Turn mixer to high speed and beat well. Spread meringue over cooled pie filling. Bake at 350°F. for 10 minutes or until meringue is golden brown. This meringue cuts beautifully and never gets sticky.

Red Deer, Alta.
Branch No. 35

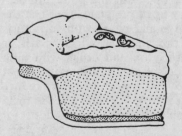

Pumpkin Chiffon Pie

1 tbsp. gelatin
½ cup cold water
1½ cups cooked pumpkin
1 cup brown sugar
3 eggs yolks, well beaten
2 tsp. cinnamon
½ tsp. ginger
¼ tsp. nutmeg
½ tsp. salt
3 egg whites
2 tsp. sugar

Sprinkle gelatin over water and let set. Combine remaining ingredients except egg whites and 2 tsp. sugar. Cook on top of stove in heavy pot or double boiler until slightly thickened, then add gelatin. Set this in fridge while you beat up the egg whites and 2 tsp. sugar until stiff, but not dry, fold egg whites into pumpkin mixture. Pour into baked pie shells. Place in fridge to set (approx. ½ to 1 hour.

Strathclair, Man.
Branch No. 154

Old Fashioned Saskatoon Pie

pastry for 9" double pie crust
4 cups fresh or frozen saskatoons
2 tbsp. water
2 tbsp. lemon juice
¾ cup sugar
1½ tbsp. Minute Tapioca
1 tbsp. butter or margarine

Simmer berries, water and lemon juice over low heat for 4 to 5 minutes. Remove from heat and stir in sugar, tapioca and butter. Cool and pour into pastry lined pie plate. Dampen the edge and cover with top crust. Trim and seal edges. Gash or prick top and brush with milk and sprinkle with sugar. Bake at 450°F. for 15 minutes; reduce heat to 350°F. and bake 30 to 35 minutes longer or until done.

Benito, Man.
Ladies Auxiliary
Branch No. 228

Cherry Cheese Tarts

1 box vanilla wafers
2-8 oz. pkgs. cream cheese
¾ cup white sugar
2 eggs
1 tbsp. lemon juice
1 tsp. vanilla
cherry pie filling

Cream cheese, beat in sugar; add eggs, one at a time. Beat in lemon juice and vanilla. Put vanilla wafer in small cupcake liner. Cover with cheese mixture. Bake at 375°F. for 15 minutes. Top with cherry pie filling. Makes 3 dozen. Freezes well.

Mahone Bay, N.S.
Ladies Auxiliary
Branch No. 49

Cheese Pastry

1¾ cups flour
½ cup sugar
½ tsp. salt
1 cup orange marmelade
2 tsp. baking powder
1 cup butter
1 cup grated cheese
¼ cup milk
1 egg

Mix flour, sugar, salt and baking powder. Add butter and cut in finely with pastry blender. Stir in cheese with a fork. Mix milk and egg together with a fork and then combine all ingredients. Chill for one hour. Heat oven to 350°F. Lightly grease 13x9x2" pan. Roll dough on floured board until slightly smaller than bottom of pan. Lift dough into pan and press with hand into corners and up the sides. Keep ¼ of the dough. Spread marmelade over dough in pan. Roll remainder very thin and cut in strips. Lay over top of marmelade.

Deer Lake, Nfld.
Branch No. 3

Flaky Pie Crust

5 cups sifted flour
1 tsp. salt
1 tbsp. white sugar
¼ tsp. baking soda
1 lb. lard
1 egg
3 tbsp. vinegar or fresh lemon juice
cold water

Combine flour, salt, sugar and baking soda together. Cut in lard in fairly large pieces with pastry blender. Beat together egg, vinegar and enough cold water to fill one cup. Add all at once to flour mixture. Work only until mixture comes away from bowl. Makes 5 or 6, 9-inch pie shells.

St. Paul, Alta.
Branch No. 100

Prize Pumpkin Pie

1 tbsp. flour
½ tsp. salt
¼ cup brown sugar
¼ cup maple syrup
½ tsp. ginger
½ tsp. mace
½ tsp. nutmeg
1 tbsp. melted butter
1 cup milk
2 eggs, well beaten
1½ cups pumpkin

Prepare pie shell. Mix together all ingredients. May use canned or steamed pumpkin. Pour mixture into pie shell and bake at 425°F. for 10 minutes; reduce heat to 325°F. and continue baking about 50 minutes or until firm and cracked. Serve with whipped cream.

To prevent soggy pie crust place pie crust in cold place to allow evaporation of moisture from shell and a crusting of dough before baking.

Steinbach, Man.
Branch No. 190

Lemon Tarts

pastry for pie shells
1 cup margarine or butter
1 tbsp. cornstarch
½ cup icing sugar
1¾-2 cups flour

Beat butter, add cornstarch, icing sugar and mix well. Add flour. Chill. Press a small piece of dough into small tart tins and shape. Prick with fork and bake at 400°F. till nicely browned.

Filling:
2 cups sugar
¼ cup butter
6 eggs, beaten
Rind and juice of 3 lemons

Cook in double boiler, cool and fill baked shells.

Minetonas, Man.
Branch No. 47

Prize Butter Tarts

pastry
2 eggs, beaten
⅔ cup butter
2 cups brown sugar
3 tbsp. milk
1 cup raisins
2 tsp. vanilla

Roll pastry 1/8″ thick and cut into 4″ rounds. Press into tart pans. Mix all ingredients together. Fill tart shells ⅔ full. Bake at 350°F. for 20 to 25 minutes or until pastry is delicately brown. Yields 2 dozen.

Pointe du Bois, Man.
Branch No. 70

Apple Tarts

¾ cup brown sugar
¾ cup Crisco
2 cups flour
1 egg
1 tsp. baking powder
½ tsp. salt

Combine ingredients and knead as for short bread, until no longer sticky. Roll out and cut to fit muffin tins. Fill with 1 tbsp. applesauce and put top on. Bake at 400°F. till brown.

Cumberland, B.C.
Branch No. 28

Amaretto Coconut Cream Pie

1 cup graham crumbs
¼ cup sugar
1 cup sugar
¼ cup melted butter
4 eggs
2 tbsp. gelatin
1¼ cups shredded sweetened coconut
⅓ cup cold water
½ cup Amaretto
1/8 tsp. almond extract
1 qt. whipping cream
12 fresh strawberries to garnish

Preheat oven to 300°F. Grease botten of 10″ spring form pan. Combine graham crumbs, sugar and butter; press evenly on bottom of pan to form a crust. Set aside. Toast coconut on baking sheet for 15 minutes and set aside. Beat eggs with electric mixer and add 1 cup sugar until fluffy. Sprinkle gelatin over cold water in measuring cup and let stand to soften, about 5 minutes. Set cup in a saucepan of hot water over direct heat until gelatin is completely dissolved. Fold gelatin, Amaretto and almond extract into egg mixture. Let stand until slightly thickened. Beat whipping cream until soft peaks form. Fold into coconut, reserving small amount to garnish. Fold whipped cream into thickened egg mixture and blend thoroughly. Pour into spring form pan and hill. Just before serving, remove sides of pan. Top with the remaining toasted coconut and garnish with fresh strawberries.

Coquitlam, B.C.
Ladies Auxiliary
Branch No. 263

Rhubarb Pie

1-9″ baked pie shell
1½ cups rhubarb
1 cup water
1 cup sugar (or less)
3-4 tbsp. custard powder
2 egg yolks

Boil sugar and water for 5 minutes. Thicken with egg yolk and custard powder. Add rhubarb. Cool and pour into pie shell. Top with meringue and bake until golden.

Gander, Nfld.
Branch No. 8

Cream Cheese Pastry

1½ cups flour
½ tsp. salt
½ cup shortening
4 oz. or 125 g cream cheese (room temperature)

Combine flour and salt. Cream together shortening and cheese, add flour gradually, blending with wooden spoon. Press into a ball. Chill one hour. Roll 1/8″ thick, cut and put in muffin tins and prick with fork. Bake at 400°F. for 10 minutes. Cool before filling. Either strawberry or lemon fillings are delicious.

Salmo, B.C.
Ladies Auxiliary
Branch No. 217

Nova Scotia Cranberry Pie

3½ cups cranberries
1½ cups white sugar
1½ tbsp. flour
¼ tsp. salt
3 tbsp. water
2 tbsp. melted butter

Chop cranberries and mix with remaining ingredients. Fill an unbaked pie shell with the mixture and arrange strips of pie crust criss-cross over the top. Bake at 450°F. for 10 minutes; reduce heat to 350°F. and continue baking for 40 minutes. Very good.

Canning, N.S.
Habitant Branch No. 73

Orange Pie
(Florida Chiffon Pie)

1 pkg. instant vanilla pudding
½ cup frozen orange juice
½ cup water
1 envelope Dream Whip
2 tbsp. grated orange rind
baked pie shell

Combine all ingredients and put in baked pie shell. Serve chilled.

Lockeport, N.S.
Ladies Auxiliary
Branch No. 80

"Never Fail" Pie Crust Mix

1 cup shortening
½ cup margarine
1 tsp. salt
3 cups flour
½ cup cold water

Cream shortening and margarine to a liquid form. Add dry ingredients. Mix well. Add water and stir in completely. Chill in fridge until a nice handling compound. Even children can roll and reroll this pie crust and it is flaky.

Onanole, Man.
Branch No. 191

Ritz Apple Pie

2 cups boiling water
1½ cups white sugar
2 tsp. cream of tartar
22 whole Ritz Crackers
1-9″ unbaked pie shell
½ tsp. cinnamon
½ tsp. nutmeg
lemon juice
butter

Bring water, sugar and cream of tartar to a boil. Add Ritz Crackers, do not stir. Cook 2 minutes. Pour into unbaked pie shell and sprinkle with cinnamon, nutmeg and lemon juice. Dot with butter. Cover with pastry and bake at 450°F. for 10 minutes. Reduce heat to 350°F. and continue baking for 30 minutes. Use your favorie recipe for the pie crust.

Milltown, N.B.
Milltown Branch No. 48

Impossible Buttermilk Pie

1½ cups sugar
1 cup buttermilk
½ cup Bisquick baking mix
⅓ cup margarine or butter
1 tsp. vanilla
3 eggs

Grease 9″ pie plate. Beat all ingredients until smooth (approx. 30 seconds in blender; or 1 minute with hand mixer). Pour into pie plate. Bake until knife inserted in centre comes out clean, approx. 30 minutes. Cool 5 minutes. Serve with mixed fresh fruit if desired.

St. Andrews, N.B.
Passamaquoddy Branch No. 8

Cake-Topped Fruit Pie

1-9″ unbaked pie shell
2-2½ cups homemade or canned pie filling (cherry is very good)
¼ cup soft butter
½ cup sugar
1 egg
½ tsp. grated lemon rind
¾ cup unsifted pastry flour
1 tsp. baking powder
¼ tsp. salt
¼ cup milk

Sprinkle pie shell with 1 tbsp. flour and spread with pie filling. Beat the butter, sugar and egg together until fluffy. Stir in flavoring, then sifted dry ingredients alternately with the milk. Spread batter over fruit filling right to the edges. Bake at 400°F. for 20 minutes. Reduce heat to 350°F. and continue baking for 35 to 40 minutes longer. Cool and garnish with whipped topping or cream.

Lawrencetown, N.S.
Branch No. 112

Impossible Pie

4 eggs
½ cup margarine
1 cup sugar
2 cups milk
½ cup flour
1 cup coconut
1 tsp. vanilla

Combine all ingredients in blender for a few seconds until well blended. Pour into a 10″ greased pie plate. Bake at 350°F. for one hour. The flour will settle to form a crust, the coconut forms a topping and the centre is a custard filling.

Dalhousie, N.B.

Pineapple Cream Filling

½ cup white sugar
1/8 tsp. salt
6 tbsp. flour
1 cup crushed pineapple
2 eggs, beaten
3 tbsp. butter
1-1¼ cups milk

Mix ingredients; add milk and cook until thick. Pour into graham wafer crust. Top with whipped cream.

Sinclair, Man.
Ladies Auxiliary
Branch No. 243

Pickles, Relishes, Jams, Preserves & Candy

Pickles Relishes

Bread and Butter Pickles

2-3 overgrown-forgotten-in-the-garden zucchini squash sliced and quartered as necessary
8 small onions
2 green peppers, or 1 red and 1 green, for color, sliced thinly

Mix ingredients together and salt. Leave 2 to 3 hours or overnight.

Syrup:
5 cups white sugar
5 cups vinegar
1½ tsp. turmeric
2 tsp. mustard seed
1 tsp. celery seed

Boil syrup together for a few minutes. Put in drained and rinsed pickles. Scald for 20 minutes. Seal in sterilized jars.

Great Village, N.S.
Ladies Auxiliary
Mayflower Branch No. 72

Best Ever Bread and Butter Pickles

6 qts. sliced cucumbers
1 qt. sliced onions
1 cup pickling salt
9 cups water

Make brine, but do not cook. Soak vegetables for 3 hours. Drain well.

1½ qts. vinegar
6 cups sugar
¼ cup mustard seed
½ tsp. celery seed
1 tsp. turmeric

Boil syrup for 5 minutes. Add vegetables and heat just to boiling. Do not boil. Bottle in sterilized jars. For best crispness, use small cucumbers.

Pilot Mound, Man.
Branch No. 62

Pickled Cole Slaw

1 large cabbage, shredded
several stalks of celery, chopped
1 tsp. salt
2 medium onions, sliced
2 carrots, grated
1 green pepper, chopped
¾ cup white sugar
3 tsp. celery seed
2 tsp. prepared mustard
1 cup white vinegar
¼ cup white sugar
¾ cup Mazola oil

Toss cabbage, onion, ¾ cup sugar, salt, green pepper and carrots. Let stand. Mix vinegar, mustard, ¼ cup sugar and celery seed with oil and bring to a boil. When bubbling pour over vegetables. Stir well and let stand overnight. This will keep crisp if sealed tightly and kept in fridge for up to 4 to 5 weeks.

Lac du Bonnet, Man.
Branch No. 164

Lady Ashburn Ham Pickles

6 large cucumbers
½ cup pickling salt
1 qt. onions, chopped fine
1 pt. white vinegar
2 cups sugar
3 tbsp. flour
1½ tbsp. flour
1½ tsp. dry mustard
1 tbsp. turmeric
1 tsp. mustard seed
1 tsp. celery seed

Peel cucumbers and remove seeds. Slice and add salt. Let stand overnight. Drain the next day. Add vinegar and dry ingredients. Cook for 1 hour and bottle.

Whycocomach, N.S.
Ladies Auxiliary
Branch No. 123

Three Minute Pickles

24 small cucumbers
2 cups vinegar
1 cup water
3 cups white sugar
1 tsp. mustard seed
¼ tsp. tumeric
1 tsp. celery seed
2 tbsp. pickling salt

Slice cucumbers thinly. Bring syrup to a boil and add cucumbers immediately and let boil 3 minutes. Pack into jars.

Sperling, Man.
Ladies Auxiliary
Branch No. 155

Frozen Pickles

3 qts. thinly sliced cucumbers
1 bunch celery, cut thin
2 pimentos, cut diagonally into ½" pieces
2 green peppers, cut thin
1½ lbs. onion, sliced
¼ cup pickling salt
6 cups sugar
4 cups vinegar

Mix together the pickling salt, sugar and vinegar and pour over remaining ingredients. Don't boil, just warm enough to dissolve sugar. Put in jars or plastic containers, cool, then freeze.

Morden, Man.
Branch No. 11

Mustard Beans

3 pts. vinegar
5 cups sugar
3 tbsp. turmeric
1 cup mustard
1 cup flour
celery seed
3 qts. beans, cooked

Boil together the vinegar, celery and salt. Combine dry ingredients and mix with vinegar to form a paste. Add to boiling mixture. Add cooked beans and simmer for 15 minutes.

Lower Sackville, N.S.
Calais Branch No. 162

Icicle Pickles

2 gallons cucumbers, cut in chunks
1 gallon boiling water
1 cup salt
1 tbsp. alum
3 tbsp. green food coloring
2 qts. vinegar
8 cups white sugar
3 tbsp. whole mixed spices
2 cups sugar
2 cups sugar
2 cups sugar
2 cups sugar

Stir together salt and boiling water. Place cucumbers in a crock and pour salt water over. Let stand four days. The brine will ferment. On the fifth day, drain the brine and cover with clean boiling water. On the sixth day, drain brine from cucumbers. Dissolve alum in boiling water, then add green food coloring and let stand 24 hours. On the seventh day, drain cucumbers and make a syrup from vinegar and 8 cups white sugar and pickling spice. Heat to boiling and pour over cucumbers. On the eighth day, drain cucumbers, saving syrup. Heat to boiling and add 2 cups sugar. Repeat this same process again on the nineth and tenth days. On the eleventh day, drain and put in jars. Heat syrup and add 2 more cups of sugar. Pour over cucumbers in jars and seal.

Wawanesa, Man.
Branch No. 28

Rhubarb Relish

1 qt. rhubarb, cut in 1" pieces
1 qt. onions
2 cups vinegar
4 cups brown sugar
1 tsp. salt
1 tsp. cinnamon
½ tsp. allspice
¼ tsp. pepper

Boil all ingredients together for 35 minutes. Put in jars and seal.

Milltown, Bay D'Espoir, Nfld.
Centennial Branch No. 61

Dill Pickles

1 gallon water
2 cups vinegar (Heinz 5% Acetic Acid white for extra crispness)
¾ cup pickling salt

Bring to a boil and boil for 5 minutes, making sure that salt is dissolved. Let cool to almost tepid. Wash and drain cucumbers, choosing them about 2 to 3" in length. Pierce a hole through at both ends with plastic toothpick or large darning needle. In sterilized jars, pack cukes, 2 cloves garlic (1 on bottom, 1 on top), 1 tsp. pickling spice, 1 small bayleaf and fresh picked dill. Pour brine to the top of jars and seal. Once the jars are sealed, run very hot water on top of each jar and tighten again. This helps ensure that the tops are well sealed.

Terrace Bay, Ont.
Ladies Auxiliary
Branch No. 223

Tomato Plus

Wash 7 qt. jars. Put 1 tsp. salt in each. Add 3 or 4 peeled tomatoes to each jar, pressing down to leave as little air space as possible. Prepare vegetable mixture by cooking approximately 1 cup each (more or less to suit individual taste) celery, onion, pepper and carrot, finely diced, in small amount of water until almost tender. Divide vegetable mixture evenly among the 7 jars. Fill the jars with more tomatoes, pressing gently when full till the juice is ready to overflow. Remove air bubbles with a knife. Adjust the lids according to the type of closure used. Process in boiling water bath for 45 minutes. Seal and cool.

Point du Bois, Man.
Branch No. 70

Eating With Relish

Tomatoes are red-ripe on the vines, and it's time for canning our favorite mixture from the garden's odds and ends. I call it Tomato Plus because of the added celery, onion, green pepper and carrots. It's delicious as a sauce for meat balls, also makes an excellent spaghetti sauce and is a flavorful addition to soups and casserole dishes.

Green Tomato Chow

1 medium cabbage
4 qts. green tomatoes
2 qts. onions
¼ cup pickling salt
1 qt. vinegar
3 cups brown sugar
½ cup pickling spice

Cut cabbage, tomatoes and onions into coarse pieces. Soak overnight with the ¼ cup pickling salt. Drain well. Place pickling spice in cheesecloth bag and add to vinegar, sugar and vegetable mixture. Cook until tender. Remove spice bag and bottle in sterilized jars.

Squamish, B.C.
Branch No. 277

Tomato and Pineapple Relish

2 cups tomatoes
2 tbsp. vinegar
2 tsp. Worcestershire Sauce
½ tsp. allspice
6 cups sugar
1½ cups crushed pineapple undrained
½ tsp. cinnamon
¼ tsp. cloves
1 bottle Certo

Chop tomatoes and cook 10 minutes. Drain to make 2 cups. Combine all ingredients and boil hard for one minute. Remove from heat and add Certo.
Certo.

Milltown, N.B.
Branch No. 48

Crab Apple Ketchup

12 cups crab apple pulp
8 cups white sugar
½ tbsp. cinnamon
½ tbsp. black pepper
½ tbsp. ground cloves
7 cups vinegar

Combine all ingredients and bring to a rolling boil. Remove from stove and seal in bottles.

Oyama, B.C.
Branch No. 189

Zucchini Relish

12 cups chopped Zucchini
4 large onions, chopped
2 red peppers, chopped
2 green peppers, chopped
⅓ cup pickling salt
3 cups white vinegar
4 cups white sugar
3 tbsp. cornstarch
2 tsp. celery seed
2 tsp. mustard seed
2 tsp. turmeric

Combine vegetables with pickling salt and leave overnight. Drain and rinse. Combine remaining ingredients with vegetables and boil 20 minutes. Put in sterilized jars.

Qualicum Beach, B.C.
Branch No. 76

Chow Chow

15 lbs. green tomatoes
1 cup salt

Soak tomatoes and salt overnight. Remove tomatoes and press out to remove water and salt. Add:

6 large onions, cut small
2 cups celery, chopped
3 pears, chopped
3 apples, chopped
3 green peppers, chopped
3 red peppers, chopped
2 oz. mixed pickling spice
6 cups sugar
1½ pts. vinegar

Cook all ingredients together for 2 hours. Fill jars and seal.

Dalhousie, N.B.

Chutney

12 green apples
6 tomatoes
2 sweet peppers
1 hot pepper
6 small onions
1 cup seeded raisins
2 tsp. salt
2 cups brown sugar
3 pts. vinegar

Put apples, raisins and vegetables through food chopper. Mix all together and simmer about 50 minutes. Pour into sterilized jars and seal.

Murdochville, Que.
Branch No. 218

Cranberry Mincemeat Relish

2 cups fresh cranberries or
1-16 oz. can whole berry
    cranberry sauce
1-20 oz. can crushed pine-
    apple
1 cup prepard mincemeat
1 tbsp. rum extract

Combine all ingredients in large saucepan and simmer for 10 minutes, stirring occasionally. Serve warm or chilled. Excellent condiment to serve with poultry, pork, beef or game. Makes 5 cups.

Montreal, Que.
Maisonneuve Branch No. 66

Chili Relish

7 cups tomatoes
½ cup onions
1 cup apples
1½ cups celery
1 cup vinegar
1½ cup sugar
2 tsp. salt
½ tsp. cayenne pepper
1 tsp. allspice
12 whole cloves (tied in bag)

Cook 1½ hours on medium-low heat.

Salisbury, N.B.
Ladies Auxiliary
Branch No. 31

Thousand Island Relish

6 large cucumbers, peeled
6 large onions
1 green pepper
1 sweet red pepper
¼ cup pickling salt
2½ cups cold water

Combine above ingredients and let stand one hour. Drain well. Mix together:

3 cups sugar
½ cup flour
1½ tsp. turmeric
1½ tsp. mustard seed
1½ tsp. celery seed.

Add:

3 cups white vinegar
1 cup water

Add vegetables and bring to a boil; then simmer for 30 minutes. Bottle.

Salisbury, N.B.
Branch No. 31

Six Day Pickles

cucumbers
onions
cauliflower
9 cups water
1 cup salt

Syrup for 4 qts. vegetables:

1 qt. vinegar
1 qt. water
2 heaping cups white sugar
½ cup pickling spices in bag

Cut vegetables and place in water and salt overnight. Drain and rinse well with cold water. Make syrup for 4 qts. vegetables. Boil and pour over pickles. Next day drain syrup and add 1 cup sugar; bring to a boil. Add 1 heaping cup sugar each day until you reach 6 cups. Last day bring to a boil and pour over pickles in jars and seal. Green food coloring may be added on the last day. Makes a very crisp pickle.

Oak River, Man.
Branch No. 150

Tomato Chutney

4 lbs. ripe tomatoes
1 lb. apples, finely chopped
3 large onions, finely chopped
1 pt. vinegar
½ tsp. cayenne pepper
2 tbsp. coarse salt
2½ cups brown sugar
1 cup seeded raisins
1 tsp. cinnamon
1 tsp. dry mustard

Chop the tomatoes, add apples and onions. Add the remaining ingredients and cook until the chutney is thick and clear, about 3 hours, stirring occasionally. Seal in hot sterilized jars. Makes 5 pints.

Sioux Lookout, Ont.
Branch No. 78

Cucumber Relish

12-14 large cucumbers, peeled, seeded and diced
4 cups finely chopped onion
½ cup pickling salt

Combine the above mixture and let stand overnight. Next morning heat at medium temperature until steaming, remove from heat and drain. Add the following mixture which has been previously cooked.

1 qt. vinegar
5 cups white sugar
1 cup flour
1 tsp. celery seed
1 tsp. mustard seed
1 tsp. turmeric

Boil the above mixture 10 minutes. Combine both mixtures and stir. Pour into sterilized jars and seal while still hot.

Lwr. Sackville, N.S.
Calais Branch No. 162

Beet Relish

6 cups beets, diced
4 cups white sugar
2 cups vinegar
2 pkgs. strawberry Jello

Boil beets, sugar and vinegar for 20 minutes. Add Jello. Stir and seal. This relish is delicious!

Oak River, Man.
Branch No. 150

Pickled Small Sweet Green Peppers Stuffed With Cabbage

5 large onions, shredded
4 heads cabbage, shredded
2 large carrots, shredded (if desired)
1 qt. Mazola oil
10 cups vinegar
10 cups water
1 cup mixed pickling spice, in cheesecloth
3 cups white sugar
1½ tbsp. salt
5-6 dozen peppers

Boil vinegar, water, pickling spices, sugar and salt for 10 minutes. Combine shredded vegetables. Salt well and let stand for 4 hours. Squeeze well and add 1½ cups oil. Mix thoroughly. Clean peppers and fill with cabbage mixture. Wash and sterilize jars. Fill with stuffed peppers. Add 1 tbsp. oil to each jar. Then pour syrup over peppers. Seal and steam 15 minutes.

Montreal, Que.
Mazeppa Branch No. 183

Mustard Relish

12 large cucumbers, diced small
6 large onions, diced
2 sweet red peppers, diced
¼ cup salt
3 cups vinegar
¾ cup water
3 cups sugar
½ cup flour
2 tbsp. cornstarch
1 tsp. celery seed
2 tbsp. turmeric
2 tbsp. dry mustard

Combine vegetables and let stand 2 hours, covered with salt; drain and rinse well. Add vinegar and boil for 30 minutes. Mix together remaining ingredients and add to vegetables. Cook 15 minutes and bottle.

Ont. Provincial Command
Ladies Auxiliary

Harvest Pickle

8 cups sliced cucumbers
1 cup sliced onion
2 large green peppers, sliced
1 tsp. celery seed
4 tsp. salt
1 tsp. mustard seed
2 cups white sugar
1 cup vinegar

Place in crock or ice cream pail in order given. Stir and store in refrigerator. These are quick to make and very handy in harvest time.

Langruth, Man.
Ladies Auxiliary
Branch No. 162

Jams Preserves

Zucchini Apricot Jam

6 cups zucchini, peeled and grated
6 cups white sugar
¾ cup crushed pineapple and juice
½ cup lemon juice
1-6 oz. pkg. apricot Jello

Cook zucchini and sugar for 15 minutes; add pineapple and juice, and lemon juice; continue cooking for 6 minutes. Remove from heat and add Jello; stir well. Seal in jars. Makes 5 pints.

Hamiota, Man.
Ladies Auxiliary
Branch No. 174

Strawberry Preserves

4 cups strawberries
1 tbsp. vinegar
3 cups sugar

Wash and hull strawberries, add vinegar and bring to a boil, cover and boil for one minute. Add sugar, bring to boil and cook gently for 20 minutes longer, uncovered. Stir occasionally to prevent sticking. Pour the hot berries into a bowl and let stand overnight at room temperature.

Oak River, Man.
Branch No. 150

Pear Conserve

12 medium size pears
1-14 oz. can pineapple tidbits
Juice and rind of 1 orange
8¼ cups sugar
1-3 oz. jar maraschino cherries

Peel pears and chop. Chop pineapple. Add sugar, orange juice and rind. Let stand overnight. Cook slowly until thick, about 2½ hours. Add chopped cherries. Pour in hot sterile jars and seal. Yields 9-6 oz. jars.

Windsor, N.S.
Ladies Auxiliary
Branch No. 9

Marmalade

1 grapefruit
1 apple, peeled
2 oranges
1 lemon
7 cups water
10 cups sugar

Put fruit through food chopper. Add water and boil hard for 30 minutes, uncovered. Add sugar, boil hard for 20 minutes, uncovered. Seal in jars.

Winnipeg, Man.
Ladies Auxiliary
Branch No. 1

Zucchini Jam

16 cups zucchini, grated
6 cups ground lemons
3-12 oz. cans crushed pineapple
3 pkgs. Certo crystals
12 cups white sugar

Bring zucchini, lemon and pineapple to a rapid boil. Reduce heat and add Certo; continue boiling for 15 minutes. Add sugar and boil for one minute. Seal in sterilized jars. Makes approx. 8 to 10 pints. For a nice change, substitute oranges for lemons.

Sanford, Man.
Ladies Auxiliary
Branch No. 171

Ripe Tomato Jelly

5 cups ripe tomatoes
4 cups white sugar
1-6oz. pkg. Jello, any flavor

Bring tomatoes to a boil, then add sugar and cook 15 minutes or until tomatoes are soft. Take from stove. Add Jello and stir well. Put in jars and seal.

Gladstone, Man.
Ladies Auxiliary
Branch No. 110

Grape Jelly

4 large beets, peeled and sliced thin
1 pkg. Certo crystals
Juice of 1 lemon
4 cups white sugar
1 pkg. grape Jello

Cover beets with water and boil till beets are pale. Take 3 cups beet juice, add Certo crystals and juice of lemon. Bring to a boil, add sugar and Jello. Boil one minute. Put in jars and seal.

Oak River, Man.
Branch No. 150

Mock Mincemeat

4 tart apples
1½ cups seeded raisins (375 ml)
grated rind of 1 orange
½ cup fruit juice (125 ml)
¾ cup sugar (180 ml)
½ tsp. cinnamon (2 ml)
½ tsp. cloves (2 ml)
½ tsp. nutmeg (2 ml)
2-3 tbsp. (30-45 crackers, finely crushed (40 ml)

Combine apples, raisins, orange rind and fruit juice. Simmer until apples are soft. Blend in remaining ingredients. (Crackers absorb liquid if apples are watery.) Cook for 20 minutes. Put into jars and seal, or in container in freezer.

Port Hawkesbury, N.S.
Branch No. 43

Heavenly Jam

5 cups rhubarb, uncooked
5 cups sugar
1 can crushed pineapple
2 large pkgs. strawberry Jello

Boil rhubarb, sugar and pineapple together for 20 minutes. Remove from heat and add Jello; stir well. Set five minutes, then bottle.

Halifax, N.S.
Ladies Auxiliary
Scotia Branch No. 25

Pear Mincemeat

7 lbs. under ripe pears
3 lbs. raisins
3 lbs. sugar, brown or white
1 cup vinegar
1 lemon
1 tbsp. cloves
1 tbsp. cinnamon
1 tbsp. allspice

Put pears, raisins and lemon through chopper. Add remaining ingredients. Cook in heavy pot to avoid sticking. Bring to a boil; reduce heat and let cook slowly until thick, about 2 hours. Put in sterilized jars and seal.

Brandon, Man.
Branch No. 247

Green Tomato Mincemeat

6 cups chopped apples
6 cups chopped green tomatoes
4 cups brown sugar
1½ cups vinegar
3 cups raisins
1 cup currants
1 tbsp. cinnamon
1 tsp. powdered cloves
¾ tsp. allspice
¾ tsp. mace
¾ tsp. pepper
2 tsp. salt
¾ cup butter

Bring all ingredients, except butter, to a boil. Simmer for 3 hours and add butter. Pour into 6 one-pint jars. Seal and store.

Antigonish, N.S.
Arras Branch No. 59

Rhubarb-and-Carrot Marmalade

4 cups carrots
4 cups rhubarb
2 oranges
2 lemons
6 cups sugar
1½ cups water

Peel carrots. Wash and dry rhubarb, oranges and lemons. Cut rhubarb into ½″ lengths. Shred carrots, oranges and lemons very thinly. Combine all ingredients and bring to a boil, stirring to prevent scorching. Boil for one hour. Pour into hot sterilized jars and seal.

Springdale, Nfld.
Branch No. 40

Rhubarb Orange Marmalade

4 cups rhubarb, diced
2 oranges
1 fresh pineapple or 1 can cubed or sliced pineapple
1 cup seedless raisins
4 cups sugar
½ cup walnuts, chopped

Wash and dice the unpeeled rhubarb. Grate rind of the oranges into long shreds. Remove all the white membrane possible and with a sharp knife slice the pulp thinly. Peel, core and dice the pineapple. Place the prepared fruits and orange rind in a large bowl. Add the raisins and sugar. Stir until well mixed. Cover with a cloth and let rest overnight. The next day, rub a saucepan with salad oil, add the fruit mixture. Bring to a boil, while stirring. Simmer until thick and transparent, about 1½ hours. Add the chopped walnuts. Simmer 10 minutes. Pour into hot sterilized jars, cool slightly and seal.

Montreal, Que.
Maisonneuve Branch No. 66

Homemade Mincemeat

1¼ cups suet
1½ lbs. raisins
½ lb. currants
1½ lbs. finely chopped apples
¼ lb. mixed fruit
½ lb. glace cherries, wet
⅓ cup brown sugar
1 cup white sugar
1 tsp. cinnamon
¼ tsp. mace
¼ tsp. nutmeg
½ tsp. cloves
1 cup grape juice
1 cup sherry wine or grape juice

Prepare fruit and mix together. Mix sugars and spices and add to fruit. Add suet, Add jam and liquid. Mix every two or three days. If dry, add jam or juice to taste. Let ripen two to three weeks before use.

Emerson, Man.
Branch No. 77

Mother's Fudge

3 cups white sugar
1 cup brown sugar, packed
1 cup milk or cream
3 tbsp. butter
1 tsp. vanilla
2 tbsp. corn syrup
1 cup any fruit or nuts

Combine milk and corn syrup. Bring almost to a boil, stirring constantly. Add sugar slowly, stirring constantly until sugar is dissolved and mixture boils. Continue cooking without stirring until small amounts of mixture forms a very soft ball in cold water. Remove from heat, add butter and flavouring and cool to lukewarm. Beat until mixture thickens and looses its gloss. Add fruit or nuts and pour at once in greased cookie sheet, patting evenly with hands. When cold, cut in squares.

Chester Basin, N.S.
Ladies Auxiliary
Everett Branch No. 88

Mock Raspberry Jam

3 cups green tomatoes, grind and use juice
3 cups white sugar
1-3 oz. pkg. raspberry Jello
a bit of red food coloring

Boil tomato juice and sugar for 15 to 18 minutes. Add remaining ingredients. Bottle. This recipe makes only a small batch of jam and can easily be doubled.

Havelock, N.B.
Branch No. 86

Marrow Marmalade

4 cups marrows
2 oranges
1 lemon
1 cup water
6 cups sugar

Put marrows, oranges and lemon through food chopper. Boil altogether until a golden brown, stirring often as it burns very easily. Put in sterilized jars. A can of crushed pineapple may be added for variety.

Shoal Lake, Man.
Branch No. 72

Candy

Marshmallows

2 pkg. Knox gelatin
½ cup cold water
2 cups sugar
½ cup hot water

Soak gelatin in cold water. Boil sugar and hot water. Let come to a boil and boil for only 2 minutes. Pour over soaked gelatin and beat until very stiff. Put in 8″ pan lined with browned coconut or cornstarch. Cool for 2 hours, then cut in squares and roll in browned coconut or cornstarch. Keep in fridge. To cut marshmallows, dip sharp knife in hot water.

Ste. Rose, Man.
Ste. Rose Branch No. 232

Poppy Cock

6 qts. popped corn
1-2 lbs. peanuts or mixed nuts
1 cup margarine
2 cups brown sugar
½ cup corn syrup
pinch salt
½ tsp. baking soda
1 tsp. vanilla

Boil margarine, brown sugar, syrup and pinch of salt together, without stirring. Add baking soda and vanilla. Pour over popcorn and stir well. Pour out on cookie sheets. Place in 250°F. oven for one hour, stirring occasionally.

Hythe, Alta.
Ladies Auxiliary
Branch No. 93

Vinegar Candy

1 cup brown sugar
1 cup white sugar
1 tbsp. butter or margarine
½ cup vinegar

Boil to hard ball stage; then pour into a buttered pan and let set.

Sanford, Man.
Branch No. 171

Fudge

1 cup chunky peanut butter
1 cup margarine
1 lb. icing sugar
½ tsp. vanilla
2-8 oz. Hershey bars
¼ cup peanut butter

Cream peanut butter, margarine, icing sugar and vanilla together. Pour in a 9'x13" pan. Melt remaining ingredients and spread on top of creamed layer. Refrigerate.

Passamaguoddy, N.B.
Branch No. 8

Candy Bars

1-6 oz. pkg. chocolate chips
1-6 oz. pkg. caramel chips
½ cup peanut butter
1 pkg. peanuts or chopped nuts
1 bag colored marshmallows

Melt chocolate chips, caramel chips and peanut butter together. Add remaining ingredients and pour into a 9x13" pan.

Roblin, Man.
Ladies Auxiliary
Branch No. 24

Mallow Fudge

2 cups sugar
¼ cup butter or margarine
¾ cup evaporated milk
9 marshmallows, cut into eighths
1 pkg. (8 squares) semi-sweet chocolate

Combine sugar, butter, evaporated milk and marshmallows in saucepan. Place over low heat, stirring until sugar is dissolved and marshmallows are melted. Bring to a boil and boil 4 minutes, stirring constantly. Add semi-sweet chocolate. Stir until chocolate is partly melted. Remove from heat and stir rapidly until chocolate is entirely melted. Pour into a greased 9" square pan. Cool and cut into 1" squares. Makes about 2 lbs. fudge.

Whitehorse, Yukon
Branch No. 254

Chocolate Easter Eggs

1 pkg. semi-sweet chocolate
½ cup margarine
1¾ cups sifted icing sugar
¼ cup cocoa
½ tsp. vanilla
2 tbsp. light cream

Melt chocolate and margarine over hot water. Add sugar, cocoa, vanilla, and cream, blend well. Chill 30 minutes or till firm enough to shape. Form into eggs. Decorate and store in fridge.

Frosting:
1 tsp. butter and food coloring
¾ cup icing sugar
vanilla

Soften butter, add icing sugar and blend well. Add milk gradually until frosting is soft enough to go through a piping bag. Yields 8 to 10 eggs. Good!

Enderby, B.C.
Branch No. 98

Preserving Choice Children

Take a large grassy field, ½ dozen children, 2 or 3 small dogs, a pinch of brooks and some pebbles. Mix children and dogs together well and put them in the field, stirring constantly. Pour the brook over pebbles, sprinkle the field with flowers, spread over all a deep blue sky, and bake in the hot sun. Then thoroughly brown, remove and set away to cool in a bathtub.

Steinbach, Man.
Branch No. 190

Chocolates

3 lbs. icing sugar
1 can Eagle Brand sweetened
condensed milk
½ cup melted butter
6 tsp. corn syrup
1 tsp. vanilla

Take 2½ lbs. icing sugar and approx. ¾ can of milk heated (stand can of milk in hot water until warm). Add melted butter, heated corn syrup and vanilla. Mix well. Divide batter into 5 parts. *First*: Add 8 drops peppermint extract. Form into patties. *Second*: Add 2 tsp. maple extract and 2 oz. ground-up walnuts. Shape into cubes. *Third*: Add 6 cherries, chopped, 2 tsp. cherry juice, 3 oz. coconut. Shape into balls. *Fourth*: Put one cherry in centre of each ball. *Fifth*: Add 3 tbsp. cocoa, 1½ oz. coconut and small amount of condensed milk. Shape oblong. Let stand overnight. Next day, dip with a fork in 1 pkg. melted Baker's semi-sweet or unsweetened chocolate and ½ cake melted parawax.

New Ross, N.S.
Branch No. 79

Peanut Butter Cones

⅓ cup margarine
½ cup peanut butter
1¼ cups brown sugar
2 eggs
1 tsp. vanilla
2 cups flour
½ tsp. salt
2½ tsp. baking powder
¾ cup milk
24 flat bottom ice cream
cones
strawberry jam

Cream margarine and peanut butter, add sugar, beat till light and fluffy. Add eggs and vanilla. Beat well. Sift dry ingredients together and add alternately with milk to egg mixture. Divide half of mixture between cones. Place 1 tsp. jam on each cone. Fill cones with remaining batter. Place cones in muffin tins. Bake at 350°F. for 25 minutes. Cool. Frost with butter icing in different colours. Ideal for children's birthday parties.

Cumberland, B.C.
Branch No. 28

Walnut Cream Fudge

1 cup butter
2 cups brown sugar
½ cup milk

Bring the above ingredients to a rapid boil. Remove from heat and add:

4 cups icing sugar
1 cup chopped walnuts
1 tbsp. vanilla

Mix until smooth, spread in greased 9x13" pan. Let cool, then cut.

New Glasgow, N.S.
Ladies Auxiliary
Normandy Branch No. 35

Two-Layer Fudge

3 cups sugar
¾ cup margarine
⅔ cup evaporated milk
6 oz. chocolate chips
1-7 oz. jar marshmallow fluff
1 tsp. vanilla
½ cup peanut butter

Bring 1½ cups sugar, 6 tbsp. margarine, ⅓ cup milk to a boil. Boil 4 minutes over medium heat, stirring constantly. Remove from heat, stir in chocolate chips. Stir until blended. Add half of the fluff, ½ tsp. vanilla and mix until blended. Pour into a greased 9x13" pan. Repeat with remaining 1½ cups sugar, 6 tbsp. margarine, ⅓ cup milk as above. Boil 4 minutes. Remove from heat, add peanut butter and blend. Add ½ tsp. vanilla and remainder of fluff. Pour over first layer, cool. Cut in squares.

Salisbury, N.B.
Branch No. 31

Honey Fudge

2 cups white sugar
¼ cup honey
¼ cup butter or margarine
½ cup milk or light cream

Do not stir after sugar, butter and honey are dissolved over low heat. Boil to soft ball stage; cool to lukewarm and beat. Pour into buttered pan. Mark in squares.

Bow Island, Alta.
Branch No. 197

Butterscotch

2 cups white sugar
½ cup brown sugar
1 cup butter
1 tbsp. vinegar
4 tbsp. boiling water
½ tsp. salt

Boil until it forms a very hard ball in water (265°F.) Pour into a greased pan and break when set.

Salisbury, N.B.
Ladies Auxiliary
Branch No. 31

Quantity, Low Calorie & Diabetic

(for 50 people)
Chocolate Cake
1 cup shortening
9 eggs, separated
2½ tsp. salt
2 cups milk
1 tbsp. vanilla
6 cups sugar
8 cups flour
4 tbsp. baking powder
9 oz. chocolate or 9 rounded
    tbsp. cocoa

Cream shortening, sugar and egg yolks together. Mix and sift flour, salt and baking powder and add alternately with milk to the first mixture, add melted chocolate and vanilla and beat thoroughly. Fold in stiffly beaten egg whites. Pour into greased pans and bake at 350°F. Serves 50 people. If margarine is used, omit the salt. Serves 50.

Summerland, B.C.
Ladies Auxiliary
Branch No. 22

Chili (for 50 people)
6 lbs. ground beef
6 large onions
4 green peppers
5 large cans tomatoes
3 tbsp. salt
1 tbsp. paprika
2½ tbsp. Worcestershire
    Sauce
2½ tbsp. sugar
1 tsp. oregano
10 tbsp. chili powder, or to
    taste
12 small cans kidney beans
4 large cans tomato soup

Brown beef in pan. Sauté vegetables and add to browned beef. Add soup, tomatoes and kidney beans; cook for 10 minutes. Make a paste of seasonings with flour and water. Blend into mixture. Season with salt. Cook over low heat for 45 minutes. Stir to prevent sticking or place pan in oven (375°F.) for 1 hour. Serves 50.

Chemainus, B.C.
Ladies Auxiliary
Branch No. 191

Sweet and Sour Meatballs for 200

2 lbs. brown sugar
32 oz. ketchup
1-17 oz. jar soya sauce
24 cups water
4 cans pineapple bits
2-3 cups cornstarch
5 cups white vinegar
green peppers (optional)
celery salt to taste
garlic salt to taste

Bring all ingredients, except cornstarch, to a boil. Then add a small amount of water to the cornstarch and stir into mixture until thickened. Pour over prepared meatballs. Serves 200 people.

Meatballs:
30 lbs. hamburger
2 dozen eggs
bread crumbs
milk
chopped onions
garlic powder
salt and pepper

Mix together and shape into small meatballs. Fry.

Peachland, B.C.
Ladies Auxiliary
Branch No. 69

Tea Biscuits

6½ qts. flour
¾ cup baking powder
2 qts. milk
½ cup salt
3 cups shortening

Mix and sift flour, salt and baking powder. Cut in shortening, or mix with fingers. Add milk slowly to make a soft dough. Roll out on floured board to ¾" thick and cut. Bake at 425°F. for 10 to 15 minutes. Yields 100 biscuits.

Summerland, B.C.
Ladies Auxiliary
Branch No. 22

Jellied Salad
(for 200 guests)
20 pkgs. Jello, any flavor
    (mixed fruit is good)
20 cups hot water
10 cans crushed pineapple
10 cups grated carrots
10 cups grated celery
1 cup vinegar
scant ¼ cup salt

Dissolve Jello in hot water. Add vinegar and salt and let partially set. Add remaining ingredients. Serves 200.

For at home:
2 pkgs. Jello
2 cups hot water
1 can crushed pineapple
1 cup grated carrots
1 cup grated celery
1 tbsp. vinegar
pinch salt

Grand Manan, N.B.
Branch No. 44

Bean Salad
(for 60)
5-14 oz. cans red kidney beans
5-14 oz. cans cut green beans
5-14 oz. cans cut yellow beans
3-14 oz. cans lima beans
2-14 oz. cans french cut green
    beans
3 green peppers, cut in thin
    strips
3 large Spanish onions, cut in
    rings and separated

Dressing:
2½ cups sugar
2½ cups vinegar
2½ cups Crisco oil
5 tsp. salt
2½ tsp. dry mustard
2½ tsp. tarragon leaves
2½ tsp. sweet basil
3 tbsp. dried parsley

Bring the dressing to a boil and let sit until thoroughly cooled. Meanwhile drain the beans and prepare the pepper and onion. Mix together and let stand overnight in the fridge.

Stettler, Alta.
Branch No. 59

Sugarless Diabetic Christmas Cake
(No eggs, no sugar)

3 cups raisins
2 cups hot water
1 cup cooking oil
1 tsp. nutmeg
½ tsp. low sodium
1 cup dates
1 tsp. cinnamon

Put the above ingredients in a saucepan and boil about 30 minutes. Let cool and add:

3 cups sifted flour
2 tsp. baking soda
1 tsp. baking powder
2 tsp. vanilla
¾ cup chopped cherries
¼ cup walnuts
¼ cup lemon peel
⅓ cup citron peel

Bake at 350°F. for 30 minutes. Reduce heat to 325°F. and bake for 45 minutes or until test shows done. Yields 2 two-lb. loaves. May use tin pans or long angel food cake pans. This recipe uses no sugar or eggs. Also for a change or darker cup use 2 cups whole wheat flour and 1 cup white flour (or reverse). Real good.

Holland, Man.
Victoria Branch No. 121

Apple Strudel

2½ cups flour
½ cup lard
½ cup margarine
1 tsp. salt
1 tbsp. sugar
1 egg yolk plus enough milk
   to make ⅔ cup
1½ cups crushed Corn Flakes
2-19 oz. cans apple pie filling
½ tsp. cinnamon
1 lightly beaten egg white
½ cup icing sugar
2 tbsp. lemon juice

Sift flour, salt and sugar, cut in lard and margarine as for pastry. Add egg yolk and milk, mix and round up into ball. Chill for one hour. Divide dough for top and bottom of 12x16" pan, lightly greased. Roll dough and fit into bottom and sides of pan, spread crushed Corn Flakes lightly over dough, spread pie filling over Corn Flakes, sprinkle with cinnamon. Roll remaining dough to fit top, cover and moisten edges; press together, make slashes in top. Brush lightly with beaten egg white over top. Bake at 400°F. for 30 to 35 minutes. While strudel is still warm, glaze with ½ cup icing sugar mixed with 2 tbsp. lemon juice. This dessert cuts into 35 servings. Mincemeat can be substituted for apple pie filling.

Salmon Arm, B.C.
Ladies Auxiliary
Branch No. 62

Meatballs with Aloha Sauce
(Serves 100)
Meatballs:
8 lbs. ground beef
4 eggs
4 cups bread crumbs
2 tsp. salt
2 tsp. ginger
2 tsp. pepper
2 tsp. soya sauce

Combine all ingredients and shape into balls. Brown and drain off any fat. Arrange in pans and cover with Aloha Sauce. Bake at 300°F. for one hour. Serves 100.

Aloha Sauce:
6 bottles (12 cups) ketchup
2 cups vinegar
2 cups pineapple juice
6 cups crushed pineapple
6 cups pineapple tidbits
6 tbsp. soya sauce
6 tbsp. brown sugar
6 tbsp. cornstarch
½ tsp. salt

Combine first six ingredients. Combine sugar, cornstarch and salt. Add to ketchup mixture. Blend well. Cook until thick, simmer and pour sauce over browned meat balls.

Chemainus, B.C.
Ladies Auxiliary
Branch No. 191

Nut Cookies
(For diabetics)

10 tablets artificial sweetener
1 tsp. orange juice
1 cup sifted flour
¼ tsp. baking powder
½ cup butter or margarine
½ cup walnuts
½ tsp. vanilla
1 tsp. grated orange rind

Crush the tablets in the orange juice. Sift dry ingredients together. Cream butter with orange juice. Add dry ingredients and blend thoroughly. Add walnuts, vanilla and rind. Form into a roll and wrap in wax paper. Chill. When chilled, slice and bake at 350°F. for 12 minutes or until slightly browned.

Killarney, Man.
Branch No. 25

Diabetic Chiffon Cake

7 eggs, separated
½ cup cold water
3 tbsp. non-caloric sweetener
½ tsp. vanilla
2 tbsp. lemon juice
¾ tbsp. cream of tartar
1½ cups sifted cake flour
¼ tsp. salt

Beat egg whites, sweetener, salt and vanilla until stiff. Beat egg yolks, water, lemon juice and cream of tartar. Add egg yolks, then flour to egg whites. Fold, do not stir. Put in chiffon pan. Bake at 325°F. for 75 minutes.

Maple Creek, Sask.
Branch No. 75

Sugarless Beet Pickles

2 cups water
2 cups white vinegar
pinch salt
¼ cup liquid sweetener, or
   to taste
2 tbsp. mixed pickling spice
   (in cloth bag)

Pour over prepared beets and simmer 15 minutes. Pack in sterilized jars and seal.

Ste. Anne, Man.
LaVerendrye Branch No. 220

Sugarless Gum Drop Cake

½ cup margarine
½ cup Sugar Twin or sweetener to equal
2 eggs
2 cups flour
1 heaping tsp. baking powder
pinch salt
¾ cup milk
¾ cup light raisins
¾ cup sliced dietetic gum drops (no black)
½ tsp. almond flavoring

Cream margarine and sugar. Add lightly beaten eggs. Add flavoring. Add gum drops and raisins which·have been sprinkled with flour. Add dry ingredients alternately with milk. Bake 1 hour at 350°F.

Chester Basin, N.S.
Ladies Auxiliary
Everett Branch No. 88

Low Calorie Cupcakes

1 cup sifted enriched flour
1 tsp. baking soda
½ tsp. salt
½ tsp. nutmeg
1 tsp. cinnamon
⅓ cup brown sugar, firmly packed
3 tbsp. soft shortening
2 eggs, unbeaten
¾ cup buttermilk
1 cup rolled oats, uncooked
¼ cup raisins

Mix and sift flour, baking soda, salt and spices in a bowl. Add sugar, shortening, eggs and about half the buttermilk. Beat until smooth; about 2 minutes. Fold in remaining buttermilk, rolled oats and raisins. Fill small paper baking cups or small greased muffin cups half full. Bake at 375°F. for 12 to 15 minutes. Makes about 20 cupcakes.

Winnipeg, Man.
Branch No. 1

Peanut Butter Nuggets

These crispy nuggets are a tasty addition to a cookie tray for parties and desserts also.

⅔ cup crushed Corn Flakes (175 ml)
½ cup unsweetened shredded coconut (125 ml)
½ cup plain or crunchy peanut butter (125 ml)
2 tbsp. liquid honey or corn syrup (25 ml)

Combine ½ cup (125 ml) Corn Flakes crumbs, coconut, peanut butter and honey; mix thoroughly. Measure out 2 tsp. (10 ml) portions; shape into balls. Roll in remaining Corn Flakes crumbs. Place on plate. Chill until firm. Store in a covered container in fridge. Makes 18 nuggets. Each serving: 1 Nugget, ½ fruits and vegetables choice, 1 fat and oils choice.

Riding Mountain, Man.
Branch No. 202

Low Calorie Baked Spareribs

2 lbs. spareribs, cut into 4 equal servings
1 lemon, sliced
½ cup ketchup
1 tsp. chili powder
2 dashes Tabasco sauce
1 onion, sliced
1 tbsp. Worcestershire sauce
1 tsp. salt
2 cups water

Place ribs in shallow baking pan, top with lemon slices and onion slices, secure with toothpicks. Bake at 450°F. for 30 minutes. Combine remaining ingredients and heat to boiling. Pour over spareribs, reduce oven temperature to 350°F. Bake for one hour, basting every 15 minutes. (Exchange: 1 serving for 3 meat exchanges and 1 calorie per food List B). Makes 4 servings.

Slave Lake, Alta.
Branch No. 110

No Sugar Cake For Diabetics

3 cups raisins or currants
1 cup oil
1 tsp. nutmeg
½ tsp. salt
1 cup chopped dates
2 cups hot water
2 tsp. cinnamon

Put the above ingredients in a saucepan and boil for 30 minutes. Let cool. Add:
3 cups sifted flour
2 tsp. baking soda
2 tsp. vanilla
1 tsp. baking powder
¾ cup maraschino cherries, drained and cut up

This makes a large cake, but if you wish, you can use two loaf pans. Line tins with wax paper. Bake at 350°F. until cake tester comes away clean.

Roblin, Man.
Ladies Auxiliary
Branch No. 24

Shortbread
(For Diabetics)

½ lb. soft butter (250 g)
½ cup sugar (125 ml)
½ cup rice flour (125 ml)
1¾ cups flour (450 ml)

Cream butter and sugar in a mixing bowl until soft and fluffy. Stir in both flours until well blended. Roll out on a lightly floured board ¼" (6 mm) thick. Cut in 1½" (4 cm) rounds. Place on ungreased cookie sheets. Prick with a fork to form a design. Bake at 325°F. (160 °C.) for 22 to 25 minutes or until golden. Makes 60 shortbread.
Each serving: 3 shortbread, 1 starchy choice, 2 fats and oils choice. 15 g carbohydrate, 2 g protein, 10 g fat, 660 kilojoules (158 calories).

Riding Mountain, Man.
Branch No. 202

Lo-Cal Jello Salad

1 pkg. Weight Watcher's or
  Esteé gelatin (suggestions:
  orange, lemon or lime)
1 cup boiling water
4 oz. 2% cottage cheese
1 tbsp. yogurt
1 cup unsweetened, crushed
  and drained pineapple
1 cup whipped topping

Dissolve gelatin in water. Puree cottage cheese and yogurt and add to gelatin. Chill till shakey. Add pineapple. Gently fold in topping and chill till set. Serves four at 77 calories per person.

Provost, Alta.
Branch No. 85

Double Good Fresh Fruit Mousse

1 envelope unflavored gelatin
1 cup fresh orange juice
½ cup mashed banana or
  strawberries
juice of ½ a lemon
grated peel of ½ an orange
low calorie substitute to equal
  ¼ cup sugar
1 envelope whipped topping
  mix
½ cup cold water
4 egg whites

Soften gelatin in ½ cup orange juice in saucepan. Stir over low heat to dissolve gelatin. In large bowl combine mashed banana or strawberries, lemon juice, orange peel, sugar substitute and remaining ½ cup orange juice. Stir in gelatin mixture, chill until it is the consistency of unbeaten egg whites. Add cold water to whipped topping mix and beat until stiff. Beat egg whites until soft peaks form (do not overbeat). Gently fold into gelatin mixture, then fold in whipped topping. Spoon into 6 cup serving bowl. Garnish with orange slices or sliced strawberries. Less than 50 calories per serving.

Sanford, Man.
Branch No. 171

Chocolate-Nut Brownies
(For Diabetics)

1 square unsweetened chocolate
⅓ cup butter or margarine
2 tbsp. sweetener solution or
  48 tablets, crushed
2 tsp. vanilla
1 cup sifted cake flour (7/8
  cup all-purpose flour)
½ tsp. salt
½ tsp. baking soda
¾ cup chopped walnuts
2 eggs

Melt chocolate and butter in saucepan over low heat. Remove from heat; add artificial sweetener, vanilla and eggs. Stir till well blended. Add flour, salt and baking soda. Stir in nuts. Pour into a greased and floured 9″ square pan. Level batter. Bake at 350°F. for 20 minutes. Cut into squares when cool.

Killarney, Man.
Branch No. 25

Weight Watcher Dessert

Base:
1 cup graham cracker crumbs
2 tbsp. melted margarine
2 tbsp. brown sugar substitute

Pack in a 9x13″ pan and cool.

Center:
1 Weight Watcher's instant
  vanilla pudding
500 g plain yogurt
1-19 oz. can drained crushed
  pineapple

Combine and spread over crumb bottom. Place in fridge to set. Top with Lucky Whip and serve. This may be frozen.

Lockeport, N.S.
Ladies Auxiliary
Branch No. 80

"Diabetic" Tomato French Dressing

2 cans condensed tomato
  soup, undiluted
2 cups water
8 tbsp. or ½ cup vinegar
1 tsp. onion powder
3 tbsp. finely chopped green
  pepper (optional)
4 tsp. Worcestershire sauce
2 tsp. low sodium
2 tsp. dry mustard
1 tsp. garlic powder
1 tsp. artificial liquid sweetener

Beat all ingredients together until smooth, preferably in an electric blender. Shake well before using. Exchange 1 tbsp. for 1 calorie per Food List B.

Holland, Man.
Victoria Branch No. 121

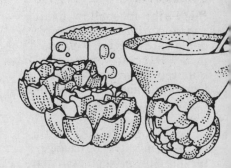

Microwave

Beef

Beef Hawaiian

2 tbsp. cooking oil
2½-2¾ lbs. boneless beef round steak, cut into thin strips
1 tsp. salt
1 tbsp. soya sauce
½ tsp. pepper
½ cup brown sugar, packed
¼ cup vinegar
3 tbsp. cornstarch
1-13¼ oz. can pineapple chunks, undrained
1 medium green pepper, cut into thin strips
2 tomatoes cut into wedges

Measure oil in 2 qt. glass casserole. Microwave on High for 2 to 3 minutes or until hot. Stir in beef and continue cooking on High for about 6 minutes or until no longer pink. Stir in soya sauce, salt pepper, brown sugar and vinegar. Cover with glass lid or plastic wrap. Microwave on Simmer for 20 minutes. Blend cornstarch and pineapple juice in 2-cup measure. Stir into meat mixture. Mix in pineapple chunks, green pepper and tomatoes. Recover and continue cooking on Simmer for 8 to 10 minutes or until hot and meat is fork tender. Let stand, covered, 5 minutes before serving. 4 to 6 servings.

Hazelridge, Man.
Branch No. 146

Beef Stew

2 lbs. beef cubes, cut into 1" pieces
2 cups water
1 envelope onion soup mix
4 carrots, thinly sliced
2 potatoes, peeled and cut into 1" cubes
1 bay leaf
1-8 oz. can green peas
¼ cup flour

Combine beef, 1½ cups water, soup mix, carrots, potatoes and bay leaf in 4 qt. casserole. Heat covered at High 13 to 15 minutes. Heat covered at Power Select Low 1-1¼ hours or until beef and vegetables are tender, stirring occasionally. Add peas and flour blended with remaining water. Heat at High 4 to 5 minutes or until stew is thickened, stirring once.

Port Morien, N.S.
Ladies Auxiliary
Branch No. 55

Quick Beef Stew

3 cups diced cooked roast beef
¾ cup chopped onion
1 cup sliced carrots
1 cup diced potatoes
½ cup chopped celery
1 cup cold water
¼ cup flour
1¼ tsp. salt
3 beef bouillon cubes
2 cups boiling water

Dissolve beef bouillon cubes in boiling water. Place meat and vegetables in a 3 qt. casserole. Blend flour, salt and cold water together, stirring until smooth. Add bouillon cubes and flour mixture to meat and vegetables. Microwave covered on Full Power for 25 to 30 minutes or until vegetables are tender. Stir each 10 minutes during cooking time.

Sinclair, Man.
Branch No. 243

Rolled Rib Roast

4-5 lbs. rolled rib roast
1 clove garlic (optional)
seasoned salt

In bottom of 2 qt. (8x8") baking dish, place an inverted saucer or small casserole cover to hold meat out of juices. Place thin slices of garlic under string holding meat together. Sprinkle roast with seasoned salt. Place roast, fat side down, on saucer and cook, uncovered for half of the time. Turn fat side up, baste and cook covered with wax paper, for remainder of time. Let stand, covered with foil, 20 minutes before carving. 8 to 10 servings. This is excellent, brush with Kitchen Bouquet.

Minutes per lb. Internal temp.

Rare — 5 minutes, 30 seconds, 120° — will increase to 140°
Medium — 6 minutes, 30 seconds, 140° — will increase to 160° during standing
Well — 7 minutes, 30 seconds, 160° — will increase to 170° during standing

Red Lake, Ont.
Ladies Auxiliary
Branch No. 102

Meatballs

1 lb. ground beef
1 egg
½ pkg. onion soup mix
½-¾ cup bread crumbs
garlic salt (optional)

Mix together and shape into meatballs. Cook 8 minutes. Start at 6 minutes. Let stand at Medium Power.

Chile Sauce for above:

3 tbsp. oil
⅓ cup vinegar
½ cup water
1 cup ketchup
2 tbsp. brown sugar
1 tbsp. dry mustard
2 tbsp. Lea Perrins

Gilbert Plains, Man.
Ladies Auxiliary
Branch No. 98

Sweet and Sour Hot Dogs

Juice of 1 lemon
2 tbsp. prepared mustard
1 cup grape jelly
1 lb. hot dogs, cut into 1″ pieces

Combine juice of lemon, mustard and jelly in a 1½ qt. casserole dish. Cover with wax paper. Cook 2 minutes. Stir and add hot dog pieces and recover. Cook another 3 minutes, or until the hot dogs are heated through. Serves 4 to 6.

Pictou, N.S.
Branch No. 16

Lasagna

6 cups water
8 oz. lasagna noodles
1 tsp. salt.
1 tbsp. oil
1 lb. lean ground beef
½ cup diced onion
1-32 oz. jar spaghetti sauce
1-4 oz. jar sliced mushrooms, drained
2 cups cottage cheese
1 egg, slightly beaten
8 oz. Mozzarella cheese, sliced

Place water and salt in glass baking dish. Cover; cook on High (9) for 10 to 12 minutes or until boiling. Add lasagna noodles and oil. Cover; cook on Simmer (3) for 11 to 13 minutes or until tender. Drain water and separate noodles to avoid sticking together. In glass casserole, cook beef and onions on Roast (7) for 6 minutes or until beef is no longer pink. Drain. Mix together egg and cottage cheese. In glass baking dish, layer ¼ noodles, ¼ sauce, ½ cottage cheese mixture. Repeat layers three more times, omitting cottage cheese from fourth layer. Cover; cook on Reheat (8) for 10 minutes, arrange Mozzarella cheese on top during last five minutes of cooking. Total cooking time 41 minutes. Serves 4 to 6.

Jacquet River, N.B.
Durham Branch No. 77

Sukiyaki

1½-2 lbs. beef tenderloin steak, cut into thin strips
½ cup soya sauce
3 tbsp. sugar
½ cup water
½ cup sliced green onion
1-4 oz. can mushroom stems and pieces, drained
1-5 oz. can water chestnuts, drained and sliced
1-5 oz. can bamboo shoots, drained
1-16 oz. can bean sprouts, drained

Combine steak, soya sauce, water and sugar in 2 qt. (12x7″) glass baking dish. Cover with plastic wrap. Marinate 3 to 4 hours at room temperature. Place remaining ingredients in rows across meat and sauce (with mushrooms and onions in center rows). Recover. Microwave on High for 10 to 12 minutes. Let stand covered for 2 minutes before serving. 4 to 6 servings.

Pipestone, Man.
Branch No. 230

Round Steak Stew

2 beef bouillon cubes
2 cups water
2 lbs. round steak, cubed
¼ cup cold water
3 tbsp. cornstarch
2 large potatoes, cut up
1 cup sliced carrots
½ cup sliced celery
1 medium onion, sliced
1½ tsp. salt
¼ tsp. pepper
1-10 oz. pkg. frozen peas

Place bouillon cubes in 3 qt. casserole. Add water and cover. Microwave on High (Power Level 10) for 3 to 4 minutes. Stir. Add round steak to bouillon. Cover and continue to microwave at Low (Power Level 3) for 1 hour and 45 minutes, stirring every 30 minutes. In a small bowl stir together water and cornstarch. Slowly add to hot mixture, stirring well. Add potatoes, carrots, celery, onion, salt and pepper. Stir to distribute evenly. Cover. Microwave at High 10 minutes. Add peas and stir well. Cover. Microwave at High 5 to 10 minutes, until vegetables are tender. Makes 6 to 8 servings.

Ste. Rose, Man.
Ste. Rose Branch No. 232

Salisbury Steak

1½ lbs. ground beef
1-10¾ oz. can condensed cream of mushroom soup
1-4 oz. can sliced mushrooms, drained
1 egg
¾ cup milk
½ cup dry bread crumbs
¼ cup finely chopped onion
1/8 tsp. pepper

Set Power Select at Medium High. Combine ground beef, ¼ soup, ½ mushrooms (chopped), egg, ¼ cup milk, bread crumbs, onion and pepper. Shape into 6 patties and arrange in oblong dish. Heat covered with wax paper 13 to 14 minutes, turning patties over (if desired, brush top of patties with browning sauce blended with water) and rearranging once. Drain and let stand covered for 5 minutes. Meanwhile in a small glass bowl, combine remaining soup, mushrooms and milk. Heat 2 to 3 minutes, stirring once. Pour sauce over patties and garnish, if desired, with parsley.

Shoal Lake, Man.
Branch No. 72

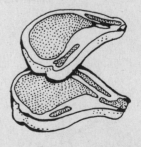

Chili

1 lb. ground beef
1 medium onion, chopped
¼ cup chopped green pepper
1-6 oz. can tomato paste
1-16 oz. can whole tomatoes
1 can kidney beans
½ cup water
1 tsp. salt
¼ tsp. garlic powder
2-3 tsp. chili powder

Crumble ground beef in 2 qt. glass casserole, stir in onion and green pepper; cover with glass lid. Microwave 6 to 8 minutes on High or until meat is browned. Drain and stir in remaining ingredients and re-cover. Microwave 20 to 25 minutes on Medium or until hot. Standing time 5 minutes. Good served with hot rice and sprinkle shredded cheese over bowls if desired.

Ste. Rose, Man.
St. Rose Branch No. 232

Bacon Topped Meat Loaf

1 lb. ground beef
1-8 oz. can tomato sauce
1-5.3 oz. can evaporated milk
1 egg
1 cup bread crumbs
1 medium onion, finely
    chopped
1 tsp. salt
¼ tsp. pepper
4-5 slices bacon

Mix all ingredients together except bacon. Pat into 9x5x2" loaf pan. Top with bacon slices. Cook on Full Power for 14 to 15 minutes. If oven has an automatic temperature control system, cook until temperature reaches 160°F.

Onanole, Man.
Branch No. 191

Cocktail Meatballs

1 lb. lean ground beef
1 tbsp. instant minced onion
1 tbsp. parsley flakes
1½ tsp. salt
1/8 tsp. allspice
pinch cloves
¼ tsp. garlic salt
½ cup dry bread crumbs
1 egg
2 tbsp. milk

Combine all ingredients in a large mixing bowl. Form into 1" meatballs. Place 8 to 10 meatballs on a paper towel lined plate. Cover with paper towel to prevent spatters. Meatballs may be refrigerated and cooked just before serving. Cook 3 minutes on Medium. Serve hot with cocktail picks.

Pictou, N.S.
Branch No. 16

Chow Mein

½ lb. lean ground pork
½ lb. lean ground veal or beef
1 medium onion, sliced
2 cups celery, diagonally
    sliced
1-4 oz. can mushroom stems
    and pieces, drained
3 tbsp. cornstarch
3 tbsp. soya sauce
1-16 oz. can Chow Mein vege-
    tables, rinsed and drained
1-8½ oz. can water chestnuts,
    drained and sliced
1 cup water
½ tsp. ginger

Combine meat, celery, onion and mushrooms in a 2 qt. casserole. Cover and cook 4 to 6 minutes or until meat loses its pink color. Dissolve cornstarch in soya sauce and stir into meat mixture. Mix in Chow Mein vegetables, water chestnuts, water and ginger. Cover and cook 4 to 6 minutes or until vegetables are tender-crisp. Serves 4.

Domain, Man.
Branch No. 208

Short Ribs with Barbeque Sauce

4 lbs. beef short ribs
1 medium onion, sliced
½ cup sliced celery
1¼ cups ketchup
¼ cup brown sugar
¼ cup cider vinegar
¼ cup flour
1 tbsp. Worcestershire sauce
½ tsp. salt
¼ tsp. dry mustard

Set Power Select at Medium. In oblong baking dish, arrange ribs, onion and celery. Heat, covered for 10 minutes. Meanwhile combine remaining ingredients; pour over ribs. Set Power Select on High. Cook, covered for 5 minutes. Set Power Select on Low. Heat, covered, for 1 hour or until ribs are tender, rearranging ribs once and basting with sauce occasionally.

Ste. Rose, Man.
Ste. Rose Branch No. 232

Onion Steak

¼ cup flour
¾ tsp. salt
¼ tsp. pepper
1½ lbs. marinated round
    steak
½ pkg. (1⅓ oz.) onion soup
    mix
1 onion, sliced
chopped parsley

Mix flour, salt and pepper. Pound the steak with the back of a heavy knife, working in half of the flour mixture per side. Cut meat into 4 pieces and put in baking dish. Sprinkle any remaining flour over top of meat. Add 1 cup water to onion soup mix and pour over meat. Cook, coverd for 14 minutes on High. Stir and rearrange meat in sauce occasionally. Place sliced onion on top and sprinkle with chopped parsley. Cook, covered for 10 minutes on High.

Lac du Bonnet, Man.
Branch No. 164

Ranch Meat Loaf

1½ lbs. ground beef
2 cups soft bread crumbs
½ cup ketchup
1 onion, cut fine
1 egg, beaten
1 tsp. salt.

Combine all ingredients in medium mixing bowl. Mix well. Pat into a 8x4″ glass loaf dish. Microwave on Defrost for 35 to 40 minutes or until well done. Let stand covered for 5 minutes before serving. Makes 5 to 6 servings.

Caledonia, N.S.
Patterson Branch No. 87

Hamburgers in Mushroom and Wine Gravy

½ cup finely chopped onion
½ cup butter
2 tbsp. flour
½ cup beef consommé, undiluted
½ cup sherry or dry white wine
½ lb. fresh mushrooms
2 tbsp. chopped parsley
1 bay leaf
¼ tsp. nutmeg
1 lb. lean ground beef
½ cup bread crumbs
1 egg, beaten
¼ tsp. garlic powder
salt and pepper to taste

Microwave onions and butter, uncovered, on High for 5 minutes. Stir in flour. Gradually add consommé and wine until blended. Stir in mushrooms, parsley, bay leaf and nutmeg; microwave, uncovered on Roast for 6 to 7 minutes, stirring once. Combine ground beef, bread crumbs, egg, garlic powder, salt and pepper. Form into 4 hamburger patties. Microwave on High, covered, on a platter, for 3 minutes. Drain juices. Pour sauce over hamburgers and microwave, on Bake for 3 to 4 minutes. Makes 4 servings.

Ignace, Ont.
Ladies Auxiliary
Branch No. 168

Meatloaf

1½ lbs. ground chuck beef
¾ cup chopped onions
½ cup fine dry bread crumbs
1 egg
2 tbsp. ketchup
1 cup milk
1 tsp. salt
¼ tsp. pepper
1/8 tsp. paprika

Combine all ingredients and pat evenly into a round ring mold. Spread 2 tbsp. ketchup evenly over top of loaf. Cover with wax paper. Cook on High for 15 to 20 minutes, checking for doneness after 15 minutes. If needed, return to oven for 2 to 5 minutes.

Terrace Bay, Ont.
Ladies Auxiliary
Branch No. 223

Meat Loaf

1½ lbs. ground beef
1 egg, slightly beaten
1 cup oatmeal
⅔ cup milk
1 small onion, chopped
salt and pepper to taste
1 can cream or potato or cream of mushroom soup

Combine all ingredients. Place in loaf pan and cover with wax paper. Cook on medium for 22 to 24 minutes or until no longer pink. Let stand for 5 minutes with cover on.

Sioux Lookout, Ont.
Branch No. 78

Pork
Fresh Ham

5-6 lb. cook-before-eating ham

Place ham on roasting rack in a 2 qt. glass baking dish. Cover corners or shank end with foil. Do not allow foil to touch walls inside microwave oven. Cook 40 to 50 minutes, allowing 8 to 9 minutes per lb. Turn ham over and rotate dish ¼ turn halfway through cooking time. Rest 10 to 15 minutes before carving or serving.

L'Ardoise, N.S.
Branch No. 110

Chinese Pork Chops

4-¾″ thick pork chops
  (1½ lbs.)
1 tbsp. flour
1 tbsp. oil
¼ cup soya sauce
¼ cup vinegar
½ tsp. ginger
⅓ cup sugar
¼ cup water

Flour chops on both sides. Preheat casserole type browning dish on High for 5 minutes; add oil. Brown chops on one side and turn. Cook on High for 5 minutes. (Chops may be browned on a convectional range. Transfer to a 9x11″ glass baking dish. Cover with plastic wrap and cook on Medium as shown above.) Combine remaining ingredients and pour over chops. Cover with glass lid. Reduce setting to Medium and cook 25 to 30 minutes or until meat is fork tender. Serves 4.

Ladies Auxiliary
Imperial Veterans in Canada
Branch No. 84

Apple Stuffed Pork Chops

(Microwave)

1 cup bread crumbs
1 cup pared and cubed cooking apples
2 tbsp. butter
1 tsp. salt
4-6 medium pork chops

In small bowl, combine bread crumbs, apples, butter and salt. Cook 2 to 3 minutes, stirring after every minute. Cut a slit in each pork chop and stuff with bread crumb mixture. Arrange in a 2 qt. glass baking dish. Cook, covered, 16 to 20 minutes, rotating dish ¼ turn halfway through cooking time. Rest, covered, 10 minutes, before serving. 4 to 6 servings.

L'Ardoise, N.S.
Ladies Auxiliary
Branch No. 110

Fried Rice

**2 pork chops, cut into small
  pieces**
Marinade:
  ½ cup soya sauce
  1 tsp. ground ginger
  1 clove garlic, crushed

Marinate in refrigerator 4 or 5
hours or 1 hour at room temperature. Drain about half of
the marinade before cooking. If
desired, this can be thickened
with cornstarch and used as
extra sauce. Place in a bowl and
cover. Cook at High for 2
minutes. Stir. Cook for another
minute. Check to see if cooked.
If not, cook longer.

  ¼-½ cup chopped celery
  **¼-½ cup chopped green
    onions**
  1 cup sliced mushrooms
  1 tsp. oil

Place in bowl and cover. Microwave on High for 1½ minutes.

  **1 egg, scrambled in micro-
    wave on High for 1 minute**
  4 cups cooked rice

Mix meat, vegetables, scrambled egg and rice. If necesarry,
reheat on Medium.

Morris, Man.
Branch No. 111

Ham and Noodle Casserole

1 medium onion, chopped
1 tbsp. margarine
**1-10 oz. can cream of mush-
  room soup**
½ cup milk
1-6 oz. can flaked ham
1-10 oz. can peas, drained
½ cup crushed potato chips

Place onion and margarine in
1½ qt. casserole. Microwave
for 2 to 3 minutes. Stir until
onion is soft. Combine soup,
ham, noodles and peas. Sprinkle with chips. Microwave 8 to 10
minutes or until bubbly. Rotate
dish half a turn after 5 minutes.

Trenton, N.S.
Branch No. 29

Barbequed Pork Chops and Rice

  ½ cup Minute Rice
  ½ cup water
  ¼ tsp. salt
  dash chili powder
  **2 pork chops, cut ½" thick
    (about 5 oz. each)**
  2 thin slices onion
  **3 tbsp. bottled barbeque
    sauce**
  1 tbsp. water

Combine rice, ½ cup water, salt
and chili powder in 6½x6½x2"
ceramic baking dish. Place pork
chops atop rice. Season chops
with salt. Place an onion slice
atop each chop. Combine
barbeque sauce and 1 tbsp.
water. Spoon over chops. Micro-
cook, covered, till chops and
rice are done, about 9 to 10
minutes, giving dish a half turn
after 5 minutes. Makes 2 servings.

Clarks Harbour, N.S.
Branch No. 148

Stuffed Pork Chops

  ½ cup milk
  ¼ cup butter or margarine
  **2 cups dry bread stuffing (as
    for poultry)**
  1 envelope brown gravy mix
  **8 thin rib pork chops (approx.
    1½ lbs.), trim off fat**

Combine butter and milk in
glass mixing bowl. Microwave
on Roast (4) until butter is melted. Stir in stuffing and mix
well; set aside. Sprinkle one side
of four chops with half of dry
gravy mix, place seasoned side
down in glass baking dish.
Spoon dressing on top of each
chop. Place remaining chops on
top of dressing. Sprinkle with
dry gravy mix. Cover with plastic wrap. Microwave on Roast
(4) for 12 to 15 minutes or until
fork tender. Let stand covered
for 5 minutes. Serves 4.

New Richmond, Que.
Bay Chaleurs Branch No. 172

Sweet and Sour Pork Chops

  2 tbsp. cornstarch
  6-8 thin pork chops
  3 tbsp. soya sauce
  ¼ cup brown sugar
  **½ tsp. finely grated fresh
    ginger**
  ¼ cup cider vinegar
  ½ cup water
  1-14 oz. can pineapple chunks
  1 medium onion

Toss pork chops in cornstarch
in a 2 qt. casserole until coated.
Add remaining ingredients and
toss together. Cook covered
with wax paper for 10 to 12
minutes, stirring twice. Let
stand 3 minutes. Stir well.

Thompson, Man.
Branch No. 246

Spare Ribs

  **3 lbs. spare ribs, cut in serving
    pieces**
  1 medium onion, chopped
  1 clove garlic, minced
  ¼ cup vinegar
  ¾ cup chili sauce
  1-7½ oz. can tomato sauce
  2 tbsp. brown sugar
  1 tbsp. Worcestershire sauce
  1 tsp. salt
  ¼ tsp. pepper

Place ribs in 9x13" glass baking
dish. Cover with plastic wrap.
Cook 15 minutes in microwave.
Drain off fat. Turn ribs over.
Arrange onion and garlic on
top. Combine remaining ingredients in small bowl. Pour sauce
over ribs. Cover with plastic
wrap. Cook 30 minutes or until
tender. Allow to stand 5 minutes before serving. Yield: 4 to 6
servings. Cook in microwave at
a Medium-High heat.

Brandon, Man.
Wheat City Branch No. 247

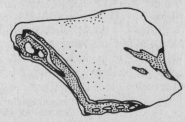

Sweet and Sour Spareribs

¾ cup chopped onion
1 cup ketchup
1 cup water
1½ tsp. dry mustard
¼ cup brown sugar
¼ cup vinegar

Mix together and pour over browned spareribs. Heat covered for 10 minutes on High. Reduce setting to Low and continue cooking 20 to 25 minutes or until ribs are tender. Conventional oven — Bake at 375°F. for 1 hour.

Elkhorn, Man.
Ladies Auxiliary
Elkhorn Branch No. 58

Barbequed Spareribs

2 tbsp. cooking oil
½ cup minced onion
2-8 oz. cans tomato sauce
2 tbsp. lemon juice
2 tbsp. brown sugar
1 tbsp. white sugar
2 tsp. Worcestershire sauce
1 tsp. prepared mustard
1 tsp. salt
¼ tsp. black pepper
1½ lbs. spareribs

Put oil and onion in a 1 qt. casserole. Cook, covered, on High for 3 to 4 minutes. Add 2 tbsp. water and remaining ingredients, except spareribs. Cover and cook on High for 3 minutes. Let stand. Cut ribs apart between bones and place in a 3 qt. casserole. Cook, covered on Roast for 15 minutes. Pour off fat and juices. Cover ribs with ¾ cup of barbeque sauce mixture. Cook, uncovered on Roast for 15 minutes. Turn ribs over. Spoon ½ cup sauce over top. Cook on Roast for 10 to 20 minutes or until meat is tender. Let stand 5 minutes before serving. Note: This recipe makes about 2½ cups sauce. Save remainder for other ribs, chicken or steak.

Schreiber, Ont.
Branch No. 109

Chicken

Roast Chicken

Dry chicken thoroughly. If desired, rub skin with browning liquid — soya sauce or Kitchen Bouquet. Chicken will brown on its own.
Place breast side down in baking dish. Microwave on High (Full Power) for 3 minutes. Reduce power to 50% (Medium) and microwave for ½ of time. Turn chicken breast side up. Microwave second ½ of time, or until leg moves easily and juices run clear. Calculate cooking time at 10 to 12 minutes per pound.

Souris, Man.
Branch No. 60

Sweet 'n Sour Chicken Thigh-Legs

4 chicken thigh-legs (9 oz. each)
1 tsp. poultry seasoning
2 tsp. salt
¼ tsp. pepper
1-10¾ oz. can condensed cream of mushroom soup
1-4 oz. can mushroom stems and pieces, drained
½ cup sour cream
½ cup water
½ tsp. finely chopped garlic

Place chicken thigh-legs skin side down and thick edges toward outside, in 2 qt. (7x12″) glass baking dish. Season with poultry seasoning, salt and pepper. Cover with plastic wrap. Microwave on High for 15 minutes, drain. Combine remaining ingredients in small mixing bowl. Turn chicken over, pour on soup mixture, recover and continue cooking on Roast for 6 to 8 minutes or until fork tender. Let stand, covered for 5 minutes before servings. Serves 4.

Cartwright, Man.
Branch No. 86

Turkey and Ham Casserole

1½ tbsp. butter or margarine
½ cup bread crumbs
2 tbsp. butter or margarine
½ cup chopped onion
3 tbsp. flour
½ tsp. salt
1-3 oz. can sliced mushrooms, undrained
1 cup light cream
2 cups cooked turkey, cubed
1 cup cooked ham, cubed
1-5 oz. can water chestnuts, drained and sliced (optional)
½ cup shredded cheese
paprika

In small bowl, melt 1½ tbsp. butter in oven for 30 seconds. Mix with bread crumbs and set aside. In 2 qt. casserole melt 2 tbsp. butter in oven for 1 minute. Stir in onion and cook 1 minute. Blend in flour, salt and pepper. Stir in mushrooms and cream. Cook for 1 minute. Stir well and cook 3 minutes more. Gently stir in turkey, ham and water chestnuts. Cook in oven for 7 minutes, stirring every minute. Top with cheese and wreathe with buttered crumbs. Return to oven for 1 minute. Sprinkle with paprika.

Cranberry Portage, Man.
Ladies Auxiliary
Branch No. 137

Chicken Rice Casserole

1 cup Minute Rice (250 ml)
¾ cup water (180 ml)
½ can cream of mushroom soup
½ pkg. onion soup mix
sprinkle paprika
1 pkg. chicken legs or breast

Put rice in round baking dish. Add water and soup. Place chicken on top of rice after rice is done. Cook at power level 9 for 12 minutes.

Port Hawkesbury, N.S.
Branch No. 43

Turkey Oriental

2 tbsp. cooking oil
1 cup finely chopped onion
1 cup finely chopped celery
2 cups cooked turkey, cubed
1-6 oz. can water chestnuts, drained and sliced
1-10¾ oz. can condensed chicken broth or 2 chicken bouillon cubes dissolved in 1½ cups boiling water
2 tbsp. cornstarch
1 tbsp. soya sauce
hot cooked rice

Combine oil, onion and celery in 2 qt. glass casserole. Microwave on High for 4 to 5 minutes or until onions are partly cooked. Stir in remaining ingredients, except rice. Mix well. Cover with glass lid or plastic wrap. Microwave on High for 10 to 12 minutes or until heated through and thickened. Let stand covered for 5 minutes. Serve with hot cooked rice.

Erickson, Man.
Branch No. 143

Stroganoff Casserole

A complete meal. Also great with leftover turkey.

1 can cream of celery or chicken soup
½ cup sour cream
1 cup milk
1 cup chicken, turkey or tuna
2 tbsp. parsley
2 tbsp. chopped pimento
¼ tsp. salt
1/8 tsp. pepper
2 cups egg noodles, cooked
2 tbsp. cracker crumbs

Blend all ingredients except cracker crumbs. Pour into 1½ qt. casserole. Top with cracker crumbs. Microwave on Full Power uncovered for 6 to 9 minutes. Serves 4.

Elkhorn, Man.
Branch No. 58

Parmesan Chicken

3 lbs. broiler-fryer, cut up
1 egg, beaten
½ cup cornflakes crumbs
½ cup grated parmesan cheese
¼ tsp. ground oregano
dash ground thyme
dash garlic salt
dash pepper
1 can Golden cream of mushroom soup
⅓ cup milk
2 tbsp. snipped parsley

Dip chicken in egg and roll in mixture of crumbs, cheese and spices. Coat thoroughly. Arrange chicken in 10" ceramic skillet or 2 qt. dish with larger pieces, such as thighs and breasts at corners, skin side down. Place wings and legs at centre. Cook in microwave, covered, on Full Power for 10 minutes. Turn chicken pieces over halfway through cooking time. Combine soup and milk. Pour over chicken. Cook in microwave covered on Full Power for 4 to 6 minutes or till chicken is tender. Garnish with remaining cheese mixture and parsley.

Roblin, Man.
Ladies Auxiliary
Branch No. 24

Crumb Coated Chicken

2 eggs
⅓ cup melted butter
1 tsp. salt
1½ cups buttery cracker crumbs (about 50)
3½ lbs. chicken, cut up with skin removed

Beat together eggs and melted butter. Coat chicken with cracker crumbs, then egg mixture. Place in a 12x8x2" glass pan or dish with meatiest pieces to outside edge of dish. Cover with wax paper. Microwave on High for 18 to 2 minutes, rotating dish ½ turn after 10 minutes. Makes about 4 servings. This is very good.

Miami, Man.
Ladies Auxiliary
Branch No. 88

Fried Chicken

Simply roll chicken pieces in melted butter. Dredge in one of the crumb based coatings. We recommend microwaving the chicken on a non-metallic rack to prevent the bottom from getting soggy, as the chicken will crisp and there is no need to turn pieces over.

2 chicken legs with thighs
1 whole chicken breast, split (about 2 lbs. total)
2 tbsp. butter or margarine
crumb coating

Rinse chicken pieces. Pat dry and set aside. Butter a 7x11" microwave baking dish. Microwave butter uncovered on High for 30 seconds or until butter is bubbly. Roll chicken pieces in butter and drain briefly. Shake in crumb coating or press coating evenly on to chicken. Arrange skin side up on non-metallic rack placed in baking dish. Breasts in centre, thighs to the outside. Microwave uncovered at 100° for 7 to 9 minutes. Rotate ¼ turn after 3½ minutes or until juices run clear and meat is no longer pink. Let stand for 5 minutes before serving. Serves 4 to 5.

Parmesan Coated Chicken:
2 tbsp. grated parmesan cheese
2 tbsp. yello meal
3 tbsp. finely dried bread crumbs
½ tsp. garlic salt
½ tsp. oregano leaves
¼ tsp. paprika

Combine ingredients in a bag.

Stuffing Coated Chicken:
⅔ cup finely crushed packaged stuffing mix or herb seasoned croutons
1 tsp. parsley flakes

Combine ingredients in a bag.

Winnipeg, Man.
Brooklands Weston Branch No. 2

Chicken Cacciatore

2½-3 lb. quartered frying chicken
1 small onion, thinly sliced and separated into rings
½ medium green pepper, cut into strips
1-28 oz. can whole tomatoes

Mushroom Sauce:
2 tbsp. cornstarch
¼ cup water
1 tsp. sugar
½ tsp. salt
2 cups reserved chicken broth
1-4 oz. can mushroom stems and pieces, drained

Arrange chicken pieces, skin side up and thick edges toward outside in 2 qt. glass baking dish. Place onion, green pepper and tomatoes over chicken. Cover with wax paper. Microwave for 35 to 40 minutes on High or until meat cut near bone is no longer pink. Drain, reserving 2 cups broth. Let stand, covered, for 5 minutes before serving.

To make mushroom sauce, combine all ingredients except mushrooms and broth in 4 cup glass measure, beat with rotary beater until smooth, beat in reserved broth. Microwave for 2 minutes on High. Beat, add mushrooms and continue cooking for 2 or 3 minutes on Roast, or until thickened. Stir well and pour over chicken to serve.

Winnipeg, Man.
Kent Memorial Branch No. 119

French Fish Fillets

1 lb. fish
¼ cup French dressing
½ cup cracker crumbs
paprika

Dip fish in French dressing, then in crumbs. Place in greased shallow baking dish. Sprinkle with paprika and cover with wax paper. Microwave 4 to 6 minutes, turning dish after 2½ minutes. Serves 2 to 3.

Stewiacke, N.S.
Branch No. 70

Fish

Fish Roll-ups in Vegetable Sauce

2 stalks celery, thinly sliced
2 onions, thinly sliced
1 clove garlic, minced
1 tbsp. butter
1-14 oz. can tomatoes, drained and chopped
1 cup or ½ lb. fresh mushrooms, sliced
¼ cup dry white wine
½ tsp. basil
6 flounder or cod fillets (2 lbs.) fresh, or frozen thawed

Combine celery, onion, garlic and butter in microwave baking dish. Cover and cook 4 minutes on High. Stir in tomatoes, mushrooms, wine and basil. Cook covered, on Medium for 3 minutes. Roll fish skin side in. Fasten with toothpicks. Stand rolls on end in dish. Spoon sauce over. Cook covered on High for 10 minutes. Turn dish ½ round through cooking period. Let stand 5 or 10 minutes. Remove toothpicks. Spoon sauce over rolls and serve. Makes 6 servings.

Justice, Man.
Branch No. 233

Filet of Sole in Almond Butter

½ cup slivered almonds
⅓ cup butter
3 tbsp. lemon juice
2 tbsp. dry sherry
½ tsp. salt
1 lb. sole filet, or other

In an 8x8″ baking dish, mix almonds and butter. Cook on Medium setting, uncovered for 5 minutes until golden brown. Add lemon juice, sherry and salt. Add filets and coat with some sauce. Cook, covered, with wax paper for 5 minutes or until fish flakes easily. Let stand, covered, for 2 minutes before serving.

Hartney, Man.
Branch No. 26

Shrimp Mornay

1 cup water
½ cup dry white wine
1 tsp. instant chicken bouillon granules
¼ tsp. dry mustard
dash pepper
12 oz. fresh or frozen shelled shrimp
2 carrots, cut into matchstick pieces
½ cup green onions, cut into 1″ pieces
⅔ cup skim milk
2 tbsp. cornstarch
1 cup or 4 oz. shredded process Swiss cheese
2 oz. linguine noodles
1 cup frozen peas, thawed

Combine water, wine, bouillon granules, dry mustard and pepper in a saucepan; bring to a boil. Add shrimp, carrots and onion. Return to boil. Cover and simmer for one minute. Remove the shrimp and vegetables with a slotted spoon; set aside. Boil liquid, uncovered for 5 to 10 minutes or till reduced to ¾ cup. Combine milk and cornstarch; add to liquid. Cook and stir till thickened and bubbly; cook 2 minutes more. Stir in cheese till melted. Remove from heat. Cool.

Cook linguine in lightly salted boiling water till barely tender, about 5 to 7 minutes; drain. Divide linguine among 4 shallow individual baking dishes. Combine shrimp and vegetables, sauce and peas; spoon mixture over linguine. Cover with foil and freeze. Makes 4 single-serving entrées.

Conventional oven: Bake, covered, at 375°F. for 45 minutes or till mixture is hot.

Microwave oven: Remove foil; cover with vented plastic wrap or wax paper. Cook, covered, at Medium High for 5 minutes, stirring once. 331 calories per serving.

Valemount, B.C.
Branch No. 266

Cumberland Fish Bake

1 lb. fresh or frozen fillets
1 lb. fresh or frozen scallops
1 cup coarse bread crumbs
1½ cups boiling water
¼ cup melted butter
salt and pepper

Thaw frozen fish in a deep dish. Pour boiling water over fish and let stand one hour. Drain off water, reserving one cup. Arrange fish in casserole, salt and pepper to taste. Cover with bread crumbs. Pour mixture of melted butter and water over crumbs. Bake for 10 minutes in microwave oven. Brown top under broiler. It is good baked at 350°F. for one hour. Serve with baked potatoes and tossed salad.

Amherst, N.S.
Ladies Auxiliary
Branch No. 10

Coquilles St. Jacques

1 tbsp. margarine or butter
1 tbsp. chopped onion
1 lb. scallops
1 cup fresh mushrooms, sliced
⅓ cup white wine
1½ tsp. lemon juice
¼ tsp. salt
dash marjoram
dash paprika
3 tbsp. margarine or butter
2 tbsp. flour
½ cup whipping cream
1 tbsp. snipped parsley

Combine 1 tbsp. margarine and onion in 1½ qt. casserole. Microwave on High for 1 minute. Stir in scallops, mushrooms, wine, lemon juice, salt, marjoram and paprika. Microwave covered on High for 3 minutes. Drain and reserve liquid.
Place 3 tbsp. margarine in small bowl. Microwave on High for 30 seconds to one minute until melted. Blend in flour. Stir in ½ cup reserved liquid, cream and parsley. Microwave on Medium

High (70%) until thickened, 3 to 5 minutes, stirring once. Stir sauce into scallops.
Spoon scallop mixture into 4 ramekins or small bowls. Microwave on Medium High (70%) until heated through, 2 to 3½ minutes. If using oven without carousel, rearrange bowls after one minute. Do not overcook.

Bridgetown, N.S.
Ladies Auxiliary
Branch No. 33

Baked Frozen Fresh Fillets

1 lb. frozen fillets
  (sole, flounder, perch or
  cod)
2 tbsp. melted butter or lard
dash salt
dash pepper
dash paprika

Place frozen fillets in a 2 qt. glass baking dish. To defrost, cook in microwave for 9 minutes. Cut block of fish in half; place center pieces to side of dish. Brush with melted butter. Sprinkle with salt and pepper; and generously with paprika. Cover and bake in microwave for 8 minutes.

Yarmouth, N.S.
Branch No. 61

Fish in Lemon Parsley Butter

½ cup butter
2 tbsp. cornstarch
3 tbsp. lemon juice
1 tsp. dried parsley flakes
1/8 tsp. celery salt
dash pepper
2 lbs. fish fillets, completely
  thawed

Place butter in a 2 qt. baking dish. Microwave about 2 minutes or until melted. Blend in cornstarch, lemon juice, parsley, celery salt and pepper. Dip each piece of fish in seasoned butter. Arrange fillets with thick edge toward outside f dish. Cover with plastic wrap or paper towel. Microwave for 8 to

9 minutes or until fish flakes easily. Let stand, cover for 5 minutes before serving.

Kelwood, Man.
Branch No. 50

Vegetables, Eggs, Cheese

Fluffy White Rice

2¼ cups boiling water
1 tsp. salt
2 tsp. butter
1 cup Uncle Ben's converted
  rice

Combine rice, water and salt in a large bowl. Cover with Saran Wrap, but leave an opening. Microwave 10 minutes on High. Remove from oven, cover completely with Saran Wrap and let stand 15 minutes.

Winnipeg, Man.
Imperial Veterans
Branch No. 84

Peas 'n Onions with Mushrooms

2 tbsp. butter
¼ cup chopped onion
1-4 oz. can mushroom stems
  and pieces, drained
1-10 oz. pkg. frozen peas
¼ tsp. salt
dash pepper
dash allspice

Combine butter and onion in a 1 qt. glass casserole. Cover with plastic and cook 3 minutes on High. Add mushrooms, frozen peas, salt, pepper and allspice. Recover and continue cooking 4 minutes on High. Stir and continue cooking 3 to 4 minutes or until peas are tender-crisp. Let stand covered 3 minutes before serving.

Miami, Man.
Ladies Auxiliary
Branch No. 88

Carrot-Asparagus Salad

Because this colorful salad can be made ahead, it's an excellent addition to a cold buffet. Be sure to cut the vegetables on the diagonal. They look prettier and cook faster and more evenly because there's a larger surface area.

3 carrots
½ cup water (125 ml)
½ lb. fresh asparagus (250 g)
8 black olives, pitted
4 tsp. vinegar (20 ml)
1 tbsp. salad oil (15 ml)
1 tbsp. sugar (15 ml)
½ tsp. salt (2 ml)
¼ tsp. garlic salt (1 ml)

Slice carrots diagonally into ¼" (1 cm) wide strips. In 8-cup (2 l) casserole, micro-cook carrots and water, covered, at high for 4 minutes. Slice asparagus diagonally into pieces 1" (2.5 cm) thick. Add to casserole along with carrots; stir and micro-cook, covered, at high for 6 to 8 minutes or until vegetables are just tender. Rinse and drain. Cut olives in half and add to carrots. Combine remaining ingredients and add to vegetables, tossing gently to coat. Chill. Makes 4 to 6 servings.

Winnipeg, Man.
Kent Memorial Branch No. 119

Vegetable Rice Pilaf

⅓ cup butter or margarine
1½ cups uncooked rice
1 onion, finely chopped
½ cup celery
3 cups water
2 tsp. Chicken-in-a-mug

Place rice, onion and celery in a 2 qt. casserole. Cook uncovered 5 minutes. Stir well. Add remaining ingredients and cook covered 10 minutes, stirring twice. Let stand covered 10 minutes to finish cooking. Serves 6.

Oak Lake, Man.
Ladies Auxiliary
Branch No. 79

Poached Eggs

1½ tsp. butter or margarine
3 eggs
salt and pepper

In every other muffin cup, place ½ tsp. butter. Break 1 egg into each cup. Cover entire muffin pan with plastic wrap. Microwave 1½ to 2½ minutes on full power. Allow to stand for 2 minutes in muffin pan prior to serving. Season with salt and pepper. Serves 3.

Clarks Harbour, N.S.
Branch No. 148

Crustless Quiche Lorraine

¾ cup minced onion
10 slices or ½ lb. bacon, cooked and crumbled
1 cup grated Swiss cheese (I use medium cheddar)
1 can or 1 lb. evaporated milk
4 eggs
¾ tsp. salt
1/8 tsp. cayenne

In 9" glass pie plate, microwave the onion, covered for 2 to 2½ minutes on full power or until tender. Spread bacon and cheese evenly over cooked onion. In a 4 cup glass measure, microwave milk 2 to 3 minutes on full power or until almost boiling. Beat eggs, salt and cayenne. Gradually add hot milk, stirring constantly. Pour over ingredients in pie plate. Microwave uncovered 6 to 7 minutes on full power. Stir 3 times during this cooking period (after 2, 4, and 5 minutes), drawing cooked portions from edges to centre. Smooth with back of spoon to prevent a lumpy surface. Quiche is cooked when it is set but still jiggles slightly when shaken. Let stand, uncovered 5 to 10 minutes before serving. Makes 4 to 5 servings. Good with a salad.

Deloraine, Man.
Ladies Auxiliary
Branch No. 83

Macaroni Bake

2 tbsp. butter or margarine
4 cups cooked macaroni
½ cup sour cream
1-4 oz. pkg. sliced ham, cut into pieces
¼ tsp. dried parsley flakes
salt and pepper

Combine all ingredients in 2 qt. glass casserole. Cover with glass lid or plastic wrap. Put microwave on Roast for 4 minutes, stir and recover. Continue cooking 4 to 6 minutes on Roast or until hot. Makes 4 to 6 servings. Can substitute leftover cooked ham for pkg. ham, sliced.

Western Shore, N.S.
Ladies Auxiliary
Branch No. 144

Vegetable Platter with Cheese Sauce

cauliflower
broccoli
zucchini
carrots

Cut cauliflower and broccoli into flowerettes; slice zucchini and cut carrots in thin strips. Arrange vegetables on a platter, placing the thicker parts of the cauliflower and broccoli towards the outside. Insert carrot sticks between pieces of cauliflower and broccoli, arrang zucchini in the centre. Dot with butter. Cover with plastic wrap and cook 10 minutes on High or 6 minutes per lb. of vegetables. Let stand 5 minutes.

Cheese Sauce:
1 tbsp. butter
1 tbsp. flour
⅔ cup milk
½ cup grated cheese
salt and pepper
dry mustard
garlic powder

Melt butter, stir in flour, add seasonings and milk. Cook 2½ minutes, stirring once. Add cheese and stir until melted. Serve with vegetable platter.

Oak Lake, Man.
Ladies Auxiliary
Branch No. 79

Scalloped Potatoes

3 tbsp. butter
3 tbsp. flour
1 tsp. salt
½ tsp. pepper
3 cups milk
1 medium onion, sliced thinly or diced, if preferred
4 medium potatoes, peeled
1 small pkg. Mozzarella cheese, shredded

In glass casserole, combine all ingredients except potatoes. Cover and cook on Roast (7) for 10 to 12 minutes, or until thickened; stirring twice. Cut potatoes in half lengthwise, then into ¼" slices. Add to thickened sauce. Spread Mozzarella cheese over top. Cover and cook on High (9) for 17 to 20 minutes or until potatoes are tender, stirring once. Total cooking time 37 minutes. Serves 4 to 6.

Saulnierville, N.S.
Branch No. 52

Deep Browned Potatoes

2 tbsp. margarine or 4 tbsp. roast drippings
½ tsp. Kitchen Bouquet
¼ tsp. paprika
¼ tsp. herb of your choice (e.g. garlic powder, basil or onion powder)
4 potatoes, peeled and cubed

Mix the first 4 ingredients and cook on High for 1 minute. Roll potatoes in mixture and coat well. Cook, covered with Saran Wrap for 4½ minutes on High. Stir, bringing potatoes toward outer edge of dish toward center. Cook uncovered for an additional 4 to 5 minutes on High or until tender. Serves 4.

Lac du Bonnet, Man.
Branch No. 164

Cheese Strata

8 slices day-old bread
1 cup Cheddar cheese, shredded
4 eggs
2½ cups milk
1 small onion, finely minced
½ tsp. prepared mustard
1 tsp. salt.
1/8 tsp. pepper
paprika

Trim crusts from bread. Place 4 slices of bread in the bottom of an 8" square glass baking dish. Cover with shredded cheese. Top with remaining 4 slices of bread. Beat eggs lightly. Beat in milk, onion, mustard, salt and pepper. Pour over top of bread slices. Sprinkle with paprika. Cover with wax paper and let stand at room temperature at least one hour. Cook on Bake for 25 to 28 minutes, or until a knife inserted in centre comes out clean. Let stand 3 minutes before serving.

Pine Falls, Man.
Ladies Auxiliary
Branch No. 64

Medium White Sauce

2 tbsp. butter
2 tbsp. flour
½ tsp. salt
1 cup milk

Place butter in 1 qt. casserole and melt for 30 seconds on High. Blend in flour and salt. Gradually add milk. Cook uncovered for 2 to 3 minutes or until thickened. Makes 1 cup.

Cheese Sauce:
Add ½-¾ cup shredded cheese.

Mushroom Sauce:
Add 1-4 oz. can sliced mushrooms.

Light Sauce:
Reduce butter and flour in half.

Heavy Sauce:
Add double butter and flour.

Waskada, Man.
Ladies Auxiliary
Branch No. 92

Browned Potatoes

2 or 3 large potatoes, peeled and cut in serving size pieces
1 tsp. cooking oil
1 tsp. Kitchen Bouquet

Place potatoes in greased casserole. Pour the oil and Kitchen Bouquet over potatoes and stir to coat the potatoes well. (They will look terrible, but don't worry.) Cover casserole and microwave on High about 10 to 12 minutes, stirring two or three times during cooking to keep potatoes coated with mixture. Let stand a few minutes to finish cooking.

Bowsman, Man.
Branch No. 51

Spinach Souffle

2-10 oz. pkg. frozen chopped spinach
¼ cup margarine
2 cups process American cheese, shredded
4 eggs
2 tbsp. dry parsley flakes
½ tsp. nutmeg
2 cups cooked rice
½ cup finely chopped onion
1 tsp. salt
⅔ cup milk
¼ tsp. leaf thyme

Place frozen spinach, icy side up in 2 qt. glass casserole, cover with plastic wrap. Microwave 8 to 10 minutes on High. Drain well through sieve. Stir in margarine until melted. Add rice and cheese. Combine milk and eggs in 4 cup glass measure. Blend in remaining ingredients. Stir into spinach mixture until well blended, cover with plastic wrap. Microwave on Roast for 25 minutes or until knife inserted near center comes out clean. Let stand covered 5 minutes before serving. Makes 6 to 8 servings.

Cartwright, Man.
Cartwright-Mather Branch No. 86

Chow Mein

1/3 cup soya sauce
3 tbsp. cornstarch
2-5 oz. can water chestnuts, sliced and undrained
1 can or 1 lb. bean sprouts, undrained
1-7 oz. can mushroom stems and pieces, undrained
2 cups diced cooked meat
2 cups celery, sliced in 1/2" diagonal pieces
1 cup thinly sliced onions

Stir together soya sauce and cornstarch in 3 qt. casserole. Stir in water chestnuts, bean sprouts and mushrooms; then add meat, celery and onion. Microwave 20 to 22 minutes on High. Stir thoroughly and serve over cooked rice or chow mein noodles.

Long Grain Rice:
1 cup rice
2 1/2 cups cold water
1 tsp. salt
1 tbsp. butter

Combine all ingredients in a 3 qt. casserole and cook for 12 to 15 minutes. Cover casserole with wax paper or Saran Wrap. Remove from oven and stir. Allow to stand covered for 5 minutes. Stir again before serving. Serves 6.

Rapid City, Man.
Branch No. 49

Rueben Sandwiches

8 slices rye bread
mayonnaise
thinly sliced corned beef
sauerkraut, well drained
4 slices Swiss cheese

Toast bread; spread 4 slices with mayonnaise and place on paper towels. Top each slice with thinly sliced corned beef, sauerkraut and a slice of Swiss cheese. Place remaining slices of toast on top. Microwave on Medium Power (50%, Roast) 3 1/2 to 4 minutes. Makes 4 sandwiches.

Carberry, Man.
Branch No. 153

Macaroni and Cheese

1-8 oz. pkg. elbow macaroni, cooked and drained
3/4 lb. pasteurized process cheese, cut into cubes
3/4-1 cup milk
1/2-3/4 tsp. salt
1/4 tsp. onion powder
1/4 tsp. pepper
1/8 tsp. dry mustard
buttered bread crumbs

Combine macaroni, cheese, milk, salt, onion, pepper and mustard in 3 qt. casserole. Heat covered 9 to 10 minutes on High, stirring twice. Top with bread crumbs and heat uncovered 3 minutes on High.

Port Morien, N.S.
Ladies Auxiliary
Branch No. 55

Swiss Scalloped Corn

3 slices bacon
2-16 oz. cans whole kernel corn, drained
1 cup or 4 oz. Swiss cheese, shredded
1/2 tsp. onion powder
1/8 tsp. pepper
1 1/2 tsp. flour
1 egg
1-5 1/3 oz. can evaporated milk
1/4 cup bread crumbs
1 tbsp. butter or margarine, melted
dash paprika

Set power select on High. Arrange bacon between layers of paper towels in an oblong baking dish. Heat 2 1/2 to 3 minutes, or until bacon is crisp. Remove paper towels and crumble bacon. Stir in corn, cheese, onion powder, pepper and flour blended with egg and milk. Top with bread crumbs blended with butter and paprika. Set power select at Medium-High. Heat 10 to 12 minutes or until corn is set. Let stand, covered, 5 minutes before serving.

Shoal Lake, Man.
Branch No. 72

Broccoli Au Gratin

1 pkg. frozen broccoli
1/4 cup butter, divided in two (60 ml)
2 tsp. flour (10 ml)
1/4 tsp. salt (1 ml)
1/8 tsp. pepper (1/2 ml)
1 cup milk (250 ml)
1/2 cup shredded cheese (125 ml)
1/3 cup bread crumbs (80 ml)

Place broccoli on plate in oven on High for 6 minutes; set aside. Put 2 tsp. butter in casserole dish and cook 1 minute on High. Stir in spices, blend well. Mix in milk and cook on power level 7 for 4 to 6 minutes. Stir in cheese and add broccoli. Place rest of butter in a small dish; melt and stir in bread crumbs. Sprinkle on broccoli. Return casserole to oven for 2 minutes on power level 9.

Port Hawkesbury, N.S.
Branch No. 43

Cheesy Potatoes

4 cups thinly sliced potatoes
3/4 cup chopped onion
3/4 tsp. salt
1-10 oz. can condensed cheddar cheese soup
1/2 cup milk
1 1/2 tsp. Worcestershire sauce

Layer 1/3 potatoes, onions and salt in a buttered 1 1/2 or 2 qt. casserole. Repeat 3 times. In a small casserole, heat soup, milk and Worcestershire sauce. Stir, then place in microwave for 3 minutes on power level 9 or high heat until smooth when stirred and hot. Pour over potatoes and onions. Cover with casserole lid or paper towel and place in microwave for 25 to 30 minutes on power level 9 or high heat, turning dish often. Let stand 5 minutes before serving.

Kelwood, Man.
Branch No. 50

Asparagus Supreme

1-10 oz. pkg. frozen asparagus, chopped
½ cup mayonnaise
1 tsp. melted butter
1 tsp. flour
3 eggs, well beaten
½ pt. light cream
½ tsp. salt
¼ tsp. basil
¼ tsp. onion puree

Place asparagus in a 1 qt. casserole. Cook covered 7 to 8 minutes or until done, stirring once. Drain and add mayonnaise, butter and flour mixture. Add eggs, cream and seasonings. Pour into greased 1 qt. mold. Cook 12 to 14 minutes or until pick inserted in centre comes out dry. Serves 4.

Domain, Man.
Branch No. 208

Company Rice

1 cup long grain rice,
   uncooked
2 tbsp. finely chopped celery
3 tbsp. green onion, finely
   chopped
1¾ cups water
2 tbsp. soya sauce
2 chicken bouillon cubes
⅓ cup fresh mushrooms,
   sliced
½ cup frozen peas

Combine rice and butter in 1½ qt. casserole dish and cook uncovered for 3 to 4 minutes on High or until rice is browned, stirring twice. Stir in celery and green onion, cook an additional minute. Add water, soya sauce and bouillon cubes; mix well. Cover with casserole lid and cook on high power for 5 minutes, then on Medium for 13 to 14 minutes, or until most of the liquid is absorbed. Stir in mushrooms and frozen peas. Let stand, covered for 10 minutes, cook an additional 3 minutes. Fluff with fork. Serves 4 to 6.

Mafeking, Man.
Branch No. 93

Broccoli Casserole

2 cups cooked rice
¼ cup butter
1 pkg. frozen broccoli or
   fresh cooked
1 can mushrooms, drained
1 cup chopped onion
6 oz. Cheese Whiz
1 can cream of mushroom
   soup

Mix all ingredients together in a medium size casserole. Bake 30 minutes at 350°F. or cook covered on Medium for about 15 minutes in microwave.

Red Rock, Ont.
Branch No. 226

Hot Potato Salad

4 cups mashed potatoes
1 egg, beaten
½ cup chopped celery
¼ cup chopped onion
3 tbsp. butter
1 tsp. mustard
2 tbsp. vinegar
salt and pepper to taste

Blend together well. Bake in buttered casserole at 350°F. for 30 minutes or 10 minutes in microwave on High.

Foxwarren, Man.
Branch No. 152

Zucchini Combo

3 medium zucchini, sliced
1 cup sliced mushrooms
¼ tsp. garlic powder
¼ tsp. salt
¼ cup butter
2 medium size tomatoes, cut
   in wedges
¼ cup Parmesan cheese,
   grated

Combine zucchini and mushrooms in 1½ qt. baking dish. Sprinkle with garlic powder and salt. Dot with butter. Cook covered 7 to 8 minutes. Stir in tomatoes and sprinkle cheese on top. Cook on full power 3 minutes.

Thunder Bay, Ont.
Ladies Auxiliary
Ortona Branch No. 113

Browned Potatoes

2 tbsp. butter or margarine
4-5 medium size potatoes,
   cut into pieces
¼-½ tsp. Kitchen Bouquet
¼ tsp. paprika
¼ tsp. herbs
2 tbsp. Lipton onion soup
   mix

Place all ingredients except potatoes into 1½ qt. casserole. Cool one minute and stir. Roll potatoes in mixture until well coated. Cook covered for 6 minutes. Stir potatoes to coat with mixture again. Cook uncovered for an addition 6 to 8 minutes, or until potatoes are tender.

Killarney, Man.
Ladies Auxiliary
Branch No. 25

Desserts

Chocolate Toffee Bars

11 graham cracker squares
½ cup butter
½ cup brown sugar
½ cup icing sugar
1 tbsp. cornstarch
¼ tsp. salt
1 cup coconut
½ cup chopped nuts
1 cup semi-sweet chocolate
   chips

Arrange graham cracker squares in a 12x8x2″ pan. Microwave butter and sugar together on High for 2 minutes. Stir well. Blend remaining ingredients except chocolate chips into butter and sugar mixture. Spread evenly over the graham crackers. Sprinkle the chocolate chips over top and microwave at High 2 to 2½ minutes. Let stand a few moments, then spread chocolate over bars. Cool. 24 bars. Delicious!

Boissevain, Man.
Branch No. 10

Jam

2 cups or 2 pts. strawberries, crushed
½ box or 2 tbsp. Certo crystals
3 cups sugar

Combine berries and Certo in a 2 qt. glass bowl. Stir well and cook at full power 5 to 6 minutes or until mixture comes to a full boil, stirring once. Add sugar and stir well. Cook 3 to 4 minutes until mixture comes to a full boil, stirring once. Set bowl on counter; then skim and stir about 5 minutes. Makes about six 6 oz. jars.

Plumas, Man.
Branch No. 189

Peanut Brittle

1 cup white sugar
½ cup syrup
1 cup salted peanuts
1 tsp. butter
1 tsp. vanilla
1 tsp. baking soda

Stir together sugar and syrup in a 2 qt. casserole. Cook at high heat for 4 minutes. Stir in peanuts and cook another 4 minutes. Add butter and vanilla. Cool 1 to 2 minutes. Add 1 tsp. baking soda and stir until foamy. Pour onto a greased cookie sheet and cool.

Pilot Mound, Man.
Branch No. 62

Can't Fail Fudge

⅔ cup evaporated milk
1⅓ cups granulated sugar
½ tsp. salt
1½ cups diced marshmallows
1½ cups semi-sweet chocolate chips
1 tsp. vanilla
½ cup chopped walnuts
½ cup coconut

Mix evaporated milk, sugar and salt in a 2 qt. casserole. Microwave on High 2 to 3 minutes until boiling; stir. Microwave on high for 5 minutes. Add remaining ingredients and pour into a 9″ square pan. Cool.

Perth Andover, N.B.
Branch No. 36

Caramel Corn

1 cup brown sugar
1-4 oz. stick butter
¼ cup white corn syrup
½ tsp. salt
½ tsp. baking soda
3-4 qts. popped corn

Combine all ingredients except baking soda and popcorn in a large dish. Bring to a boil and cook on full power for 2 minutes. Remove from microwave and stir in baking soda. Place popcorn in brown paper bag. Pour syrup over and shake. Cook in bag on full power in microwave for 1½ minutes. Shake and cook 1½ minutes more. (May need a bit more.) Cool.

Hartney, Man.
Branch No. 26

Raisin Bran Muffins

1¼ cups Bran Flakes cereal
1 cup milk
1 egg
½ cup raisins
½ cup brown sugar, firmly packed
⅓ cup vegetable oil
1 cup flour
2½ tsp. baking powder
1 tsp. salt

Mix cereal and milk together in a medium bowl. Let stand 2 to 3 minutes or until cereal softens. Stir in egg, raisins, sugar and oil. Sift dry ingredients together and add to batter. Stir just until flour disappears. Place 2 paper cupcake liners in 6 oz. glass custard cups. Fill each cup half full with batter. Microwave as directed below. Immediately remove muffins from custard cups and cool on rack.

2 muffins — full power ¾ to 1 min., and bake (7) 1 to 1¼ min.

4 muffins — full power 1 to 1½ min., bake (7) 2 to 2½ min. Makes 16 to 18 muffins.

Ignace, Ont.
Ladies Auxiliary
Branch No. 168

Bran Muffins

2 cups boiling water
4 cups all-bran cereal
2 cups 100% bran flakes
1 qt. buttermilk
3 cups sugar or ½ cup Sugar Twin
4 eggs, beaten
1 cup margarine
5 cups flour
5 tsp. baking soda
1 tsp. salt

Pour hot water over cereals in large mixing bowl, stir in buttermilk and remaining ingredients. Mix until just blended. (This batter can be refrigerated between 3 and 4 weeks.) Spoon 2 tbsp. batter into six 6 oz. glass custard cups lined with paper liners, arrange the 6 cups in a circle in oven. Cook full power for 1 minute, 10 to 20 seconds. 4 muffinds — 1 min.; 2 muffins — 35 to 45 sec.

Onanole, Man.
Branch No. 191

Peanut Butter Cookies

½ cup butter
½ cup brown sugar
½ cup white sugar
½ cup peanut butter
1 egg
1½ cups flour
¼ tsp. baking soda
¼ tsp. salt
1 tsp. vanilla

Cream butter, sugar and peanut butter together. Add egg; blend in flour, baking soda, salt and vanilla. Stir well. Shape dough in 1″ balls. Arrange in rows on wax paper covered microwave baking tray. Space 2″ aprt and press down with fork. Microwave at power level 12 for 2½ to 3 minutes.

Langruth, Man.
Ladies Auxiliary
Branch No. 162

Crunchy Apple Crisp

6 cups cooking apples, peeled, cored and sliced
⅔ cup quick-cooking rolled oats
⅓ cup flour
¾ cup brown sugar, packed
½ tsp. cinnamon
½ tsp. nutmeg
¼ cup butter or margarine

Place apple slices in a 8x8″ glass baking dish. Combine remaining ingredients, except butter, in medium mixing bowl. Cut in butter until crumbly. Sprinkle over apples. Microwave for 16 to 20 minutes on High (100%) or until apples are tender. Makes 6 servings.

New Ross, N.S.
New Ross Branch No. 79

Date Squares

1 cup margarine or butter
1 cup dark brown sugar, packed
1½ cups flour
1 tsp. baking powder
¼ tsp. salt
1½ cups rolled oats

Cream margarine and sugar, add flour, baking powder and salt sifted together; then the oats. Put half the crumbly mixture into the bottom of a greased 8″ square glass pan. Spread the date filling over it and cover with the remaining oat mixture.

Date Filling:
1 lb. pitted dates
1 cup crushed pineapple, undrained

Combine dates in 1½ qt. glass casserole, stir in pineapple. Cook for 4 minutes on high power stirring once.

Cook squares for 7 to 9 minutes on high power, rotating pan once if squares are not rising evenly. Let cool before cutting.

Sydney, N.S.
Ladies Auxiliary
Branch No. 128

Brownies

2 eggs
½ tsp. salt
½ cup or ¼ lb. melted butter
½ cup cocoa
1 cup sugar
1 tsp. vanilla
¾ cup unsifted flour
1 cup chopped nuts

Beat together eggs, sugar, salt and vanilla at medium speed, about one minute until light. Add melted butter. Continue beating until thoroughly blended. Mix in flour and cocoa at low speed. Stir in nuts and spread evenly in 8″ dish. Microwave at High Power 6 to 7 minutes, rotating dish ¼ turn every 2 minutes. When done, top looks dry and will spring back when lightly touched. Cut when cool.

Gilbert Plains, Man.
Branch No. 98

Peach 'n Cherry Cobbler

1 can cherry pie filling
1-16 oz. can sliced peaches, drain and reserve ⅔ cup syrup
2 tbsp. lemon juice
½ tsp. cinnamon or nutmeg
1¼ cups prepared biscuit mix
2 tbsp. sugar
3 tbsp. milk
1 egg, slightly beaten

Combine pie filling, peaches, ⅔ cup syrup, lemon juice and cinnamon in 2 qt. casserole. Microwave, covered, 8 to 9 minutes or till bubbly. Combine biscuit mix, sugar, milk and egg till moistened. Drop dough by tablespoons around edge of hot mixture, leaving an opening in centre. Spoon some fruit mixture over dough. Microwave, uncovered, 3½ to 4½ minutes or till topping is no longer doughy, rotating dish once. Serve warm. Can be made about 40 minutes ahead.

Roblin, Man.
Ladies Auxiliary
Branch No. 24

Steamed Carrot Pudding

½ cup brown sugar (125 ml)
½ cup grated peeled carrot (125 ml)
½ cup grated peeled potato (125 ml)
⅓ cup salad oil (75 ml)
½ tsp. baking soda (2 ml)
½ tsp. cinnamon (2 ml)
¼ tsp. ground cloves (1 ml)
¼ tsp. nutmeg (1 ml)
¼ tsp. salt (1 ml)
½ cup flour (125 ml)
2 tsp. chopped candied peel (10 ml)
2 tbsp. chopped candied cherries (25 ml)
1 cup raisins (250 ml)
2 tbsp. chopped nuts (25 ml)

Combine sugar, carrot, potato and oil. Combine dry ingredients and add to sugar-carrot mixture. Stir in fruit and nuts. Spread batter into lightly greased 1 qt. (1 l) casserole or microwave mold. Cover tightly. To trap all the steam while baking, cover casserole completely with plastic wrap and secure with a plate or lid. Micro cook at medium (50%) for 8 minutes or until toothpick inserted in centre comes out clean. Uncover. Cool directly on flat surface for 10 to 15 minutes. Unmold. When cool, wrap well and allow to age at least one week in refrigerator.

To reheat, place on serving plate and micro cook, covered, at medium high (70%) for 5 to 6 minutes or until hot. Let stand, covered, for 2 minutes. Makes 8 servings. Serve with Butterscotch Sauce.

West Pubnico, N.S.
Ladies Auxiliary
Branch No. 66

Strawberry-Banana Cobbler

3 firm medium bananas
1-12 oz. can strawberry pie filling
1 tbsp. lemon juice
½ tsp. vanilla
9 coconut bar cookies crumbled (1 cup)
¼ cup chopped pecans
vanilla ice cream or light cream

Peel and slice bananas, place in 10x6x2″ baking dish. Mix pie filling, lemon juice, and vanilla. Spoon over bananas. Micro-cook uncovered, 6 minutes turning dish every 2 minutes. Mix cookies and pecans, sprinkle over fruit. Cook uncovered 1 minutes. Serve warm with ice cream or light cream. Serves six.

Cheticamp, N.S.
Branch No. 32

Cheesecake Tarts

3 tbsp. butter or margarine
½ cup graham cracker crumbs
1½ tsp. sugar
1-8 oz. pkg. cream cheese, softened
¼ cup sugar
1 egg
1 tsp. vanilla
1 can cherry pie filling

Place butter in a 10 oz. custard cup. Microwave, uncovered, on High (100%) for 1 minute. Blend in cracker crumbs and the 1½ tsp. sugar.
Line six 6 oz. custard cups with paper baking cups; spoon crumb mixture equally into cups. With a spoon, press mixture firmly over bottom and slightly up sides of cups. Arrange cups in a circle on a large flat plate.
In a small bowl, beat cream cheese and the ¼ cup sugar until smooth. Beat in egg and vanilla, blending well. Spoon mixture equally into crumb-lined cups.
Microwave, uncovered, on High (100%) for 2½ to 3½ minutes, rotating each cup ½ turn after 1½ minutes. Tarts should look slightly dry on top. Let stand for 10 minutes on plate and refrigerate for one hour. Remove tarts from cups (peel off paper liners, if desired) and serve; or cover and refrigerate. Just before serving, spoon cherry pie filling over each cheesecake. Makes 6 servings.

New Ross, N.S.
New Ross Branch No. 79

Rhubarb Crunch

Serve on a chilly evening at the cottage or make ahead for a cold dessert on a sizzling summer day.

Fruit Base:
4 cups sliced rhubarb (1 l)
1 cup crushed pineapple with liquid (250 ml)
1 cup granulated sugar (250 ml)
2 tbsp. orange liqueur or orange juice (25 ml)
2 tbsp. cornstarch (25 ml)

Topping:
¼ cup butter (50 ml)
2 tbsp. flour (25 ml)
¼ tsp. ground cinnamon (1 ml)
2 cups bran flakes (500 ml)
½ cup dessicated coconut (125 ml)
⅓ cup brown sugar (75 ml)

Fruit Base: In 8-inch (2 l) square dish, combine rhubarb, pineapple with liquid, granulated sugar, liqueur and cornstarch. Cover with plastic wrap, turning back one corner to vent. Micro-cook at high for 8 to 10 minutes or until rhubarb is tender, stirring once or twice.
Topping: In 4-cup (1 l) dish, melt butter for 1 minute. Add flour and cinnamon and stir to combine. Toss in remaining ingredients. Sprinkle on top of rhubarb mixture. Micro-cook at High for 2 minutes or until bubbly and hot. Serve warm or cold. Makes 6 to 8 servings.

Winnipeg, Man.
Kent Memorial Branch No. 119

Black Forest Cake

1 layer pkg. of chocolate cake mix

Follow directions on package but use ¼ less liquid. Bake in microwave in either microwave Bundt dish or a round pyrex dish. Put a fitted piece of paper towel in bottom of dish. Bake with cake dish elevated (sitting in microwave oven on a saucer or other small dish) and cover with a piece of waxed paper. Bake for 3 minutes on medium and then for 2½ minutes on High or until toothpick comes out clean. Invert and put on large plate or tray. Repeat above procedure to make second layer of cake. Spread a can of cherry pie filling on bottom layer of cake. Then place the top layer of cake on the cherry filling. Ice the cake with Dream Whip (takes 2 pkg.). Decorate with cherries and almond halves.

Miami, Man.
Ladies Auxiliary
Branch No. 88

French Apple Pie

1-9″ pastry shell, microwaved
Filling:
5-6 cups apples
1 tbsp. lemon juice
½ cup sugar
2 tbsp. flour
½ tsp. cinnamon or nutmeg
Topping:
¼ cup margarine
½ cup flour
¼ cup brown sugar
½ tsp. nutmeg

Toss filling ingredients together. Pile high in pastry shell. Cut margarine into other topping ingredients until crumbly. Sprinkle over filling. Place wax paper under plate while microwaving. Microwave on High for 8 minutes. Rotate ½ turn. Microwave 6 to 10 minutes until apples are tender.

Pilot Mound, Man.
Branch No. 62

Easy Fruit Cobbler

1-14 oz. can drained fruit packed in juice (398 ml)
1 cup biscuit mix (250 ml)
3 tbsp. sugar (45 ml)
¼ tsp. almond extract (1 ml)
⅓ cup milk (80 ml)
1½ tsp. butter (7 ml)
½ tsp. cinnamon (2 ml)
¼ cup chopped nuts (50 ml) (optional)

In 8″ (20 cm) round glass dish spread fruit evenly on bottom. A little juice may be left with fruit, if desired for spooning over top after cooking. In small mixing bowl blend biscuit mix, 2 tbsp. sugar (30 ml), almond extract and milk; drop evenly over fruit. Dice butter on top. Combine cinnamon, remaining sugar and nuts. Sprinkle on top. Microwave, uncovered, at Full Power 4 to 5 minutes, rotating ¼ turn halfway through cooking. Most fruits (apricots, peaches, cherries, etc.) may be substituted, either fresh or canned. Cooking Time: 4 to 5 minutes. Standing Time: 5 minutes.

Souris, Man.
Branch No. 60

Impossible Pie

4 eggs
½ cup shortening
½ cup all-purpose flour
2 tbsp. vanilla
2 cups milk
1 cup white sugar
1 cup shredded coconut

Place all ingredients in blender. Blend at high speed for 2 minutes. Pour mixture into greased 10″ pie plate immediately after blending. Cook at High for 13 minutes. Gently lift edges to spread uncooked portions. Cook at High for 7 minutes longer. Cover with plastic wrap and let stand for 5 minutes. Top with toasted coconut flakes and/or well drained peach slices. This pie makes its own crust.

Hantsport, N.S.
Lucknow Branch No. 109

Plum Pudding

2 cups bread crumbs
½ cup flour
½ cup currants
½ cup raisins
2 tbsp. brown sugar
½ tsp. baking soda
¼ tsp. nutmeg
¼ tsp. salt
½ tsp. cinnamon
¼ cup butter or margarine
½ cup milk
2 tbsp. cherry juice
1½ tbsp. molasses
1 egg

Grease 2 cup glass measuring cup, cover bottom and sides with wax paper. Mix as given and pour in cup. Cover with plastic. Microwave 50% 8 to 12 minutes let stand 5 minutes pour 2 tbsp. brandy over top and light.

Canning, N.S.
Habitant Branch No. 73

Pecan Pie

1 basic pastry shell, uncooked
1 egg yolk
2 tbsp. dark corn syrup
¼ cup butter
3 whole eggs plus extra egg white
1 cup dark corn syrup
⅓ cup brown sugar, packed
1 tbsp. flour
1 tsp. vanilla
1½ cups pecan halves

Place pastry in 9″ pie plate. Brush with mixture of egg yolk and corn syrup on inside of shell. Microwave at High for 6 to 7 minutes. Rotate dish after first 3 minutes. Place butter in large glass bowl. Microwave at High for ½ to 1 minute. Add eggs to melted butter. Mix well; then add syrup, sugar, flour and vanilla. Mix in pecan halves and pour into crust. Microwave at Medium 12 to 15 minutes, rotating one half turn after 5 minutes. When done, top surface is dry and puffed, and filling is set.

Rapid City, Man.
Branch No. 49

Cranberry-Yogurt Coffee Cake

Cook on high power 15 to 17 minutes. Makes 8 servings.

Topping:
¼ cup white sugar
⅓ cup firmly packed dark brown sugar
1 tsp. ground cinnamon
1 cup chopped pecans or walnuts

Batter:
2 cups all-purpose flour sifted
1 tsp. baking soda
1 tsp. baking powder
¼ tsp. salt
½ cup butter or margarine room temperature
1 cup white sugar
1 cup plain yogurt
1 tsp. vanilla
1-16 oz. can whole berry cranberry sauce

Combine the ingredients for topping in a small bowl. Grease bottom of 8x8x2″ baking dish. Sift flour, baking soda, baking powder and salt onto waxed paper. Beat butter and the sugar in large bowl until creamy. Add eggs one at a time, beating in well after each addition. Beat in yogurt and vanilla alternately with flour mixture until thoroughly combined. Spread half of the batter evenly in dish. Spoon on ½ cup of the cranberry sauce and sprinkle with ⅓ of the topping mixture. Spread with remaining batter; top with ½ cup more of sauce and sprinkle with ⅓ cup of the topping. Swirl topping and cranberry sauce into batter, using a knife. Sprinkle with remaining topping. Cook on high power 15 minutes rotating dish ½ turn every 5 minutes. Check with wooden stick, if it comes out clean it is done, otherwise return and cook for 2 minutes longer. To serve, heat remaining sauce in oven for 1 to 2 minutes on high power. Cut cake into square and serve with sauce, yogurt and more nuts if you wish.

Tantallon, N.S.
St. Margaret's Bay branch No. 116

Bread and Raisin Pudding

1 cup milk (250 ml)
3 eggs
¼ cup sugar (60 ml)
1 tsp. cinnamon (5 ml)
½ tsp. vanilla (2 ml)
2 tbsp. butter or margarine (30 ml)
3 slices bread, cubed
½ cup raisins (125 ml)

Microwave milk in 2 cup (500 ml) glass measure on Full Power for 2½ to 3 minutes or until it begins to boil. Meanwhile, in a 1½ qt. (1½ L) casserole, beat eggs, sugar, cinnamon and vanilla. Add butter to hot milk. Microwave on Full Power 45 to 60 seconds until butter melts. Gradually add hot mixture to egg mixture, stirring constantly. Stir in bread and raisins. Place casserole in another dish. Pour hot water into dish to depth of 1 inch (2.5 cm). Microwave, uncovered on Full Power 8 to 10 minutes. At 3, 5 and 7 minutes draw cooked pudding towards centre of casserole allowing uncooked portion to flow to the edges. Rotate dish ¼ turn. Pudding is cooked when it is set but jiggles when shaken. Allow to stand in hot water 15 minutes before serving. Serves 4 to 5.

Souris, Man.
Branch No. 60

La Carrot Cake

3 eggs
1½ cups sugar
1 cup oil
1 tsp. vanilla
1½ cups flour
¾ tsp. salt
1¼ tsp. baking soda
2½ tsp. cinnamon
1¼ tsp. cloves
2½ cups grated carrots
¾ cups coarsely chopped walnuts

In large mixing bowl combine eggs, sugar, oil and vanilla. Blend in flour, salt, cinnamon and cloves. Fold in carrots and nuts. Pour into 12-cup Bundt pan. Microwave (high) 12 to 14 minutes, rotating ¼ turn every 4 minutes — rest 10 minutes. Loosen sides and centre, invert on serving plate. Frost with Cream Cheese Frosting.

Cream Cheese Frosting:
4 oz. softened cream cheese
3 tbsp. softened butter
½ lb. powdered sugar
1 tsp. vanilla

In a small bowl soften cream cheese and butter (high) ½ to 1 minutes. Blend in powdered sugar and vanilla until light and fluffy. Makes 1½ cups.

Swan River, Man.
Ladies Auxiliary
Branch No. 39

Easy Company Cake

¼ cup butter or margarine
¾ cup sugar
2 eggs
¼ tsp. vanilla
¾ cup unsifted all-purpose flour
½ tsp. baking powder
¼ tsp. salt
¼ cup milk

Topping:
¼ cup butter or margarine
¼ cup sugar
1 tbsp. milk
1 tbsp. flour
⅓ cup slivered almonds

Place butter in large mixing bowl. Microwave on Roast (4) for 30 seconds or until softened. Beat in sugar, eggs and vanilla until light and fluffy. Stir in dry ingredients alternately with milk, beating well after each addition. Pour into 9″ round glass baking dish. Microwave on Simmer (3) for 7 minutes or until toothpick comes out clean. Combine butter, sugar and milk in glass measuring cup, stir until blended. Blend in flour, stir in almonds. Microwave on Roast (4) for 1 to 2 minutes or until slightly thickened. Stir to blend. Pour over top of cake.

New Richmond, Que.
Bay Chaleurs Branch No. 172

Two-Layer Pineapple Upside-Down Cake

4 tbsp. butter or margarine
1 cup firmly packed dark brown sugar
2-15¼ oz. cans sliced pineapple, drained
22 maraschino cherries, drained
1-8½ oz. pkg. yellow cake mix and ingredients as called for on cake pkg.

1. Place ½ of the butter in each of two 8″ round non-metallic cake pans.
2. Heat each pan, uncovered in Microwave oven for 40 seconds or until butter is melted.
3. Blend ½ of the brown sugar with the melted butter in each pan. Spread mixture evenly over bottom of cake pans.
4. Drain pineapple juice into a measuring cup and reserve. Arrange pineapple slices and cherries over brown sugar mixture in each pan.
5. Prepare cake mix according to package directions substituting the reserved pineapple juice for the liquid called for on the package. Add water if necessary for full measure.
6. Pour ½ of batter over pineapple slices in both pans. Spread evenly.
7. Heat each layer uncovered in Microwave oven for 10 minutes turning pan ¼ turn after each 2½ minutes.
8. Invert 1 layer onto serving plate. Invert the second layer on top of the first. Serve warm. Serves 8.

Gladstone, Man.
Branch No. 110

Carrot Spice Cake

1¼ cups flour
1 cup brown sugar
1 tsp. baking powder
1 tsp. baking soda
1 tsp. ground cinnamon
½ tsp. ground allspice
½ tsp. salt
1 cup shredded carrot
⅔ cup oil
2 eggs
½ cup crushed pineapple with syrup
1 tsp. vanilla extract

In large bowl, with electric mixer, combine flour, sugar, baking powder, baking soda, cinnamon, allspice, salt and carrot. Stir in remaining ingredients and beat 2 minutes at medium speed. Pour batter into a greased 8 or 9″ round baking dish with small glass inverted in center.

To Heat By Auto Sensor: Cover completely with 2 overlapping pieces of plastic wrap. Heat on Cook A4. After heating, release plastic. Time: about 10 minutes.

To Heat By Time: Heat at Medium 10 to 11½ minutes.

To Complete: Let stand, covered, 10 minutes. Store covered until ready to serve.

Wolfville, N.S.
Branch No. 74

Devil's Food Cake

2 cups sifted all-purpose flour
1¼ tsp. baking soda
¼ tsp. salt
½ cup shortening
2 cups sugar
½ cup cocoa
1 tsp. vanilla extract
½ cup buttermilk
2 eggs lightly beaten

1. Grease the bottoms of two 8″ round cake dishes. Line the bottoms with 2 layers of wax paper.
2. Sift together flour, baking soda, and salt. Set aside.
3. Cream together shortening, sugar, cocoa, and vanilla until light and fluffy.
4. Measure 1 cup water in a 2 cup measuring cup. Cook for about 2½ minutes, or until water comes to a boil. Let stand.
5. Stir boiling water, buttermilk and eggs into creamed mixture and beat well. Add sifted dry ingredients all at once and beat well.
6. Divide mixture between prepared cake dishes.
7. Cook, uncovered, one layer at a time on bake for 5 minutes.
8. Cook on high for 4 minutes. Remove from oven and let stand until cake is cool.
9. Turn out of dishes and cool thoroughly. Frost as desired.

Schreiber, Ont.
Branch No. 109

Christmas Cake

2 eggs
¾ cup brown sugar
2 tbsp. molasses
⅓ cup oil
1½ cups flour
1 tsp. baking powder
½ tsp. salt
¼ tsp. allspice
¼ tsp. nutmeg
2 cups raisins
½ cup juice (orange or pineapple)
8 oz. glazed cherries
8 oz. mixed peel
1 cup sliced almonds
½ cup brandy (rum)
8 oz. mixed fruit

Combine eggs, brown sugar and molasses in a large bowl, beat well. Beat in oil. Stir dry ingredients alternately with juice, mix well after each addition. Stir in fruit and nuts. Line sides of a 9x5x3″ glass loaf pan with wax paper (or brown butcher paper). Lightly grease sides of pan to hold paper in place. Paper should extend at least 2″ above the rim of the pan. Pour in batter. Cook uncovered for 30 minutes on Defrost or until a toothpick inserted in center comes out clean. Turn onto a rack to cool. Once cool wrap cake in cheese cloth or layers of J-cloth. Soak with brandy. Store in tightly sealed container to hold moisture.

Soak fruit, peel and cherries in enough brandy to cover them overnight. Use this brandy for the ½ cup in the recipe.

Napinka, Man.
Branch No. 89

Zucchini Chocolate Cake

This super moist and very rich cake is a favorite with our staff.

½ cup butter or margarine
1½ cups sugar
½ cup cooking oil
2 eggs
1 tsp. vanilla
3 cups shredded, unpeeled zucchini
¼ cup milk
2½ cups unsifted all-purpose flour
¼ cup unsweetened cocoa
1 tsp. baking soda
1 tsp. salt
½ cup semi-sweet chocolate pieces

1. Microwave (high) butter in glass mixing bowl 20 to 30 seconds or until softened. Blend in sugar and oil; beat well. Add eggs, one at a time, beating well after each. Stir in vanilla, zucchini and milk. Add flour, cocoa, baking soda and salt; mix well. Stir in chocolate pieces.
2. Generously grease a 12-cup fluted plastic tube cake dish. Sprinkle with sugar; shake out excess sugar. Spoon batter into dish, spreading evenly.
3. Microwave (medium—50%), uncovered, 12 minutes, rotating dish once. Rotate dish. Then, Microwave (high) 6 to 8 minutes or until no longer doughy, rotating dish once. Cool 10 minutes; invert onto serving plate. If desired, glaze or sprinkle with powdered sugar. About 16 servings.

Teulon, Man.
Branch No. 166

Chocolate Cake

1½ cups flour
1 cup brown sugar
¼ cup cocoa
1 tsp. baking soda
½ tsp. salt
½ cup water

In a mixing bowl stir together all ingredients. Add water and stir to a stiff shiny batter.

½ cup water
⅓ cup cooking oil
1 tbsp. vinegar
½ tsp. vanilla

Add additional ½ cup water, oil, vinegar and vanilla. Stir till smooth and well blended. Pour batter into greased 8″ round pan. Microwave at Power Level (10) 8 to 10 minutes. Let stand on wooden board to cool.

Langruth, Man.
Ladies Auxiliary
Branch No. 162

Reindeer Toffee

1 can condensed milk
1 cup brown sugar
5 tbsp. syrup
½ lb. butter or margarine

Mix all ingredients together in a large bowl. Put in microwave on high until it bubbles, about 3 minutes. Stir. Then boil for 12 minutes, stirring three times every three minutes. Grease a cookie sheet and pour in centre, or on buttered tin foil. Cool and cut in pieces. Delicious.

Grandview, Man.
Branch No. 14

Miscellaneous

Hints

Always undercook and check, start w/minimum time, check, then add more time as required. It is better to overstand than overcook. Remember that baked goods will continue to cook during standing time.

Dunrea, Man.
Napinka Auxiliary
Branch No. 89

Cooked Salad Dressing

1 cup vinegar
½ cup sugar
1½ cups water
3 tbsp. flour
1 tsp. mustard
6 egg yolks
1 tsp. salt

1. Combine vinegar, sugar, and 1 cup water together in 2 qt. glass casserole. Heat with microwave energy 6 minutes or until it boils.
2. Mix flour and mustard with ½ cup water and stir into hot vinegar mixture. Cook 3½ minutes; stirring at end of each 30 seconds.
3. Beat egg yolks well, stir some of the hot mixture into egg yolks, then stir all together. Cook 1½ minutes.
4. Remove from oven, add salt and stir well. Recipe yields 1 qt. If too thick when ready to use, thin with cream.

Deloraine, Man.
Ladies Auxiliary
Branch No. 83

Fresh Strawberry Jam

4½ cups crushed fresh strawberries
1 box powdered fruit pectin
7 cups sugar

In 3 qt. casserole place berries and pectin. Stir well. Cover. Microwave at High 8 to 10 minutes, until mixture is at a full rolling boil. Add sugar to boiling mixture and stir well. Microwave at High 8 to 10 minutes, uncovered, stirring after 5 minutes, until mixture reaches a full rolling boil. Then, time for 1 minute of boiling. Skim off foam with metal spoon, stirring jam about 5 minutes before ladling into prepared glasses. Seal. Makes about 8 cups.

San Clara, Man.
Branch No. 237

Sloppy Joes

Total cooking time: 11 minutes
Serves 4
1½ qt. glass casserole dish
13x9″ glass dish

1 lb. ground lean beef
4 slices uncooked bacon, diced
1 small green pepper, finely chopped
1 small onion, diced
1-15 oz. can chili beans
1-8 oz. can tomato sauce
1 tbsp. chili powder
1 tsp. garlic powder
1 tsp. salt
4 hamburger buns
½ cup grated Cheddar cheese

In glass casserole, combine ground beef, diced bacon, green pepper and onion. Mix well. Cook on Roast (7) for 6 minutes or until meat is no longer pink, stirring once during cooking. Drain. Add remaining ingredients except hamburger buns and cheese. Mix well. In glass dish, place open hamburger buns and heap each half with an equal amount of beef mixture. Sprinkle with grated cheese. Cover; cook on High (9) for 4 to 5 minutes or until cheese is melted.

Fort Frances, Ont.
Branch No. 29

Thick Hamburger Soup

1 lb. ground chuck
2 qts. water
3 bouillon cubes
3 onions, sliced
3 carrots, sliced
1-1 lb. can chopped tomatoes
3 stalks celery, chopped
1 tbsp. salt
1 tsp. MSG
¼ cup quick-cooking rice
½ cup quick-cooking barley

Place meat in a 4 qt. casserole. Microwve 5 minutes, stirring twice. Add remaining ingredients and cover. Microwave 45 minutes, stir every 15 minutes. Let stand, covered, 30 minutes before serving. Serves 6 to 8.

Stewiacke, N.S.
Branch No. 70

Quick Tomato-Venison Stew

Cook on high power 37 minutes — makes 6 servings

1 can condensed tomato soup
½ cup canned beef broth
2 tbsp. butter or margarine
1½ lbs. boneless venison, cut in ¾″ cubes (tenderized if you wish)
¼ tsp. salt
1/8 tsp. pepper
¼ tsp. leaf thyme crumbled
4 medium white onions, peeled and root end scored
4 medium carrots, halved lengthwise, then crosswise (I use frozen baby carrots)
3 medium potatoes, quartered
1 lb. fresh green beans, trimmed and cut in 1½-inch pieces (frozen green beans can be used)

Mix tomato soup and beef broth in a 2 cup measure. Put butter in a 3 qt. glass baking dish and cook on high power 45 to 60 seconds, until melted. Add venison; sprinkle with salt and pepper; stir. Put tomato-broth mixture and venison mixture in oven at same time. Cook 4 minutes, stirring meat after 2 minutes. Pour hot broth mixture over meat, sprinkle with thyme, stir. Cover with plastic wrap and cook 8 minutes, stir and cook 8 minutes longer. Arrange vegetables in a circle around meat, cover and cook 8 minutes. Rotate dish ½ turn and cook 8 minutes longer. Remove from oven and cover dish tightly with aluminum foil. Let stand 10 minutes. Note: when using frozen vegetables cook about ½ the time required for regular use before adding to the recipe.

Tantallon, N.S.
St. Margaret's Bay Branch No. 116

Denver Brunch Sandwich

8 slices bacon
6 eggs
⅓ cup milk
½ cup salad dressing or mayonnaise
¼ cup pimento, chopped
¼ cup chopped green pepper
¼ tsp. salt
6 tomato slices

In 1½ qt. baking dish, cook bacon between layers of paper towel until crisp, about 4 minutes. Remove bacon, paper towels and excess drippings from dish; crumble bacon. Meanwhile beat eggs, milk and salad dressing until well mixed. Stir in pimento, green pepper, salt and bacon.Pour into baking dish. Cover tightly with plastic wrap. Cook 3 minutes, stir, moving cooked portion to center. Cover again and cook 2 minutes or until center is almost set. Arrange tomato slices on top and cook 30 seconds. Let stand, covered, 2 minutes to finish cooking. 5 to 6 servings.

Red Lake, Ont.
Ladies Auxiliary
Branch No. 102

Teenage Snack

1 slice of bread
spaghetti sauce or mayonnaise
chopped meat — any kind
sliced tomato
1 cheese slice

Spread spaghetti sauce on bread. Cover with chopped meat. Add a layer of sliced tomato. Top with cheese slice. Microwave on High for 30 to 40 seconds or until cheese is melting.
My teenage sons would have 2 or 3 of these for an evening snack. Also a nutritious lunch for school children.

Erickson, Man.
Branch No. 143

Teriyaki Burgers

½ cup soya sauce
3 tbsp. sugar
3 green onions, sliced
½ tsp. ground ginger
1/8 tsp. instant minced garlic or 1 clove garlic, minced
1 lb. ground beef
1-8¼ oz. can pineapple (4 slices)
4 hamburger buns, split and toasted

In 2 qt. (8x8) baking dish, combine soya sauce, sugar, onions, ginger and garlic; mix well. Shape beef into 4 patties. Add to soya sauce mixture, turning over to coat. Cook, uncovered 6 minutes or until done, turning once during last half of cooking time. Top with pineapple slice and cook, uncovered for 30 seconds to warm pineapple. Serve on toasted buns.

Ste. Anne, Man.
Ladies Auxiliary
LaVerendrye Branch No. 220

Baked Onions in Tomato Juice

12 small onions (approx. 1½ lbs.)
¼ cup tomato juice
salt
pepper
½ tsp. Worcestershire Sauce
2 tbsp. chopped fresh parsley
2 tbsp. butter

Place peeled onion in greased casserole. Combine tomato juice with seasonings and pour over onions. Dot with butter and cover. Microwave on High for 3 minutes and then on medium for about 10 minutes. Stir occasionally during cooking. Note: If fresh parsley is not available, a small amount of dried may be used.

Bowsman, Man.
Ladies Auxiliary
Branch No. 51

Miscellaneous & Hints

Miscellaneous

Deep Pit Barbeque

25 lbs. beef, boned and rolled
½ cup salt
¼ cup pepper
¼ cup sugar
1 tbsp. garlic salt, or less

Put holes in the meat with a butcher knife. Mix the seasonings and rub into the holes and on outside of the meat. Wrap in cheesecloth, then in aluminum foil (wide works best). Fold in at top and ends to keep in juices. Roll in burlap and tie with baler wire, tying both ways, and leaving wire long enough for handles to remove from the pit. Put meat in rock lined pit after at least 4 hours of firing so that there is a good bed of coals. When you put the meat in, cover immediately with a metal lid, and 12 to 16 inches of earth. Remove in 15 to 20 hours. Never put more than 25 lbs. to a bundle. Add 2 feet in length to pit for each additional bundle. Never put more than 8 bundles to a pit.

Abbey, Sask.
Branch No. 222

Freezing Corn

10 cups corn
1 tbsp. salt
1 pt. hot water
¼ cup sugar
2 tbsp. butter

Cook in roaster in oven at 375°F. till it begins to boil. Stir occasionally. Cool and bag. Results are best if corn is picked and cut off cob and frozen the same day.

Justice, Man.
Branch No. 233

Barbeque Spice

½ tsp. chili powder
½ tsp. nutmeg
¼ tsp. cayenne
2 tbsp. brown sugar
2 tsp. curry powder
2 tsp. garlic salt
2 tsp. onion powder
2 tsp. dry mustard
2 tsp. black pepper
6 tbsp. paprika
½ tsp. thyme
½ tsp. tarragon
½ tsp. marjoram
½ tsp. basil
2½ cups salt

Put all ingredients in blender and pulverize. Great on anything. This salt is close to Laury's Salt. Makes about 3 cups.

Wells, B.C.
Branch No. 128

Summer Sausage

3 lbs. ground beef, not too lean
3 tbsp. liquid smoke
1 tsp. mustard seed
3 tbsp. Martin's tender quick salt
1 cup water
¼ tsp. garlic powder
½ tsp. onion powder
1/8 tsp. black pepper

Mix well, using masher or hands. Take three sheets of aluminum foil 12x13", dull side up. Form meat into 3 rolls. Roll up and seal ends; refrigerate 24 hours. Remove from fridge and punch holes in one end with fork. Place on cookie sheet, one that has sides, and bake at 325°F. for 1¼ hours. Let cool in the foil. Discard foil, replace the meat in fresh foil. Cool in fridge. Slice and use as you wish.

Russell, Man.
Ladies Auxiliary
Branch No. 159

Spiced Brisket

4-5 lbs. beef brisket
6 tbsp. pickling spice
2 tsp. saltpetre
3 tsp. salt
pinch pepper
5 tbsp. brown sugar
¼ tsp. cinnamon
clove garlic, crushed

Mix spices together. Lay a large piece of wax paper on table and sprinkle with half the spiced ingredients. Place meat on top and spread the rest of spices on top and sides. Wrap meat with wax paper and tape in place. Wrap this in foil, tightly sealing. Then wrap in brown paper and seal tightly with tape. Place in fridge on lower shelf, turning over once a day for ten days. Remove from fridge and unwrap. Place on foil in roaster; cover with foil and bake 3 to 4 hours at 375°F. until tender. Slice and serve. This can be frozen.

Tantallon, N.S.
St. Margaret's Bay Branch No. 116

Homemade Salami

2¾ lbs. ground beef
2 tbsp. liquid smoke, mixed in 1 cup water
½ tsp. garlic powder
1/8 tsp. mustard seed
¼ tsp. onion powder
1/8 tsp. celery seed
3 tbsp. Martins tender quick salt

Mix together thoroughly. Form into long rolls. Wrap individually in foil. Refrigerate 24 hours. Prick holes in bottom of foil. Put some water in bottom of broiling pan. Set rolls with holes down on a rack in pan and bake for 90 minutes at 350°F. Cool and refrigerate or freeze. Freezes well for six months.

Winnipeg, Man.
Charleswood Branch No. 100

Homemade Yogurt

3 cups instant powdered milk
1 pkg. Knox gelatin
1 tbsp. sugar (optional)
1 large can evaporated milk
3 tbsp. commercial yogurt
water

Soften gelatin. Add enough boiling water to make one cup and add sugar (takes edge off). Let cool.Preheat oven to 275°F. Mix 3 cups powdered milk with 3 cups cold water. Add 1 cup evaporated milk, 2 more cups cold water and gelatin mixture. Add 3 tbsp. yogurt. Stir well and cover bowl. Put in oven, turn heat off. Leave in overnight or 6 to 7 hours. May add strawberries, blueberries, etc.

Trenton, N.S.
Branch No. 29

Fruiti-freeze Pops

1 envelope Knox unflavored
gelatin
½ cup water
1 cup unsweetened fruit juice,
heated to boiling
1 tbsp. lemon juice
⅓ cup sugar, use more or less
according to taste
1 cup pureed unpeeled fresh
peaches, plums or necta-
rines

In a large bowl sprinkle gelatin over water and let stand 1 minute, add hot juice and stir until gelatin is completely dissolved. Stir in remaining ingredients and pour into six 5 oz. paper cups. Freeze until partially frozen. Insert wooden ice cream sticks and freeze. 5 minutes before serving peel off paper cup. Makes 6 pops. Kids love them!

Montreal, Que.
Mazeppa Branch No. 183

Potato Sausage

5 lbs. potatoes, peeled
5 lbs. fresh pork shoulder
5 lbs. beef round
1 onion

Grind all ingredients together. Mix in:

2 tbsp. pepper
2 tsp. allspice

Cut casing into 24″ lengths. Tie one end. Fill lightly with meat mixture so it can expand during cooking. Prick air bubbles as you fill casing so casing won't break. Use a darning needle. Tie other end of casing. Simmer about 2 hours, drain broth and cool. Keep in refrigerator. Can also be canned in jars. Very nice for luncheon.

Steinbach, Man.
Branch No. 190

Potted Meat

2 pork hocks
1 beef shank, approx. 2 lbs.
2 tsp. salt

Place in large pot, covering with water. Simmer until meat falls from bones easily. Remove meat from pot, reserving liquid. Discard all bones, fat, rind and gristle.
Chill the liquid overnight. Remove hardened fat from surface. The liquid, when chilled, should be firmly jelled. Heat the liquid and strain to remove any particles of bone. Return strained liquid to pot. Grate 2 medium onions. Add to liquid and simmer. Put meat through food chopper using coarse blade. Add to heated liquid. Then add:

¼ tsp. cinnamon
¼ tsp. allspice
¼ tsp. cloves
½ tsp. poultry seasoning
black pepper to taste

This mixture should be moist. Simmer a few minutes to marinate flavours. Spoon into plastic containers. Cover and chill.

New Glasgow, N.S.
Ladies Auxiliary
Normandy Branch No. 34

Pop Corn Tree

Step one: Cut wax paper circles, one each of 12″, 10″, 8″, and 4″. Fill a 1 lb. plastic cheese container with sand or salt. Make a round hole in the middle of the lid to fit a roll out of a foil wrap — cover with foil and insert into hole of the container; this is the stem of the tree.

Syrup:
2 cups white sugar
½ cup Lily white syrup
½ cup water
½ cup butter
2 tsp. salt

Cook over low heat until the soft crack stage is reached. In large oiled bowl put 4½ cups of popcorn, pour syrup over it and mix quickly - put out on the 12″ paper form and form into a circle with a hole in the middle — save some for a ball that is fitted over the centre post, form into a slight peak (top of tree.) Make a second batch of syrup to make the other four circles with holes in the centre (wear well buttered gloves). To assemble: Slip the 12″ circle over stem, crumple up a piece of foil and wrap around the stem, proceed with the rest of the circles, with crumpled foil between each circle, ending with the top. Presto, an edible Christmas tree. Sounds complicated but really isn't.

Winnipeg, Man.
Transcona Branch No. 7

Eagle Brand Milk

1 cup dry milk powder
⅔ cup sugar
3 tbsp. margarine
⅓ cup boiling water

Combine all ingredients. Blend until smooth. Makes 1½ cups.

Oak River, Man.
Branch No. 150

Kitchen Hints

1. Cigarette ashes on a damp cloth will remove glass rings on furniture. Rub until spot is gone.

2. If short one egg in a recipe, substitute 1 tsp. cornstarch. It's an almost perfect replacement.

3. Add a few drops of castor oil to the dirt around plants to make the leaves greener.

4. Weight-Watching Tip: Sprinkle a few drops of vinegar on any food; it curbs the appetite.

5. Get rid of onion or garlic odor on hands by rubbing them with vinegar, a slice of lemon, mouthwash or rubbing wet hands with salt.

6. Chew fresh parsley to get rid of garlic on breath.

7. Refresh dried out bread and rolls by reheating in a paper bag which has been sprinkled with water. Heat at 400°F. for 10 minutes.

Sydney, N.S.
Branch No. 12

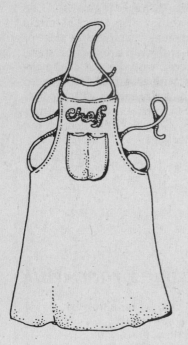

To keep whipped cream from going watery, add icing sugar instead of granulated sugar.

Kenton, Man.
Branch No. 118

Household Hints

Sprinkle table salt all over a rug, vacuum thoroughly to freshen colors and loosen dirt.

Blankets will be fluffy if a little liquid ammonia is added to the water.

When camping without refrigeration, coat eggs with shortening. It will help preserve them by sealing out air.

To keep mold from cheese or bacon, wrap in cheesecloth or muslin dipped in vinegar and wrung out.

Write recipes that are frequently halved or doubled in one color ink, their altered quantities in a second color for easy-to-read-no-error computation.

Did you know that chili powder, cayenne pepper and paprika need to be refrigerated?

A truly unusual way to clean pewter is to rub it with cabbage leaves.

Mothballs in the bottom of the garbage will help minimize odors.

If you put a solid room deodorizer next to the air-return vent of a forced-air heating system, the fresh smell will be carried through the ducts into every room.

Hazelridge, Man.
Branch No. 146

Recipe for Friendship

2 heaping cups patience
1 heart full love
2 handfuls generosity
dash of laughter
1 full cup understanding
2 cups loyalty

Mix well and sprinkle generously with kindness. Spread this irresistable delicacy over a lifetime and serve everybody you meet.

Foxwarren, Man.
Branch No. 152

Horseradish Hints

Cough, choke and gag when grinding horseradish roots? No need to! After cleaning roots, place plastic freezer bag over mouth of grinder, secure with heavy elastic band.

Horseradish freezes very well. Add 1 tbsp. sugar, ½ tsp. pickling salt and ¼-½ cup vinegar, 1 qt. bag of ground fresh horseradish. Expel excess air carefully, and knead to blend. Pat flat and freeze. Chop or break off amount needed for winter recipes, or use as fresh.

Hands burn when cleaning and seeding hot red peppers? Place cooking oil in saucer and keep fingers and hands oiled.

Want to save time and energy preparing cabbage leaves for cabbage rolls (Holupchi)? Remove core from cabbage and place in plastic bag in freezer for a day or two. Remove from freezer and thaw. Leaves separate very easily from head and are ready to use. Remove heavy spine from leaves for easier rolling.

Hazelridge, Man.
Branch No. 146

Recipe for a Happy Day

1 cup friendly words
4 tsp. time and patience
heaping dash of humour
2 cups understanding
large pinch warm personality

Measure words carefully, add heaping cups of understanding. Stir, using generous amounts of time and patience. Keep temperatures low, do not boil. Add a dash of humour, and a pinch of warm personality often. Season to taste with the spice of life. Serve in individual molds to all your friends.

Terrace Bay, Ont.
Branch No. 223

Recipe for Friendship

You take a bit of sunshine,
and you mix it with a smile,
add human understanding
as you travel every mile.
And then you add some loyalty,
which mingles in so well
and blend it with a voice
that has some cheery news to
        tell.
And don't forget some
        sympathy,
for other people's woes,
and lots of human nature,
everywhere a person goes.
Plus love for ordinary folks
who have no wealth to give
and dignity with which all men
have got the right to live.
Then add to these a hand clasp
        strong,
and measure out some truth,
and willingness to help the old
plus time for eager youth.
Now stir them all together,
and your task is at an end.
For all these combine
to make life's greatest gift —
a friend.

Steinbach, Man.
Branch No. 190

Metric Weight Conversions

1 oz. = 28.35 g
1 lb. = 0.45 kg
1 ton = 0.91 tonne (t)
1 g = 0.04 oz.
1 kg = 2.21 lb.
1 t = 1.10 ton

Temperatures

32°F = 0°C
212°F = 100°C
300°F = 150°C
325°F = 160°C
350°F = 180°C
375°F = 190°C
400°F = 204°C
425°F = 220°C
450°F = 230°C
500°F = 260°C

Metric Volume

1 fl. oz. = 28.4 ml
1 pt. = 570 ml (0.57 L)
1 qt. = 1.14 L
1 Imp. gal. = 4.54 L
1 ml = 0.04 fl. o.z
1 L = 1.75 pt.
1 L = 0.88 qt.
1 L = 0.22 Imp. gal.
1 tsp. = 5 ml
1 tbsp. = 15 ml
1 cup = 250 ml

Length Measurement

1 in. = 2.54 cm
1 ft. = 0.30 metre
1 yd. = 0.91 metre
1 mi. = 1.61 km
1 cm = 0.39 in.
1 m = 3.28 ft.
1 m = 1.09 yd.
1 km = 0.62 mi.

Equivalents

3 tsp. = 1 tbsp.
2 tbsp. = ⅛ cup
4 tbsp. = ¼ cup
5 tbsp. & 1 tsp. = ⅓ cup
8 tbsp. = ½ cup
4 oz. = ½ cup
8 oz. = 1 cup
16 oz. = 1 lb.
1 oz. = 2 tbsp. fat or
  liquid
2 cups fat = 1 lb.
2 cups = 1 pt.
2 cups sugar = 1 lb.
⅝ cup = ½ cup &
  2 tbsp.
1 lb. butter = 2 cups
2 pt. = 1 qt.
1 qt. = 4 cups
A few grains = less than
  ⅛ tsp.
Pinch = As much as can
  be taken between tip of
  finger and thumb.

Substitutions

1 tbsp. cornstarch (for thickening) = 2 tbsp. flour or 4 tsp. quick cooking tapioca.
1 cup sifted all-purpose flour = 1 cup plus 2 tbsp. sifted cake flour
1 sq. chocolate (oz.) = 3 or 4 tbsp. cocoa plus ½ tbsp. fat
1 tsp. baking powder = ¼ tsp. baking soda plus ½ tsp. cream of tartar
1 cup bottled milk = ½ cup evaporated milk plus ½ cup water
1 cup sour milk or buttermilk = 1 tbsp. vinegar or lemon juice plus sweet milk to make 1 cup (let stand 5 minutes)
1 cup molasses = 1 cup honey
1 small fresh onion = 1 tbsp. instant dry onion, rehydrated
1 tsp. dry mustard = 1 tbsp. prepared mustard
1 clove garlic = ⅛ tsp. garlic powder
1 cup tomato juice = ½ cup tomato sauce plus ½ cup water
1 bouillon cube dissolved in 1 cup boiling water or 1 cup consomme = 1 cup meat stock
For orange or lemon extract = grated orange or lemon peel